W9-AVS-407

FIFTH EDITION

Public Personnel Management
Contexts and Strategies

Donald E. Klingner
University of Colorado at Colorado Springs

John Nalbandian
University of Kansas

Prentice
Hall

Upper Saddle River, New Jersey 07458

Library of Congress Cataloging-in-Publication Data

Klingner, Donald E.
    Public personnel management : contexts and strategies/Donald E. Klingner, John
Nalbandian.—5th ed.
        p. cm.
    Includes bibliographical references and index.
    ISBN 0-13-099307-7
    1. Civil service—Personnel management.   I. Nalbandian, John, (date)   II. Title.

JF1601 .K56 2003
352.6—dc21   2002074857

VP/Editorial Director: Charlyce Jones Owen
Senior Acquisitions Editor: Heather Shelstad
Associate Editor: Brian Prybella
Editorial Assistant: Jessica Drew
Marketing Manager: Claire Bitting
Marketing Assistant: Jennifer Bryant
Prepress and Manufacturing Buyer: Benjamin Smith
Cover Art Director: Jayne Conte
Cover Designer: John Christiana
Cover art: Martial Colomb/Getty Images, Inc./PhotoDisc, Inc.

This book was set in 10/12 New Baskerville by TSI Graphics
and was printed and bound by Courier Companies, Inc. The cover was
printed by Coral Graphics.

© 2003, 1998, 1993, 1985, 1980 by Pearson Education, Inc.
Upper Saddle River, New Jersey 07458

Printed in the United States of America

10   9   8   7

ISBN 0-13-099307-7

Pearson Education LTD., London
Pearson Education Australia PTY, Limited, Sydney
Pearson Education Singapore, Pte. Ltd
Pearson Education North Asia Ltd, Hong Kong
Pearson Education Canada, Ltd, Toronto
Pearson Educación de Mexico, S.A. de C.V.
Pearson Education—Japan, Tokyo
Pearson Education Malaysia, Pte. Ltd
Pearson Education, Upper Saddle River, New Jersey

To my parents Ruth and Evans, who have shown by their own live's work how the twin professions of social work and accounting can contribute to public administration. To my wife Janette, who has defined with me the meaning of dual careers. To my colleagues throughout the world, who have helped me understand why public personnel management is so vitally tied to building democratic institutions. And to my children, who are all that will survive, other than my writings, beyond this life.

Don Klingner
Colorado Springs, CO

This is a very special dedication to my grandchildren, George and Jane, born since the last edition was published. Their vitality encourages me to continue to think in terms of beginnings and to wonder if I ever was as patient as their loving parents. With my wife, Carol, my family brings out the best in me.

John Martello is a graduate student in the MPA program at the University of Kansas. It is hard to imagine completing this edition without his help. He provided essential research and helped rewrite several of the chapters. Thank you, John.

John Nalbandian
Lawrence, KS

Contents

4   Planning, Budgeting, Productivity, and Information Systems   84

5   Defining and Organizing Work   110

6   Rewarding Work: Pay and Benefits   131

PART III: ACQUISITION

7   The Saga of Social Equity: EEO, AA, and Workforce Diversity   160

8   Recruitment, Selection, and Promotion   184

PART IV: DEVELOPMENT

9   Leadership and Employee Performance in Turbulent Times   213

10   Training, Education, and Staff Development   238

14 Collective Bargaining   348

Preface

Public Personnel Management: Contexts and Strategies was first published in 1980. It continues to sell well, and we are gratified that readers and reviewers confirm its strengths. One reviewer characterized the book as having

> clearly stated learning objectives at the beginning of each chapter, with relevant practical examples, figures, and diagrams that summarize key concepts and relationships in a comprehensive yet readable manner; challenging case studies and exercises at the conclusion of each chapter to facilitate application; a comprehensive list of study questions to reinforce learning, and a listing of key concepts to guide study. Hence, the text is very student and user friendly.*

Every few years, we have revised this text in response to changes in the environment (social, economic, political, and technological) of the field, changes in law, and changes in organizational policy and practice. We have tried in this edition to focus more on the manager's perspective on human resources management rather than the personnel specialist's. With a new chapter, we have provided an explicit focus on strategic thinking in human resources management and throughout the book we relate how several human resource management activities are and should be related to the strategic goals and objectives of public employers. In addition, we have gradually increased our treatment of human resources management in developing countries, taking advantage of Professor Klingner's consulting experiences in Latin America and in Egypt. Each chapter has also been

---

*Roberts, Gary (September 2000). Book Review, *American Review of Public Administration*, 344–352.

updated with current references, illustrations, and some new case studies that come out of out consulting and teaching experiences.

But along with the changes, we also have tried to keep the familiar foundations. We are mindful that since its first edition this book has emphasized a coherent values perspective and is organized around four personnel functions that must be fulfilled in any complex organization. The values and the functions remain, and that framework continues to set this book apart from others.

Here are some of the changes you will see.

- Chapter 1 (The World of Public Personnel Management) discusses the continued conflict and interaction among fundamental values, including the impact of performance contracting and privatization as alternatives to traditional civil service. And it discusses the evolution of public personnel systems under diverse conditions in developing countries, including the link between government capacity and democratization.
- Chapter 2 (Doing Public HRM in the United States) focuses on the practice of public personnel management in public agencies, including the roles of supervisors and managers in implementing the personnel policies approved by elected officials and designed by personnel specialists.
- Chapter 3 (Strategic Thinking about HRM) is a new chapter that focuses on the importance and interrelated impact of personnel functions on organizational effectiveness.
- Chapter 4 (Budgeting, Planning, Productivity, and Information Systems) puts more emphasis on privatization.
- Chapter 5 (Defining and Organizing Work) emphasizes the continued transition from position-based to performance- and employee-based jobs, underscoring the importance of job descriptions to performance contracting, service contracts, and other alternative personnel systems.
- Chapter 6 (Rewarding Work: Pay and Benefits) highlights the continued movement toward flexible performance-based rewards for individual and teams, and toward individually tailored benefits that emphasize family-work balance, flexibility, and cost-containment.
- Chapter 7 (The Saga of Social Equity: Equal Employment Opportunity) focuses on the continued transition from EEO and AA to workforce diversity, and from employment-related to contract-related diversity issues.
- Chapter 8 (Recruitment, Selection, and Promotion) highlights the importance that external factors have on hiring practices and includes a new case study on recruitment in the field of information technology. The chapter also explores the importance of competencies as a concept.
- Chapter 9 (Leadership and Performance in Turbulent Times) highlights the importance to human resources managers of being aware of the ways that expectations and obligations of employees and managers interact.
- Chapter 10 (Training, Education, and Staff Development) and 11 (Performance Appraisal) reflect the importance of connecting these development functions to strategic thinking of the organization and how focusing on the concept of competencies have helped do that.
- Chapter 12 (Safety and Health) focuses on management's responsibilities to provide a safe and healthy workplace.
- Chapter 13 (Organizational Justice) updates judicial decisions relating to human resources management and orients the chapter more towards managers.

- Chapter 14 (Collective Bargaining) focuses on the evolving role of public unions, including their efforts to emphasize employee rights in the face of global economic pressures.

The new millennium marked the distribution of this text in Spanish and Chinese, as well as the English-speaking world. Under agreement with Prentice-Hall/Simon & Schuster, McGraw-Hill Interamericana published *La Administracion de Personal Publico* in Mexico City for distribution throughout Latin America; and Renmin University Press (Beijing) announced plans to distribute it in China. Given our understanding of the relationship between public personnel management and democratization and the importance of human resource management to organizational effectiveness, we are both gratified at this interest and humbled by the responsibility it entails.

We hope that you will find the book useful and a significant improvement over previous editions. As always, we invite you to share your comments and concerns with us.

Donald E. Klingner
Graduate School of Public Affairs
University of Colorado
  at Colorado Springs
1420 Austin Bluffs Parkway
P.O. Box 7150
Colorado Springs, CO
80933-7150
719-262-4012
dklingne@uccs.edu

John Nalbandian
Department of Public Administration
University of Kansas
1541 Lilac Lane, #318
Lawrence, KS
66045-3177
785-864-3527
nalband@ku.edu

1

The World of Public Personnel Management

INTRODUCTION

Public **personnel management** has been studied extensively, from at least four perspectives. First, it is the *functions* needed to manage human resources in public agencies. Second, it is the *process* by which public jobs are allocated. Third, it is the interaction among fundamental societal *values* that often conflict over who gets public jobs and how they are allocated. Finally, public personnel management is personnel *systems*—the laws, rules, organizations, and procedures used to express these abstract values in fulfilling personnel functions.

In the United States, public personnel management is widely recognized as a critical element of democratic society and effective public administration. The development of public personnel management in the United States is complex because there are multiple levels of government plus thousands of governments, each with its own personnel system. Today, public personnel management in the United States may be described as a dynamic equilibrium among competing values, each championed by a particular personnel system, for allocating scarce public jobs in a complex and changing environment. As one might expect, this conflict exhibits a commingling of technical decisions (*how* to do a personnel function) with political ones (*what* value to favor or *what* system to use).

Internationally, the millennium has been characterized by dramatic political changes, notably the demise of international Communism and the emergence of democratic institutions in much of Latin America, in the former Soviet Union, and in parts of Africa. The global nature of these changes, and the similarity of the transitional process from authoritarian to democratic regimes, raises the intriguing possibility that there is a general pattern for the relationship between public personnel management and democratization in developing countries.

By the end of this chapter, you will be able to:

1. Define the functions needed to manage human resources in public agencies (planning, acquisition, development, and sanction—PADS).
2. Explain why public jobs are scarce resources, and how scarcity causes competition over who gets government jobs, and how they are allocated.
3. Describe the four pro-government values that have traditionally underlain the conflict over public jobs in the United States (responsiveness, efficiency, individual rights, and social equity).
4. Discuss the contemporary shift toward three emergent anti-government values (individual accountability, limited and decentralized government, and community responsibility).
5. Define a personnel system as the set of laws, policies, and practices used to fulfill the four public personnel functions (PADS), and give examples of the four traditional personnel systems now operating in the United States (political appointments, civil service, collective bargaining, and affirmative action).
6. Discuss two contemporary alternatives (alternative mechanisms for providing public services, and flexible employment relationships); how and why they have emerged; and what has been their impact on traditional values and systems.
7. Discuss conflict and compromise among alternative personnel systems.
8. Describe the history of public personnel management in the United States as a conflict among competing personnel systems and values.
9. Propose a general model for the relationship between public personnel management and democratization in developing countries.
10. Explain why developing countries are different from developed ones, and propose an agenda for strengthening civil service in developing countries.

PUBLIC PERSONNEL MANAGEMENT FUNCTIONS

Public personnel management consists of four fundamental functions needed to manage human resources in public organizations. These functions, designated by the acronym **PADS**, are planning, acquisition, development, and sanction. They are shown in Table 1–1, along with the activities that comprise them.

PUBLIC JOBS AS SCARCE RESOURCES

Basic decisions about public personnel management are important because jobs are the most visible way we measure economic and social status for individuals and groups. Public jobs are scarce resources because tax revenues limit them, and their allocation is of enormous significance for the course of public policy making generally. Because public jobs are scarce and important, there is competition for them among individuals and more broadly among advocates of competing public personnel values and systems.

TABLE 1–1   Public Personnel Management Functions

Function	Purpose
PLANNING	Budget preparation and human resource planning; dividing tasks among employees (job analysis, classification, and evaluation); deciding how much jobs are worth (pay and benefits)
ACQUISITION	Recruitment and selection of employees
DEVELOPMENT	Orienting, training, motivating, and evaluating employees to increase their competencies
SANCTION	Establishing and maintaining expectations and obligations that employees and the employer have toward one another; discipline, grievances, health and safety, and employee rights

THE FOUR TRADITIONAL VALUES: RESPONSIVENESS, EFFICIENCY, INDIVIDUAL RIGHTS, AND SOCIAL EQUITY

Public personnel management may be seen as the continuous interaction among fundamental **values** that often conflict. Traditionally, conflict in the United States centered around four values: political responsiveness, organizational efficiency and effectiveness, individual rights, and social equity.

Political responsiveness is the belief that government answers to the will of the people expressed through elected officials. Applicants' political and personal loyalty is best ensured through an appointment process that considers political loyalty, along with education and experience, as indicators of merit. Often, in order to promote responsive government, elected officials are authorized to fill a certain number of **exempt positions** through political appointments.

Organizational efficiency and **effectiveness** reflect the desire to maximize the ratio of inputs to outputs in any management process. This means that decisions about who to hire, reassign, or promote should be based on applicants' and employees' competencies, rather than political loyalty.

Individual rights emphasizes that individual citizens will be protected from unfair actions of government officials. Public employees' rights to job security and due process are maintained through **merit system** rules and regulations that protect them from inappropriate partisan political pressure (such as requiring them to campaign for elected officials, or contribute a portion of their salary toward election campaigns, or run the risk of losing their jobs if they refuse). In a parallel fashion, public employees who are union members will have recourse to work rules, contained in collective bargaining agreements that protect them from arbitrary management decisions.

Social equity emphasizes fairness to groups like women, racial minorities, the disabled, and veterans, that would otherwise be disadvantaged by a market economy that accepts the legitimacy of discrimination in hiring and in pay. Like individual rights, social equity is concerned with fairness. But unlike individual rights (which are based on personal attributes like education, experience, or seniority), social equity is concerned with employment preferences based on membership in a protected class or group.

ANTI-GOVERNMENT VALUES: INDIVIDUAL ACCOUNTABILITY, LIMITED AND DECENTRALIZED GOVERNMENT, AND COMMUNITY RESPONSIBILITY

Underlying the four traditional values is an implicit endorsement of collective action through government.[1] It is difficult to pinpoint the precise point at which this consensus began to be altered. But one key event was the 1976 presidential campaign, won by Jimmy Carter, who ran against the national government as a Washington "outsider." Beginning in 1980, the Reagan administration, though starting from fundamentally different values and policy objectives, continued to cast government as part of the problem, and to campaign against the infrastructure of public agencies and public administrators.

The anti-government assumptions behind this shift were paralleled by a related transition from political to economic perspectives on public policy. This shift in perspectives emphasized the role of market forces on individuals and the economy, rather than program implementation by government agencies and employees, as the most efficacious tools of public policy.[2] While public administration retained its role as the "great compromiser" among competing values, economic perspectives and the value of administrative efficiency clearly reflected these intense political and economic pressures on the public sector to "do more with less."

Since from 50 percent to 75 percent of public expenditures go toward employee salaries and benefits, efforts to increase accountability and reduce expenditures have focused on those managerial functions subsumed by public personnel management. The shift focused on philosophies and techniques used to enhance accountability in previous eras (such as the 1930s and the 1960s) by emphasizing program outputs and by rationally tying program inputs to outputs. Examples of these trends were program budgeting, human resource forecasting, job evaluation, management by objectives, objective performance appraisal, training needs assessment, cost-benefit analysis, and gain-sharing (productivity bargaining). As the information systems revolution expanded access to information formerly used by management for coordination and control, this pressure has also been reflected in organizational restructuring and "downsizing" middle managerial positions.

These underlying contemporary political, social, and economic forces shaped three emerging anti-government values: personal accountability, limited and decentralized government, and community responsibility for social services. First, proponents of **individual accountability** expect that people will make individual choices consistent with their own goals, and accept responsibility for the consequences of these choices, rather than passing responsibility for their actions onto the rest of society. Second, proponents of **limited and decentralized government** believe, fundamentally, that government is to be feared for its power to arbitrarily or capriciously deprive individuals of their rights. Proponents also believe that it is easier to connect public policy, service delivery, and revenue generation in a smaller rather than a larger unit of government. Decision makers are known, revenues are predictable, and services are directly visible. And for some, the reduction in size and scope of government is justified by the perceived ineffectiveness of government; by the high value accorded to individual freedom, responsibility, and accountability; and, finally, by a reluctance to devote a greater share of personal income to taxes. Third, proponents of **community responsibility** for social services believe that governmental agencies' efforts need to be supplemented by **not-for-profit, non-governmental organizations** responsible for social services, recreation, and community-development activities. For public personnel management, the most significant consequence of emergence of this value has been the creation of thousands of nonprofit organizations that routinely provide local government social services funded by taxes, user fees, and charitable contributions.

PERSONNEL SYSTEMS

In public policy making generally, values are ultimately reflected in laws and policies. Values in public personnel management are not articulated directly, but rather through personnel systems—the laws, policies, rules, regulations, and practices through which personnel functions are fulfilled.[3]

Traditional Systems: Political Patronage, Civil Service, Collective Bargaining, and Affirmative Action

There are four basic public personnel systems within the traditional model of public personnel management: political systems, civil service, collective bargaining, and affirmative action.

Political patronage means legislative or executive approval of individual hiring decisions, particularly for policy-making positions, based on the applicant's political or personal loyalty to the appointing official. Political appointees may be fired at any time; they serve at the discretion of those who appoint them.

Civil service system proponents favor a professional public service as the best way to achieve the values of efficiency and individual rights and a bureaucracy responsive to political direction. They think that staffing public agencies rationally, based on jobs needed to carry out specific programs and the competencies needed to accomplish these goals, and treating employees fairly are the best ways to maintain an efficient and professional public service. This means giving them good pensions and health benefits; giving them equal pay for work of comparable worth; hiring and promoting them on the basis of competencies; treating them impartially once on the job; and protecting them from partisan political influences. Overall policy objectives of civil service systems are controlled by elected officials, who often appoint agency heads responsible for managing the bureaucracy. The legislature maintains control over resources by limiting the total number of employees an agency can hire, staffing levels in particular agencies or programs, and the personnel budget. These tools help ensure political responsiveness. Civil service systems are supported by citizens and groups who want to keep "politics" out of public personnel decisions and to manage public agencies rationally and efficiently. But, because advocates of privatization and "cutting the fat out of big government" also believe in running government rationally and efficiently ("like a business"), there are some conflicts among proponents of this objective.

Collective bargaining systems exist within civil service systems. They reflect the value of individual rights (of union members), achieved by basing personnel decisions like promotion on seniority. Even though collective bargaining is commonly associated with negotiation over wages and benefits, the primary motive is to ensure equitable treatment by management. Contracts may also provide additional protection for individual employees against disciplinary action or discharge. In all cases, contracts negotiated between an agency's managers and leaders of the union representing its employees are subject to legislative approval.

Affirmative action systems usually exist within civil service systems. For the affirmative action system to operate, the governmental jurisdiction must have acknowledged an imbalance in the percentage of minorities in its workforce and those qualified minorities in a relevant labor force. Alternatively, members of a group protected against discrimination may have sued the public employer, resulting in a judicial ruling or consent decree requiring the agency to give special consideration to members of the "protected class" in various personnel decisions, especially hiring and promotion. Affirmative action is supported by members of underrepresented classes (such as female, minority, and disabled job applicants and employees), and by advocates who contend that the effectiveness of representative democracy depends upon the existence of a representative bureaucracy.

Contemporary Systems: Alternative Mechanisms and Flexible Employment Relationships

The rise of anti-government values has led to the emergence of their own personnel systems. These contemporary public personnel practices have had a fundamental impact on the way public services are delivered. Two trends are apparent: (1) reducing the role of government and the number of public employees by using alternative organizations or mechanisms for providing public services,[4] and (2) increasing the flexibility of employment relationships for the public employees that remain.

These alternative mechanisms include purchase-of-service agreements, privatization, franchise agreements, subsidy arrangements, vouchers, volunteerism, and regulatory and tax incentives.

Purchase-of-service agreements with other governmental agencies and **nongovernmental organizations (NGOs)** have become commonplace.[5] They offer municipalities a way of reducing capital costs, personnel costs, political issues associated with collective bargaining, and legal liability risks. Also, the use of outside contractors increases available expertise *and* managerial flexibility by reducing the range of qualified technical and professional employees that the agency must otherwise hire to provide training.

Privatization, as the term is generally used in the United States, means that, while a public agency *provides* a particular service, the service is *produced* and *delivered* by a private contractor. Privatization may result in the abolition of the agency (sometimes as an intended ideological goal). It offers all the advantages of service purchase agreements, but on a larger scale. It has become commonplace in areas such as solid waste disposal, where there is an easily identifiable "benchmark" (standard cost and service comparison with the private sector), and where public agency costs tend to be higher because of higher pay and benefits.[6]

Franchise agreements often allow private businesses to monopolize a previously public function within a geographic area, charge competitive rates for it, and then pay the appropriate government a fee for the privilege. Examples are cable TV and jitneys as a public transit option. Municipalities often encourage the procedure because it reduces their own costs, provides some revenue in return, and results in a continuation of a desirable public service.

Subsidy arrangements enable private businesses to perform public services, funded by either user fees to clients or cost reimbursement from public agencies. Examples would be airport security operations (provided by private contractors and paid for by both passengers and airlines), some types of hospital care (e.g., emergency medical services provided by private hospitals and reimbursed by public health systems), and housing (subsidizing rent in private apartments by low-income residents as an alternative to public housing projects).

Vouchers enable individual recipients of public goods or services to purchase them from competing providers on the open market. Under proposed educational voucher systems, for example, parents would receive a voucher that could be applied to the cost of education for their child at competing institutions (public or private), as an alternative to public school monopolies.

Volunteers provide contributed services otherwise performed by paid employees, or not at all. These include community crime-watch programs (in cooperation with local police departments), teachers' aides who provide tutoring and individual assistance in many public schools, and community residents who volunteer services as individuals or through churches, and other nonprofit service agencies. Frequently, such contributions are required to "leverage" a federal or state grant of appropriated funds.

Regulatory and tax incentives are typically used to encourage the private sector to perform functions that might otherwise be performed by public agencies with appropriated funds. These include zoning variances (for roads, parking, and waste disposal) granted to condominium associations. In return, the condominium association provides services normally performed by local government (security, waste disposal, and maintenance of common areas).

Increasing the Flexibility of Public Employment Relationships

Increasingly, public employers reduce costs and enhance flexibility by meeting minimal staffing requirements through career (civil service) employees, and by hiring other employees "at will" into **temporary** or **part-time positions**.[7] These "temps" *usually* receive lower salaries and benefits than their career counterparts and are *certainly* unprotected by due process entitlements or collective bargaining agreements. Conversely, where commitment and high skills are required on a temporary basis, employers may use contract or leased employees in positions exempt from civil service protection. Managerial and technical employees hired into these types of contracts usually receive higher salaries and benefits than can be offered to even highly qualified civil service employees, and they enhance managerial flexibility to trim personnel costs quickly should this be necessary, without having to resort to the bureaucratic chaos precipitated by the exercise of civil service "bumping rights" during a layoff situation.

The impact of these two devices—market mechanisms and flexible employment relationships—is accelerated by retirement "buyouts," which offer employees close to retirement age an incentive to retire early within a limited period of eligibility ("window"). If the plan is designed properly—so that enough employees retire to provide substantial savings, but enough stay to provide for organizational continuity and skills, both employer and employee benefit.

Impact of Emergent Systems on Traditional Values

Employee rights are diminished by the new systems. It is more likely that employees hired "at will" into temporary and part-time positions will receive lower pay and benefits, and will be unprotected by civil service regulations or collective bargaining agreements.[8] Whether or not the political neutrality of public employees suffers in this environment is unknown presently, but it seems logical to assume that as the criteria for success become more arbitrary or capricious, civil service employees—particularly those in mid-management positions—will begin to behave more like the political appointees whose jobs depend on political or personal loyalty to elected officials.[9]

Social equity is also diminished by the new systems. Comparisons of pay equity over the past twenty years have uniformly concluded that minorities and women in public agencies are closer to equal pay for equal work than are their counterparts in the private sector. Managerial consultants are overwhelmingly white and male. Many part-time and temporary positions are exempt from laws prohibiting discrimination against persons with disabilities or family medical responsibilities.

The impact of the emergent systems on public agency efficiency has been mixed. On the plus side, the change in public agency culture toward identifying customers and providing market-based services increases productivity. And the threat of privatization or layoffs has forced unions to agree to pay cuts, reduced employer-funded benefits and changes in work rules.[10] But the personnel techniques that have become more common under these emergent systems may actually increase some personnel costs, particularly those connected with employment of independent contractors, reemployed annuitants, and temporary employees.[11] **Downsizing** may eventually lead to higher recruitment, orientation, and training costs, and loss of organizational memory and "core expertise" necessary to effectively manage service contracting or privatization initiatives.[12] Maintaining minimum staffing levels also results in increased payment of overtime and higher rates of employee accidents and injuries. As the civil service workforce shrinks, it is also aging. This means unforeseen increases in several critical areas: pension payouts, disability retirements, workers' compensation claims, and health-care costs. Increased outsourcing (**contracting out**) makes contract compliance the primary control mechanism over the quality of service, rather than traditional supervisory practices. This creates a real possibility of fraud and abuse.[13]

The impact of non-governmental personnel systems on political responsiveness is problematic. If public problems are viewed as the results of individuals' personal choices, then the responsibility for dealing with the consequences of these problems is individual rather than societal. Downsizing and decentralization reduce the comparative importance of government in society, and refocus governmental activity from a national to a state and local level. Continual budget cuts and pressure to "do more with less" result in agencies that are budget driven rather than mission driven. And budget-driven agencies that address public problems with short-term solutions designed to meet short-term legislative objectives are not likely to be effective.

CONFLICT AND COMPROMISE AMONG ALTERNATIVE PERSONNEL SYSTEMS

Conflict among values and public personnel systems is limited and regulated by the dynamic realities of the competition itself. Because jobs and resources are finite, advocates of each system strive to minimize the influence of others. But each value, carried to its extreme, creates distortions that limit the effectiveness of human resource management because other values are suppressed. So attempts by each system or value to dominate lead inevitably to stabilizing reactions and value compromises. Responsiveness carried to extremes results in the hiring of employees solely on the basis of patronage (**spoils system**), without regard for other qualifications, or in the awarding of contracts based solely on political considerations (graft and **corruption**). Efficiency, carried to extremes, results in over-rationalized personnel procedures—for example, going to decimal points on test scores to make selection or promotion decisions, or making the selection process rigid in the belief that systematic procedures will produce the "best" candidate. Individual rights, carried to extremes, result in overemphasis on seniority or on due process and rigid disciplinary procedures. Social equity, carried to extremes, results in personnel decisions being made solely on the basis of group membership, disregarding individual merit or the need for efficient and responsive government. And it might be expected that anti-government values, carried to extremes, would eventually result in the emergence of a society dominated by markets rather than communitarian values or the public policy-making process. And the weaknesses of market models—primarily their inability to address issues such as distributive equity or indivisible public goods—act to limit reliance on service contracting, privatization, user fees, and other "anti-government" personnel systems.

A HISTORICAL ANALYSIS OF PUBLIC PERSONNEL MANAGEMENT IN THE UNITED STATES

Political Patronage Systems

First, public jobs were allocated primarily among elite leaders—the small group of upper-class property owners who had led the fight for independence and

established a national government. Next, the emergence of political parties created a patronage system that rewarded party members and campaign workers with
jobs once their candidate was elected. The spoils system expanded as the functions
of government and the number of government employees grew after the Civil War
(1861–1865). Political "machines" developed in big cities, supported by newly arrived immigrants. These systems were designed from the street level up, in a sort
of political hierarchy whose mission was to nominate candidates and win elections.
With electoral victory of candidates who had been nominated in conventions of loy-
alist delegates came the opportunity and obligation to dispense patronage or public jobs to those who had worked hardest for the party. In return the new jobholder
would "contribute" (often monthly) a "voluntary" assessment to pay the party officials who had provided the job and to finance future election campaigns.

The patronage system did help millions of immigrants make the transition to
life in a complex urban society. Effective party machines, partisan political leaders
(often serving as role models because they were of the same culture and language
as the immigrants they represented), and local precinct workers brought government to these people. While it does not necessarily result in the selection of highly
qualified employees or provision of efficient government services, the patronage
system does enable elected officials to achieve political objectives by placing loyal
supporters in key positions in administrative agencies. And it increases political responsiveness, because elected officials get reelected by providing voters with access to bureaucrats who often don't seem to understand that rules must sometimes
be bent or broken for voters to feel that justice has been done.

Civil Service Systems

The period between 1883 and 1937 is important in the development of public personnel administration based on merit principles. These principles of merit
and political neutrality reflect what Hugh Heclo has identified as the civil service
ideal—the principle that a competent, committed workforce of career civil servants
is essential to the professional conduct of the public's business.[14] A civil service system grows out of the principles listed in Table 1–2.

While the **Pendleton Act of 1883** espoused efficiency as well as the elimination of politics from personnel decisions, it was some years before efficient methods of recruiting, selecting, and paying employees were available. **Scientific
management**—the application of science to administration in the twentieth century—began to provide the tools, for example, in the areas of selection and position classification.

Position classification is often cited as the cornerstone of public personnel
management, not only because of its centrality among personnel functions but also
because it epitomizes the connection between efficiency and the elimination of
politics from administration. It suggests that public personnel management can
be conducted in a routine and politically neutral fashion, a belief that is philo-
sophically attractive, even if less than accurate in practice. Position classification
offers management a uniform basis for grouping jobs by occupational type and
skill level and an equitable and logical pay plan based on the competencies needed

TABLE 1–2 Civil Service System Principles[15]

1. Recruitment should be from qualified individuals from appropriate sources in an endeavor to achieve a workforce from all segments of society, and selection and advancement should be determined solely on the basis of relative ability, knowledge, and skills, after fair and open competition which assures that all receive equal opportunity.
2. All employees and applicants for employment should receive fair and equitable treatment in all aspects of personnel management without regard to political affiliation, race, color, religion, national origin, sex, marital status, age, or handicapping condition, and with proper regard for their privacy and constitutional rights.
3. Equal pay should be provided for work of equal value with appropriate consideration of both national and local rates paid by employers in the private sector, and appropriate incentives and recognition should be provided for excellence in performance.
4. All employees should maintain high standards of integrity, conduct, and concern for the public interest.
5. The workforce should be used efficiently and effectively.
6. Employees should be retained on the basis of the adequacy of their performance, inadequate performance should be corrected, and employees who cannot or will not improve their performance to meet required standards should be separated.
7. Employees should be provided effective education and training in cases in which such education and training would result in better organizational and individual performance.
8. Employees should be:
    a. protected against arbitrary action, personal favoritism, or coercion for partisan political purposes.
    b. prohibited from using their official authority or influence for the purpose of interfering with or affecting the result on an election or a nomination for election.
9. Employees should be protected against reprisal for the lawful disclosure of information which the employees reasonably believe evidences:
    a. a violation of any law, rule, or regulation,
    b. mismanagement, a gross waste of funds, an abuse of authority, or a substantial and specific danger to public health or safety.

to perform each job; it translates labor costs (for pay and benefits) into impersonal grades that can be added, subtracted, averaged, and moved about to create organizational charts.

At the same time, it can be used to minimize political or administrative abuse and protection of individual rights with regard to personnel functions. Pay rates are tied to positions and thus individual favorites cannot be paid more than others. The work to be performed is specified in a job description. Hiring people at a high salary and asking them to assume few if any responsibilities—which occurs frequently in political patronage positions—is minimized.

The relationship between political patronage systems and civil service systems is intermittently marked by intense conflict, for both systems represent powerful and legitimate values. For example, the tremendous economic, military, and social problems confronting the United States during the New Deal and World War II (1933–1945) brought about the emergence of administrative effectiveness, which combines the scientific principle of efficiency with the political principle of accomplishing objectives demanded by events. This combination of efficiency and effectiveness required that most positions be covered by the civil service system, but that sensitive or policy-making positions be filled by political appointees who were either personally or politically responsive. It resulted in programs consistent with elected officials' philosophy and vision of government, and with administrators' ability to make operational plans and manage resources efficiently (including human resources).

Given the obvious need for politically responsive agency management, one might wonder why civil service systems pay so much attention to protection from political influence.[16] The reason is that incidents frequently indicate that elected officials consider political loyalty the most important criterion for selection to administrative positions, regardless of the applicants' qualifications.[17] Much of the history of public personnel management can be viewed as efforts to reconcile civil service and patronage systems at an operational level. The Pendleton Act (1883) created the civil service system at the federal level, leading eventually to the development and implementation of civil service systems for a majority of professional and technical positions. The **Civil Service Reform Act (CSRA) of 1978**, passed almost a century later, was designed to maintain bureaucratic responsiveness but still protect the career civil service from political interference. It created a **Senior Executive Service (SES)** of high-level administrators who voluntarily elected to leave their civil service positions in return for multiyear performance contracts and the possibility of higher salaries and greater career challenge and flexibility.

As might have been expected, the results of the CSRA are mixed. Some administrators successfully made the transition to SES appointments and received performance bonuses. Other administrators, and impartial observers, felt that the system was flawed from the beginning because of inadequate rewards, unclear performance standards, political pressure on career civil servants to join the SES, and inadequate training for new SES members to teach them how to function in an environment where productivity and control over expenses were more important than they had been in traditional civil service positions. The CSRA did establish that public personnel management agencies had at least two contradictory objectives—protecting employee rights and making agencies politically responsive—which required that the old federal Civil Service Commission be split into two agencies, the **Merit Systems Protection Board (MSPB)** and the **Office of Personnel Management (OPM)**. The MSPB is responsible for hearing appeals from employees alleging that their rights under civil service system laws and rules have been violated[18]; the OPM is responsible for developing, implementing, and evaluating personnel policies within federal agencies.

Collective Bargaining and Affirmative Action Systems

While all public employees covered by collective bargaining agreements are also covered by civil service systems, under collective bargaining the terms and conditions of employment are set by direct contract negotiations between agency management and unions (or employee organizations). This is in contrast to the patronage system, where they are set and operationally influenced by elected officials, or the civil service system, where they are set by law and regulations issued by management and administered by management or an outside authority (such as a civil service board). Collective bargaining in the public sector has many of the same procedures as its private sector counterpart, such as contract negotiations and grievance procedures. But fundamental differences in law and power outweigh these similarities. The right to approve (or disapprove) negotiated contracts is reserved to the appropriate legislative body (such as the city council, school board, or state legislature) because only legislatures are policy-making bodies with the authority to appropriate money to fund contracts. This means that both labor and management realize that ratification of negotiated contracts is more critical than negotiation of them, and they both set their political strategies accordingly.

During this same period, affirmative action emerged to represent social equity through voluntary or court-mandated recruitment and selection practices to correct the underrepresentation of veterans, minorities, and women in the workplace. (Ironically, those who now oppose employment preferences for minorities forget that wartime veterans and disabled veterans—predominantly white males—were the beneficiaries of the first federal affirmative action program). But regardless of their origin, affirmative action systems arose as a direct result of the civil rights movement of the 1960s and the women's rights movement of the 1970s. They were supported by the fundamental beliefs that a representative bureaucracy was essential for our government to function as a democracy; and that other personnel systems had not been effective at ensuring proportional representation.[19]

State and federal administrative agencies, which are responsible for monitoring compliance with affirmative action laws, control affirmative action systems by public agencies or contractors. This system takes effect when a gross disparity exists between the percentage of minority or female employees in an agency and their percentage in a relevant labor pool (such as the community served by that agency, or the percentage of applicants qualified for the position), and when the agency has resisted the voluntary adoption of techniques (such as recruitment, selection, training, or promotion) that would reduce this disparity. In such a case, members of the affected class may sue the agency to force it to take affirmative action in the selection or retention of women or minority group members. If successful, these court efforts may result in considerable judicial control of the agency's personnel system. The court can require an agency to hire or promote specific numbers or percentages of underutilized groups (qualified females or minority group members) until their representation in the agency workforce is more proportionate with their representation in the labor market.

But there are limits to this control. Courts cannot compel affirmative action compliance for legislative or judicial positions. They cannot require an agency to hire minority or female employees if agency managers elect not to fill any vacancies, or to retain minority and women employees in civil service positions if funds are not available to do so.

Alternative Mechanisms and Flexible Employment Relationships

The shift from pro-government to anti-government values leaves the fundamental issue of the appropriate role of government unresolved. Both the ways the debate is framed in the minds of partisans on both sides and the outcome of the conflict are still the subject of political and social controversy.[20] Pro-government adherents see the declining quality of public life as equivalent to a declining quality of life; anti-government value adherents view it as an enhanced opportunity for individuals to make personal choices about their own spending priorities, including community responsibilities. Adherents to the emergent model see their values as liberating, in the sense that they emphasize individual choice and community responsibility. Adherents to the traditional model see the emergent values as a hypocritical overlay atop greed and self-interest.

But whatever the eventual outcome of this controversy, one thing is certain. Historically, it was taken for granted that public program innovations would be accomplished by a staff of career civil service employees, working within the structure of centralized public agencies budgeted with appropriated funds. Today, none of these are true—public programs are more than likely performed by alternative market mechanisms rather than directly by public agencies; and when public agencies are used, they are more likely to be staffed by temporary employees hired through flexible employment mechanisms rather than permanent employees protected by civil service regulations and collective bargaining agreements.

PUBLIC PERSONNEL MANAGEMENT VALUES
AND SYSTEMS IN THE UNITED STATES TODAY

Public personnel management in the United States has evolved as a dynamic equilibrium among competing values and systems for allocating scarce public jobs in a complex and changing environment. These stages are shown in Table 1–3.

TABLE 1–3   Evolution of Public Personnel Systems and Values in the United States

Stage of Evolution	Dominant Value(s)	Dominant System(s)	Pressures for Change
One (1789–1828)	Responsiveness	"Government by elites"	Political parties + Patronage
Two (1828–1883)	Responsiveness	Patronage	Modernization + Democratization
Three (1883–1933)	Efficiency + Individual Rights	Civil Service	Responsiveness + Effective Government
Four (1933–1964)	Responsiveness + Efficiency + Individual Rights	Patronage + Civil Service	Individual Rights + Social Equity
Five (1964–1980)	Responsiveness + Efficiency + Individual Rights + Social Equity	Patronage + Civil Service + Collective Bargaining + Affirmative Action	Dynamic equilibrium among four competing values and systems
Six (1980–now)	Responsiveness + Efficiency + Individual Accountability + Limited government + Community Responsibility	Patronage + Civil Service + Collective Bargaining + Affirmative Action + Alternative mechanisms + Flexible employment relationships	Dynamic equilibrium among four pro-governmental values and systems, and three anti-governmental values and systems

PUBLIC PERSONNEL SYSTEMS AND VALUES IN DEVELOPING COUNTRIES: DEVELOPMENT AND DEMOCRATIZATION[21]

Developing countries tend to be poorer than developed ones. But in many cases, a country rich in exported oil or other natural resources may still suffer from political, economic, or social conditions that lead to its being classified as "developing." So if the difference isn't money, or isn't *just* money, what else is it? The demise of international Communism in 1989 spurred worldwide interest in issues of international development and **democratization**. How exactly do you build government capacity? What is the relationship between effective government and public administration? How do alternative public personnel systems like civil service, unions, or privatization fit into this picture?[22]

Developing countries today face many of the same challenges the United States once faced in their personnel systems. This is understandable. The process of modernizing public management appears to be relatively uniform because pressures for modernization and democratization tend to parallel though lag behind those in the Western world; administrative reforms are introduced by Western consultants or exposure to the West; and Western lenders often mandate administrative reforms as a condition of continued credit.[23]

In the first stage, the *elite leaders* of successful independence movements establish new nations. The transition to a second stage (*patronage*) follows as these emergent nations strive to strengthen the conditions in civil society that underlie effective government (such as education, political participation, economic growth, and social justice) by refining their constitutions, developing political parties, and creating public agencies. This transition is often difficult. Arbitrary postcolonial boundaries, internal ethnic conflicts, and centralized authoritarian leadership patronage (even given its drawbacks) may prevent efforts to build a stable party system. Development of the economy may be hampered by a colonial-era focus on exporting agricultural products, minerals, or timber rather than balanced growth of domestic agriculture, industry, and tourism—or simply by domestic capital flight or lack of external investment.

The third stage, if it occurs, is a transition from patronage to *merit systems* marked by passage of a civil service law, creation of a civil service agency, and development of personnel policies and procedures. It happens due to internal pressures for efficiency (modernization) and human rights (democratization). Often, international lenders and donor governments add external pressures that emphasize government capacity, transparency, and citizen participation. Again, this transition may be difficult. Governments may be large or inefficient due to socialist traditions favoring public control of agencies (such as railroads, airlines, mining and petroleum, banking, health and hospitals, and insurance) that in the United States are part of the private sector. Pressures for transparent, honest, and efficient government may be thwarted by corruption, use of the public sector as the employer of last resort, or a "brain drain" to the private sector because of an underpaid, poorly qualified, and politically vulnerable civil service. Developing countries that lack a strong cultural tradition of the "public interest," the rule of law, or a professional public service may also suffer from administrative formalism: laws, agencies, and practices that look fine "on paper" may not function well in reality.[24] And in countries plagued by class barriers or high underemployment, pressures for employee rights or equal employment of minorities, women, or persons with disabilities are not likely to significantly impact personnel policy or practice.

If and when the transition to civil service occurs, developing countries then seek to balance conflicting values and personnel systems to achieve the contradictory objectives that characterize the fourth stage public personnel management. For example, they must establish an optimum level of public employment, maintain administrative efficiency, and protect public employee rights, and achieve both uniformity and flexibility of personnel policies and procedures. As difficult as these dilemmas are in developed countries like the United States, they may be even more difficult overseas. Colonial traditions and current political pressures tend to produce centralized political and economic systems.[25] As a result, overrigidity and uniformity outweigh administrative flexibility and diversity. "Neo-liberal" economic policies (imposed by international lenders to promote economic development by reducing public expenditures and external debt) lead to layoffs and divestiture of state agencies. While these policies do reduce external debt by cutting public employment and expenditures, they may also increase unemployment, social injustice, and popular discontent with elected leaders or the entire political system. This in turn further undermines civil society and the rule of law. These weaknesses may be accentuated by a strong military role in civil society, compounded by a history of military governments and a United States-backed focus on counterinsurgency and drug-interdiction efforts to support our own national policy objectives. International human rights pressures to reduce the role of the military may actually increase its power by leading to heavier military involvement in newly privatized businesses.

This evolutionary process for public personnel systems in less-developed countries is shown in Table 1–4.

TABLE 1–4   Evolution of Public Personnel Systems and Values
in Developing Countries

Stage of Evolution	Dominant Value(s)	Dominant System(s)	Pressures for Change
One	Responsiveness	"Government by elites"	Political parties + Patronage
Two	Responsiveness	Patronage	Modernization + Democratization
Three	Efficiency + Individual rights	Civil service + Patronage	Responsiveness + Effective government
Four	Responsiveness + Efficiency + Limited government	Patronage + Civil service + Collective bargaining + Privatization	Dynamic equilibrium among pro- and anti-governmental values and systems

The Impact of Context on National Development

So even though developing countries are on average poorer than the United States, the most significant differences are related to culture, circumstance, and power. Let's examine each of them.

Favorable Political Culture.   Our political system developed through successive (and successful) fights against the excesses of patronage, and against social pressures to be the "employer of last resort," in a well-developed economy that provides ample jobs outside government. Though our conflicts with corruption, cronyism, and nepotism are not completely resolved, we do expect that government will provide services efficiently, using honest and qualified employees. Exceptions generate cynicism or indignation precisely because they *are* exceptions. If they were the norm, they would not be news. Nor would they generate reform pressures to make government more honest or efficient.

It took us over two centuries to develop an effective balance between patronage and civil service. It is not reasonable or appropriate to insist that developing countries make this transition easily or quickly. Patronage politics characterized public personnel management at all levels in the United States until at least 1900. It continues today in many governments. In some levels and sectors of government it may not be a major issue; but cynics would respond that patronage is less serious only because it has been replaced by corrupt contracts as a more effective means of exchanging campaign contributions for access to public officials.[26]

Favorable Historical Circumstances.   In the United States, the development of public personnel management has occurred within a context of almost two centuries of democratic government under a single Constitution, and within a civil society widely considered controlled by laws rather than individuals. Though our policy-making process is costly, complex, and tortuous, it results in outcomes that are generally considered to be transparent, effective at maintaining government authority, and politically responsive to the will of the electorate. Our tax system functions well, in spite of (or because of) its voluntary nature. While our society is deeply affected by conflicts based on race, ethnicity, and class, it provides great opportunity for personal growth and economic advancement. Our political and administrative processes are generally open to public scrutiny by a free press and public records laws.

Power.   By every meaningful economic, political, and military measure, the United States is the most powerful country in the world. This power largely exempts us from influence by other nations or international agencies. Indeed, our power is so great that we can either ignore these organizations (as we characteristically do with the United Nations) or use them as instruments to accomplish our own international economic and political objectives (as we do with the World Bank and the International Monetary Fund).

By contrast, less-developed countries may be characterized by factors—mostly beyond their control—that make it difficult to establish conditions of statehood we in the United States take for granted: a national identity, the rule of law, and a self-sufficient economy. Even the development of stable patronage systems may be hampered by societal conditions (e.g., nonfunctional justice systems, inability to meet even minimum standards of education and health care, political leadership based on "cults of personality" rather than true pluralist political parties, and overly centralized and authoritarian political systems).[27] These conditions generally impede **capacity building**—the evolution of rational administrative structures and systems.[28] For example, organizations in many less developed countries share common structural and managerial attributes that differ from those typically found in North America, Europe, and Japan: *low* levels of role specialization, formalism, and morale; *high* levels of centralization, paternalism, authoritarian leadership, rigid stratification, and dysfunctional conflict.[29]

Third, clearly the most significant difference between the evolution of public personnel management in the United States and in developing countries today is that we, in this country, were able to first progress from patronage to civil service; second, to integrate them into an effectiveness model that combined efficiency and patronage; then to integrate affirmative action and collective bargaining into the mix; and finally to establish the boundaries between public personnel management and emergent market-based techniques like privatization and service contracting.[30] By contrast, fledgling personnel systems in less-developed countries are likely to face obstacles—pressure for patronage, underpaid and poorly qualified civil servants, and inadequate public program planning, budgeting, management, and evaluation. A less-developed country that has successfully moved from patronage to civil service still faces pressure from unions and the emergent middle class for high levels of public employment, *and* pressure from lenders to reduce public employment and favor export-oriented agriculture, mining, and logging activities over the domestic industries and services needed to achieve economic and social development. As hard as this evolution has been for us, think how much harder it is for developing countries to establish functional civil service systems, combat patronage, deal with politically powerful unions, and balance demands for contracting and divestiture from international lenders and corporations.[31] How well would we have done if we had had to develop in the same way, facing these conflicts simultaneously rather than sequentially? To put this question another way, consider Fred Astaire and Ginger Rogers, the ballroom dance couple immortalized by the golden age of Hollywood cinema. Both are considered elegant and graceful. But while Fred is more famous, Ginger's job was harder—she did everything he did, only she had to do it backwards and wearing high heels! These factors are shown in Table 1–5.

Doing More with Less—A Lesson We Learn from Developing Countries

A final lesson for us in the United States is that many HR innovations come from outside the United States.[32] Some come from developed countries, others from developing countries. For example: the United Stated experience with "reinventing government" owes much to the neo-liberalism of Margaret Thatcher in

TABLE 1–5 How Country Conditions Affect Public Personnel Systems

1. SUCCESSFUL TRANSITION FROM INDEPENDENCE TO A FUNCTIONAL PATRONAGE SYSTEM

Negative Indicators	*Positive Indicators*
• High reliance on charismatic leadership • Restricted freedom of speech and press • High emphasis on export of agricultural products and raw materials • Capital flight • Societal repression based on race, ethnicity, or class • Inadequate electoral process	• Stable political parties • Open information and free media • Balanced, domestically focused economic growth, including professional/technical • Domestic reinvestment of capital • Some social justice, including minorities and women • Functioning electoral process

2. SUCCESSFUL TRANSITION FROM PATRONAGE TO A FUNCTIONAL CIVIL SERVICE SYSTEM

Negative Indicators	*Positive Indicators*
• Government process considered low on effectiveness, rationality, transparency • Widespread patronage appointments, and job retention based on salary "kickbacks" • High unemployment or underemployment • Public sector the "employer of last resort" • Underpaid, underqualified public employees • Widespread employment discrimination based on race, gender, or ethnicity • High degree of administrative formalism • High role of the military in civil society and government • Government reforms generated mainly by international economic and political pressure	• Government process considered high on effectiveness, rationality, transparency • Civil Service law, public personnel agency, and policies and procedures • Low unemployment or underemployment • Balanced economic growth/development • Adequately paid, qualified civil service • Low level of employment discrimination based on race, gender, or ethnicity • Low degree of administrative formalism • Reduced role of the military in civil society and government • Government reforms due mainly to domestic political, social, and economic pressure

3. SUCCESSFUL TRANSITION BEYOND CIVIL SERVICE TO A MATURE PUBLIC PERSONNEL SYSTEM

Negative Indicators	*Positive Indicators*
• Overrigidity, uniformity, and centralization of personnel policies and practice • Overemphasis on employee rights or on managerial efficiency • Over- or underemployment in the public sector	• Balance of flexibility/rigidity, centralization and decentralization, and uniformity and variation • Balance between employee rights and managerial efficiency • Balanced public and private employment

England[33]; many recent suggestions for Social Security reform are derived from the market-based public employee pension systems long used in Chile[34]; students of race relations in the United States are intrigued by South Africa's structural and behavioral transition from apartheid toward democratic pluralism[35]; and democratic theorists study the high rate of political participation in Costa Rica, achieved through political education in schools, youth elections, and literacy. The point is that as we seek to innovate, and to "do more with less," it is always useful to consider what we can learn from others, as well as what they can learn from us.

SUMMARY

Public personnel management can be viewed from several perspectives. First, it is the *functions* (planning, acquisition, development, and sanction) needed to manage human resources in public agencies. Second, it is the *process* by which a scarce resource (public jobs) is allocated. Third, it reflects the influence of seven symbiotic and competing *values* (political responsiveness, efficiency, individual rights, and social equity under the traditional pro-government model; and individual accountability, downsizing and decentralization, and community responsibility under the emergent anti-government model) over how public jobs should be allocated. Fourth, it is the laws, rules, and regulations used to express these abstract values— personnel *systems* (political appointments, civil service, collective bargaining, and affirmative action under the traditional model; and alternative mechanisms for providing public services, and flexible employment relationships under the emergent anti-government model).

The history of public personnel management in the United States can be understood conceptually as conflict and compromise among competing personnel systems and values. Administrative systems in general (and public personnel systems in particular) in less-developed countries tend to evolve along a single track toward the model of increased rationality and transparency valued by international lenders as indicators of effective government and economic development. With respect to personnel systems, this generally involves a sequential transition from statehood to patronage, from patronage to civil service, and from civil service to a range of alternative personnel systems.

The evolution of public personnel management in developing countries reflects a process similar and yet different from that we are familiar with in the United States. On the one hand, pressures for modernization and democratization tend to parallel though lag behind those in the Western world; Western consultants tend to introduce administrative reforms; and Western lenders often mandate them as a condition of continued credit. On the other hand, each country's administrative systems and innovations reflect its own history, culture, and conditions. Yet beyond this, most developing countries face the difficult prospect of developing civil service systems to move past patronage, curbing the power of politically influential unions while maintaining employee rights, and achieving the benefits of privatization while avoiding its pitfalls. Privatization may be justified *administratively* by claims that it will reduce costs and provide better service. But *political* objectives (such as the demands of outside donor agencies, or internal political pressures to divest assets to enrich potential purchasers) are likely to dominate the debate. And in any case, privatization in less-developed countries is not likely to be effective at reducing costs and providing better service unless the country has already made successive (and successful) transitions from independence to statehood, to patronage, and to civil service. Until these transitions occur, it is not likely that country's government has adequate administrative capacity to manage the process. If it does not, privatization is more likely to suffer from crony capitalism, military diversification into the civil economy, or administrative formalism.

So for us living and working at the dawn of a new millennium, responsible professionalism means first that we become more aware of what is happening in developing countries, and then that we act in support of their own development efforts.

KEY TERMS

affirmative action system
capacity-building
Civil Service Reform Act (1978)
civil service system
collective bargaining system
community responsibility
contracting out
corruption
democratization
downsizing
exempt positions
franchise agreements
free enterprise capitalism
individual accountability
individual rights
limited and decentralized government
merit system
Merit Systems Protection Board (MSPB)
non-governmental organizations (NGOs)
not-for-profit organizations
Office of Personnel Management (OPM)
organizational efficiency and
effectiveness

PADS (planning, acquisition,
development, and sanction)
part-time positions
Pendleton Act (1883)
personnel management
political patronage systems
political responsiveness
privatization
public personnel system
purchase-of-service agreements
regulatory and tax incentives
representative bureaucracy
scientific management
Senior Executive Service (SES)
social equity
spoils system
subsidy arrangements
temporary positions
values
volunteers
vouchers

DISCUSSION QUESTIONS

1. Identify and describe the four public personnel management functions (PADS).
2. Why are public jobs scarce resources? What is the significance of this observation?
3. What are the four competing values that have traditionally affected the allocation of public jobs? What are the three more recently emergent "anti-government" values that conflict with them?
4. What is a personnel system?
5. Identify and describe the four traditional competing public personnel systems. What are the two emergent anti-government personnel systems that have recently been added to them?

6. Why is it possible to trace the development of public personnel management as conflict and symbiosis among alternative personnel systems?
7. What values and systems have dominated public personnel management in the United States over the past two centuries?
8. In what respects is the evolution of public personnel management in developing countries similar to, and different from, its evolution in the United States? Why?
9. What can we learn from developing countries that might help us with our own developmental issues?
10. As responsible public administrators and public personnel managers, what can we do to promote the development of rational and transparent government, at home and abroad?

CASE STUDY 1: VALUES AND FUNCTIONS IN PUBLIC PERSONNEL MANAGEMENT

Identify the appropriate value(s), systems, and functions in these examples. Explain your choices.

1. A state is going to fill a vacancy in its community-development agency. The state representative who controls the appropriations committee for all legislation involving the agency has suggested that an applicant from her district fill a high-level position in the civil service. A major contributor to the governor's reelection campaign contends that the job ought to be filled by a prominent real estate developer. Neither candidate has the education or experience specified as desirable in the job description.
2. A federal agency is considering a layoff. It anticipates a budget shortfall that is going to require cutbacks in personnel since the legislature has shown no indication that it is willing to raise taxes. The agency director has suggested that a layoff score be computed for each employee, based primarily on the person's performance appraisal. The Federation of Employees, which is the recognized bargaining agent for the agency's employees, strongly objects and proposes that the layoffs be based on seniority.
3. A county anticipates a request by surrounding cities to provide water services for all county residents. This will require upgrading the skills of a substantial number of county employees and will provide those employees with opportunities for advancement. The union insists that the training slots be allocated to current employees on a seniority basis. The affirmative action officer, seeing this as an opportunity to increase the number of minorities in higher-paying positions, proposes that several of the openings be set aside for current minority employees.
4. A city government is looking for ways to reduce costs. The city commission amends its charter to remove the sanitation department from the civil service system. This in effect nullifies the collective bargaining agreement between the city and its unionized sanitation employees. The city lays off all these employees and contracts instead for solid waste services provided by an outside private contractor.
5. Here is a scenario that takes the values beyond a human resources management perspective:

   A state government closes many of its public parks and recreation areas because prison construction has taken an increasing share of state revenues and caused corresponding budget cuts in many other state agencies. It has increased user fees at others, in an effort to generate revenues sufficient to keep the parks open. The three results from this are all predictable: The number of visitors at state parks and recreation areas declines, as many people are excluded by higher user fees; those visitors that do come to the parks complain increasingly about inadequate facilities and maintenance; and attendance and profits at private recreation theme parks within the state (Disney World, Busch Gardens, etc.) increase dramatically.

CASE STUDY 2: POLITICAL CLEARANCE FOR "BUCK" PLEAKE

Reaction against political patronage systems focused at the federal level in 1883, when the assassination of newly elected President Garfield by a disappointed job seeker caused an outpouring of criticism against the inefficiencies of the spoils system. But patronage remained a powerful force at the state and local levels, especially in agencies like corrections, public works, transportation, and county sheriff. During the 1960s and 1970s, newly elected officials routinely discharged the patronage employees appointed by their predecessors and replaced them with their own appointees, who received their jobs on the basis of having supported the newly elected official's candidacy—and sometimes because of an informal commitment to "voluntarily" return a percentage of their salaries as a direct political contribution or as a disguised contribution through the purchase of tickets to political dinners or other fund raising events.

Although elected officials and other supporters of patronage systems defended the contributions as voluntary, in reality employees who quit making contributions risked losing their jobs, because local party leaders declined to give them the political clearance they needed to certify their loyalty for the patronage position. This is what happened to "Buck" Pleake, a long-time employee of the Indiana State Highway Commission who was required to reapply for political clearance in order to retain his job. In fact, the requirement was impossible to meet and was imposed deliberately because he had chosen to test the "voluntary" nature of the campaign contributions required of all employees by ceasing to contribute.

After reading the background information on the case, answer the following questions.

1. Was "Buck" Pleake's political contribution voluntary or involuntary?
2. Why did the Indiana State Employees Association raise the issue with the Governor?
3. What were the Governor's conflicting responsibilities in the case? How did he resolve them?
4. What is the proper balance between competencies and political or personal loyalty in determining suitability for a government job? Why?
5. What has been the relationship between the political, social, and economic conditions in the United States and our evolution toward more diverse and elaborate public personnel systems?
6. To what extent is this U.S. experience with patronage and corruption comparable with that of developing countries?

STATE of INDIANA

INDIANAPOLIS

INDIANA STATE HIGHWAY COMMISSION
100 North Senate Avenue
Indianapolis, Indiana 46204

Greencastle, Indiana
November 8, 1974

Jewell M. Pleake
RR #1
Stilesville, Indiana

Dear Sir,

In compliance with the Indiana employee's patronage system, requiring patronage clearance, I requested on October 4, 1974 and again on October 9, 1974, that you return to me a completed patronage form.

As you have not complied with my request, I am notifying you on instructions from John Harlan, District Administrative Officer, effective November 12, 1974, that your employment, as shop foreman, from the Greencastle sub-district garage, Crawfordsville district, Indiana State Highway Commission, has terminated.

Yours truly,

Harold Baire

Harold Baire, Superintendent
Sub-District Garage
Greencastle, Indiana

cc: Thomas Milligan
     Judson Dutton
     Paul Green
     Kelsey McDaniels

POLITICAL ENDORSEMENT — INDIANA REPUBLICAN STATE COMMITTEE
(This is not an application for employment)

Dept. _____

Name _____
        (Last)   (First)   (Middle Initial)

Address _____
        (Street or Route)   (City or Town)   (Zip)

County _____ Twp. _____ Precinct _____ Cong. Dist. _____

Telephone _____ Birth Date _____ Political Party_____

Did you vote in the last Primary election?_____ If so, in what county? _____

Signature _____ Date _____

Endorsements

(2) Precinct Comm. _____   (1) Vice Comm. _____

(4) Twp. or Ward Chr. _____   (3) Vice Chr._____

(6) County Chr. _____   (5) Vice Chr._____

(7) State Chr. _____

Jewell Venice Pleake
R. R. #1
Stilesville, Indiana

Your application for political clearance has
been processed and approved by the Indiana Republican State Central Committee.

THIS CARD MAY BE USED AS PROOF OF POLITICAL
CLEARANCE.

MAR 14 1973

INDIANA STATE EMPLOYEES ASSOCIATION, INC.

632 ILLINOIS BUILDING, 17 WEST MARKET STREET, INDIANAPOLIS, INDIANA 46204 · (317) 632-7254

November 13, 1974

Governor Otis R. Bowen, M.D.
State House
Indianapolis, Indiana 46204

Dear Governor Bowen:

I am taking this opportunity to correspond with you at some length because I believe we have a matter that deserves your personal attention. I am not sure in my own mind that this matter has been brought to your attention, although I have attempted to proceed through regular channels, including Mr. William Lloyd, your Executive Assistant.

While I could complain about the many instances of what we believe to be outright harassment of state highway employees, one particular case illustrates the problem very well and raises some profound questions. I am referring to the case of Jewell V. ("Buck") Pleake, an employee of the Greencastle sub-district of the Crawfordsville District of the Indiana State Highway Commission.

Buck Pleake had been employed with the ISHC for some six years. Being promoted up to the position of Shop Foreman, Buck has proven himself to be a dependable, conscientious employee and one who is well-respected among his peers. We have encountered nothing in Highway Department records or in our discussions with Highway officials that would make us believe otherwise.

On October 4, 1974, Buck was suddenly given a new set of "Patronage Clearance" papers and told to have them completed by the following Monday--an action which requires no less than eight signatures be obtained. I will not attempt to detail all that occurred to Buck as he tried to comply. Perhaps I can illustrate how ludicrous the affair became if you can picture Buck waiting outside the Operating Room of a local hospital to get his county vice-chairperson, Mrs. Swisher, to sign. Mrs. Swisher, a nurse, was apparently very put out by the whole affair and would not sign the form and directed they be left for her to deal with later. The clearance papers did not surface again for almost two weeks. As he attempted to obtain the signatures, it became increasingly clear to Buck that he had been singled out because he was not paying "2%." Finally, Mr. Paul Green, the Sixth District Chairman, flatly refused to sign, saying that Mr. Pleake had already been replaced. On November 11, 1974, Buck received a letter notifying him he was officially terminated from his employment. His termination was solely based on his failure to complete these new clearance papers.

Lest I forget, Buck was "cleared" for his job when first employed six years ago and he also received a postcard from Republican State Central Committee in March, 1973, indicating he was "recleared" since the change to your Administration. The postcard said that it was proof of clearance. It has become very apparent to us that Buck's recent attempt at reclearance and subsequent discharge was directed by Tom Milligan, the Republican State Chairman. Mr. Milligan has been publicly quoted as saying that employees should be fired if they don't pay their "2%," job performance notwithstanding.

This situation frankly raises doubts in my mind as to who is the final authority in running the Highway Commission, a state governmental agency. The entire chain of events leads me to believe the political party runs the state Highway Commission, not the officials who were elected and appointed to do so. In these days of Watergate backlash, I am distressed to see such a situation allowed to persist. We have been told continually through this chain of events that the decisions were left in the hands of others and that even the District Engineer could not resolve the problem, but rested with the District and State Chairmen.

More important is the fact that your commitment has been that "job retention should be based on the ability to perform adequately and the quality of the work done." I quote from your letter to me dated September 27, 1974, at which time you also indicated that any employee political contributions should be strictly voluntary.

Mr. Pleake's job promotions and previous political clearance speak for themselves and would leave only this recent decision not to pay 2% as the sole reason behind this effort by the State Republican Chairman and may in fact alienate a dedicated Republican such as Mr. Pleake, and others as well. It also raises the question of integrity on the part of the Republican State Central Committee who issued a "proof of clearance" to Mr. Pleake in March 1973.

Governor, if the precedent is allowed to stand that an employee is at any time subject to sudden "reclearance" in
order to keep his job, then we have both done a disservice
to the employees. If the criterion upon which job retention
is based is politics or contribution, I foresee morale drop-
ping to an all-time low in state government. In the Highway
Department, where the problem is particularly acute, many
will begin to abandon their employment at the earliest possible opportunity, for they will know that even if they do
their job well, they will never be secure. This is particularly disturbing to me, now that the important period of
snow and ice removal is fast upon us.

I honestly believe the situation to be very critical. At
the same time, I have considerable confidence in your ability to govern and I appreciate the many fine things that
have been accomplished to better state service during your
tenure. I request that you give this situation your personal and immediate attention.

                    Sincerely,

                    Charles F. Eble

                    Charles F. Eble
                    Executive Secretary, ISEA

P.S. - This situation also involves Mr. Pleake's son.

cc: Bose, McKinney & Evans

CFE:pvt

OFFICE OF THE GOVERNOR

INDIANAPOLIS, INDIANA 46204

OTIS R. BOWEN, M. D.
GOVERNOR

November 14, 1979

Mr. Charles F. Eble
Executive Secretary
Indiana State Employees Association, Inc.
417 Illinois Building
17 West Market Street
Indianapolis, Indiana 46204

Dear Mr. Eble:

Attached is a memo that I am sending out today to
all department heads and to the Republican State
Chairman.

Sincerely,

Otis R. Bowen, M.D.
Governor

ORB:vw

TO: All Department Heads
          Mr. Thomas S. Milligan

FROM: Otis R. Bowen, M.D.
          Governor

RE: 2% Contributions

DATE: November 14, 1974

Rumors and accusations are coming to my attention that
threats of firing and replacements are being made to
patronage employees.

I want to reiterate what I have said publicly several times:

          "Job retention should be based
          on the ability to perform
          adequately and the quality of
          work done."

ORB:vw

OFFICE OF THE GOVERNOR

INDIANAPOLIS, INDIANA 46204

OTIS R. BOWEN, M. D.
GOVERNOR

September 27, 1974

Charles F. Eble
Executive Secretary
Indiana State Employees Association, Inc.
417 Illinois Building
17 West Market Street
Indianapolis, Indiana 46204

Dear Mr. Eble:

Thank you very much for your recent letter and the resolution.
Please express my thanks to the members of your association.
I appreciate your kind remarks and hope that encouragement of
voluntary contributions be continued. I feel that everyone
has an obligation to support the political party and perhaps
those who are employed by government directly or indirectly
as a result of political activity have a little more obligation
than others not so employed.

Once again, I emphasize that my remarks and my letter and my
attitude are that it should be voluntary and that I make no
threats whatsoever concerning job retention being dependent
upon contributions. Job retention should be based on the ability
to perform adequately and the quality of the work done.

Kindest personal regards,

Otis R. Bowen, M.D.
Governor

ORB:lkd

NOTES

[1]Tussman, J. (1960). *Obligation and the body politic.* New York: Oxford University Press.

[2]Beckett, Julia (2000). The "government should run like a business" mantra. *American Review of Public Administration, 30* (2): 185–204.

[3]Freyss, S. F. (Fall 1995). Municipal government personnel systems. *Review of Public Personnel Management, 16:* 69–93.

[4]International City Management Association (1989). *Service delivery in the 90s: Alternative approaches for local governments.* Washington, DC: ICMA.

[5]Mahtesian, C. (April 1994). Taking Chicago private. *Governing*, pp. 26–31.

[6]Siegel, Gilbert B. (March 1999). Where are we on local government service contracting?" *Public Productivity and Management Review, 22* (3): 365–388; O'Looney, John (1998). *Outsourcing State and Local Government Services: Decision Making Strategies and Management Methods.* Westport, CT: Greenwood; and Martin, Lawrence L. (1999). *Contracting for Service Delivery: Local Government Choices.* Washington, DC: International City/County Management Association.

[7]United States Merit Systems Protection Board (1994). *Temporary federal employment: In search of flexibility and fairness.* Washington, DC: U.S. Merit Systems Protection Board.

[8]Hsu, Spencer (September 4, 2000). Death of "big government" alters region: Less-skilled D.C. workers lose out as area prospers. *Washington Post,* p. A1+.

[9]Brewer, Gene, and Robert A. Maranto (2000). Comparing the roles of political appointees and career executives in the U.S. Federal executive branch. *American Review of Public Administration, 30* (1): 69–86.

[10]Cohen, S., and W. Eimicke (1994). The overregulated civil service. *Review of Public Personnel Administration, 15,* 11–27.

[11]Peters, B. G., and D. J. Savoie (1994). Civil service reform: Misdiagnosing the patient. *Public Administration Review, 54,* 418–425.

[12]Milward, H. Brinton (1996). Introduction: Symposium on the hollow state: Capacity, control, and performance in interorganizational settings. *Journal of Public Administration Research and Theory, 6* (4), 193–7.

[13]Moe, R. C. (1987). Exploring the limits of privatization. *Public Administration Review, 47,* 453–460.

[14]Heclo. *A government of strangers.* Washington, DC: The Brookings Institution, p. 20.

[15]Civil Service Reform Act of 1978. P.L. 95–454, October 13, 1978.

[16]Sayre, W. (1948). The triumph of techniques over purpose. *Public Administration Review, 8,* 134–137; and Fischer, J. (October 1945). Lets go back to the spoils system. *Harper's, 191,* 362–368.

[17]Hamilton, David K. (1999). The continuing judicial assault on patronage. *Public Administration Review, 59* (1), 54–62.

[18]West, William F., and Robert F. Durant (2000). Merit, management, and neutral competence: Lessons from the U.S. Merit Systems Protection Board, FY 1988–FY 1997. *Public Administration Review, 60* (2): 111–122.

[19]Mosher, F. (1982). *Democracy and the Public Service* (2nd ed.). New York: Oxford University Press.

[20]Kirlin, John J. (1996). What government must do well: Creating value for society. *Journal of Public Administration Research and Theory, 6* (1): 161–185.

[21]Klingner, Donald E. (1996). Public personnel management and democratization: A view from three Central American republics. *Public Administration Review, 56,* 390–399.

[22]Bekke, Hans, James L. Perry, and Theo Toonen, eds. (1996). *Civil Service Systems in Comparative Perspective.* Bloomington: Indiana University Press.

[23]Salgado, Rene (1997). Public administration for results: choice, design and sustainability in institutional development and civil service reform. DPP Working Paper Series No. 106. Washington, DC: Interamerican Development Bank.

[24]Kearney, Richard C. (1986). Spoils in the Caribbean: The struggle for merit-based civil service in the Dominican Republic. *Public Administration Review, 46, 2:* 66–80.

[25]Glade, William, ed. (1996). Bigger economies, smaller governments: The role of privatization in Latin America. Boulder, CO: Westview Press, 247–275.

[26]Darrough, Masako N. (2000). Privatization and corruption: Patronage vs. spoils. *International Public Management Journal, 2* (2): 273–298.

[27]Klingner, Donald E. (December 2000). South of the border: Problems and progress in implementing new public management reforms in Mexico today. *American Review of Public Administration*, 30 (4), 365–373.

[28]Ruffing-Hilliard, Karen, in Ali Farazmand (1991). Merit reform in Latin America: A comparative perspective. *Handbook of Comparative and Development Public Administration*. New York: Marcel Dekker, pp. 301–312.

[29]Kettl, Donald (1997). The global revolution in public management: Driving themes, missing links. *Journal of Policy Analysis and Management*, 16, 3, 446–462.

[30]Klingner, Donald E., and Mohamed G. Sabet (2002). Contemporary public human resource management: patronage, civil service, privatization, and service contracting, in Krishna Tummala (ed.). *Encyclopedia of Life Support Systems*. New York: UNESCO.

[31]Kearney, Richard C., and Steven W. Hays (Fall 1998). Reinventing government: The new public management and civil service systems in international perspective. *Review of Public Personnel Administration*, 40–54.

[32]Klingner, Donald, and Charles W. Washington (January 2000). Through the Looking Glass: Realizing the Advantages of an International and Comparative Approach for Teaching Public Administration, *Journal of Public Affairs Education* 6 *1*: 35–43.

[33]Savoie, Donald J. (1990). Public management development: A comparative perspective. *International Journal of Public Sector Management*, 3: 40–52.

[34]Mesa-Lago, Carmelo. Pension reform in Latin America: Importance and evaluation of privatization approaches. In Glade, William, ed. (1996). *Bigger Economies, Smaller Governments: The Role of Privatization in Latin America*. Boulder, CO: Westview Press, 89–134; and Gunter Nagel, S. (1997). Developments in social security systems: Reflections on the work of the Council of Europe in this field. *International Review of Administrative Sciences*, 63(2): 225 +.

[35]Perkins, Edward J. (1990). New dimensions in foreign affairs: Public administration theory in practice. *Public Administration Review*, 50 (4), 490–493; and Harrison-Rockey, Samantha (1999). What state has been reached in the reform and transformation of the structures and systems of government? The case of South Africa. *International Review of Administrative Sciences*, 65(2): 169 +.

2
Doing Public HRM in the United States

INTRODUCTION

While the first chapter's discussion could focus conceptually on public HRM functions, values, systems, and techniques for allocating jobs, the remainder of the book focuses on what HRM is, and how it is carried out in context.

Five key issues dominate this discussion. First, *what* is public employment in the United States? How many people are employed in which functions by what level of government, now and historically. What are the realities of public employment, particularly in light of the myths used to reinforce alternative values and systems?

Second, *who* is responsible for public HR management? The personnel department is the tip of the iceberg. Most HRM is not done by personnel managers or even by the technical specialists they supervise. Rather, it is shared among elected officials (who establish policies and fund systems), appointed officials (who design systems), personnel managers (who develop policies and procedures), and managers and supervisors (who implement these systems in the day-to-day process of working with employees and within agencies).

Third, we know from Chapter 1 that HR directors and specialists function within a variety of traditional and contemporary public personnel systems, each responsible for carrying out underlying values about who gets public jobs, and how. But we don't yet understand how the day-to-day *practice* of HR differs depending on the system—or combination of systems—under which an agency operates. This section shows how patterns of law and practice have led alternative systems to emphasize different functions and to perform them differently.

Fourth, while we know that public HR management comprises relationships among three major groups (elected and appointed officials, personnel directors and specialists, and managers and supervisors), we don't know how this translates into organizational *structures and relationships*.

Fifth, we have yet to examine how the evolution of values and systems described in Chapter 1 affects the *roles and competencies*, and therefore the requisite experience and training, required of those who aspire to careers as public HR managers. And because managers and supervisors carry out most HRM, we must examine how these changes have affected the competencies required of public administrators generally.

By the end of this chapter, you will be able to:

1. Discuss the myths and realities of public employment in the United States.
2. Explain how responsibility for public HR functions is shared among elected and appointed officials, managers and supervisors, and personnel directors and specialists.
3. Describe how public HR is done under the different systems introduced in Chapter 1.
4. Discuss contemporary HRM role expectations for politicians, HR directors and specialists, and managers.
5. Describe the four key HRM roles: technician, professional, educator, and mediator.
6. Build a career in public HRM as a HR specialist or a general administrator by learning what competencies are important, knowing how to get them, and keeping your skills current.

PUBLIC EMPLOYMENT IN THE UNITED STATES: MYTHS AND REALITIES

While in the public's view federal employees often symbolize government bureaucracy, in reality they constitute only about 17 percent of all public employees. Federal government employment peaked at 3.4 million during World War II, receded to 2.0 million in 1947, and rose again to 2.5 million in 1951. After fifteen years of minor fluctuations, federal employment gradually rose again to 3.1 million in 1987. It began to decline again in 1990, reaching a current level of 2.8 million in 1997, about the same level as in 1966.[1]

State and local government employment both grew steadily after World War II from a total of 3.6 million in 1946 to over 13.3 million in 1980. While the rate of growth has slowed since 1977, total state government employment has increased to 4.7 million and local government employment to 12.0 million in 1997. Of the 12 million local government employees (1997), 2.4 million are employed by counties, 3.2 million by cities and towns, 5.7 million by school districts, and .7 million by other special districts (such as airports). These total employee figures include hours worked by part-time employees, comprising nearly 4.5 million of the total 19.5 million public employees. Table 2–1 shows these historical trends. In 1997, these 19.5 million public employees were employed in a variety of functions, as shown in Table 2–2. The primary federal functions were national defense, postal service, and financial management; the primary state and local functions were education, police protection, highways, corrections, welfare, and utilities—with the emphasis on education. Numbers of employees are given in thousands. (Percentages will not total 100 due to rounding to the nearest whole percent.)

TABLE 2–1 Government Civilian Employment, 1940–1997[2]

	EMPLOYEES (IN MILLIONS)			
Year	Total	Federal	State	Local
1940	4.4	1.1	3.3	(includes local)
1950	6.4	2.1	1.1	3.2
1960	8.8	2.4	1.5	4.9
1970	13.0	2.9	2.8	7.4
1980	16.2	2.9	3.8	9.6
1990	18.4	3.1	4.5	10.8
1997	19.5	2.8	4.7	12.0

TABLE 2–2 Government Employment by Function and Level of Government, 1997[3]

Function	Total	%	Federal	%	State, Local, Other	%
Total	19,540	100	2,807	14	16,733	86
Education	8,969	46	11		8,958	46
Hospitals	1,223	6	163	1	1,060	5
Health	548	3	136	1	412	2
Public Welfare	507	3	9		498	3
Social Insurance Administration	165	1	69		96	
National Defense	777	4	777	4	0	
Space Research & Technology	20		20		0	
Police	951	5	95	1	856	4
Fire Protection	356	2	0		356	2
Corrections	709	4	30		679	4
Postal Service	854	4	854	4	0	
Transportation	666	4	67		599	4
Natural Resources	397	2	191	1	206	1
Parks & Recreation	354	2	24		330	2
Housing & Community Development	141	1	18		123	1
Sewerage	129	1	0		129	1
Solid Waste Management	115	1	0		115	1
Financial Administration	533	3	139	1	394	2
Judicial and Legal Administration	419	2	53		366	2
Other Government Administration	406	2	22		384	2
Water Supply	318	2	0		318	2
Electric Power	158	1	0		158	1
Gas Supply	20		0		20	
Transit	388	2			388	2
All other	417	2	129	1	288	1

SHARED RESPONSIBILITY FOR PUBLIC HUMAN RESOURCE MANAGEMENT

Three main groups share responsibility for public personnel management (or HRM, as it is also commonly termed): political leaders, personnel directors and specialists, and other managers and supervisors. Political leaders (legislators, executives, and their political appointees) are responsible for authorizing personnel systems, and for establishing their objectives and funding levels. Agencies must be created, program priorities established, and funds allocated to meet program objectives before jobs can be designed or positions filled. In addition, the personnel system itself must be designed and authorized. This is true no matter which systems dominate HR policy and practice, because the same general functions (PADS) are required regardless.

Personnel directors and specialists design and implement personnel systems, or direct and help those who do. In civil service systems, they usually work within a personnel department that functions as a staff support service for managers and supervisors. Their main responsibility is achieving agency goals within a prescribed budget and a limited number of positions. HR directors and specialists both help line managers use human resources effectively; they constrain their personnel actions within the limits imposed by political leaders, laws, and regulations.

Most HR functions (PADS) are performed by the managers and supervisors who work with employees on a day-to-day basis, not by personnel departments. Administrators (from first-level supervisors to senior directors) are responsible for the routine managerial and supervisory activities. Supervisors instruct and train employees, provide informal feedback on how they are doing, and recommend pay increases (or disciplinary action and dismissal) based on their assessment of employee job performance. Managers and supervisors thus are responsible for implementing almost all the rules, policies, and procedures that constitute personnel systems. Their behavior is critical because the relationship between individual employees and their supervisors is the key influence on how effectively employees are developed and used. This sets the climate, or culture, that embodies the organization's HRM policy. Table 2–3 shows how HRM responsibility is shared among these three groups.

HOW PUBLIC HRM IS DONE UNDER DIFFERENT PERSONNEL SYSTEMS

While the basic HRM functions remain the same under all systems, system values dictate that the relative emphasis among functions and how they are performed differ depending on the system.

HRM Under a Patronage System

HRM under a patronage system heavily emphasizes recruitment and selection of applicants based on personal or political loyalty. The other three functions are simply irrelevant or de-emphasized. The HR specialist is not a personnel di-

TABLE 2–3   Shared Responsibility for Personnel Functions

FUNCTION	LEVEL		
	Elected and Appointed Officials	*Managers and Supervisors*	*Personnel Directors and Specialists*
Planning	Estimate revenues; set program priorities	Manage to mission within a budget	Develop job descriptions, implement pay and benefit plans
Acquisition	Influence values that guide the selection process	Hire and fire employees	Develop hiring rules and procedures
Development	Define agency and program goals and priorities	Make sure employees have clear goals, skills, feedback, and rewards	Develop training and evaluation systems
Sanction	Determine appropriate personnel systems	Counsel and discipline employees and policies	Develop policies and programs for drug testing, discipline

rector, but instead a political advisor or even a political party official responsible for identifying individuals who deserve or require a political position, screening them informally to make sure that their personal and political background does not include activities or associations that might embarrass or discredit their boss politically, and then recommending who should be hired in which position. The elected official then makes the appointment (or nominates the individual, if legislative confirmation is required) based upon the candidate's competencies, political or personal loyalty, financial or campaign support for the elected official, or support by an influential interest group seeking access to the policy-making process. Nomination and appointment of women or minorities may be important as political symbolism, but affirmative action laws do not apply to judicial, legislative, or other patronage appointments. Once hired, political appointees are subject to the whims of the elected official. Few rules govern their job duties, pay, or rights, and they are usually fired at will. Nor is development a priority. Employees are hired for a current position, not for a career. Though they may end up serving in a series of progressively responsible political positions, there is no guarantee of that.

HR in a Civil Service System

In a civil service system, HR is a department or office that functions as an administrative support service to the city manager, school superintendent, hospital director, or other agency administrator. Because civil service is a complete system, HR has a balanced emphasis on each of the four major personnel functions—planning, acquisition, development, and sanction.

Planning.   HR is responsible for maintaining the system of positions that have been categorized into a plan according to criteria like degree of difficulty or type of work. The total number of positions, the types of jobs, and their pay levels are established and restricted legislatively by pay and personnel ceilings. The pay system is usually tied to the classification system, with jobs involving similar degrees of difficulty being compensated equally. Periodic checks are conducted to compare the actual work a person is doing with the duties outlined in a job description for the position. Yearly pay plan updates are also performed as budget planning exercises or in anticipation of collective bargaining negotiations. HR is also responsible for developing and updating the agency's retirement and benefits programs, and for negotiating with benefit providers. It maintains records like eligibility and use of sick leave and vacation time, enrollment and maintenance in various health insurance programs, and life insurance or savings bond purchases. It also handles calculation of authorized retirement benefits, disability retirement determinations, and monitoring of workers' compensation claims for job-related injuries and illnesses.

Acquisition.   HR is responsible for scheduling tests for jobs that are frequently available. It advertises vacant or new positions, conducts an initial review of job applications and administers written tests. HR compiles a list of those eligible for employment, maintains the list to ensure it is up-to-date as job applicants secure other employment, and provides a ranked list of eligible applicants to managers in units where vacancies actually exist. After the manager conducts interviews and selects one applicant, HR then processes the paperwork required to employ and pay the person.

Development.   HR is responsible for orienting new employees to the organization, its work rules, and the benefits it provides. It keeps track of and distributes notices of training or transfer opportunities. It may conduct training itself. HR also tracks and processes all **personnel actions**—changes in employee status such as hiring, transfer, promotion, or dismissal.

Sanction.   HR establishes and staffs an employee grievance and appeals procedure; advises supervisors throughout the organization of appropriate codes of conduct for employees; establishes the steps necessary to discipline an employee for violations of these rules and the procedures to follow in the event the employee appeals this disciplinary action or files a grievance.

HR in a Collective Bargaining System

If employees are covered by a collective bargaining agreement, the personnel department is usually responsible for negotiating the agreement (or hiring an outside negotiator who performs this function), bringing pay and benefit provisions into accord with contract provisions, orienting supervisors on how to comply with the contract, and representing the agency in internal grievance resolution or outside arbitration procedures. Because collective bargaining is a partial personnel system, civil service systems continue to provide most of the rules and procedures relating to acquisition and development.

HR in an Affirmative Action System

HR is responsible primarily for implementing human resource acquisition decision rules emphasizing social equity for protected classes. Thus, it most heavily affects recruitment, selection, and promotion policies and procedures. The affirmative action director shares responsibility with the personnel director in this area. Once members of protected classes are hired, other personnel systems (civil service or collective bargaining) influence the way in which planning, development, and sanction functions occur.

HR under Alternative Mechanisms

HR is handled differently depending on which specific alternative mechanism is used. In general, reliance on non-governmental organizations reduces the absolute number of public employees, thereby reducing the HR department's functions related to acquisition, development, and sanction of public employees. However, it does increase the importance of planning and oversight, which are necessary to estimate the type and number of contract employees needed to provide a desired level of service; develop requests for proposals to outside contractors; evaluate responses to proposals by comparing costs and services; and overseeing contract administration. HR directors, staff, and managers work increasingly with citizen volunteers and community-based organizations, much as personnel directors for not-for-profit organizations (such as community recreation programs, hospitals, and schools) have traditionally used volunteers to supplement paid staff. In these cases, public managers need to become more skilled in recruitment, selection, training, and motivation of volunteer workers.[4]

HR under Flexible Employment Relationships

Flexibility in employment relationships is achieved primarily by the increased use of temporary, part-time, and seasonal employment; and by increased hiring of exempt employees through employment contracts. This generally means less emphasis on planning and employee development, at least for these employees.

Development is largely irrelevant. Contingent workers are hired with the skills needed to perform the job immediately. Performance evaluation is unnecessary—if they do their jobs adequately, they get paid; if not, they are simply released at the end of their contract and not called back when workload once again increases. Their motivation is financial or based on work-life balance considerations, perhaps augmented by the chance of being hired into a civil service position if vacancies become available.

Nor is the sanction function particularly important with respect to these workers. Like political appointments, but unlike their civil service counterparts, at-will employees have no right to retain their jobs. They can be discharged for any reason, or for no reason, without management having to give a reason or to support the dismissal.

HR under Mixed (Hybrid) Public Personnel Systems

Thus far we have discussed HR functions under uniform public personnel systems. Since a system is by definition a set of assumptions, values, laws, rules, and procedures, HRM would be fairly routine if it all took place within the context of a single system. But in the "real world" of contemporary public HRM, political leaders often disagree about which system should predominate in determining how personnel functions are performed. In those instances where competing systems have developed and implemented contradictory rules for performing a function, it is usually the public personnel director who responds to, mediates among, or initiates conflict among competing systems. For example, the creation of a vacant position by the retirement or transfer of the incumbent will require the personnel manager to respond, propose, or attempt to mediate among competing decision rules for filling the position:

1. *Civil service.* Fill the position with one of the applicants who placed highest on the civil service test for the position.
2. *Civil service/political appointment.* Revise the minimum qualifications for the position to include the candidate with the most political support, and then pick that candidate from among the most qualified applicants for the position.
3. *Civil service/affirmative action appointment.* Conduct targeted recruitment efforts, making sure the applicant pool has a sufficient representation of women and minorities who also meet the minimum qualifications for the position. Then pick either the most qualified applicant or the most qualified minority applicant, depending on the extent of pressure and legal authority to appoint a minority group member.
4. *Civil service/collective bargaining appointment.* See if the position can be filled from within through a bidding process that emphasizes seniority, as specified by the collective bargaining agreement.
5. *Civil service/"at will" appointment.* Offer civil service employees the opportunity to compete for a promotional vacancy. The vacancy is an exempt position outside the civil service, filled through an annual employment contract. The employee has a significantly higher salary and an attractive benefit package, but no longer qualifies for civil service protection or "bumping rights" back into a classified position in the event of a layoff.
6. *Civil service/independent contractor appointment.* Highly skilled professional or technical positions (information systems, engineering, etc.) previously filled as permanent, full-time positions through civil service are abolished. In their place, independent contractors are hired on a temporary, part-time basis as needed to do this work. The hourly pay rate increases considerably, but it does not include benefits or some employer payroll taxes (worker's compensation or Social Security) that legally are the contractor's responsibility. Frequently, highly qualified civil servants will retire from their classified positions and be rehired as independent contractors or consultants to perform essentially the same duties as before, but through a distinctly different type of employment relationship.

But staffing a complex organization would become agonizingly slow and inefficient if every hiring or promotion decision involved a basic decision about competing systems or rules. While these decision choices are theoretically present in any hiring decision, groups of positions are in fact classified to fall under specific personnel systems or decision rules. When the external political context changes, exerting pressure to alter hiring criteria, then the negotiation is over the rules that apply to groups of staffing decisions (though the "trigger" event may be a specific vacancy).

HR STRUCTURES AND RELATIONSHIPS

While HR functions are uniform, the system has profound effects on their relative importance, their organizational location, and their method of implementation. The organizational structure and relationships within which public HR functions are carried out are established and regulated by law, following a pattern that is tied closely to the evolution of personnel systems themselves.

In the United States nationally, this process was represented by passage of the Pendleton Act (1883) and creation of the U.S. Civil Service Commission. This in some cases followed and in other cases encouraged the establishment of similar state and local civil service agencies. As public personnel management tried to unify the opposing roles of civil service protection and management effectiveness, the organizational location and mission of the central personnel agency became increasingly significant. In some cases it remained an independent commission. In others, it split into two agencies like the U.S. Merit Systems Protection Board and the Office of Personnel Management, one responsible for protecting employees against political interference under civil service rules, and the other responsible for administering and enforcing the chief executive's HRM policies and practices in other executive branch agencies.

As collective bargaining and affirmative action emerged as separate personnel systems, separate agencies were often created at all levels of government to focus on these responsibilities. For example, collective bargaining for federal employees is regulated by the Federal Labor Relations Agency; and affirmative action compliance for federal agencies—and all employers generally—is enforced by the U.S. Equal Employment Opportunity Commission. Other agencies like a Department of Labor (whether state or local) may regulate public employee pay, benefits, and working conditions. Often, these agencies have conflicting or overlapping roles in particular HRM functions.

Another variable that affects the structure of public HR systems is the dilemma that arises over the comparative advantages of centralization and decentralization. Inevitably as central civil service agencies mature, they may tend to become larger and more specialized. This in turn can lead to inefficiencies or delays in providing services to other agencies when universal rules become more of a hindrance than a help to service delivery. Because these agencies have developed their own internal personnel departments that assist agency managers and link with the central personnel agency on all requisite functions, they tend over time to exert pressure on the chief executive for more autonomy. And in periods of limited hiring where economies of scale do not apply, or tight recruitment markets where fast action on available and interested candidates is essential, pressures for decentralization increase. Under such conditions, the role of the central personnel agency tends to transform from direct responsibility for personnel functions to indirect responsibility and oversight of agencies' HR planning, management, and evaluation efforts. Organizational size also makes a difference. In large units, the personnel function may be staffed by hundreds of employees or divided into divisions. In a small local government, the functions may be carried out as part of the responsibilities of the chief administrative officer or an assistant. And there are many possible variants within this range.

The structure of public agency HRM also parallels private sector innovations, because both are responsive to the same changes in available technology, workforce characteristics, and other contextual variables.[5] Public agencies may choose to handle individual functions through specialized private companies. This is particularly true of activities like training, pay and benefits administration, or recruitment and selection through "headhunters" or employment services. And as public services become increasingly privatized, responsibility for the HR activities connected with that service pass from the public employer to the private contractor.[6]

HR ROLE EXPECTATIONS

Just as the structure of public HRM links to changes in values and systems, so do the role expectations and competencies required of HR professionals. There are three major groups involved in the practice of public HRM: elected and appointed officials, personnel directors and specialists, and managers and supervisors.

What We Expect of Elected and Appointed Officials

Political responsiveness is the ultimate value for elected and appointed officials. So their views of their responsibilities tend to reflect the impact of changing conditions on public personnel systems and underlying values. For example, voter discontent with high taxes or inefficient civil service agencies is likely to generate political pressure to adopt policies that favor privatization, service contracting, and use of temporary or contracted employees as alternatives to civil service. However, voter unease at reports of cost overruns at privatized prisons or sexual harassment of inmates by private contractors' employees is likely to make the pendulum swing the other way, resulting in increased political pressure in favor of retaining civil service systems and control mechanisms. And in any case, elected officials will probably ask managers and HR professionals to achieve the advantages of each competing system while avoiding their respective disadvantages. After all, it is the prerogative of elected officials to ask for solutions that represent good policy, while leaving it up to administrators and HR specialists to implement them in practice.

Hopefully the sum of all HRM policy decisions represents strategic thinking about how policies affect employees' ability and willingness to work. For example, we would hope that a legislatively approved tuition remission program for all state employees would be accompanied by sufficient funding to state universities so they could offer the public administration courses most employees want. And we would hope that these decisions would send congruent rather than conflicting messages regulating the conflict and interaction among competing personnel systems. For example, it would be unfortunate if an affirmative action plan proposing the hiring of new minority employees were approved at the same time a state budget crisis led the governor to impose a hiring freeze, or even seniority-based layoffs.

What We Expect of HRM Directors and Specialists

Over time, public and political expectations of HRM directors and specialists have evolved from the evolution of public HRM systems and has complicated what we expect of HRM directors and specialists. The primary roles have been watchdogs against the spoils systems, collaboration with legislative restrictions, cooperation with management, and compliance with legislative mandates.

"Watchdogs." During the transition from patronage to merit systems (Stage Three in the model presented in Table 1–3), public HR was generally viewed as a conflict between two systems, one evil and the other good. Public HR managers were considered responsible for guarding employees, applicants, and the public from the spoils system. This required knowledge of civil service policies and procedures, and the courage to apply them in the face of political pressure.

Collaboration. During Stage Four (1933–1964), public personnel managers sought to maintain efficiency and accountability, and legislators and chief executives sought to control the behavior of public managers through budgetary controls and position management. In effect, it was the responsibility of public personnel managers to synthesize two distinct values (bureaucratic compliance as the operational definition of organizational efficiency, and civil service protection as the embodiment of employee rights). There was tension between them because they were both symbiotic and conflicting. And together with the value of bureaucratic neutrality, they supported the concept of political responsiveness.

Consultation. During Stage Five (1964–1992), the focus of public personnel management shifted to work management as managers and public personnel specialists continued to demand flexibility and equitable reward allocation through such alterations to classification and pay systems as rank-in-person personnel systems, broad pay banding, and group performance evaluation and reward systems. This trend coincided with *employee* needs for utilization, development, and recognition.[7] The moral ambiguities of the post-modern era made life difficult for public personnel managers, because the change from compliance to consultation demanded that they work with managers to increase productivity, work with elected officials to increase political responsiveness of public agencies, and with employees to maintain their rights under civil service systems.

From Consultation to Contract Compliance. Currently, public HR managers are still required to work consultatively with agency managers and employees. But they may legitimately feel that they have fewer options and less discretion than before as to how they balance these conflicting objectives. The definition of "good management" is narrow by previous standards.

First, public personnel managers are required, more than ever, to manage government employees and programs in compliance with legislative and public mandates for cost control. The scope of their authority may be diminished by legislative micromanagement, or the value of cost control may be so dominant as to preclude other considerations—even concern for employee rights, organizational efficiency, or social equity.

Second, good management may in time comprise skills that are more directed to minimizing loss (such as risk management and contract compliance) than to maximizing human development and organizational performance for permanent employees. For example, public personnel managers will increasingly be responsible for developing and managing a range of public employment systems for contract, temporary, and at-will employees. They may more often be required to work with volunteers and community-based not-for-profit organizations that increasingly constitute the social safety net by which the value of community responsibility is carried out. Civil service and collective bargaining continue to be important for many public employees (particularly school teachers and administrators, police and firefighters) who are still covered by union contracts and collective bargaining agreements. But risk management, cost control, and management of other types of employment contracts will become more important than ever. In this sense, substituting a calculating perspective for an optimistic view of the joint possibilities for organizational productivity and individual growth represents a narrowing of the public personnel manager's perspective.

Third, and somewhat paradoxically, even as this minimalist view of personnel management emerges, there are countervailing pressures to develop an employment relationship characterized by commitment, teamwork, and innovation. Perhaps the key to the paradox is the emerging distinction between "core" employees (those regarded as essential assets) and contingent workers (those regarded as replaceable costs). Particularly for permanent employees, productivity is prized, risk taking is espoused, and variable pay systems that reward individual and group performance are touted.

The impact of changing values and systems can be seen in Table 2–4.

Managers and Supervisors

In a way, adapting to changing role expectations is hardest for managers and supervisors. First, value conflicts surrounding public administration have intensified. Elected officials understandably tend to pass the responsibility for achieving multiple and conflicting objectives on to managers and supervisors, without necessarily giving them the tools or resources needed to do them. And when revenue shortfalls or other emergencies occur, cuts are disproportionately likely to fall on internal agency staff services—like HR, information services, and budget management—less likely to affect short-term productivity than cuts to direct services. All this leaves managers and supervisors responsible for achieving, or at least attempting to achieve, many activities that were formerly left to HRM professionals. This can be risky for individual managers who must often choose between short-term productivity and long-term organizational effectiveness, between spending time with employee issues or letting employees fend for themselves while the manager focuses on planning, budget management, or crisis control.

TABLE 2–4 The Role of the Public HR Manager in the United States

Stage	Dominant Value(s)	Dominant System(s)	HRM Role
One (1789–1828)	Responsiveness	"Government by elites"	None
Two (1828–1883)	Responsiveness	Patronage	Recruitment and Political clearance
Three (1883–1933)	Efficiency + Individual rights	Civil service	"Watchdog" over agency managers and elected officials to ensure merit system compliance
Four (1933–1964)	Responsiveness + Efficiency + Individual rights	Patronage + Civil service	Collaboration with legislative limits
Five (1964–1980)	Responsiveness + Efficiency + Individual rights + Social equity	Patronage + Civil service + Collective bargaining + Affirmative action	Compliance + Policy implementation + Consultation
Six (1980–now)	Responsiveness + Efficiency + Individual accountability + Limited government + Community responsibility	Patronage + Civil service + Collective bargaining + Affirmative action + Alternative mechanisms + Flexible employment relationships	Compliance + Policy implementation + Consultation + Contract compliance + Strategic thinking about HRM

KEY HR ROLES: TECHNICIAN, PROFESSIONAL, EDUCATOR, AND MEDIATOR

Technician

Technical roles are usually performed by entry-level personnel specialists (in large HR departments) or generalists (in small ones).

- **Staffing specialists** administer examinations, establish lists of eligible applicants and refer eligible applicants to managers for interviews and selection. This requires knowledge of personnel law, affirmative action, and recruitment and selection procedures.
- **Job analysts** or **position classifiers** analyze jobs to determine the appropriate competencies and minimum qualifications, respond to managers' requests for reclassification (to determine if duties, competencies, and minimum qualifications have

changed over time), recommend the appropriate salary for a position (based on job worth factors or market conditions), and determine whether employees can perform the essential functions of a position under the Americans with Disabilities Act. This job requires task analysis and writing job descriptions.

- **Testing specialists** develop valid and reliable selection devices for positions, and defend the reliability and validity of current tests. This job requires knowledge of testing, measurement, and test validation procedures.

- **Pay and benefits specialists** administer the payroll system, enroll new employees in benefit programs, advise employees of changes in benefit programs, and ensure compliance with federal pay and benefit laws (such as FLSA and COBRA). This job requires knowledge of pay and benefit systems; employment contracts; pensions; federal laws with respect to wages, hours, and benefits; and health, life, and disability insurance.

- **Affirmative action compliance officers** are responsible for compliance with equal employment opportunity and affirmative action laws protecting minorities, women, persons with disabilities, and other protected groups. This requires knowledge of affirmative action laws and compliance agencies, and of related personnel functions like recruitment and selection.

- **Training and development specialists** determine training needs, develop programs, train, and evaluate their effectiveness. They have training or experience as adult educators.

- **Employee assistance program directors** coordinate programs offered by the organization or by contract providers, as a response to personal problems that affect work performance: alcohol and drug abuse, debt, domestic and workplace violence, life-threatening diseases, legal problems, etc. They should know federal laws protecting the rights of employees with physical or mental disabilities (such as the Americans with Disabilities Act and the Family and Medical Leave Act); be able to conduct informal counseling with supervisors and employees; and orient employees to the agency's health benefits.

- **Risk managers** are responsible for developing or enforcing personnel policies designed to limit the organization's exposure to legal or financial liability due to violations of employee rights, unsafe or unhealthy working conditions, or poor management practice. In particular, personnel managers who function as risk managers are responsible for reducing employer liability for workers' compensation, disability retirement, and negligent hiring, retention, or referral claims. This function may also be shared with the organization's attorney and budget officer. Risk managers must know personnel law, Occupational Safety and Health (OSHA), workers' compensation systems and procedures, and the Family and Medical Leave Act.

- **Contract compliance specialists'** responsibilities vary. Under collective bargaining systems they develop background information to support management's positions during contract negotiations, or administer contracts to ensure that labor and management comply with negotiated agreements. Under alternative systems, they develop and negotiate service contracts with vendors or employment contracts with individual contractors. This requires experience with business law, policy analysis, contract negotiation, or contract compliance.

Professional

The issue of whether public personnel managers are **professionals** has been debated for years. Conceptually, the issue seems to focus on the extent to which there is an identifiable body of competencies that define the occupation of the human resource manager, an accepted process of education and training for acquiring these competencies, and a standard of ethics that guides their application. There is an underlying body of theory that forms the basis for developing and implementing alternative approaches to the personnel functions, setting these approaches theoretically within the governmental context, and then describing the extent to which role strain or role conflict among the conflicting expectations of alternative systems and values are an expected part of the job.

Educator

HRM specialists, whether managers or personnel directors, are **educators** of other managers who wish to improve their ability to manage people. Fundamentally, they encourage others to see HRM as a set of strategically interrelated activities that taken together give employees the ability and willingness to work effectively together. So in addition to professional and technical responsibilities, HR managers are responsible for presenting the "big picture" of how separate personnel functions interact. They are also responsible for experimentation, technology transfer, and organizational learning.[8] Experimentation means testing personnel policies or procedures to determine their impact on a desired value (such as the effect of a new benefit, or a new performance evaluation method, on employee productivity or turnover). Lastly, organizational learning means HR managers and specialists educate employees and other managers on public personnel systems.

Mediator

Initially, civil service reformers sought to establish the professional credibility of public personnel management by emphasizing its political neutrality and focusing on administrative efficiency. This established the field as a body of techniques used to perform HRM functions, and separated public HRM from politics. As a vestige of this tradition, many public personnel managers view civil service as a moral ideal superior to other systems, whose competing claims to legitimacy are always suspect. Ironically, however, by focusing personnel management on administrative techniques instead of broad human resource policy questions, it had exactly the opposite effect desired—devaluing the status of the profession rather than affirming it.

Contemporary public personnel managers are more likely to find ethical dilemmas challenging and inevitable because they arise directly out of role conflicts implicit in their job. To succeed, public personnel managers must not only do things right, they must do the right things.[9] This means they must function as **mediators** and wrestle with choices imposed by external conflicts among competing systems and derive from these choices the existential satisfaction of each day coming closer to unattainable objectives under conditions of ethical uncertainty. The inevitability of political and ethical dilemmas for the modern HR manager is an important theme of this book. Ethical dilemmas arise inevitably out of the scarcity of public jobs and legitimate but conflicting role expectations over how to fill them.

Some Conclusions

What conclusions can be drawn from this variety of activities and role expectations? First, historical traditions emphasize the technical side of personnel management, with less emphasis on policy-related analytical work, relationships with outside organizations, and conflicting values. In addition, both employees and line management are seen as clients and are perceived as being served through the merit system. The traditional department's work includes record keeping and the processing of personnel transactions, especially in smaller government agencies or units.

A more contemporary view emphasizes different activities and relationships. While the traditional functions continue to be important, they are relatively less important than the "brokering" or mediating of conflicts among competing personnel systems. For example, the modern personnel director might be called upon to prepare cost-benefit analyses of alternative pay and benefit proposals related to collective bargaining with employees in the solid waste department. At the same time, he or she might also be asked to evaluate the comparative feasibility, productivity, and cost of privatizing or contracting out this entire function (thus making the collective bargaining analysis irrelevant). Or since the majority of employees in a department are minorities, the director might be asked to assess the impact of contracting out on the city's overall level of affirmative action compliance. Modern personnel directors do not work in isolation; rather, they work closely with other officials within their own agency (budget directors, attorneys, collective bargaining negotiators, affirmative action compliance officers, and supervisors) and outside it (legislative staff, union officials, affirmative action agencies, civil service boards, health and life insurance benefit representatives, pension boards, ethics commissions, and employee assistance programs dealing with substance abuse and other personal problems).

Most public personnel departments have moved cautiously into the modern era because of their traditional reluctance to be identified with or become involved in "politics." Yet, as their function is increasingly viewed as the development and management of human resource systems involving the reconciliation of value conflicts, they are overcoming this reluctance and working outside the confining environment of the civil service system. And they are finding that this expanded role brings benefits as well as risks. They are able to bring their expertise to bear on a range of critical human resource issues in a variety of contexts—issues traditional personnel managers might define as falling outside their area of responsibility. For example, they can work with legislators on privatization and benefits issues, with labor negotiators on alternative pay and grievance procedures, and with affirmative action compliance agencies on affirmative action proposals or minority business contracting procedures. By continuing to assert their central role in the most critical issues of agency management, they are developing not only their own professional status but also the status of their profession.[10]

BUILDING A CAREER IN PUBLIC HRM

Given the previous discussion about change and instability in public administration in general and HRM in particular, it may seem nonsensical to talk about a career in public HRM. On the contrary, it is precisely because of this conflict and instability that there is a high demand for HRM professionals in public and private organizations, whether they work as HR directors or as managers with specific HRM competencies. Three issues are relevant: (1) what competencies do HRM professionals need, (2) how can they get them, and (3) how can they maintain their skills in a complex and changing environment?

What Competencies Do Public HR Managers Need?

Traditional public HR requires that personnel directors and other managers know the laws and regulations that affect HR policy and practice within civil service systems and the techniques used within that system. For managers, this means learning how to "work the system" to reward good employees and get rid of bad ones. This involves rewriting job descriptions to increase an employee's pay level, reaching quality applicants on a list of eligibles, or giving outstanding performance evaluations to high-quality employees.

Public managers in general, and HR directors in particular, must be sensitive to the need for administrative systems to be responsive to legitimate political values and public participation in governance, especially in local government. These kinds of changes inevitably challenge the shield that the rhetoric of merit has provided the traditional manager. First, theirs is a world in which trends such as privatization and service contracting have blurred distinctions between public and private. Second, their world is controlled by a myriad of complex and conflicting laws involving affirmative action, labor relations, personal/professional liability, employee privacy, due process, and pay equity. Potentially, the power of public personnel managers in public organizations is increasing. This is a *potential* consequence resulting from their successful ability to move from a traditional view of the field (involving primarily technical skills) to a modern view (involving primarily professional skills as an interpreter of conflicting interests and mediator among them). At the same time, they will be called upon to protect the integrity of merit systems.

Today's public HR manager needs several general types of competencies to perform well in this enhanced role. Public personnel managers must exhibit continued concern for productivity and effectiveness. They must become and remain competent in law, technology, and quantitative/analytic skills. They must have a humanistic orientation toward employees, a positive orientation to managerial objectives, and close working relationships with other professionals inside and outside the organization. No one manager can possess expertise in all these areas, but no complex public agency can overlook them in their complement of competencies.

How Do They Get these Competencies?

While all public managers need to know something about HRM because it is an important part of the field, many students have a more specific interest—they want a job. Their interest in what public HR managers do is followed by these two questions: As a student, what courses should I be taking to qualify myself for an HR position? As an applicant, how do I get a job?

While HRM is a recognized profession, its members have followed a variety of career paths. Some started as entry-level specialists. Most have degrees and training in public management or business administration. This may include course work in personnel management from a private-sector perspective, or in public personnel management from the perspective of civil service and collective bargaining systems. There are specialized graduate curricula in personnel management taught by a number of programs: information on public administration programs can be obtained from the National Association for Schools of Public Affairs and Administration (NASPAA); information on business administration programs can be obtained through the American Association for Schools and Colleges of Business (AACSB).

In addition to a required course in HRM, many graduate and undergraduate degree programs also offer an optional specialization in HRM. While programs differ among institutions, the following topics are usually included, either as separate courses or as elements in a curriculum.

- *Administrative law:* impact of rules and regulations on public administration, including HRM.
- *Collective bargaining:* impact of unions on public personnel management, legal and political antecedents, contract negotiation, and administration procedures.
- *Test development:* development and validation of devices for selection, promotion, and placement (sometimes offered by the psychology department).
- *Pay and benefits:* job analysis, classification, and evaluation; setting wages and salaries through job evaluation and/or market surveys; statutorily required employee benefits (workers' compensation, Social Security), and optional ones (health insurance, pensions, etc.).
- *Training and employee development:* design, implementation, and evaluation of orientation, training, and career development programs (sometimes taught in an adult education department).
- *Affirmative action compliance:* work force diversity, equal employment opportunity, affirmative action, and employment equity without respect to gender, race, national origin, age, religion, or disability.
- *Organizational development and change:* assessing organizational performance and changing structure and culture to make it more effective.
- *Role of women and minorities:* changing organizational culture to make it more equitable for women and minorities.
- *Vocational rehabilitation:* career counseling and placement, particularly in response to issues involving disability, ADA accommodation, and other medical conditions (sometimes offered through a program in health services or public health).
- *Productivity improvement:* making organizations more efficient and effective through the application of policy-analytic techniques.
- *Comparative or development administration:* offered through public administration, business administration, economics, or international relations programs.
- *Third-party government:* using alternative mechanisms such as privatization and service contracting to accomplish public program objectives.

University training (a BPA, a Master's degree, or even a graduate professional certificate program in public personnel management) will give personnel specialists added knowledge that can enhance their performance as specialist, professional, mediator, or human resource management expert, thereby enhancing their career options. And because public personnel functions involve others besides personnel specialists (such as managers, supervisors, and appointed officials), many human resource management courses have more general usefulness for anyone considering a career in public policy or management.

Those without significant HRM experience as managers or as personnel specialists may have a harder time breaking into the field. Worldwide changes in labor markets, plus the changing political conditions under which public administrators work today, mean that there is more competition for professional jobs in many fields, including public personnel management. Often, recent college graduates without significant public personnel management experience are competing against experienced professionals who are on the job market because they have been laid off (or, if you prefer current terminology, "outplaced" or "reengineered" out of their jobs). Under pressure to "do more with less," employers will seek to hire employees who will not incur start-up costs. They may prefer to hire the experienced professional to the recent graduate. How do you "get your foot in the door" under these conditions?

The first suggestion is to take courses that offer the competencies HR managers need, particularly the entry-level positions discussed above. Take enough courses (usually semester credit hours) and the right courses so that you can apply for a major, a minor, or a certificate in human resource management or personnel management.

Second, include an internship as part of your university curriculum. Make sure it is with an organization that is looking for employees—one that uses internship programs as a recruitment mechanism rather than just as a source of temporary, free labor. Your best gauge of this is by asking your university's internship placement coordinator, your professors, or current employees who started work there as interns. While a formal internship option may not be feasible for the mid-career student, expressing interest and aptitude on-the-job may help with a lateral transfer into personnel work. With some creative thinking and job design, it may be possible to share some time in the personnel office or to gain experience by seeking out personnel-related tasks in your own office.

Third, tailor your résumé so it highlights the education, experience, skills, and knowledge needed for a job in personnel management. Identify related courses in management, computer sciences, statistics, psychology, law, or other fields.

Fourth, practice applying for jobs and taking interviews so you know how to respond to questions interviewers ask. Why do you want this job? What work experience have you had that shows your aptitude or ability for personnel work? If you lack related experience, what skills and abilities do you have that would make it easy to learn? Why are you the best candidate for the position? Good luck!

Keeping Current as a Public HRM Professional

Training begins to become obsolete the moment the course is over. Clearly, HR professionals—whether specialists or supervisors—need to take charge of their own career development. Suggested methods are professional associations, research libraries, and the Internet.

Professional associations offer the opportunity to network with other professionals locally, to attend national and regional conferences, and to receive free member services such as newsletters or professional journals. All offer continued education and career advancement options for working professionals.[11] Universities, professional associations, and private professional development institutes provide training courses and seminars for public personnel practitioners. Check the continuing studies or university outreach programs of local universities, or the calendars of local chapters of professional associations.

Research libraries are indispensable for students or practitioners seeking to keep their knowledge of law and practice up to date. People tend to think of libraries as places where books are kept, but in reality, the past ten years has witnessed their transformation into sources of information, much of it stored or transmitted electronically rather than on paper. A generation ago, students researched papers by checking books out of the library or by photocopying journal articles. They took the materials home, wrote a draft of the paper, and typed the final copy. Books are a good source of historical data, but they are rarely useful for researching the latest developments on current topics because of the long lead-time between writing and publication (usually a minimum of two years). Books are cataloged by subject area, usually according to the Library of Congress cataloging system.

Research is totally different today. It's possible to research excellent papers without using books at all, by utilizing alternative information sources: **reference books**,[12] loose-leaf services, indexes, professional journals, and government documents. **Loose-leaf services** are serial publications issued on a regular basis to provide researchers, lawyers, and practitioners with current information on specified areas of personnel practice and procedure.[13] **Indexes** are bound books or CD-ROM disks that provide bibliographic sources on human resource management topics from a range of professional journals and other periodicals. Data are arranged so that author, publication, key word, etc., may locate references. They are published monthly, quarterly, or annually.[14] Many professional associations publish **professional journals** to keep members informed about current law, practice, innovations, and issues in the field. These are sent to members, or are available through research libraries. Generally, periodicals in the human resource management area are found in the HF5549.5 area (Library of Congress cataloging system).[15] The federal government, and many state and local governments, routinely send publications to so-called repository libraries throughout the country. These **government documents** are sometimes hard to locate because they are not indexed by Library of Congress codes (as are books and professional journals). But reference librarians can help you if you can't locate what you need through the indexes of public documents.[16] Or you may contact these agencies directly to request specific documents; most are free or low-cost.[17]

It's also possible to research a popular current topic through newspapers and magazines. While the quality of news magazines and newspapers is uneven, some periodicals (such as *The New York Times* and *The Wall Street Journal*) are noted for their thoughtful, well-researched coverage. Frequently, this is the only source you can use for current topics, as the lead-time to publication in professional journals is often over a year. Some periodicals (including the two mentioned above) have their own indexes. If your library subscribes to a comprehensive index of periodicals (such as **LEXIS/NEXIS**), you will be able to search the whole universe for material on a specific topic. Some popular magazines are also indexed in the indexes mentioned previously.

While it is of course possible to do research by visiting the library and browsing through these information sources there, all this information—and a lot more—is available on the Internet using a computer, a phone or cable modem, and an Internet service provider. Using these tools, it's possible to use four major applications of the Internet: e-mail, list servers, search engines, and websites (home pages). But just because information is available "on the web" does not mean it is current or accurate. Trained librarians have carefully chosen journals and books for library purchase. No such screening process occurs with material posted on the Internet. Sites may not be updated, and there is no guarantee of the centralized quality control or accountability that we assume (with relative certainty) exists with print media.

E-mail (electronic mail) is fundamental to Internet connections, since it provides the computer address from which and to which messages are sent through each computer's modem, using phone lines or wireless transmission across distances. E-mail has several critical advantages over conventional communication by memo, fax, or voice communication by telephone. First, it is paperless, meaning less waste and less transmission time. Second, messages are received and stored automatically for the recipient, who can "pick up the mail" and read it from any software-compatible computer using the individual's e-mail address and a confidential access code. This avoids playing "phone tag," because the complete message or question is stored, waiting to be accessed by the recipient. It also avoids long-distance phone charges since information is transferred instantaneously from computer to computer. Messages can be sent to lists of recipients simultaneously, creating the opportunity for a true communications net among people with common interests. Of course there are numerous challenges to the use of e-mail, including open records law requirements and privacy concerns.

List servers are tools that organize and expand the usefulness of e-mail by providing an easy way for persons with common interests to share information. Once people join a listserv, they are automatically sent every message sent on the Internet to every other member of that listserv; and a message they send to that listserv is automatically referred to all other members as well.

The positive implications of the Internet are enormous and obvious. It enables students and scholars to communicate easily and directly around the world. The problems are equally obvious: organization and quality control. With all this data floating around in cyberspace, how do users know where to look for it, and how do they evaluate the correctness or quality of the data out there? **Browsers** are automated search engines used to locate materials on a particular subject, using branching logic trees and key-word addresses in a fashion similar to CD-ROM indexes used by reference libraries. Many government agencies, the Library of Congress, and universities engaged in public management research maintain browsers to help scholars find their way around the web. Individuals, organizations, or agencies may create their own **home page**, a web site identified with their particular e-mail address. For example, readers who wish to ask questions, suggest changes, or communicate information to other readers may do so by contacting either author's e-mail address (dklingner@uccs.edu or nalband@ku.edu).

SUMMARY

There are about 18.6 million public employees in the United States. While it is widely believed that most work for the national government in social welfare programs, in fact 15.7 million, including 3.5 million part-time employees, work for state and local governments, primarily in education.

Public personnel management consists of the functions needed to manage human resources in public agencies. These functions are shared among political leaders, line managers and supervisors, and the personnel department. Civil service systems are the predominant public personnel system because they have articulated rules and procedures for performing the whole range of personnel functions. Other systems, though incomplete, are nonetheless legitimate and effective influences over one or more personnel functions. While personnel functions remain the same across different systems, their organizational location and method of performance differ, depending upon the system and on the values that underlie it.

Public personnel managers may be viewed as technicians, professionals, mediators, and human resource management specialists. Traditional personnel managers (those who operate within a consensus on one system and its underlying values) tend to define themselves, and to be defined by others, as technical specialists working within a staff agency. Contemporary personnel managers (those who operate as human resource management experts or as mediators among competing systems and values) tend to define themselves, and to be defined by others, as professionals whose role involves a blend of technical skills and ethical decision making. They educate other managers in thinking strategically about HRM and mediate conflicts among competing values and systems.

Public personnel managers normally receive specialized undergraduate or graduate training. But it may take a combination of specialized experience and education to advance into the profession. And rapid changes in the field require lifelong learning and career development through such mechanisms as professional associations, research libraries, and the Internet.

KEY TERMS

affirmative action compliance officer
browsers
contract compliance specialist
educators
employee assistance program director
government documents
home page
indexes
job analyst
LEXIS/NEXIS
list servers
loose-leaf services
mediator
pay and benefits specialist

personnel actions
personnel director
position classifier
professionals
professional association
professional journal
reference books
research library
risk manager
staffing specialist
technician
testing specialist
training and development specialist

DISCUSSION QUESTIONS

1. How many public employees are there? How many work for each level of government (national, state, and local)? What functions does each level of government specialize in?
2. What does each of these three groups (politicians, managers, and HR specialists) have to do with public personnel management?
3. Describe similarities and differences in the way managers and HR specialists function in different public HR systems.
4. What are the six stages in the development of the role of the public HR manager? What different expectations have people had for them in each stage?
5. What are some examples of ethical dilemmas HR professional face? How can they resolve them?
6. What competencies do public HR managers need, and where can they get them?
7. What suggestions would you offer persons who want to enter the HR field? How might they use professional associations, university courses, libraries, and the Internet for career development?

CASE STUDY: CHOOSING A MUNICIPAL PERSONNEL DIRECTOR

A south Florida city needed a new HR director. It advertised in the local newspaper and in the *Recruiter* section of the *IPMA News & Views*.

Director of Human Resources
City of Sunny Skies

Sunny Skies is a city of 60,000 with 650 employees. It has a mayor-council form of government. It is primarily residential, with population shifting from older Anglo retirees to a broader mix of working-class families from a range of racial and ethnic groups. The city police department's officers are covered by a collective bargaining agreement with the PBA; a three-year contract was negotiated last year. The city's civil service system covers 400 employees. Others, including all managers, are in exempt positions filled through performance contracts.

The city seeks a human resource director with the proven ability to manage a personnel department responsible for testing, selection, affirmative action, job analysis, salary and benefits, performance evaluation, and collective bargaining. Excellent benefits, including an employer-funded 457 pension program. Salary range $60,000 to $85,000, dependent upon qualifications. Proof of citizenship required. We are a drug-free workplace and an AA/EEO employer.

Two hundred persons applied. An outside consultant firm conducted initial screening based on the following criteria:

- *Experience:* Ten to fifteen years of progressively responsible personnel experience, including at least three years as a personnel director. Municipal experience preferred.
- *Education:* BA/BS degree in human resource management or a related field (public administration, business administration, organizational psychology). MA/MS in public administration, human resource administration, or related field preferred.

After the outside consultant firm had selected the twelve most qualified applicants, a representative interview panel headed by the assistant city manager asked each applicant these questions.

First, tell us something about your career:

1. What is your most innovative accomplishment in your present position?

2. Describe the most difficult personnel problem you have faced. How did you resolve it? How did you communicate your decision to employees and/or other managers? How did they respond? If you faced the problem now, how would you handle it differently?
3. What has been your greatest professional disappointment or setback? How did you respond to it? What did you learn from the experience?
4. Where do you see yourself working in five years?

Next, please tell us something about your human resource management style:

5. What kind of supervisor do you like, and why?
6. When evaluating the performance of your subordinates, what factors are most important to you?
7. What methods do you use to keep informed of personnel issues or problems coming up in your organization? How have these methods worked for you?
8. What do you perceive affirmative action to be? What general policies do you establish to achieve it?

Briefly describe your work experience with each of these specific personnel issues:

9. collective bargaining contract negotiations
10. workers' compensation issues or claims
11. termination of civil service employees
12. sexual harassment issues and policies
13. disciplinary action and grievances

If you were personnel director, how would you deal with each of these issues the city now faces?

14. Compliance with the drug and alcohol testing requirements of the Omnibus Transportation Employee Testing Act of 1991?
15. What is the best balance between flexibility and uniformity of personnel policies and procedures?
16. The city hires contract attorneys to handle some personnel-related legal issues and handles others in-house through the city attorney. In your view, which issues should be handled which way? If it is determined that the city's reliance on contract attorneys' services is excessive, what would you do to reduce this reliance?
17. As a representative of the city in contract negotiations, you may be required to conduct collective bargaining negotiations when you do not have authorization to offer a COLA increase or any other increase in benefits to the union. Have you ever been in such a situation? How would you conduct the negotiation?
18. The city's shrinking tax base could result in civil service layoffs. If cuts could not be met through attrition or by not filling vacant positions, what alternatives to layoffs are there? If layoffs are unavoidable, how would you do them?
19. Bringing employees on the job after their interviews sometimes takes several months. What timetable is reasonable? What methods would you consider to speed up this process?
20. A promotional exam was administered, and an eligibility list established and published, for a contract position. A person on that list claims that the employee at the

top of the list has been given answers to the questions by the department head of that unit. What would you do?

21. A female employee tells you in confidence that she feels a male co-worker is sexually harassing her. She has not mentioned this problem to anyone else. She insists that she wants no action taken against the offending employee and that she can handle the situation on her own. What do you do?

22. Same as above, except now the offending party is her immediate supervisor. Would you handle the issue any differently?

23. The city has several different types of employees (civil service, contract, no benefits, etc.). Performance evaluation and reward systems differ for each group, which causes frustration for employees and equity issues for the personnel department. What would you do about this, if anything?

Discussion Questions

After reading this case study, answer the following questions:

1. Why did 200 people apply for this job? How qualified are the top applicants likely to be?

2. What do you think the primary duties of the HR director will be?

3. Based on the background information and interview questions, what are the shared HR roles of the personnel director, managers, and the city manager in this city? Who does what?

4. What specific competencies are important in doing this job well? What would be most important to you if you were the city manager? If you were a department director? An employee? A taxpayer?

5. Which of these competencies is likely to be gained through formal education and degrees? Which through experience?

6. This case study is an example of how public HRM has changed recently. What changes can you identify with respect to each of the following variables:
   - Required competencies?
   - Required education and experience?
   - Selection methods?
   - Environmental change and uncertainty?

NOTES

[1]U.S. Census Bureau (2000). *Compendium of Public Employment: 1997.* Series GC97 (3)–2. Washington, DC: U.S. Department of Commerce, p. 2.

[2]Ibid., p. 2.

[3]Ibid., p. 3.

[4]Pynes, Joan (1997). *Personnel Administration in Non-Profit Agencies.* San Francisco: Jossey-Bass.

[5]Sampson, Charles (1998). New manifestations of open systems: Can they survive in the public sector? *Public Personnel Management,* 27(3): 361–383.

[6]Siegel, Gilbert B. (2000). Outsourcing personnel functions. *Public Personnel Management,* 29(2): 225–236.

[7]National Performance Review (1993). *Reinventing human resource management.* Washington, DC: Office of the Vice President.

[8]Stehr, Steven D., and Ted M. Jones (spring 1999). Continuity and change in public personnel administration. *Review of Public Personnel Administration,* pp. 32–49.

[9]Bennis, W., and B. Nanus (1985). *Leaders: The strategies for taking charge.* New York: Harper & Row.

[10]Klingner, D. (September 1979). The changing role of public personnel management in the 1980s. *The Personnel Administrator, 24,* 41–48; and Nalbandian, J. (Spring 1981). From compliance to consultation: The role of the public personnel manager. *Review of Public Personnel Administration, 1,* 37–51.

[11]Chief among these are the International Personnel Management Association (IPMA), 1617 Duke Street, Alexandria, VA 22314, (703) 549–7100, www.ipma-hr.org; the American Society for Public Administration (ASPA), Section on Personnel Administration and Labor Relations (SPALR), 1120 G Street, NW, Suite 700, Washington, DC 20005, (202) 393–7878, www.aspanet.org; and the National Academy of Public Administration, 1120 G Street, NW, Suite 850, Washington, DC 20005–3801, (202) 347–3190, www.napawash.org.

[12]Good public HR reference books are:

American Salaries and Wages Survey HD4973.A67

The Compensation Handbook HF5549.5C67H36 1991

Consultants and Consulting Organizations Directory HD69.C6R4C647

Employee Benefits Dictionary HD4928.N6B75 1992

Inter-City Cost of Living Index HD6977.C63

Job Analysis Handbook for Business, Industry and Government HF5549.5.J6J63 1988

Occupational Outlook Handbook HD8051.A62

Occupational Outlook Quarterly DOC PER L2.70/4

Occupational Safety and Health HD7654.P43 1985

Training and Development Organizations Directory HD30.42.U5T72.

[13]Loose-leaf services. Current employment law; published by West, Bureau of National Affairs (BNA), Prentice Hall (PH) and Commerce Clearing House (CCH). Examples:

Americans with Disabilities, BNA Vol. 1-present BUS KF3469.A5A45

Collective Bargaining Negotiation & Contracts, BNA BUS HD6500.B8

EEOC Compliance Manual, CCH BUS KF3464.A6C6

EEOC Decisions, CCH BUS KF3464.A56E65

Employment Practices Decisions, CCH Vol. I-present BUS KF3464.A6E46

Employment Practices Guide, CCH BUS KF3464.A5C65

Fair Employment Practice Cases, BNA Vol. 1-present 3 BUS KF3464.A6E46

Human Resources Management, CCH HF5549.H865

Individual Employment Rights Cases, BNA Vol. 1-present BUS HD6971.8.15

Individual Retirement Plans, CCH BUS KF3510.A615

Labor Arbitration Reports, BNA Vol. 56-present

Labor Relations Reference Manual, BNA Vol. 61-present BUS HD5503.A7224

Labor Relations Reporter, BNA BUS KF3385.L3

Occupational Safety & Health Cases, BNA Vol. 1-present BUS KF3568.A2B87

Occupational Safety & Health Reporter, BNA 1973-present BUS KF3570.Z9B9

Payroll Management Guide, CCH BUS KF6436.A6C6

Pension Plan Guide, CCH BUS HD7106.U5C6

Wage and Hour Cases, BNA Vol. 19-present BUS HD4974.W3.

[14]Indexes: bound books or CD-ROM disks. Examples: *ABI/Inform, Business Periodicals Index,* HF5001.B845; *Personnel Management Abstracts,* HF5549.P452; *PAIS (Public Affairs Information Service)* (H1.B8); *Psychological Abstracts,* BF1.P652; *Social Sciences Index,* H1.S63; and *Sociological Abstracts,* HM1.S67.

[15]Professional journals: *Review of Public Personnel Administration, Public Personnel Management, American Review of Public Administration, Personnel Journal, Compensation and Benefits Review, Training and Development Journal, Public Productivity Review,* the *IPMA Newsletter,* and *Public Administration Review.*

[16]Indexes to government documents: *Government Publications Index, Government Periodical Index, Congressional Masterfile* and *Statistical Masterfile.*

[17]Suggested agencies are:

The U.S. Office of Personnel Management (OPM)
Office of Systems Innovation and Simplification
1900 E Street, NW
Washington, DC 20415–0001
(202) 653–2511

U.S. Merit Systems Protection Board (MSPB)
Office of Policy and Evaluation
1120 Vermont Avenue, NW
Washington, DC 20419
(202) 653–7208

U.S. Equal Employment Opportunity Commission (EEOC)
Office of Communications and Legislative Affairs
1801 L Street, NW
Washington, DC 20507
(800) 669–EEOC

3

Strategic Thinking about Human Resources Management

INTRODUCTION

In the 1990s, the primary focus of personnel systems changed from defending merit system principles to a concern for maximizing productivity. In part this change signifies an understanding that merit systems no longer are defined exclusively in moral terms in contrast to patronage systems. Merit systems now are evaluated as a means to an end rather than ends in themselves. This emphasis is part of a growing realization that organizations must continually align their administrative systems in ways that allow employees to complete their work effectively. This requires designing and managing administrative systems in response to changes in external environments, including pressure for responsiveness and political accountability. Effective human resource management is defined by how well employees are completing work that (1) advances existing agency goals and (2) that positions the organization to respond to present and future external environmental changes.

The focus is changing from management of "positions," which implied an internal organizational focus for personnel management, to managing "performance" and more directly facilitating accomplishment of the agency's mission. In part, this requires continuing emphasis on traditional merit-system values and commitment to human resources as assets; but more importantly it also emphasizes strategic thinking about human resources issues. These requirements highlight the responsibility of managerial cadre as well as personnel specialists; there is no substitute for leadership that evaluates human resources management practices against the axiom that human resources are assets.

For many organizations with civil service systems the changes have required increased flexibility and experimentation in many areas: with privatization, contracting out, and utilization of part-time and temporary workers; rank-in-person versus rank-in-job personnel systems; work classification and evaluation versus job classification and evaluation; increasing adaptation to a tight labor market and recognition of the impact of the person on the job; team as well as individual performance evaluation; and experimentation with variable pay based on performance. For managers and supervisors this means obtaining the highest performance and commitment from employees while remaining cognizant of the need to restructure, reorganize tasks, and even downsize in the face of rapidly changing environmental conditions. The challenge places managers squarely in the middle of the clash between traditional values of civil service systems and the market-based values underlying alternative methods for delivering public service. It challenges personnel specialists and managers to align personnel systems and practices with agency mission and objectives, mindful of conflicting values and often-divergent perspectives of political leaders, appointed executives, professional managers, and employees.

By the end of this chapter, you will be able to:

1. Identify traditional civil service system assumptions.
2. Describe the ways that contemporary work and organizations, demographic trends, and market-based values challenge the assumptions of traditional civil service systems.
3. Describe the consequences of these challenges for human resources management.
4. Describe the framework that links these challenges with values, functions, organizational mission, and multiple perspectives on human resources management.
5. Describe three approaches to human resources management.
6. Describe the integrated approach to human resources management.
7. Identify strategic human resources issues.

THE ASSUMPTIONS OF TRADITIONAL CIVIL SERVICE SYSTEMS

Civil service systems grew up in response to patronage challenges. They balance the values of efficiency and individual rights and rest on a foundation of assumptions about work that were developed when civil service systems were developed decades ago.

- Public sector work is organized around the role of government as a deliverer of services.
- This work can be divided into individual packets of duties and responsibilities called jobs.
- Duties and responsibilities remain stable over time because government work is performed in bureaucratic organizations designed to promote predictability and reliability, stability and routine.
- Knowledge, skills, and abilities of workers are valued and assessed in relationship to particular jobs, and personnel functions are oriented around positions rather than the people who occupy those positions.

- The analytical focus on individual jobs and the relationship of one job to another provide a rational system for pay, recruitment, and selection, and appraisal of employee performance.

These **assumptions about civil service systems** were essential to successful transition from the era of patronage, and they have provided sound guidance for the design and implementation of civil service systems for years. But today, some argue strenuously that they seem less appropriate and less able to guide elected officials, agency heads, managers, and employees through environmental and political turbulence. For these critics, contemporary challenges undermine the assumptions underlying civil service systems.

The challenges fall into three categories: **contemporary work and organizations, demographic trends,** and **market-based, anti-governmental values.**

CHALLENGES TO THE TRADITIONAL ASSUMPTIONS

Contemporary Work and Organizations

Increasing specialization of work and the rapidity of change characterize *contemporary work and organizations.* While the knowledge needed to address today's problems becomes more specialized, the problems themselves remain broad, requiring teams of specialists. The practice of medicine is an example that is easy to relate to. But other examples are plentiful. Public responses to gangs involves families, social service agencies, the courts, the police, recreation specialists, teachers and school district personnel, as well as the employment of both volunteers and professional workers. This complexity and specialization requires teams of people working together, often in temporary arrangements, until the particular problem they are dealing with changes and the composition of the team must be revised.

The concept of working in teams is very different from the idea that work can be divided discretely into little packages of duties and responsibilities. Rather than managing individual workers, many of today's managers are responsible for teams of workers, where the focus is on the group as well as the members. In teams, the interpersonal skills that used to be less relevant to individual work become crucial. Good citizenship behaviors and personal attributes like courtesy, friendliness, conflict resolution, effective listening, persuasiveness, and speaking ability become assets to teams even if they often are difficult to measure and are absent from traditional job descriptions and appraisal instruments. Rather than a job description determining what the employee does, increasingly, the person with specialized knowledge, working in concert with others, heavily influences his or her own job by helping define what the duties and responsibilities ought to be or at least how the job ought to be carried out.

The rapidity of change largely corresponds to the rate of innovation in the technological software and hardware utilized for work and also to the degree of dynamism in the marketplace. The more competitive the marketplace, the more responsiveness private business expects from government. For example, when developers put all the pieces into place—the land, the tenants, the architects and planners, the financing, and so on—they want a responsive city hall that will process a rezoning application and site plan and issue building permits in a timely fashion; and they want the city's work oriented toward the developers' needs, not vice versa, so the project can be built on schedule and the developer can get on to the next project.

Demographic Trends

The single biggest influence on human resources management today is the scarcity of labor, all kinds, but particularly those with specialized knowledge and the capacity to learn. Whether public or private, the need for labor dominates strategic thinking as well as the day-to-day pressure to fill vacancies. Recruitment, training, and retention of employees is on every list of human resources issues employers are facing now and in the foreseeable future, as the ratio of retires to new workers adds to the scarcity of labor.

The fact that virtually all adults, whether married or not, are working outside the home has made balancing work and family obligations a critical challenge for today's worker, manager, and employer. Today's *demographic trends* show that super pop has joined super mom. Women have become all too familiar with the stressful responsibilities for nurturing a family and working outside of the home, and now their husbands are experiencing similar demands and the stress associated with having to balance family needs, work responsibilities, and personal interests. Working too hard in organizations that are downsizing or understaffed, perhaps holding a part-time job as well, shuffling kids around day care, soccer matches, and music lessons have to change one's expectations about work and one's perspective on what it means to be an employee today. The call for a return to "family values" at a time when balancing family and work obligations has never been harder creates incredible stress in some individuals and families, stress that is bound to carry into the workplace through demands for family-friendly benefits, flexible work arrangements, and less commitment to those organizations where employees are viewed simply as factors of production rather than assets.

Market-Based Values

The now familiar anti-governmental rhetoric is matched by a resurgence of political support for *market-based values.* If government cannot solve certain problems, then let the marketplace try, advocates argue. Privatization, contracting out, and staffing by part-time and temporary workers result from this kind of sentiment accompanied by and encouraged in an environment where raising taxes is difficult. In this kind of environment, where organizations cannot be depended upon to foster long-term employment, and where employment opportunities are plentiful, employees become career entrepreneurs, responsible for managing their own successes, failures, and future.

At no time in recent memory have the distinctions between public and private sectors seemed less appreciated or important—a surging economy in the 1990s where fewer and fewer people depended upon government is important in this trend. The role of government as a deliverer of services at state and federal levels is yielding to the concept of government as "guarantor" of services, as services are contracted out. Agency managers have had to adjust their thinking from the management of people and services to the management of contracts, knowing full well that they still are going to be held politically accountable for the quality of service delivery.

The blending of public and private work is reflected in expectations of citizens who receive public services, regardless of who delivers them. No amount of explanation will satisfy a citizen who has to stand in line at the county treasurer's office or the department of motor vehicles office and then goes to the bank and receives instant service or, better yet, goes to an ATM. Similarly, the popularity of FedEx or UPS has challenged the Postal Service. These expectations require more funding for personnel and better wages to attract better people, but they also require more delegation of authority to those actually serving the public. At the same time that expectations for rapid, customized responses have increased, the traditional role of government, as arbiter of political values, has not decreased. Working through questions of values takes time, and developing managers who can understand "customer service" values with traditional "community building" values is a challenge for ways an agency thinks about its human resources needs.

CONSEQUENCES OF THESE CHALLENGES FOR HUMAN RESOURCES MANAGEMENT

This clash of new forces with traditional civil service assumptions creates incredible political and managerial challenges. Among the human resources management challenges are the following.

First, the traditional employment contract between public employees and the public has fundamentally been affected by market-based values in two critical respects. The most obvious is that because of a dynamic environment, government work is less secure than it used to be, even where the demand for labor exceeds the supply. There are changes in the perceived equity of public employment, in that public employees have traditionally been willing to trade lower pay for better benefits and greater job security. Less well understood, but probably more significant in the long run, is that anti-government values also call into question whether government work is a worthwhile vocation. Traditionally, public service was considered desirable because it offered the opportunity to serve the public. But after twenty years of being told that they are part of the problem rather than part of the solution, public employees are finding it difficult to believe that others understand that their motive is public good rather than private gain. And as a public employee, it is increasingly difficult to embrace that motive when one feels under attack by citizens or elected officials.

Second, the resurgence of market-based values and the accompanying implementation of privatization and contracting out cause most reflective human resource managers at times to question their calling. Are there *any* critical differences between the values, job objectives, and competencies required of personnel managers in business and in public agencies? Is there *anything* about civil service system values or principles that contributes to the unique nature of public work and that cannot be privatized? If most personnel functions are contracted out or decentralized to managers, what impact will this have on delivery of personnel services or the internal debate over the values underlying public employment?

Third, the flexibility demanded by specialization, rapidity of change, and the balancing of family and work, challenges the impersonal, routine, stable, and position-oriented character of civil service systems. A bedrock value of civil service systems is fairness and equity, insured through legal and quasi-legal restrictions on managerial discretion. Managing in an environment that demands flexibility, responsiveness, and efficiency has led to attempts to streamline disciplinary and appeals procedures and has placed traditional personnel techniques— oriented in large measure towards eliminating favoritism—under substantial scrutiny.

And finally, the demands to do more with less have affected elected officials as well. They are called upon to make increasingly more difficult decisions—ones that not only require compromise among the four traditional values but also with the emergent anti-government values that result (for example) in privatization

TABLE 3–1 Shifting from a Traditional Public Sector System to a System for the Twenty-first Century

Traditional Public Service Systems	*Public Service Systems for the Twenty-first Century*
1. Single system in theory; in reality multiple systems not developed strategically	1. Recognize multiple systems, be strategic about system development, define and inculcate core values
2. Merit definition that had the outcome of protecting people and equated fairness with sameness	2. Merit definition that has the outcome of encouraging better performance and allows differentiation between different talents
3. Emphasis on process and rules	3. Emphasis on performance and results
4. Hiring/promotion of talent based on technical expertise	4. Hiring, nurturing, and promoting of talent to the right places
5. Treating personnel as a cost	5. Treating human resources as an asset and as an investment
6. Providing job for life/lifelong commitment	6. Involving both inners and outers who share core values
7. Protection justifies tenure	7. Employee performance and employer need justifies retention
8. Performance appraisal based on individual activities	8. Performance appraisal based on demonstrated individual contribution to organizational goals
9. Labor-management relationship based on conflicting goals, antagonistic relationship, and ex-post disputes and arbitration on individual cases	9. Labor-management partnership based on mutual goals of successful organization and employee satisfaction, ex-ante involvement in work-design
10. Central agency that fulfilled the personnel functions for agencies	10. Central agency that enables agencies, especially managers, to fulfill the personnel function for themselves

Abramson, Mark A. (Editor). *Towards a Twenty-first Century Public Service: Reports from Four Forums.* The PricewaterhouseCoopers Endowment for the Business of Government. January 2001, p. 29.

decisions. They may even be tempted to run against "the bureaucracy"—even though these are the people they will later need, if elected, to carry out their campaign promises. And at the same time elected officials think about a reduced role for government, somehow they are challenged to realize that the best and brightest still need to be attracted to government work. Citizens deserve the best talent available for dealing with complex environmental issues, international diplomacy and trade, immigration, and so on.

A MODEL OF HUMAN RESOURCES MANAGMENT

Table 3–1 shows the differences between traditional human resources management systems and those of the twenty-first century. We propose the following model to describe how contemporary human resources management works. The model is captured in Figure 3–1.

The model consists of the environmental forces, political values, and human resources functions we already have discussed. After describing the perspectives of elected officials, senior administrative staff, managers, and line workers, we will identify the strategic issues and how the model works. According to Wilson,[1] an organization's hierarchy is divided into **operators**, (employees), **managers**, and **executives**.

FIGURE 3–1   Strategic Thinking about Human Resources Policy and Management

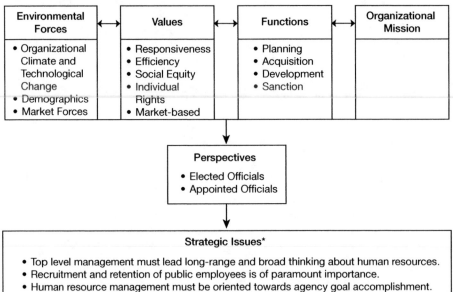

Environmental Forces	Values	Functions	Organizational Mission
• Organizational Climate and Technological Change • Demographics • Market Forces	• Responsiveness • Efficiency • Social Equity • Individual Rights • Market-based	• Planning • Acquisition • Development • Sanction	

Perspectives

• Elected Officials
• Appointed Officials

Strategic Issues*

• Top level management must lead long-range and broad thinking about human resources.
• Recruitment and retention of public employees is of paramount importance.
• Human resource management must be oriented towards agency goal accomplishment.
• Experimentation in how to organize, plan for, and manage human resources must be subjected to evaluation.

* National Academy of Public Administration. Fall 2000 Annual Meeting, Washington, DC.

Operators are those responsible for completing the core work of the agency. In a small police department, these would be the officers on the street, the detectives, and those that support them; in a hospital these would be the nurses, the physicians, and support personnel primarily responsible for treating and caring for patients; for the park service these would be the rangers and personnel that help with and support the ranger's work. From the *operator's perspective*, wages, working conditions, and benefits are important; but operators also are concerned with having the opportunity to do their work well. This could mean good management and supervision, the right tools for the job and up-to-date training, adequate staff and work loads, and how their job is designed. They want some influence over the conditions that influence their ability to do their work, and they want to be recognized and treated equitably.

But employees are not uniform in their perspective which depends upon their status as full or part-time, permanent or temporary, civil service or contract, unionized or not. The terms of the employment contract—expectations and obligations of employee and employer—changes, depending upon one's status. Employees are beset by work/life balance issues, the continual need to upgrade technological skills, and what often seem like incredible demands from the public for customized services delivered in a timely fashion—"timely" as determined by the citizen.

Managers bring a different *perspective*, according to Wilson. They find themselves between the operators and the executives of an agency. They are responsible for conveying the needs of operators to executives and for translating the policy interests of executives to the operators. Wilson sums up the manager's perspective by saying that they are responsible for dealing with the constraints that operators have to work under: the sometimes vague or conflicting directives, procurement, personnel, accounting, and budgeting processes that do not always facilitate the operator's work but make sense from other perspectives.

Managers find themselves facing continuing obstacles as they attempt to align organizational structure, administrative systems, and the motivation and abilities of employees in order to facilitate goal accomplishment. For example, a tight labor market dictates the need to shorten recruitment and selection processes so other employers do not hire the best candidates. At the same time, there is pressure not to short-circuit hiring processes to insure equal access to jobs and fairness in hiring.

Executives may be politically appointed or career civil servants. They are primarily responsible for handling the agency's external relationships. This means that they are continually alert for external forces—like legislatures and interest groups—that might place the agency under undue scrutiny and thus limit its autonomy to do its work. Autonomy is crucial to an agency, enabling it to adapt to changing conditions. For example, it is much different working under a procurement policy that requires all purchases over $5,000 to be approved hierarchically than one which delegates this authority to line departments. Tight procurement rules often result from scrutiny by critics outside the agency. In short, the work of the executive is to build and maintain credibility for the work the operators are performing. The more credibility, the more flexibility the agency will be allowed, which theoretically will promote productivity.

Elected officials bring yet another **perspective**. Their concerns may or may not be directed at a specific agency or policy area. Inevitably, they will reflect the interests and concerns of their constituents. Political accountability is very important to them, and in addition to their policymaking or legislative role, most take their oversight role very seriously. Elected officials and agency directors are challenged to confront the ways their perspectives have been bounded by traditional views of personnel management. Elected officials are largely responsible for the creation of position management through their focus on external control of agency resources (for example, through line-item budgets, control over appropriations, and control over number of positions and average grade level). Elected officials are responsible for setting agency missions and objectives legislatively, for engaging administrative officials, hopefully in a partnership, to achieve those objectives, and for expecting agency leadership to develop and implement administratively sound and politically sensitive human resources plans that reflect strategic thinking.

Now that we have described these perspective, let's look at the model. It shows that environmental forces are filtered through the political values we described in the first chapter. These forces affect the way the four functions are carried out which, in turn, often produce human resources issues that have an impact on agency mission accomplishment. These issues are processed through the various perspectives just described.

In fact, the dynamic is never linear. Mostly, it starts with the problems an agency faces in the short term. Let's say that the legislature has voted low wage increases for several years, and agency managers are having difficulty accomplishing their work because quality employees are moving to jobs that pay more attractively. The inability to complete work at an acceptable standard is what causes an agency to react, to focus its time and energy. Often, this draws the attention of those outside the agency, including interest groups. Then, the analysis begins, the problem is defined based on the perspectives of those who see the problem as important, alternatives are sought, larger issues may be recognized, and environmental forces identified as having a more or less direct effect on an agency.

Here is a real example. A gap in revenue needed to provide public transportation in Los Angeles finds its way as an issue into the collective bargaining that occurred in Fall 2000.[2] The Transit authority's position is to reduce overtime, hire more part-time drivers, and create more transit districts, which will have the effect of creating a partially nonunionized work force. The efficiency and rights issues abound here, affecting both the sanction and planning functions. But driving some of this is the profound emphasis that the embrace of the market place has given to the Transit Authority's alternatives. In the midst of this struggle are found people of lower socioeconomic status who rely on public transportation to get to work. The political pressures to settle the strike are immense, but financial implications of alternative settlements are significant, and the struggle for power between the union and the Transit Authority underlies it all.

As another example, in November of 2000 teachers and the city of New York were reported to be far apart on a labor contract.[3] The backdrop is a national movement favoring performance-based incentive systems. The city and the mayor saw this as an opportunity to gain more control over contractual issues that, in the past, they felt made it difficult to promote productivity. The union saw this as an attempt to deflect attention from a wage structure that has made central city school-teacher salaries noncompetitive with suburban districts. The larger issues here were teacher shortages now and projected, competitive wages, the relative power of Mayor Giuliani compared to the union, and traditional contract provisions challenged by contemporary trends in performance-based pay nationwide.

As these issues are faced and dealt with, the environmental forces become more recognizable and they are more likely to enter into broad human resources decisions. The key is whether or not the agency is able to engage in noncrisis strategic planning that, in its broadest sense, will incorporate environmental forces into the agency's thinking about its mission. The strategic thinking will link the two—environmental forces and agency mission—through the identification of problems and possible solutions. The problems will reflect more than a short-term reactive perspective; they will be future oriented. The greater the potential impact these broad forces have on the core personnel functions of the agency— planning, acquisition, development, and sanction—the more important thinking strategically about human resources issues becomes.

Figure 3–1 also summarizes some of the strategic issues relative to human resources management that we will be discussing throughout the book.

THREE APPROACHES TO HUMAN RESOURCES MANAGEMENT

The model and examples show the dynamism present in human resources management. As we begin a new decade, we can see three ways of approaching human resources management. The first is an approach that reflects the anti-government values so prominent in the late 1990s.[4] Advocates of this approach criticize public personnel management as being rule bound, inflexible, driven by legal mandates, risk averse, and a constraint on managers. Seeing little connection between personnel management and organizational mission, their response to the contemporary challenges is to minimize or do away with the in-house personnel function and outsource everything feasible to contract out. An example of this sentiment comes from Drnevich and Crino, who argue, "It is our position that with some exceptions, little is sacrificed and much may be gained by outsourcing most HRM activities."[5] Another example is found in Exhibit A at the end of the chapter.

A second approach responds to contemporary challenges by focusing on the traditional civil service values. Advocates of this approach value the expertise embodied in human resources professionals, and they understand the value of consistency in personnel policies as well as the necessity and importance of compliance with legal mandates. But most importantly, this approach is based upon traditional principles of merit—personnel practices based on knowledge, skills, and abilities; and fairness and social equity in the treatment of employees and job applicants.[6] Additionally, in this approach public service itself is valued.

While advocates of this approach are not opposed to outsourcing some personnel functions, they do see the importance of in-house personnel professionals who remind organizational leaders of their commitments to public service values and practices. This approach is captured in Exhibit B at the end of this chapter.

The third approach is one that views the essence of human resources management as workforce planning. The response to contemporary challenges is to act upon them through planning, not letting the short-term challenges dictate an organization's actions. The essence of this approach is a plan that identifies and connects present and future competencies with the outcomes identified in an organization's strategic plan. It includes an inventory of what is available in the current workforce and what is needed, and it develops a plan to close the gap. The plan is crucial, and other human resources functions could be contracted out. An example of this approach is found in Exhibit C at the end of this chapter. The importance of workforce planning as a key ingredient in human resources management also is captured in a document like "Building Successful Organizations: A Guide to Strategic Workforce Planning," produced by the National Academy of Public Administration.[7]

AN INTEGRATED APPROACH TO HUMAN RESOURCES MANAGEMENT

Looking over the three approaches to human resources management that we have just described, one can find attractive features in each. The first offers a healthy dose of criticism and questions the value of human resources management professionals and offices. What do they do? What value do they add? The second reminds us that there is value in public service, and that human resources professionals are in an ideal position to advance those values through value-based personnel practices. And the third approach reminds us more than anything that the internal operations of an agency have to be geared to sensing periodically and systematically what is going on in the agency's external environment.

An integrated approach takes from all three perspectives. It is unafraid to outsource traditional personnel functions like benefits management, payroll, training, and so on. It is value based, focused on equity and employee development, as well as efficiency in agency operations, and it is future oriented and finds ways to link personnel practices with agency goals. This integrated approach can be labeled *strategic human resources management.*

The City of Minneapolis provides an example of this approach.[8] They have identified four major human resources goals: improve quality of city services and customer orientation; clarify responsibilities and improve accountabilities for all city employees; minimize problems that may have resulted from inconsistent human resources practices; and recognize that city employees are a primary resource and make a commitment to their personal and professional development. There are fourteen objectives listed as part of the reform as well as a key initiative relating to workforce planning. The federal government has produced a similar comprehensive strategic plan.[9]

STRATEGIC HUMAN RESOURCES MANAGEMENT

Strategic human resources management is the purposeful resolution of human resource administration and policy issues so as to enhance a public agency's ability to accomplish its mission in an efficient and equitable way. The key to strategic thinking is connecting human resources management with agency goals without losing sight of public service values like individual rights and social equity. This is not simple! It highlights an age-old debate about the role of staff functions like personnel administration. How independent should personnel administrators be in order to enhance the quality of personnel services? How subservient should they be in order to aid agency managers? Strategic thinking requires an *understanding* of how organizational human resource management functions relate to one another, to their environmental context, and to agency goals; a *vision* of the importance of human resources in goal accomplishment and in building a workforce committed to public service values; and a *commitment* on the part of elected officials, personnel administrators, managers, and employees to work for the kinds of changes that will enhance concern for human resources issues.

In Fall 2000 the National Academy of Public Administration (NAPA) convened its annual meeting in Washington. It set out to establish strategic guidelines for a new presidential administration. Its recommendations, shown in Table 3–2, illustrate how strategic thinking can be applied to human resources management. The issues and recommendations are listed below. Even though they are targeted to human resource policy and administration in the federal government, there are many recommendations that are applicable at all levels.

These issues and recommendations raised in the National Academy of Public Administration's 2000 annual fall meeting boil down to four areas that are applicable to any large employer—public, private, or non-profit:

1. To deal with human resources issues, agency heads must lead strategic thinking; it cannot be left to personnel specialists.
2. Recruitment and retention of employees are of paramount importance.
3. Human resource management should be oriented towards agency goal accomplishment.
4. Experimentation in how to organize to plan for and manage human resources should be subject to evaluation.

To provide more practical understanding of these four broad issues and to incorporate the equity issues that seem to be missing, we have broken them down into more specific concerns that are addressed throughout the remaining chapters. They are listed below and followed with brief discussion.

1. Recognition that human resource management is a critical organizational function;
2. The need to balance the importance of employee rights and due process with the flexibility managers need to make timely responses in service delivery;
3. Developing the knowledge, skills, abilities, and values to work in teams along with administrative systems that facilitate the work of teams;

TABLE 3–2   Reforming the People Side of Government

ISSUE PRIORITIES AND RECOMMENDATIONS FROM THE NATIONAL ACADEMY OF PUBLIC ADMINISTRATION
In order to improve fundamentally the human resources future for the federal government, Presidential leadership in cooperation with key stakeholders such as federal employee unions, managers, executives, senior political appointees, is essential. The four key recommendations for reforming the people side of government follow:

1. **Human capital needs to be top priority (not just an HR issue, but an executive priority—White House and every agency)**
   a. Assign lead responsibility to senior WH aide and COO in every agency
   b. OMB, OPM, and executive branch agencies should work closely with Capitol Hill on human capital issues
   c. OMB should be more involved in human capital planning/process, linked to budget process and the GPRA (strategic planning and results-oriented management) process, with the support of OPM
   d. OPM should focus more on tools not rules (e.g., workforce planning, helping agencies, technical assistance, best practices, streamline regulations)
2. **Recruit, retain, and develop a skilled and diverse workforce, including redefining public service careers and promoting public service**
   a. President and key government leaders must speak out about the importance and value of public service on a continuing basis
   b. Require agencies to develop and implement workforce analysis and plans (e.g., what competencies exist now, what are needed in the future to achieve agency missions, what are the gaps?)
   c. Develop policies and encourage inter/intra-governmental and private sector mobility
   d. Improve and promote quality of work place (e.g., rewarding initiative, motivating workers, encourage risk-taking, stimulate intellectual growth)
   e. Improve and promote quality of work life balance through family-friendly policies (e.g., flextime, flexiplace, virtual office)
   f. Increase educational outreach efforts
   g. Streamline the hiring process to respond to changing market competition
3. **Modernize the performance management and training/development systems**
   a. Link performance management systems to the strategic plan and make it results oriented
   b. Adopt a balanced scorecard approach (e.g., results, client feedback, employee feedback)
   c. Adopt a more performance-based incentive and reward system for individuals, teams, and agencies
   d. Enhance information systems to support improved performance management systems
   e. Invest in human capital development necessary to achieve organizational goals, drawing examples of levels of investment from private sector best practices
4. **Decide how much standardization is necessary in the human capital system**
   a. White House should lead an expedited assessment of the effects of the implementation of individual agency personnel systems and their results (e.g., achievement of agency mission)
   b. Simultaneously review the existing regulations associated with Title V to simplify/streamline/improve the human capital system
   c. Determine the opportunities for more comprehensive improvements necessary to achieve organizational goals

4. A shift in the focus of public management from position management to work management and employee management;

5. Clear differentiation between "core" and "contingent" jobs based on divergent underlying values about costs;

6. For core jobs, a clear focus on employee training and development;

7. For core jobs, a clear focus on employee involvement and participation;

8. For core jobs, a shift in focus from EEO/AA compliance to workforce diversity;

9. For core jobs, an emphasis on performance-based compensation systems that emphasize achievement of mission through the use of variable pay;

10. For core jobs, an emphasis on family-centered leave and benefit policies;

11. Enhanced investment in human resource management information systems;

12. Entrepreneurial behavior by public personnel managers.

Recognition that Human Resource Management is a Critical Organizational Function

In an environment where politics, administration, and markets are joined on various issues, a premium is placed on strategic thinking. Public personnel management consists of the techniques and policy choices related to agency human resource management. Taken together, these techniques and choices send messages to employees, mangers, and external stakeholders about the value the agency places on human resources. In an organization with an effective human resource management capability, these messages are clear and positive. For managers and employees within the agency, this is the message: "Human resources are assets." But the message goes further. "And, we will evaluate our human resources policies and practices against this criterion." For elected officials outside the agency, the message is: "Employees are a cost and an asset. Through progressive personnel management, agencies reduce costs and maintain assets." And for the personnel director, the message is: "You are the key member of the management team in developing, implementing, and evaluating human resource policies and programs so as to develop assets and cut costs. Part of your job is to engage top management in strategic human resources issues."

Balancing Legal Requirements with the Manager's Need for Flexibility

Increasingly the rights of employees are captured in law. The provisions in these laws act to limit the discretion of managers. That is their intent. They are designed to prevent those with authority over human resources decisions from acting in ways contrary to the interests of employees as reflected in law or union contracts. At the same time that human resources specialists are required to monitor supervisory behavior in light of the law, they are expected to help managers accomplish agency goals. Sometimes, the two expectations conflict. For example, in order to comply with the law, agency procedures may require managers to follow a step-by-step recruitment and hiring procedure. This may work well with many jobs, but with jobs where applicants are scarce, short circuiting the standard recruitment and selection procedure, as well as the pay schedule, may be necessary in order to hire a top-flight applicant.

Aligning Administrative Procedure with a Team Approach to Organizing for Work

As work becomes increasingly specialized, the need for teams becomes more apparent. Problems do not present themselves in ways suitable to specialized skills. Problem solving requires the application of multiple skills and knowledge, in other words, teams of individuals. Traditional approaches to personnel administration focus on the individual job. Job analysis, classification, evaluation, appraisal are all geared towards individual jobs. The human resource specialist of the future will be able to identify ways that human resources policies and procedures can accommodate the transitions from individual work to people working in teams.

Shift from Position Management to Work Management and Employee Management

Due to a variety of political and economic pressures, the focus of public personnel management changed from management of positions, as was the case under traditional civil service systems, to accomplishment of agency mission through work management and employee management.[10] For public personnel managers accustomed to working primarily within civil service systems, this has meant recognizing the need for increased flexibility and experimentation in many areas such as rank-in-person personnel systems, broad pay banding, and group performance evaluation and reward systems. Outside civil service systems, it includes contracts, leased employees, and other secondary labor market mechanisms.

Clear Differentiation between Core and Contingent Jobs Based on Divergent Concerns for Asset Accountability and Cost Control

Another strategic human resources management issue relates to the financial costs of public employees. Enhanced sensitivity to personnel budgets are focused on the differences between traditional, full-time permanent, civil service employees and contingent workers. Strategic human resources planning anticipates total compensation costs and concerns for risk management as they relate to full-time and contingent workers. On the one hand, hiring contingent workers can reduce compensation and benefit costs and can reduce employer liability in some cases, but productivity and employee loyalty may suffer.

For Core Jobs, a Clear Focus on Employee Training and Development

Employers accept the human resource asset assumptions underlying core jobs filled through primary labor market mechanisms. That is, employees *in these jobs* are human capital whose retention and utilization depend on appropriate placement and continued development. A close relationship between employee development and corporate human resource policy helps the organization in three respects: (1) It focuses planning and budget analysis on human resources; (2) it facilitates cost-benefit analysis of current training and development activities; and (3) it facilitates communication and commitment of organizational goals through employee participation and involvement.[11]

For Core Jobs, a Clear Focus on Involvement and Participation

The strategic importance of involvement and participation stems from two factors. First, to the extent that employees value involvement and participation, it is crucial to their satisfaction and, therefore, retention. While job satisfaction does not always translate into added employee motivation, it does affect an employee's decision of whether to stay or leave a job. Second, a major concern for organizations in changing environments is how to plan, learn, and adapt as an organization. The learning organization defies strict organizational hierarchy. Knowledge relevant to improvements in organizational processes is available at all organizational levels, and without involvement and participation, valuable knowledge is not accessible. A key strategic concern is how an organization moves from a traditional hierarchy to a structure that encourages employee involvement and participation.

For Core Jobs, a Shift in Focus from EEO/AA Compliance to Workforce Diversity

Workforce diversity is not just a variant on civil rights or affirmative action. While the two concepts are related, they differ in three important respects. Workforce diversity is broader. It focuses on accomplishment of agency mission rather than compliance with sanctions; and, as a result, its locus of control is internal rather than external.

The link between diversity and strategic planning is reflected in the Secretary of the Navy, Richard Danzig's, story about the future Navy that requires planning and action now.[12] It takes twenty to thirty years, he reminds us, to move from an entry-level officer rank to admiralty rank. In twenty to thirty years, the civilian political elite in America will include many more minority influentials than today. Working with a minority-influenced political elite, the Navy of the future would be advantaged by an officer corps that reflects the diversity of the country as a whole. The Navy must think about and anticipate that situation now if it wants to effectively deal politically twenty years from now. It must do this at a time when the armed forces, just like any other employer, are having difficulty recruiting and retaining its members.

For Core Jobs, Emphasis on Family-Centered Leave and Benefit Programs

Family-centered leave and benefit programs are integrally related to employee involvement and participation, and to workforce diversity. They represent organizational adaptations to the changing demographics described earlier in this chapter. First, the productivity of core employees is directly related to their involvement and participation, which is in turn related to the extent to which the employer provides services and benefits, which help employees, meet family obligations. Second, because women are the traditional caregivers in our society, the effectiveness of an employer in attracting a diverse workforce depends upon the provision of these same services and benefits. Major components of a family-centered corporate human resource policy for core employees are: (1) flexible benefits, (2) family leave, (3) childcare support programs, (4) alternative work locations and schedules, and (5) employee-centered supervision.

Investments in Human Resources Management Information Systems

The ability to think and plan strategically depends in part on access to reliable information about the past, present, and future and the ability to integrate information produced in the past by separate administrative processes. As a simple example, knowing the age breakdown of an organization's workforce will alert managers to staffing issues associated with retirements and anticipated personnel outlays. The ability to break that information down by skill level and an understanding of the market value of those skills and their availability will enhance human resource planning. Of course, none of this makes any difference if the organization itself does not know where it is headed, which makes a connection with legislative or political intent crucial.

Public Personnel Managers as Entrepreneurs

Contemporary public personnel managers tend to see themselves, and to be viewed by others, as interpreters or mediators among competing systems, stakeholders, and values. They see themselves as professionals whose role involves a blend of technical skills and ethical decision making and as key players in developing corporate human resource management strategy. The essence of this emergent professional public personnel management role is *synergy*, the exploitation of pressure points where conflicting systems compete and converge and the reconciliation of conflicting values, changing conditions, competing stakeholders, and a diverse workforce into a coherent and dynamic whole.

SUMMARY

Strategic human resource management is the purposeful resolution of human resource program and policy issues in order to enhance a public agency's ability to accomplish its mission and promote equity and fairness in human resources management. Contemporary work and organizations, demographic trends, and market-based values challenge traditional views of public personnel management as they alter both external and internal organizational environments.

The most important message in this chapter is that human resources management issues are strategic in nature as long as labor is considered an asset in addition to a cost. But strategic thinking must go beyond simple workforce planning. It must incorporate, as well, a critical view to what human resources managers can add to an organization, what personnel functions can be outsourced, and how public service values can be reflected in human resources planning. Once seen in this way, human resource concerns transcend what a personnel department can accomplish on its own. The strategic issues outlined in this chapter require top management attention.

KEY TERMS

Assumptions about civil service systems	Managerial perspective
Contemporary work and organizations	Market-based values
Demographic trends	Operator (employee) perspective
Elected officials' perspective	Strategic human resources
Executive perspective	management

DISCUSSION QUESTIONS

1. What are the assumptions that underpin traditional public personnel management systems?
2. Give examples from your own experience of how contemporary work and organizations, demographic trends, and market-based values challenge the assumptions of traditional public personnel systems.
3. Identify four of the consequences of these challenges.
4. Identify the components of the human resources model and how the components interact. After reviewing the examples in the book of how the model works, give an example of your own, either real or hypothetical, focusing on one or more of the strategic issues identified toward the end of the chapter.
5. Describe and discuss the operator, manager, executive, and political perspectives on human resources management. If you are now working outside of school, which perspective best describes your position? Give one example of how two of the perspectives might coincide and an example of how they might clash.
6. Use Exhibits A, B, and C at the end of the chapter to illustrate three approaches to human resources management.
   a. How does the role of the personnel manager change depending upon the approach?
   b. Make an argument in favor of each approach. Show the shortcomings of each approach.
   c. Which approach would you favor if these were your only choices? Why?
   d. Which approach most characterizes the agency you work for? The agency you would like to work for?
7. Describe the integrated or strategic thinking approach to human resources management and be able to show how it incorporates parts of each individual approach.
8. Review (a.) the twelve human resources issues identified in this chapter as well as (b.) the National Academy of Public Administration recommendations for human resources management and (c.) the characteristics of Public Service Systems for the Twenty-first Century. Find four to six common elements in the three lists. Where are the differences? What do you think is driving these attempts to modernize human

resources management? Which element is most important to an agency you are familiar with? Which would you be most interested in writing a research paper about?

EXHIBIT A: "PERSONNEL MANAGEMENT: PART OF THE PROBLEM OR PART OF THE SOLUTION?"

The article summarized below appeared recently in a national management magazine.[13] After reading it, answer the following questions:

1. Why does the author think human resource departments should be eliminated?
2. What evidence does he offer to support his assertions?
3. What alternative does he propose?
4. Are the author's suggestions consistent or inconsistent with the recommendations offered in this textbook? Defend your answer, citing specific functions and recommendations.
5. Do you agree or disagree with his assessment of the problem? With the solution he proposes? Defend your answers.
6. How does the message in this article compare with Tom Lewinsohn's message in Exhibit B?

Why Not Abolish the Human Resources Department?

People need people—but do they need personnel? Your company's human resources (HR) department employees spend 80 percent of their time on routine administrative tasks. Chances are its leaders are unable to describe their contribution to value added except in trendy, unquantifiable terms. Yet the department frequently dispenses to others advice on how to eliminate work that does not add value.

Nearly every major HR function now done in-house can be done better and cheaper by private contractors—benefits design and administration, payroll, information systems and record keeping, OSHA compliance, and EAPs. None have much potential to produce competitive advantage for a company that does them in-house; all offer economies of scale to outside suppliers; and some reduce risk by offloading exposure to liability or regulatory claims.

HR still has a useful compliance role in monitoring diversification and EEO/AA compliance, but recruitment and selection are best left to line managers because they know most about the job.

Few companies have the skill to develop and implement complex performance and reward systems that reconcile such elements as encouraging cooperation in work teams, yet rewarding individual performance in hierarchies. It is far better to buy high-quality systems from outside, and leave line managers and supervisors responsible for discipline and rewards.

Most "canned" training programs are also irrelevant and wasteful. The best training is OJT, which is done on-site when needed.

HR directors say that human resources are of great strategic importance to the company. This may be true, but it is all the more reason to turn HR functions over to line managers. They, after all, are the ones who are most concerned with productivity improvement.

So there are two possible futures for HR. One is to become a highly automated employee services operation that functions primarily as a conduit for outsourced personnel functions. The other is to become proactive custodians of strategic human capital, holders of the keys to core competencies and competitive advantages in the global marketplace. And companies clearly need to demand that their HR departments focus on their own future, not that of other units.

EXHIBIT B: LEWINSOHN MEMORANDUM

July 5, 1996
TO: John Nalbandian and Donald Klingner
FR: Tom Lewinsohn, Former Personnel Director, Kansas City, Missouri, and Past President, International Personnel Management Association
RE: The Staffing Function

I was taught and believed that the public service was a career that truly practiced equal employment opportunity for entry into the service and for subsequent promotional opportunities. I started my career as an intern with the state of Kansas and retired as Director of Personnel for Kansas City, Missouri. I am an advocate of merit principles as defined by the Office of Personnel Management.

In the last few years, the personnel function relabeled itself to the human resources function. In my opinion, the purpose was for personnel to become more "management" oriented and to add "value" to the organization. It sounds terrific, and I am sure that there are human resources departments that accomplish those goals. I am also seeing the basic function of recruitment and selection contracted out to the private sector which can result in pre-selection and circumventing of equal employment opportunity. On the one hand, this practice concerns me because it goes around the "open" process, but on the other hand, I can understand that the operating departments welcome this kind of outsourcing since they no longer have to interview the "unknown" masses from the eligible register. After all, hiring temporaries, which is occurring in an ever-increasing variety of positions, has become a common practice at all levels of government. It's simple and quick, and all we have to do is call the agency and say, "send another one." The private sector thrives on this practice. What is good for business should be good for government, shouldn't it? It is expedient preselection without accountability. It is *not* a merit system that affords equal employment opportunity.

In a recent exposé of city workers goofing-off and sleeping on the job, the operating department responded by stating that the workers caught on the cameras were "temporaries" and that the city will not pay the agency for hours not worked!

What are the consequences of this accelerated privatization? I think it impacts negatively on the very foundation that attracted persons to the public service. With the "temporaries" there is no job security and in turn no loyalty to the public service. The supervisors of these temporaries have complete discretion as to who comes back or not and who will be rewarded by permanent appointments. It is employment "at will," with considerably less legal consequences to complaints by these non-employees.

Over the past few years, many vital personnel functions, especially those that have fiscal ramifications like insurance programs, have been contracted out to the private sector for the appearance of businesslike practices as opposed to "politics." Recruitment and selection, based on a current grade classification system with a competitive wage and benefits program, is the core of the human resources function. When this function is contracted out for administration and enforcement of EEO principles, we abate the management function of personnel.

Questions

1. How would you summarize Lewinsohn's message?
2. Do you agree that privatization of personnel functions diminishes merit principles?
3. Is the core of merit-based human resources management recruitment and classification based on a current grade classification system with a competitive wage and benefit program?
4. Do you think that EEO principles are more likely to be followed by a government personnel department than they would be by a private employment agency?

EXHIBIT C: HOWZE SHIPLETT MEMORANDUM

December 17, 2000
To: John Nalbandian and Donald Klingner
Fr: Myra Howze Shiplett, Deputy Director, Center for Human Resources Management, National Academy of Public Administration

The human resource function of an organization should exist only if it provides value by direct contribution to the organization's strategic mission, its goals and objectives. For most public sector organizations, direct compensation, benefits, and related expenses consume 70 to 90 percent of the agency's budget. To justify such a major expenditure, the organization must have "the right people, in the right place, at the right time, with the right skills." For this to occur each organization must have a strategic plan, and it must identify the human resources goals and objectives required to accomplish the substantive work of the organization. The methodology to accomplish this is strategic human resources, or workforce, planning. The workforce plan is directly linked to the organization's strategic plan. It identifies the:

- competencies required for the workforce to accomplish the outcomes identified in the strategic plan;
- number and level of employees;
- degree to which the current workforce possesses those competencies;
- way in which the gap between what exists and what is needed can be closed through human capitol development or through recruitment.

The workforce plan must be reviewed annually and updated whenever the conditions and requirements of the organization have changed. All other human resources functions—from processing personnel actions such as hiring, promotion to downsizing the workforce—can be contracted out.

Part of the strategic human resources planning process is to assess the human resources management functions that the organization requires and then to decide how these might best be accomplished. In many public organizations today, particularly at the federal level the number of employees in the human resources function has been reduced to such a point that it is not possible to do the human resources work that is required effectively and efficiently. Contracting out offers a viable alternative and can be used in several different ways. These can be:

- Literally the contracting out of the various functions to other public sector agencies or to the private sector;

- Putting contracts in place to provide assistance if the volume of work in a particular function exceeds the staff capacity to perform effectively and efficiently (using contracting as a safety net);
- Putting contracts in place for selected functions to be performed.

Any of the three approaches can be used successfully if they are linked to the organization's strategic human resources plan and through that directly to the organization's overall strategic plan.

Questions

1. What emphasis on human resources management is reflected in this letter?
2. How does this emphasis differ from those reflected in exhibits B and C?
3. What ideas do you find attractive in this letter?
4. What ideas do you disagree with?
5. Under what environmental conditions is workforce planning important? Under what conditions is it most feasible?

NOTES

[1]Wilson, J. Q. (1989). *Bureaucracy*. Basic Books: New York.

[2]Rabin, J. L., and N. Riccardi (October 18, 2000). Strike Settled: Bus Service to Resume Today. *Los Angeles Times*. www.latimes.com.

[3]Greenhouse, Steven (November 13, 2000, A28). New York City and Teachers Far Apart on Money Issues and Tenure in Contract. *New York Times*.

[4]Peters, R. G, and D. J. Savoie (1994). Civil Service Reform: Misdiagnosing the Patient. *Public Administration Review, 54*, 5, 418–425.

[5]Drnevich, P. L., and M. D. Crino (no date available). Rethinking HRM. *Public Administration and Management: An Interactive Journal*. www.pamij.com/drnevich.html.

[6]Kearney, R. C., and Hays, S. W. (1998). Reinventing Government, The New Public Management and Civil Service Systems. *Review of Public Personnel Administration, 18*, 4, 38–54.

[7]National Academy of Public Administration (May 2000). *Building Successful Organizations: A Guide to Strategic Workforce Planning*. Washington, DC.

[8]HR Reform: Investing in Human Capital (October 2000). *IPMA News*. www.ci.minneapolis.mn.us.

[9]U.S. Office of Personnel Management (November 1990). *Strategic Plan for Federal Human Resources Management*. PSO 216.

[10]Abramson, Mark A. (editor) (January 2001). *Towards a 21st Century Public Service: Reports from Four Forums*. The PricewaterhouseCoopers Endowment for the Business of Government. January 2001.

[11]Bernhard, H., and C. Ingols (September-October 1988). Six lessons for the corporate classroom. *Harvard Business Review, 88*, 40–48; and Rosow, J., and R. Zager (1988). *Training—The Corporate Edge*. San Francisco: Jossey-Bass.

[12]Danzig, R. (November 17, 2000). Presentation at the annual meeting of the National Academy of Public Administration. Washington, DC.

[13]Stevens, T. (January 15, 1996). Taking on the last bureaucracy. *Fortune, 133*, 105–108.

4
Planning, Budgeting, Productivity, and Information Systems

Through the budget process, political differences are debated and transformed into new, expanded, reduced, or eliminated government programs. The budget preparation and approval process brings human resource management into a larger political context. Because pay and benefits can constitute some 70 percent of an agency's budget, the most vital budgetary items often are the number of personnel and the costs associated with their employment. **Human resource planning** is that aspect of public personnel management that mediates between the external political environment and core activities such as job analysis, job classification, job evaluation, and compensation. In brief, human resource planning matches "wish lists" proposed by agency managers with political realities generated by projected revenues and political philosophies and goals. For the line manager, the process begins with a request from the budget office: "What kind and how many positions do you need in order to meet program objectives?" In many jurisdictions, this request is preceded by some kind of strategic planning and goals-setting process that helps establish priorities and goals. It ends with legislative authorization of programs and funds connected to these requests and others initiated at the legislative level.

Refusals to allocate requested funds focus attention on doing more with less or simply the desire to reduce the size and scope of government. At best this stimulates productivity with innovations in service delivery, technology, and personnel practices; but in many cases it also has resulted in decreased quality and quanity of public services.

By the end of this chapter, you will be able to:

1. Explain why budgeting and financial management are of critical importance to public personnel management.
2. Describe various methods of forecasting future human resource needs.

3. Evaluate the pressures for downsizing and impact of uncertainty on the human resource planning process; and assess its impact on underlying values.
4. Define productivity as efficiency, effectiveness, and responsiveness.
5. Identify the elements in a human resource management information system and the importance of such a system.
6. Discuss the pros and cons of contracting with private firms for public services.
7. Identify ways of expanding the human resource manager's role in productivity programs.

THE CRITICAL LINK: WHY BUDGETING AND FINANCIAL MANAGEMENT ARE ESSENTIAL TO PUBLIC PERSONNEL MANAGEMENT

A **budget** is a document that attempts to reconcile program priorities with projected revenues. It combines a statement of organizational activities or objectives for a given time period with information about the funds required to engage in these activities or reach these objectives. A budget has many purposes: information, control, planning, and evaluation.[1]

Purposes of a Budget

Historically, the most important purpose of a public-sector budget has been external control—that is, limiting the total resources available to an agency and preventing expenditure for activities or items not allowed by law. This control has applied to both money and jobs. The type of budget used for control purposes is called a **ceiling budget**: It controls an agency directly by specifying limits to expenditures through appropriations legislation or indirectly by limiting agency revenues.

Other types of budgets have been developed for different purposes. A line-item budget, which classifies expenditures by type, is useful for controlling types of expenditures as well as their total amount. Performance and program budgets are useful for specifying the activities or programs on which funds are spent, and thereby assist in their evaluation. By separating expenditures by function (such as health or public safety) or by type of expenditure (such as personnel and equipment) or by source of revenue (such as property tax, sales tax, or user fees), administrators and legislators can keep accurate records of an agency's financial transactions for the maintenance of efficiency and control.

Budgeting is like a game in that all players usually know its participants, rules, and time limits in advance.[2] The primary participants are interest groups (including employees), public agency administrators, the chief executive, and legislatures and their committees.

Shared Roles: Preparation Approval, Management and Audit

Although each participant's game plan will differ with circumstances, each has a generally accepted role to play. Interest groups exert pressure on administrators and legislators to propose or expand favorable programs. Department administrators use these pressures and their own sense of their department's mission, goals, and capabilities to develop proposals and specify the resources (money, time, and people) needed to accomplish them. Chief executives coordinate and balance the requests of various departments. After all, resources are limited and departmental objectives should be congruent with the overall objectives of the city, nonprofit agency, state, or national government. In many cases, the chief executive has a staff agency responsible for informing departments or agencies of planning limitations, objectives, and resource limits. In smaller jurisdictions, the chief administrative officer individually may perform this coordinating function. And, in other cases, there may be a budget task group or department representatives that cooperatively seek to align budget requests with revenue forecasts. The chief executive or chief administrative officer presents the combined budget request of all departments within the executive arm to a legislature or board (city council, county commission, nonprofit board, state legislature, or Congress).

Legislative action on appropriations requests varies, depending on the legislature's size and the staff's capabilities. At the national and state levels, committees consider funding requests from various agencies. These committees examine funding requests in the light of prior expenditures, testimony from department heads and lobbyists, and the committee members' own feelings about the comparative importance of the agency's programs and objectives. Appropriations requests are approved (reported out of committee) when the committee agrees on which programs should be funded and on the overall level of funding.

The entire legislature usually approves committee proposals, unless the funding relates to programs that affect the interests of groups that have not expressed their opinions adequately during committee hearings. Legislation authorizing new programs is usually considered separately from bills that appropriate funds for those programs.

In an elementary view, after new programs are authorized, funded, and signed into law, the executive branch is responsible for executing them. The chief executive is responsible for administering the expenditure of funds to accomplish the objectives intended by the legislature; department administrators are responsible for managing their budgets and programs accordingly.

Financial management is the process of developing and using systems to ensure that funds are spent for the purposes for which they have been appropriated. Through an accounting system, each agency keeps records of financial transactions and compares budgets with actual expenditures. Agency managers engage in financial management when they take steps to limit expenditures, when they transfer funds from one budget category to another to meet program priorities, or when they borrow or invest idle funds.

Audit, the last step in the budget cycle, is the process of ensuring that funds were actually spent for the intended purpose and in the prescribed manner. Controller's offices inside the organization, and auditors outside, review expenditures for compliance with legislative mandates and prescribed procedures. In the case of waste, fraud, and abuse, agencies may be required to return funds; and responsible officials may be subject to organizational reprimand and criminal prosecution by state authorities.

FIGURE 4–1   The Budget Process (*Source:* Donald E. Klingner, *Public Administration: A Management Approach* © 1983 by Houghton Mifflin, Boston, Mass. All rights reserved)

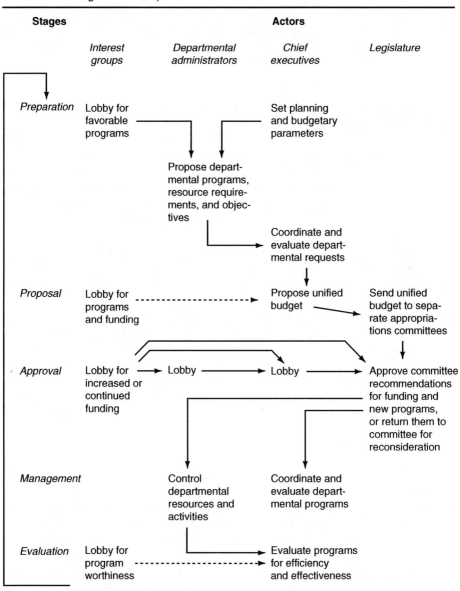

The process of budget preparation, approval, and management is shown in Figure 4–1. This process is a recurrent ritual whose frequency depends on the length of the appropriations cycle. Most governments budget annually, although the problems associated with continually developing and evaluating programs have led some states to develop biennial budgets (every two years). In the typical annual budget cycle, an agency or a department normally is developing the next year's budget a year in advance of the period for which it is requesting funds. At the same time, it is also evaluating programs from the prior year. Although most governments follow an annual cycle, their budget years begin and end on different dates. Most state governments use a fiscal year beginning July 1 and ending June 30, while the federal government's fiscal year begins October 1 and ends September 30. Other governments use a calendar year, January 1 to December 31.

VARIOUS TECHNIQUES FOR FORECASTING HUMAN RESOURCE NEEDS

The budget preparation and approval process is, in effect, the "engine" that forces legislative and executive decisions on programs and expenditures. While the budget is a central policy making and control mechanism, as we saw in Chapter 3 human resource planning would be incomplete if it did not include a concern for the interaction among goals, budget, position allocations, workforce skills and competencies, and final products or services.

Given the extent to which public agency expenditures are comprised of pay and benefits and the use of personnel ceilings to control agency activity, human resource planning is the means by which public officials use the budget to allocate resources among competing priorities and programs in line with the strategic thinking contemporary organizations are emphasizing.

In addition, human resource planning relates to two other specific and important allocation and planning activities: job analysis and classification, and compensation and benefits. By establishing the duties and qualifications for positions, job analysis allows positions to be classified by type of occupation and level of difficulty. This in turn enables uniform and equitable pay and benefit programs to be established for each position. Without these two additional steps, it would not be possible for human resource planners to use forecasts to estimate human resource costs.

Because of the uncertainty surrounding the planning function, most human resource planning is done incrementally. But in some cases, the need for planning is so great that analytical methods must be employed even if the past is not a good predictor of the future because the contemporary economic, political, social, and technological environment is changing so rapidly. Large metropolitan police departments or the U.S. military, for example, simply cannot do human resource planning incrementally without inviting chaos in training, equipment budgets, supervisory capacity, career ladders, or racial tensions.

The primary goal of human resource planning is to match the demand for employees with the supply. In budgetary crises this requires cutbacks; in times of growth or changes in priorities, obviously, a government must plan for new employees. The larger the government unit, the more important it is to anticipate not only personnel needs but also the available supply of labor. Will the competencies be available in the market when the public employer needs them? Again, in larger government units the public personnel manager or workforce specialist could work with department heads and the budget office to forecast future human resource needs; then these combined estimates could be used to develop a coordinated staffing program for the agency or government.

Incrementalism (or **decrementalism**) is a forecasting method that projects straight-line changes in personnel needs based on various factors that influence the quality and quantity of service delivery. The defining characteristic of incrementalism in **human resources forecasting** and planning is its assumption that goals and purposes remain the same or will change only marginally. For example, an *incremental* human resource plan might call for a 5 percent increase in the number of positions allocated to each organizational unit for each 5 percent increase in population served. Similarly, a 5 percent increase in revenues might trigger requests for more personnel incrementally. A *decremental* plan might call for a 5 percent reduction in personnel for a 5 percent reduction in population served or revenue shortfall. Neither one is very effective as a comprehensively rational forecasting technique because both assume no changes in policy goals and purposes, and therefore project no changes in the kinds of people that may need to be hired or laid off.[3] The simplest version of incrementalism, and often the most frustrating to agency staff, is seen when the chief administrative officer asks the governing body what they want to see in the next budget, and the governing body members respond based on a few vocal citizen complaints rather than on a more deliberative process weighing alternatives and opportunity costs.

The most widely used forecasting technique is **collective opinion**. It involves first gathering information from a variety of sources inside and outside the agency and then reaching a group consensus about the interpretation of these data.

This information could relate to such external factors as enabling legislation, budgetary and personnel ceilings, changes in agency structure or objectives, affirmative action goals, collective bargaining, or pressures for political responsiveness. Internal factors might include current human resource utilization, projected staffing needs, or shifts in program priorities. For example, a group of agency personnel directors might conclude that a new state law, requiring the issuance of environmental impact permits for beach-front developers and the funding of the program for a certain dollar figure, would require a 20 percent increase in employees for the state environmental management agency over the next three years.

Usually, the incremental and collective opinion approaches to human resource planning process are more political than analytical/rational.[4] That is, new positions are created and abolished as a reaction to legislative funding priorities influenced by agency plans, interest group pressures, political trade-offs, and anticipated revenue, rather than to meet a systematic and multiyear analysis of legislative priorities, agency needs, and labor market supply.

More rational approaches to human resource planning are available as well. Macro-level forecasting techniques such as categorical forecasting and cluster forecasting may be used. Categorical forecasting estimates further needs for separate occupational groups, such as doctors, lawyers, and personnel managers. Cluster forecasting groups those occupations with common skill requirements and those that are required for other positions to function. These techniques are most often used by larger organizations. Regression analysis is a general statistical tool used with a number of forecasting techniques to estimate the relationships between two or more variables based on past experience. For example, through a regression analysis a police department might be able to estimate the number of new police officers required in relationship with specific levels of population growth.

Modeling, or **simulation** forecasting techniques usually require the use of mathematics and computers.[5] The simulation process requires developing a model that duplicates reality with respect to the crucial environmental, organizational, or interpersonal factors affecting a particular agency goal. A model specifies the conditions that affect the relative feasibility of procuring alternative personnel levels and skills. It requires that guidelines be established, current programs identified, and outputs determined. Next, it requires that possible alternative combinations of human resources be substituted to determine their effect on outputs.

For example, a personnel director seeking to estimate future personnel costs for a department might review the turnover rate for secretarial positions. If the rate were 20 percent annually, he or she would conclude that if the number of positions in the agency were to remain constant, one fifth of the secretarial positions would need to be filled annually. Computing the cost of recruitment, selection, orientation, and training, minus any salary dollars saved for the time positions were vacant could then project anticipated costs for this activity for new employees.

Which forecasting technique should be used? Although most organizations will continue to use nonrational, incremental approaches largely geared to revenue forecasts and the interplay of legislative and agency interests, rational techniques may be adopted fairly easily by many agencies, particularly those organizations that have adequate and competent staff, sufficient data on current programs and resource requirements, receptive management, and access to sophisticated software.[6] The administrator's skill and commitment to seeking the best solution determines the technique used and its effectiveness in forecasting. While in some cases rational planning is impractical or optional, in others it is a necessity. For example, rational planning is essential in determining staffing and skill requirements in the military where doctrine and force levels are changing, and it is not unusual at the federal level where research is done on overall demographic trends and the implications for the federal civil service.[7]

Having used a variety of techniques to forecast the demand for human resources within the agency, managers may use similar techniques to forecast the supply of qualified applicants—the potential labor market from which the agency can recruit. This is influenced by a number of factors inside and outside the agency: among them the state of the economy; the level of technology; the educational system; competing employers; the nature of the labor market; the agency's compensation system; the number of vacancies; availability of valued competencies; training and retraining opportunities; the agency's recruitment practices; affirmative action considerations; and any collective bargaining working rules regarding staffing procedures.

In theory, by subtracting the aggregate supply of human resources from the aggregate demand for these resources within the organization, human resource planners can compute the need. This figure is then used to set up programs and financial mechanisms for acquiring, developing, and utilizing human resources, and this is not as theoretical as it might seem.

For example, even in a municipality of some 100,000, governing board members often find it easier and more comfortable to fund a plan rather than incremental requests. After a while of hearing administrators talk about using overtime for police foot patrols downtown and losing officers through **attrition**—reducing the workforce permanently by not filling vacant positions—the governing body is likely to be receptive to a plan that sets out population growth, police department goals and objectives, and average annual need for new officers. The same is true for a number of departments, like fire and emergency medical services, utilities, and parks and recreation. Some kind of human resource planning will occur by necessity where reductions in revenue are projected, but it is just as important in growth communities so that citizens and governing body members, as well as staff, can feel like the ship is sailing on a course rather than wherever the wind wants to take it.

On the other hand, in a highly politicized environment where plans are utilized only when they support a partisan majority's interests, it may be rational to establish minimum staffing levels for permanent civil service positions and then respond to shifting political priorities with lower cost, temporary employees. Thus, instead of hiring new police officers, utilizing auxiliary officers might be an option for traffic control.

UNCERTAINTY IN HUMAN RESOURCE PLANNING AND DOWNSIZING

The cartoons that decorate office cubicles are often clear indicators of the differences between public management theory and practice. As one cartoon states, "It is the objective of all good managers to carefully plan their activities and to effectively allocate available resources based on program priorities—but when you're up to your ass in alligators, it's difficult to remember that your initial objective was to drain the swamp!!"

The contemporary environment in which public managers operate is filled with "alligators"—political and economic constraints that impede their ability to make rational and reflective choices. Here are several examples of how the contemporary environment negatively influences human resource planning.

The first involves the hiring of new police officers. Shortages of police officers and concerns about public safety have led to a political climate conducive to the hiring of new officers. In large municipalities, implementing this public policy initiative highlights the importance and difficulty of good planning. Mahtesian reports that "Too often, a rush to put police officers on the street has significantly diluted the quality of individual police departments."[8] He cites the cases of Washington, DC, and Miami, where political pressure to put new officers on the streets resulted in haphazard background checks and inadequate training to meet goals and timetables. Further, once on the street, supervision and oversight were lacking due to an overload of new officers in relation to the number of supervisors.

According to Mahtesian, in Houston the process has gone more smoothly but not without problems. While Houston has managed the training challenge, it has not been able to do as well integrating the racially diverse group of newcomers into a largely Anglo force. "While HPD [Houston Police Force] is looking for a few good men and women, it wants most of them to be brown or black."[9] Apparently, the faster HPD has moved to diversify in order to reflect the racial composition of the citizenry, the more racially divided the police force has become.

In Los Angeles the problem is attrition. The Los Angeles Times reported in 1996 that then Mayor Riordan pledged to expand LAPD by 3,000 officers in four years.[10] Frustrating the emphasis on hiring, LAPD was losing nearly 500 officers annually. Disputes over causes of the attrition pitted the mayor and his aides against LAPD officials. The union joined as a strained ally of the police chief. The mayor's aides intimated that the problem was with LAPD leadership; LAPD and union officials countered that the problem was with wages and benefits. One consequence of the attrition was that LAPD ended up financing the training of new officers only to lose many of them to higher-paying suburban police departments.

Cutback Management

Some commentators emphasize the importance of the "three Rs"—reading, writing, and 'rithmetic—to a high-quality elementary school education. Most public managers have been introduced, usually unwillingly and with much pain, to a different "three Rs" during the past fifteen years: re-engineer, reduce, and re-invent.

With cuts in federal spending, demands on state and local governments escalate. At the same time, taxpayers may resist increases in state and local taxes to pay for services. The problem is worsened by the regressive nature of sales and property taxes, which disproportionately affect the poor but are revenue staples for state and local governments.

Reductions in revenue often mean that public agencies are required to practice **cutback management**. This means that agencies will hire fewer permanent employees, freeze wages, or downsize by eliminating current employees, because such a large portion of a government's budget goes for salaries and benefits, especially in school districts and local governments.

A recent Wall Street Journal article reported that in Indianapolis, outsourcing work has reduced public employment 40 percent in three years; similarly, in Sunnyvale, California, 25 percent of the workforce is temporary.[11] Savings in wages and benefits are significant and often result in no reductions in service. But problems can occur when more attention is paid to the revenue side of things rather than to service delivery. For example, cuts in the school district's budget result in fewer teachers, larger classes, and less variety in course offerings; cuts in the public works department can mean haphazard pothole repair, postponed street maintenance, and less frequent trash pickup; cuts in the police department mean slower responses to calls for service, including 911 calls, less attention to minor crimes, and more time in police cars than in mixing with the community face to face; cuts at the state department of environment will mean reduced enforcement of environmental regulations; and reduction in force at the department of motor vehicles means longer lines.

These reductions in service are unnoticed by citizens until the service is needed, and then the typical response often is a complaint about response time or service quality rather than acknowledgment that lower service levels are a function of lower budgets.

Potentially, one of the benefits of the devolution of government to the local level is the relative ease with which citizens can see the connection between revenue and service. For example, reasonable citizens can understand that expecting a school district to reduce transportation costs while maintaining equity in school boundaries is probably expecting the impossible. The average citizen simply cannot make these kinds of connections with federal revenue and services or programs, making it easier to call for cuts in taxes.

At the agency level, the cutback process is felt in several ways. First, it is difficult to cut an agency's programs equitably. Both the contributions of each program to agency goals and the comparative effects of alternative cuts on public services are difficult to measure without resolving the problems related to productivity measurement and program evaluation. Furthermore, many larger agencies are likely to have multiple missions and goals, and it is impossible to assess the contribution of specific programs and divisions to the agency's mission. A second problem, one closely related to the responsibilities of the public personnel manager, is that the easiest methods of reducing agency expenditures are seldom the most appropriate from a productivity or effectiveness standpoint. A **reduction-in-force** could involve across-the-board cuts, hiring freezes, a layoff, or attrition. Across-the-board cuts, like the incremental or decremental methods discussed earlier in the chapter, are practical but non-analytic methods of reducing expenditures in the absence of more definitive program evaluation information or non-confliction politics. And layoffs often result in organizational paralysis, particularly if based on seniority: "Bumping rights" cause productive junior employees to be replaced by disgruntled managers who may lack current technical or professional expertise.

In addition to the convulsive effects of large-scale cutbacks, these allocational decisions spotlight value conflicts. Advocates of fiscal responsiveness and administrative efficiency often advocate downsizing, with consequences sharply felt not only in reduced service levels generally; but also downsizing will be a problem for proponents of social equity and individual rights. If the agency has been hiring a high percentage of minorities and/or women to redress previous patterns of discrimination, reductions in force will mean that they are the first to be dismissed, because on the whole they have less seniority than their white male counterparts. As the seniority of the average employee increases, compensation and retirement benefits likewise increase. Since most employees laid off are at the bottom of the organization, the average grade level of employees also tends to rise.

The National Academy of Public Administration identified several lessons learned from downsizing experiences. They are:

- "Restructure the organization to reflect the changed mission, staffing levels, and performance expectations before you determine staff reductions—simply cutting staff will only leave fewer employees to do the same amount of work;

- "Target separation incentives to organizations and occupations that will be downsized to minimize loss of skills in key mission areas that will carry on after the downsizing;
- "Tap employee and union knowledge and involvement when planning and undertaking downsizing;
- "Communicating honestly to everyone about the downsizing is critical—in effect, poor communications can turn downsizing into a disaster for morale;
- "Giving as much advanced notice as possible about when, who, how, and why better prepares people for taking action;
- "Use involuntary separations (reductions in force) as necessary due to mission needs or timeframes, but they should be the last resort; and
- "Address the needs of the affected employees including the survivors so that mission objectives and organizational performance are achieved."[12]

Effective human resources managers should recognize their mediating role in arranging compromises among the competing values that often accompany decisions about downsizing or privatization. If cuts are inevitable, their impact can be minimized by examining the organizational mission and limiting activities to those programs required by law; or by using the results of rational mechanisms such as cost-benefit analysis or program evaluation. Often, however, cutbacks occur in programs that serve a deserved but politically isolated or unpopular clientele or where outsourcing, privatization, or the hiring of part-timers or temporary employees is feasible.

Maintaining communication with users, clients, and employees is vital to the success of cutback management. Those who must bear the consequences of the cutback should be informed fully and frequently about anticipated actions. When clients and employees discover cutback plans on their own, the poor communication or secrecy produces distrust of virtually all elected and administrative officials.

WHAT IS PRODUCTIVITY?

The governmental response to revenue shortfalls has not only focused on downsizing. It has drawn attention more broadly to the productivity of public employees. Pay for performance, experiments with alternative work schedules, assistance programs for employees with drug and alcohol problems, and the innovative design of work to capture the motivation of employees all represent the impact of the efficiency value on human resources management.

Alternative Definitions: Efficiency, Effectiveness, and Responsiveness

Various terms like output, performance, efficiency, effectiveness, and "bang for the buck" are commonly associated with productivity. Technically, **productivity** concerns two specific assessments of performance. First, **efficiency** is measured as a ratio of outputs to inputs. In other words, measuring efficiency requires identification of a performance outcome, such as the number of school lunches served in the cafeteria or the number of arrests made by a police officer or police department, and identification of the resources used to produce the outcome, such as employee hours worked or funds allocated to meal service or to wages in the police department. The efficiency ratio then becomes:

$$\frac{\text{number of meals served}}{\text{number of cafeteria employee hours worked}}$$

The resultant ratio measures number of meals served per hour worked. Efficiency will increase in either of two ways: by increasing the number of meals served with the same number of employees, or by serving the same number of meals with fewer employees.

What if, in our example, efficiency were increased by serving more meals and making more arrests, yet the meals were unappetizing and not fully consumed and the arrests failed to lead to convictions and instead crowded the courts? Could we say that productivity had improved? Probably not.

Productivity, then, also implies **effectiveness**, a concern with the quality of the output measured against some standard. Thus, a more valid productivity measure would be:

$$\frac{\text{number of meals consumed}}{\text{number of cafeteria hours worked}}$$

where consumption is distinguished from meal preparation. Similarly,

$$\frac{\text{number of arrests leading to convictions}}{\text{salary and wages of police officers}}$$

attempts to incorporate a quality measure for the original output, number of arrests.

Concerns for efficiency focus attention on input-output ratios and answer the question "Are we getting the most for our money?" Implied in this question is the effectiveness concern, "Are we accomplishing the goal we set out to accomplish?" On top of this pyramid of questions is a **responsiveness** question, "Is the goal we set out to accomplish worthwhile in light of the other goals we might have chosen?"

Thus, in the cafeteria example, the responsiveness question might have been, "Do we want to invest public money in school lunches or library books?" Once this question is answered, the school district can attend to the effectiveness and efficiency questions. Because the responsiveness question requires explicit value judgments resulting in winners and losers, governments frequently focus on efficiency questions, such as saving money. It is a lot easier and more popular to ask why the superintendent of schools is making $120,000 a year than it is to determine whether the school district should be hiring more teachers or buying more computers. Critical responsiveness questions are often avoided until such time that losses in service become so obvious that explicit discussions of political priorities cannot be avoided.

Examples of Productivity Improvement

Productivity programs seem to cluster into three areas. The first set of projects and innovations involve changes in organizational structure, processes, and operating procedures:

1. Privatization
2. Contracting out
3. Substituting temporary and part-time employees for career employees
4. Reduction-in-force
5. Flexibility in civil service procedures
6. Selective decentralization or reorganization into homogeneous units
7. Increased use of performance measures and work standards to monitor productivity
8. Consolidation of services
9. Use of economic-rational decision models for scheduling and other problems

A second area includes increased use of technology like the following:

1. Labor-saving capital equipment—for example, shifting from three- and two-person sanitation crews to a one-person side-loaded truck;
2. More sophisticated software in areas like record keeping, payroll, and billing along with an integration of financial and human resource information data bases;
3. Electronic tools for scheduling, tracking of projects, and early warning of problems.

The third area includes personnel-related activities:

1. Job simplification
2. Job enrichment, employee empowerment, and use of teams where appropriate
3. Incentive awards
4. Increased sophistication in training
5. Competency-grounded hiring, training, and appraisal methods
6. Specification of work standards
7. Increased office communication, team building, and organizational development
8. Total quality management
9. Alternative work schedules

HUMAN RESOURCE MANAGEMENT INFORMATION SYSTEMS

It is possible to design a management information system that routinely collects information on various factors related to productivity and organizational effectiveness, and to present this information to managers in the form of reports they can use to make necessary changes in policies or procedures. A department might routinely produce information on purchasing costs, personnel costs, overtime, and productivity. If the method of collecting and compiling information into reports is systematically designed to answer the needs of planners, managers, and other evaluators, it is called a **management information system (MIS)**; those elements of the system that concern management of employees are called the **human resource management information system (HRMIS)**.

The strategic thinking described in Chapter 3 introduces us to the importance of gathering information about human resources. Now, let's look at a typical city and see specifically how its HRMIS might relate to the four personnel functions—planning, acquisition, development, and sanction—introduced in Chapter 1. The relationship between the HRMIS and planning occurs during the budget preparation and approval process. Revenue estimates are matched against program proposals. The cost of proposed programs depends upon such factors as the number and type of employees, their pay and benefits, and the training they will need. All these data are collected and stored as part of the budget and payroll system. The changes that occur throughout the year in staffing are reflected in the human resources database and routinely transferred into financial databases. In some cases, these databases themselves will be integrated.

Affirmative action is a personnel activity that influences the acquisition of human resources. The extent to which social equity considerations will influence selection is determined by the extent to which particular groups are underutilized, the validity of the selection criteria, and the emphasis on affirmative action in the law. Both utilization analysis and empirical validation techniques are dependent upon computerized applicant data such as race, sex, age, test scores, and performance evaluations and employee EEO grievances.

Employee development involves the comparison of performance and productivity data against organizational objectives. Performance appraisal systems and organizational productivity data are routinely computerized. Training needs assessment can be based on a comparison of computerized skill inventories against jobs' required competencies.

The sanction function involves organizations such as unions in personnel management. The success of a municipal negotiator, for example, will depend on how well documented the city's wage position is. An outside arbitrator will accept the position as reasonable only if comparative wage data show that the salaries and benefits the city proposes are comparable with those of employees in similar jobs in similar communities, or that the existing tax structure will not support increased personnel costs. Both require access to an HRMIS, preferably one compatible with the systems in neighboring communities.

Despite widespread recognition that an HRMIS is important, some confusion exists concerning both the criteria that should be used to select such a system and the problems associated with its use. First, public personnel managers need to specify the **data elements** that will provide the information required answering questions such as those raised above. Data are the facts on employees and positions needed to assess organizational programs. For example, **position data** might include the salary range, occupational code, and organizational location of each position. **Employee data** might include each employee's age, sex, classification, duty location, seniority, pay, benefits, skill inventory, and affirmative action status.

These data elements are summarized to form **reports**. This function is most often associated with an HRMIS. Report generation requires that personnel managers ask of themselves, but also of others, who will use the information: "What reports do we need, and how often do we need them, in order to monitor agency inputs, activities, or outputs." In this context, employee skills and tax revenues might be considered inputs; programs are activities; and program results are outputs. Here are some typical reports produced periodically by personnel departments:

1. *Payroll:* total personnel expenditures, by employee, during a pay period
2. *Human resource planning:* number and classification of all filled or vacant organizational positions; turnover rate for selected departments or occupations
3. *Affirmative action compliance:* race and sex of applicants and selections, by organizational unit or type of position
4. *Collective bargaining:* total pay and benefit costs for employees covered by a collective bargaining agreement

Last, program planners use current reports as a means of predicting the future. For example, if health-care costs for civil service employees have increased 12 percent annually over the past five years, it is reasonable to assume (barring a reduction in benefits or increased employee contributions) that they will increase 12 percent next year as well. This forecasting combines the use of current or past data with **modeling** (the development of assumptions about the future to help predict the probable outcomes of alternative policy decisions).

To sum up, an HRMIS is used to collect and store data, to produce reports used to control and evaluate current programs, and to develop estimates to support policy decisions. Therefore, a good HRMIS provides the kind of information needed to the people who need it when they need it. The personnel director must decide what the system needs to do before computer specialists decide how to do it; the HRMIS must be designed to be compatible with the larger organizational management information system (MIS), including the financial data base; and computerization should be recognized as a change in work technology that also involves such issues as employee acceptance, job redesign, and training. Because the costs of some applications are high, HRMIS designers, whether in-house employees, consultants, or vendors, need to balance them against user expectations and capabilities.

An extensive list of HRMIS applications is shown in Table 4–1.

In today's environment, the traditional role of the human resource department to recruit the best and brightest, respond quickly to employee and management inquiries, and manage personnel and legal documents, has expanded. **Enterprise resource planning (ERP)** software, long used by manufacturing and retailers to manage business processes, is becoming a core component in the public sector. ERP software packages consist of modules, each managing different business processes that are linked to deliver comprehensive and strategically useful information. In the public sector, popular modules are human resources, financial management, and purchasing/procurement. "Back in 1994, Kansas was one of the few brave public-sector jurisdictions willing to take a chance on a new kind of software application with the unwieldy name of 'enterprise resource planning,'" recalled Don Heiman, the state's CIO and the person who headed up the project. "We were a traditional mainframe shop back then, with an SNA (system network architecture) infrastructure."[13] The State of Kansas purchased and installed human resources, payroll, and benefits ERP from the vendor

---

July 19, 2001
TO: Journal Entry
FR: John Martello, Director of Human and Information Resources
RE: Integration of new Enterprise Resource Planning (ERP) system with the existing systems

The transition from the old mainframe personnel management system to the new human resources, payroll, and benefits ERP several years ago was a blessing, yet a scary transition. Though the division of the department of administration overseeing the statewide transition had the appropriate redundancies and safeguards during the conversion to ensure success, 100 percent accuracy of data following migration could not be guaranteed. As an executive of an agency responsible for employment data integrity, this was not comforting. Backup copies of critical employment history of each agency employee, position, and funding source were made as a precautionary step. And sure enough, those backups later proved useful.

Now another system is coming on-line, the annual agency budget is becoming automated. Since I've been with the state, preparing, revising, and managing the budget has been a manual, paper-intensive process. The use of spreadsheets with macros help eliminate the majority of the redundancy, but the core data still needed to be inputted. Now, the funding information associated with each position and employee will automatically migrate into a comprehensive system. A major blessing! HOWEVER, the information migrating into this new system from the existing ERP is not fully accurate, so corrections are still needed. For instance, a snapshot of all salary, benefit, and funding information is taken on July 1st from the human resource system and used by the budget system as the base to work from. Unfortunately, the majority of the staff at this agency is unclassified, and has new contracts starting at the beginning of August. The compensation rates from each of these employees do not reflect the higher rates of pay and funding codes for the remaining eleven months of the fiscal year, so the base is wrong. A significant number of manual adjustments will need to still be made despite the automation of this process. And since this system is new, accuracy cannot be assumed, thus tedious review of ALL data will be necessary. Initially, there will be little time savings, but more will be realized over time.

This just reinforces my belief that technology is not the answer, but a tool that allows us to work towards the answer.

PeopleSoft. At that time, over 2000 modifications were made to allow the commercial version of the software to properly function in the public sector.

"Those pioneering days of 1994 are long past, and today a growing number of state and local governments are building ERP applications. Companies like SAP and PeopleSoft now offer public-sector versions of their brand-name software. Government has been drawn to ERP for the same reasons businesses have installed the software.[14] It integrates data, functions and departments across the entire organization,

TABLE 4–1 HRMIS Applications to Program Evaluation

Activity	HRMIS Applications
PLANNING	
Human resource planning	Compile inventory of current employees' skills; determine whether these meet forecast future needs
Job analysis and classification	How many employees are in different occupations?
Compensation	Determine current pay and benefit costs for all employees; project the cost of alternative proposed pay and benefit packages, on-line benefits enrollment, and monitoring
ACQUISITION	
Affirmative action	Compare actual utilization of particular groups with their representation in the labor market; assess organizational affirmative action plan compliance
Recruitment	Compile new hire estimates based on anticipated staffing needs; are current recruitment efforts sufficient to meet them?
Selection	Do an applicant's qualifications meet minimum standards for a given position? Do selected applicants meet performance standards for their positions?
DEVELOPMENT	
Productivity	Record performance of organizational units; compare to other units or previous time periods
Performance appraisal	Record employee performance; compare to other employees, performance standards, or previous time periods
Training and development	Summarize training activities and costs; assess training needs by comparing skills; assess OD needs by measuring organizational climate
Employee motivation and job design	Measure employee productivity, turnover, absenteeism, and internal motivation; assess effect of changes in job design on productivity and motivation
Safety	Record injuries, accidents, and illnesses; use these data to change safety regulations, selection critiera, or employee orientation
SANCTION	
Labor-management relations	Collect and compare salary and benefit data against that of other positions or jurisdictions; compute the cost of proposed changes in pay and benefits
Discipline and grievances	Compile reports on the number and type of grievances and disciplinary actions; use these data to recommend changes in work rules, employee orientation, or supervisory training
Constitutional rights of employees	Record cases of sexual harassment or civil rights violations; use these to improve affirmative action compliance, employee orientation, or supervisory training
CONTROL AND ADAPTATION	
Evaluation	Collect data through HRMIS to evaluate all public personnel management activities

while automating previously manual tasks. Beyond these, a workforce analysis can identify symptoms and causes that may plague an organization. "Recruitment analysis goes far beyond traditional sourcing effectiveness and time-to-hire to determine what companies should really care about—the quality of hires over time. Training finally links courses taken with effectiveness, career progression and employee success."[15] "Human resources, a labor-intensive, non-revenue producing part of any organization, can benefit from the efficiencies ERP delivers by reducing the amount of staff required to process payroll, hiring and benefits. In Phoenix, for example, new hires no longer have to report to a central office to fill out forms. The work can be done from desktops anywhere in the city."[16] This trend in government will continue as "illustrated by the news that California is preparing to build a statewide payroll system for its 250,000 employees."[17]

PRODUCTIVITY AND PRIVATIZATION: WHAT'S A MANAGER TO DO?

Information systems that can gather and produce data about productivity are crucial to managerial and political decisions regarding the delivery of services, including the question of what services the government should provide and who should deliver them. Why should a city government collect trash when a private vendor could do the same? Why should the government manage lodging and concessions in public parks when private businesses could do the same?

These examples highlight the most popular form of privatization—contracting with private business to deliver services governments have been providing. Governments have contracted with private business for services like street construction and repair, tree trimming and planting, ambulance service, vehicle towing and storage, building and grounds maintenance, data processing, legal services, and tax bill processing.[18]

Human resource directors are not the primary decision makers when privatization is discussed. Elected officials, agency heads and staff, chief administrative officers, and department heads lead the discussion. But personnel directors are often asked to assess the pros and cons of privatization, especially as it affects the workforce. How should they respond to such requests?

Chandler and Feuille identify four characteristics of the services most frequently contracted for by local governments.[19] First, there is no compelling reason that government deliver the service. Second, there are usually a number of private-sector firms that could supply the service. Third, the service usually requires low levels of skilled labor. Fourth, outputs are usually easy to monitor. Elliot Sclar's recent award-winning work shows the pitfalls encountered when these guidelines are not taken seriously.[20]

Goodman and Loveman claim that the issue of public versus private gets caught up in symbolic and philosophical arguments when the real issue is "under what conditions will managers [whether public or private] be more likely to act in the public's interest. Managerial accountability to the public's interest is what counts most, not the form of ownership."[21] They continue: "Takeover artists like

Carl Icahn saw the same excesses in corporations that many people see in governmental entities: high wages, excess staffing, poor quality, and an agenda at odds with the goals of shareholders. Monitoring of managerial performance needs to occur in both public and private enterprises, and the failure to do so can cause problems whether the employer is public or private."[22]

Also, they observe that competition is likely to reduce costs. There is no more reason to believe that the public will benefit from a private monopoly driven by a profit motive than by a public monopoly oriented toward public service. According to Goodman and Loveman, the issue is competition versus monopoly not private versus public.

Contracting out for public services often is a rational way to increase government productivity. It holds the promise of saving tax dollars and providing a reasonable level of service. But in many circles it remains a controversial avenue to productivity enhancement because it involves the reallocation of jobs. Reallocation of jobs from the public to the private sector brings values and personnel systems into conflict and points out the inherently political underpinnings of public personnel policy and administration. For example, those responsible for finances may favor contracting out as a way of averting a costly union contract and work rules. But the loss of public jobs invites the political displeasure of employee unions. Even though the private contractor would hire many public employees, unions object strenuously to contracting out because their members will usually find themselves with lower wages and benefits even if they do not lose their jobs.[23]

Social equity may suffer as women and minorities who benefit from gains in government employment find themselves at a disadvantage with employers who might show less commitment to affirmative action and merit. On the other hand, as the Supreme Court has closed the door on opportunities for patronage in government jobs, contracting out provides an opportunity for rewarding political supporters. In large urban areas this may work to the advantage of minority contractors who are politically favored by an administration in power.[24]

While those who advocate contracting out point to "inflexibility" and "red tape" in government personnel systems, merit system protections for the individual rights of public employees suffer with private personnel systems, where grievance procedures are less developed. And, of course, private employers are under no obligation to provide constitutional protections to their employees or to the clients they serve.[25]

While the beginnings of an initiative to contract out a public service may simply reflect a concern to save public dollars, it is worthwhile to remember that jobs are scarce resources in our society. Any attempt to publicly manage their allocation is likely to invite strong reactions from those invested in the current distribution. As we see throughout this book, those investments reflect fundamental differences in the values that shape public personnel management.

ENHANCING THE ROLE OF HUMAN RESOURCES MANAGEMENT IN PRODUCTIVITY DECISIONS

Human resources management and productivity go hand in glove. Enthusiasm for productivity improvement in government opens opportunities for an expanded

April 5, 1996

To: John Nalbandian

Fr: Department Head

Re: Downsizing

As organizations "thin" and the competition for scarce public jobs increase, the process of filling vacancies that are retained in the budget becomes a war within the organization. If the position is actually rebudgeted and advertised, the competition for this public job now creates a large number of applications. Many times, individuals with real qualifications for the position are at a premium due to private-sector competition. Other applicants will cite that local residency, community knowledge, and even friendship with staff or local officials should outweigh required job skills. Thus, often we are confronted with a selection process with many wrong solutions and few win-win outcomes. The end result will often be a political or legal challenge to the selection decision. In addition, many public organizations are losing the "in-house generalists" in the middle management ranks of the organization through the thinning of the organization. These individuals began their careers in very technical areas. But, due to tenure, career advancement, and program needs, they have grown into positions of mid-management and effectively operate the organization day-to-day. These positions are exactly those that are at risk in each and every budget cycle. In an attempt to reduce personnel costs, we quickly rule out department heads, technical staff, and lower-level operating staff from serious consideration for a reduction-in-force. This leaves the middle management supervisors and operational generalists or program operators as the moving targets of the budget process. Each time a person like this is cut, it becomes more difficult for program staff to negotiate needed compromises within the organization.

The result is a decline in staff who share a public-sector philosophy of providing service in an equitable manner for the community. Instead, the hardcore technical staff remain and find themselves unable to communicate with other parts of the agency. The greatest challenge from this conflict is that many of the day-to-day decisions on operations are now made at the highest level of the organization, where they may become politicized. They are brokered on the top floor of city hall or among the department heads of the city. The remaining energy and time of the administrative team after these in-house wars provides little opportunity for creative solutions or ideas leading to better public services.

role for the human resources manager—whether a supervisor, manager, or personnel specialist.

Activities aimed at productivity improvement easily affect core personnel functions but do not usually fall within the formal responsibilities of the personnel department. In the productivity area, line managers connected to technological developments in their field and budget analysts concerned with financial matters consistently play a larger role than personnel specialists. In a way, this role assignment is understandable, since line managers are most familiar with daily operations and because in reality the primary motive for productivity enhancement in the public sector is saving money. In addition, the line manager and the budget analyst are familiar with numbers and ratios and tracking production figures and budgetary accounts throughout the year.

The price for entering this decision-making arena is expertise that those involved in productivity projects will value and subsequently search out. This will involve not only knowledge of technical operations and service delivery. Knowledge of the applied behavioral sciences is becoming increasingly valuable considering the impact that productivity decisions have, especially those involving privatization and downsizing, on workforce morale and commitment. Understanding organizational change processes, the conditions that ease adaptation to change, the conditions that produce resistance to change, and the competence to deal with uncertainty, conflict, and anxiety are qualities of the effective human resources manager as case study three at the end of the chapter shows.

Academically, this knowledge is found in the social sciences: psychology, sociology, anthropology, social psychology, communication studies, and political science. The application of social science knowledge to real-life problems often is referred to as **applied behavioral science (ABS)**. In the federal government, the extensive research by the Office of Personnel Management and the Merit Systems Protection Board into federal employee attitudes and the effectiveness of pay for performance fall into this category of expertise.

SUMMARY

There is a close relationship between budgeting, producing information, planning, and productivity in human resource administration, which involves both political and technical decisions. The human resource manager—supervisor, line manager, or personnel specialist—is centrally involved in both.

A budget represents compromises over political and technical issues concerning governmental programs and objectives. In part, these decisions are influenced by the demand and supply of labor connected to the achievement of government objectives. Productivity concerns focus on how to implement government programs and services with as few resources as possible. Frequently, the focus is on how to scale back on programs and service levels without damaging the quality of public services unacceptably.

One area that continues to attract advocates of administrative efficiency is the privatization of public services. But the hope that the private sector can deliver public services at lower cost is tempered by concerns that employee and client rights will be eroded, that social equity claims will receive less attention, and that accountability mechanisms like open meeting laws and open records requirements will be diminished.

KEY TERMS

applied behavioral science (ABS)
attrition
budget
ceiling budget
collective opinion
cutback management
data elements
effectiveness
efficiency
employee data
enterprise resource planning (ERP)
financial management
human resource forecasting

human resource management
 information system (HRMIS)
human resource planning
incremental/decremental planning
management information system (MIS)
modeling
position data
productivity
reduction-in-force
reports
responsiveness
simulation

DISCUSSION QUESTIONS

1. How does budgeting epitomize the impact of the value of political responsiveness on public personnel management?
2. How are human resource planning and forecasting in public agencies related to the budgetary process?
3. What are the effects of cutback management on a workforce, and how should the human resource manager respond to them?
4. Define each term and then describe the relationship among three alternative definitions of productivity (efficiency, effectiveness, and responsiveness).
5. Describe the elements in a human resource management information system and the role such a system plays in an organization's ability to meet its goals? If you are familiar with such a system, what information does it produce that is helpful to agency managers? What are the drawbacks?
6. What are the pros and cons of contracting out? If you have experience with contracting out, what challenges did you face in writing the contract specifications, and what challenges did you face in administering the contract?
7. Describe the human resource manager's enhanced role in seeking productivity improvements.

CASE STUDY 1: A DAY IN THE LIFE OF A CITY MANAGER

One year ago, in April, Cityville (population 80,000), a suburban city, hired you, Arlene Mayberry, as the new city manager. You brought a reputation for sound financial management and were chosen unanimously by the council. Cityville has experienced revenue shortfalls in the past two years due to a revenue decline in sales tax. The shortfall resulted in modest increases in the mill levy during these two years. The school board's mill levy increased substantially a year ago, due to a cutback in state aid to school districts. The county's levy is scheduled to rise modestly for the next three years, due to commitments previous commissions have made to a significant capital improvements program.

In April, Save Our City, a group dedicated to holding the line on taxes, surprised everyone, including you, by electing two of its slate of three candidates to the city council. The council now consists of these two members, Robert Pipes and Caroline Nixon, both elected to four-year terms; Jane Scott, a very politically astute middle-of-the-road council member who has two years remaining on her term; Max Laney, an ex-police officer supported by the Fraternal Order of Police, with two years remaining on the council; and Ron Reaume, who ran on a platform expressing concern for rebuilding a sense of community and respect for diversity and was elected to a two-year term. Reaume has already said he will not run for reelection. Scott and Laney have not indicated their plans.

You view this group as very diverse politically and potentially difficult to work with. You expect that a number of issues will be decided on split votes. In the summer following the election, after considerable debate and political maneuvering, the new council accepted the budget you had proposed on a 3–2 vote. The fiscal year runs from January 1 to December 31. None of the council members wanted to raise taxes, and the two mill increase you reluctantly proposed was reduced to one mill with the two Save Our City council members voting against adoption; they favored no tax increase under anything other than financial exigency.

After adoption, Pipes and Nixon jointly issued a press release calling for tightening the belt, increased productivity, and sacrifices just like those made by private-sector small businesses and ordinary citizens. The newspaper carried a front-page story without editorial comment, even though the publisher is known to be sympathetic to their cause.

After the budget was adopted, during the fall and winter it became obvious that police-community relations were showing signs of strain. A self-appointed task force representing a coalition of culturally diverse groups met and held a number of forums to gather information about how citizens felt the police were treating them. The forums were not well attended, but it was clear from those who did attend that individual members of minority populations in Cityville felt the police had treated them inequitably. For example, one African-American youth said he was walking home from a late-night job carrying a bag of groceries when he was stopped by the police and told to empty the contents of the bag.

In the spring, responding to a 911 family disturbance call, the police shot and killed a young Asian wielding a knife. The police claimed self-defense; the family, speaking little English, was distraught and suggested that the police had acted too quickly and more out of concern for their own safety than for the victim or family.

The event heightened tension in the community, even though the vast majority of Cityville supported the police. The council was aware of this majority, but Reaume in particular believed something ought to be done and urged city staff to make some suggestions. He became an occasional visitor to the meetings of the task force on police-community relations—now heavily attended—and pledged to introduce their anticipated report to the council. Laney defended the police at the next council meeting, noting that police work had become more dangerous in Cityville, and that these events, tragic as they are, happen in today's violent world.

The next week, Pipes and Nixon declared that it might be worthwhile to look into a possible contract with the sheriff's department for law enforcement. They contended that the sheriff's department was larger, had better training, and could provide law enforcement more cheaply than Cityville could on its own. Laney went through the roof! The leadership of the police union quickly set up appointments with each of the council members. Reaume backtracked a bit, suggesting that rebuilding the sense of community in Cityville required maintaining an independent police force.

As this political maneuvering was going on, the budget process was beginning. The police chief, Jack "Buck" Fishbach, requested a meeting with you. Buck is a no-nonsense law enforcement officer, professionally trained and tolerant of city managers at best. He had been one of the original founders of the Fraternal Order of Police in Cityville when he was just a corporal, years ago. He reminded the city manager that ten years ago the city had passed a half-cent sales tax to hire new police officers. You knew this. The chief added that since that time, in order to show fiscal restraint, the city had not hired a single officer, despite the addition of some 10,000 citizens. This was news to you, and you kicked yourself for not knowing it already. Further, the chief claimed that the police had become exasperated and very angry because lack of staffing had required them to cut back on the very community-oriented activities they were now being criticized for not having performed. He said he was going to develop and present to you a budget proposal designed to augment staff over a five-year period. You knew that the only way to hire more police would be to raise the mill levy.

After the chief leaves, you get a call from the newspaper publisher wanting to know how things are going.

Questions

1. What are you going to tell the publisher?
2. How are you going to approach the budget?
3. How are you going to deal with the chief of police?
4. How are you going to deal with the council?
5. Why did you want to become a city manager in the first place?

CASE STUDY 2: PRIVATIZATION

A majority of the governing body has pledged to the voters that it would explore all avenues available to privatize city services. It has directed the chief administrative officer to present council with some options. After discussion with department heads, the CAO has suggested the following: The city can save some $500,000 annually if it privatizes its sanitation service. This savings could translate into a reduction in the property tax of some 5 percent.

Council member Rodriguez asks how this savings can be achieved and whether the present sanitation workers will lose their jobs. The CAO responds that, in conversations with various private contractors, it appears that the contractor could be expected to hire all of the displaced employees who apply. "However," she adds, "a large amount of the savings probably would be achieved by reducing employee benefits, including health-care coverage. There will be no pension benefit."

Council member Johnston indicates that 70 percent of the employees who will have to change jobs are racial minorities. He noted that the skill level of the sanitation workers is such that they will not have any choice but to accept the reduced standard of living.

Council member Reyes acknowledges Johnston's concern but indicates that the savings will be reflected in a property tax reduction that should benefit the poorest landowners the most—those on fixed incomes in modest homes.

Council member Richardson suggests that the city's economic development strategy is aimed at developing good-paying jobs. He asks if the privatization of sanitation services will advance that goal, for minorities as well as other citizens and taxpayers.

Prior to the evening that the city council will discuss this item, the council members report that a number of taxpayers have called urging privatization and following through on campaign pledges. It appears to the council members that the majority of voters would favor the privatization.

At the evening meeting the item is on the council's agenda, the room is packed. On one side are members of a taxpayer's group in favor of the privatization. On the other side are about half the city's sanitation employees, and a group of African-American and Hispanic clergy and community activists who are opposed to privatization.

Questions

1. What makes this case so difficult?
2. What expressions of different values can you find?
3. Who should make the decision whether or not to privatize? Defend your choice.

NOTES

[1]Axelrod, D. (1988). Budgeting for Modern Government. New York: St. Martin's Press.

[2]Rubin, I. (1993). *The Politics of Public Budgeting* (2nd ed.). Chatham, NJ: Chatham House; Wildavsky, A. (1988). *The New Politics of the Budgetary Process.* Glenview, IL: Scott, Foresman.

[3]Duane, M. J. (1996). *Customized Human Resource Planning.* Westport, CT: Quorum.

[4]Lengnick-Hall, C. A., and M. L. Lengnick-Hall (1988). Strategic human resources management: A review of literature and a proposed typology. *Academy of Management Review, 13,* p. 457.

[5]Duane, *Customized Human Resource Planning.*

[6]Ibid.

[7]Kawecki, C., K. Cameron, and J. Jorgenson (1993). *Revisiting Civil Service 2000: New Policy Direction Needed.* Washington, DC: U.S. Office of Personnel Management.

[8]Mahtesian, C. (January 1996). The big blue hiring spree. *Governing, 9,* p. 29.

[9]Ibid., p. 30.

[10]Newton, J. (January 21, 1996). LAPD attrition may pit mayor against chief. *Los Angeles Times,* p. A-1, 20.

[11]Zachary, G. P. (August 6, 1996). Some public workers lose well-paying jobs as agencies outsource. *The Wall Street Journal,* p. A-6.

[12]National Academy of Public Administration (1995). *Effective Downsizing: A Compendium of Lessons Learned for Government Operations.* Washington, DC: National Academy of Public Administration.

[13]Newcombe, T. (August 2000). Embracing the enterprise in ERP. *Government Technology,* p. 26.

[14]Ibid.

[15]Kutik, W. (August 2000). Alive and well. *Human Resource Executive,* 58–61.

[16]Newcombe, Embracing the enterprise in ERP, p. 26.

[17]Ibid.

[18]Sharp, E. B. (1990). *Urban Politics and Administration.* New York: Longman; and Halachmie, A., and M. Holzer (1993). Towards a Competitive Public Administration. *International Review of Administrative Sciences, 59*, 29–45.

[19]Chandler, T., and P. Feuille (1991). Municipal unions and privatization. *Public Administration Review, 51*, 15–22; see also, United States General Accounting Office (March 1997). *Privatization: Lessons Learned by State and Local Governments.* Washington, DC: United States General Accounting Office. GGD–97–48.

[20]Sclar. E. (2000). *You Don't Always Get What You Pay For: The Economics of Privatization.* Ithica, NY: Cornell University Press.

[21]Goodman, J. B., and G. W. Loveman (1991). Does privatization serve the public interest? *Harvard Business Review, 69*, p. 28.

[22]Ibid., 35.

[23]Chandler and Feuille. Municipal unions and privatization; Walters, J. (November 1995). The Whitman squeeze. *Governing Magazine, 8*, p. 22.

[24]Chandler and Feuille. Municipal unions and privatization.

[25]Kettl, D. F. (1991). Privatization: Implications for the public work force. In C. Ban and N. Riccucci (Eds.). *Public Personnel Management: Current Concerns—Future Challenges.* New York: Longman.

5

Defining and Organizing Work

INTRODUCTION

The ways in which work is defined and organized tend to separate those responsible for public HRM into two camps—HR specialists and everybody else. In that respect these functions generate responses like those that accompany topics such as rotating your car's tires or flossing your teeth. Experts consider them essential, but many of us don't spend enough time on them—and we certainly don't want to spend more time talking about them.

For HR specialists, writing a **job description**—a position's duties and the minimum qualifications required to perform them—is the key to position management. And **position management** (classifying positions by job type and level of responsibility, and limiting total agency payroll to the sum of the salaries authorized for all classified positions) is the cornerstone of personnel management. Others don't see it that way. Legislators and elected officials may concede that budget management and program evaluation are useful legislative oversight tools, but writing job descriptions and classifying positions is an administrative detail they are not concerned with. Supervisors tend to consider job descriptions and position management undesirable and unnecessary restrictions on their ability to flexibly manage human resources. Their objective is to be able to shift employees from one job to another as circumstances dictate, without reference to formal job descriptions. And position management restricts managers' budget autonomy and flexibility by preventing them from hiring additional employees or paying them more, even if they have money in their budget to do so. So this chapter starts with that dilemma. How do we reconcile these competing perspectives on job analysis and classification within the context of contemporary public HRM?

By the end of this chapter, you will be able to:

1. Tell why different groups responsible for public agency HRM have different views of job analysis; and relate the historical development of the field to the conflict and interaction among underlying values and objectives.
2. Summarize why traditional job descriptions (those oriented toward position management) are unsuitable for supporting public personnel management as its focus has changed to work management and employee management.
3. Analyze work using a results-oriented description (ROD), which incorporates work management and career management into the traditional job description.
4. Understand why job descriptions are important for jobs filled through other systems besides civil service, including the alternative mechanisms and flexible employment relationships that characterize non-governmental personnel systems.

JOB DESCRIPTIONS: DIFFERENT GROUPS HAVE DIFFERENT OBJECTIVES

A job description describes a job by listing major duties and specifying the minimum qualifications needed to do it. Exactly how job descriptions are prepared and used is a complicated story that has its origins in the creation of civil service systems and merit system principles. Because different groups have been involved in HRM policy or implementation, and because these groups have different perspectives, it is not surprising that attitudes toward job descriptions differ.

- *Elected and appointed officials* have three contradictory attitudes toward job descriptions. If they are in charge of an agency, they may consider job descriptions and position management an intrusion on patronage hiring. If they are more interested in oversight, they may consider position management essential to control the size and direction of agency staff as an important aspect of budget management and program evaluation. Finally, most elected officials may consider job descriptions and classification systems to be simply irrelevant unless their primary focus is budget cutting.
- *Merit system reformers* consider analyzing and classifying positions as the key to a successful transition from the evils of the spoils system to the greater effectiveness and equity of a civil service system as the basis for responsive and professional public administration.
- *Public HRM specialists* consider job descriptions and classification systems as the key to *position management*. And they are the key to other functions like recruitment, selection, pay equity, and performance evaluation.
- *Managers and supervisors* have an ambivalent viewpoint on job descriptions. They may consider them a necessary first step to recruitment, performance evaluation, setting equitable pay, or disciplinary action. At other times, they may be an unwelcome intrusion on **work management**—their ability to creatively and flexibly use human resources to achieve program objectives.
- *Employees* view job descriptions ambivalently. A current and accurate **position description (PD)** may clarify what they need to do to succeed on their job. Otherwise, criteria established in a job description (like specific types of experience or education) may seem unfair and artificial barriers to **career development**—personal mobility and advancement based on competencies.

Elected and Appointed Officials Focus on Patronage Jobs

Jobs are not defined, analyzed, or classified at all under political patronage systems. The primary purpose of filling the job with a political supporter is the maintenance of the spoils system, not getting public work done effectively. While some minimally acceptable level of performance might be required to avoid political embarrassment for the elected official, minimum qualifications interfere with elected officials' freedom to allocate jobs to their supporters. And today two changes in the nature of work make political patronage even easier. Independent contractors can be hired to temporary or part-time positions not subject to classification; and remote ("virtual") offices allow political appointees to work with little direct oversight.

Merit System Reformers Focus on Civil Service Systems

For merit system reformers, job analysis epitomizes the principles of scientific management and budget transparency that enable them to control the spoils system. They support job analysis because it is the essential first step to ensure that employees are hired and promoted based on ability and performance, and that jobs of equivalent difficulty are paid the same salaries. Without this, it is simply not possible to hire or pay employees so as to support the values of individual rights or administrative efficiency. Again, anyone who assumes that objective and fair pay systems are inevitable, or that they are easy to achieve, has only to look at the chronic and interrelated economic, political, and social problems that plague governments in developing countries—corruption, incompetence, and "brain drain."

Operationally, creating a civil service system means identifying how many employees work for each agency by job type, geographic location, and salary. This enables personnel specialists to develop a **staffing (manning) table**, a roster of all authorized positions in an agency. Hopefully, as personnel actions result in employees being hired, transferred, or discharged, the position management information system will keep this information current. While the need to develop an adequate position management information system may seem self-evident, and the steps involved in doing so may seem childishly simple to complete, the political culture of patronage politics can make it difficult to achieve this basic administrative reform. Under patronage systems, it is difficult to determine how many employees actually work for an agency because there are three possible answers: (1) all persons on the payroll (whether or not they show up for work); (2) all persons who actually show up for work on a regular basis; and (3) all the authorized positions in an agency, whether or not they are filled and whether or not those individuals actually show up for work.

Each of these answers is the result of different pressures on patronage systems. The first option, a payroll "padded" with persons who get paid but never show up for work, results from allowing elected officials to place non-employees on the public payroll as a reward for political or personal loyalty (and perhaps to pocket a percentage of salary as a "kickback" from the non-working "employee"). The second option, a valid payroll matching the number of actual employees, is the objective of civil service reformers. The third option, a payroll inflated by showing as filled positions those that are actually vacant, allows senior managers to pocket the salaries of "ghost" employees as a reward for their own political loyalty. It is widely accepted that the first and third options are corrupt and wasteful. This tension between patronage and merit is not limited to the past or to underdeveloped countries. Local governments in the United States will often cut civil service positions to save money at the same time that they add political employees to the payroll. These may be legitimate appointments, or they may simply be positions created because a powerful elected official wants a friend to have a job and happens to control the budget of the agency in which the new job is to be created.

HR Specialists and Position Management

Once this transition from patronage to civil service is under way, merit system reformers have sought to restrict patronage by entrusting HR directors and specialists with implementing civil service through position management. This means ensuring that public agencies limit pressure by elected officials to create patronage positions. As part of public administration, position management supports rational budgeting by limiting the total amount that can be spent on salaries and benefits. And it fosters rational policy making and implementation by making the staffing of agencies consistent with the intent of the law and the objectives of public programs.

The underlying assumption of position management is that public agencies, left unprotected, will be unable to resist pressure from elected officials to add patronage positions or to fill vacant civil service positions with patronage employees. The way personnel specialists seek to protect the merit system is by working inside the agency to implement legislatively imposed **personnel ceilings**—that is, budget limits on the agency **payroll** and position management limits on the number and type of personnel they can employ. Frequently, position and budgetary controls are combined through the imposition of **average grade-level restrictions**, which limit the number of positions that can be created and filled at each level of the agency hierarchy. A low average grade-level means that most positions are low-level positions. Theoretically, at least, these position management techniques are analogous to line-item budgets in that they focus on *inputs* to the governmental process (number and type of employees). Together, line-item budgeting and position management have historically been successful at forcing compliance and accountability because the first controls the budget and policies of the executive branch, and the second controls the allocation of personnel and money to implement programs in executive agencies.

HR specialists consider job analysis the heart of personnel management because for them the ability to specify a job's duties and the **minimum qualifications ("quals")** needed to perform them satisfactorily (education and experience) is an essential prerequisite to other personnel functions like recruitment, selection, training, and performance evaluation. They regard setting minimum qualifications as essential to establishing an equitable pay range for the position and for encouraging **career development**. By creating **career ladders** (vertically linked positions within the same occupational field) employees could advance as they met the qualifications for the next higher position.

So historically, during the period of transition from patronage to merit, and even today among specialists, the ability to conduct a job analysis and write a good job description is considered an essential HRM competency. One of the authors began his career as a management intern in the federal civil service agency (now OPM, then the U.S. Civil Service Commission). But many disgruntled HR specialists had worked their way up "through the ranks" rather than through an internship program that offered what they considered an unfair promotional advantage to recent college graduates. For these specialists, the success of the entire internship could be determined by the graduate's answer to a single question: "Can you write a good job description?" Other skills and experiences might be useful, but unless an HR trainee had learned this, he or she could not be considered qualified as a technician or a professional in the field.

Managers and Supervisors Focus on Work Management

The control over program inputs that is achieved by line-item budgets and position management is less critical for managers and supervisors whose primary objective is managerial effectiveness, not legislative compliance. This is because budgets and personnel ceilings function well to control the size and direction of inputs to an agency; they are quite ineffective at making the agencies more productive, as measured by program outputs. For the work to get done with the most efficient use of human resources, the agency must hire the right number of people, with the right qualifications, for the right jobs, in the right locations. It must pay people enough money to be competitive with other employers, but not more. Under these conditions, managers need to be rewarded for flexible and responsible stewardship of personnel and financial resources. They are likely to resent legislative "micromanagement" because it restricts their flexibility and autonomy. Or, alternatively, they may be unable or unwilling to function as managers because they have for too long been accustomed to citing legislative controls as the reason for not managing resources creatively or effectively.

Employees Focus on Career Management

Employees have a different perspective than either managers or elected and appointed officials. They want to be treated as individuals, through a continual process of supervision, feedback, and reward. They want to know what their job duties are and how performance will be measured. They want to be paid fairly, based on their contributions to productivity and compared with the salaries of other employees. They want their individual skills and abilities to be fully utilized in ways that contribute to a productive agency and to their own personal career development.

Today, the current emphasis on flexible employment relationships makes us forget that civil service systems were originally created to prevent elected and appointed officials from hiring and firing public employees at will. This stability was designed to make government more efficient and to increase public confidence in the quality of public service. And today, the widely accepted notion that civil service systems provide a safe haven for lazy and incompetent employees makes us forget that civil service systems were originally created to protect employee rights by establishing clear criteria and procedures for selection, reassignment, promotion, or discharge. This is based on the assumption that people work most productively when they have adequate skills, clear objectives, adequate resources and organizational conditions to do their jobs, and clear feedback and consequences. They work not only as individuals but also as members of groups that collectively shape the culture of the agency and the ways in which together they can meet the agency's objectives.

Summary

These five different perspectives on job analysis frequently come into conflict because they embody different values and objectives about public HRM. Elected and appointed officials emphasize either the internal discretion to make patronage appointments or the external authority to control agency activities by controlling personnel inputs. Merit system reformers view job analysis as the key to effective and transparent budget management and personnel management. HR directors and specialists have traditionally allied themselves with civil service reformers, emphasizing external control over patronage through position management. Managers and supervisors consider job descriptions increasingly irrelevant to flexible use of human resources, and employees are more concerned with how minimum qualifications and classification systems impede their personal career development.

JOB ANALYSIS AND JOB DESCRIPTIONS UNDER ALTERNATIVE PUBLIC PERSONNEL SYSTEMS

So where does all this lead us? It means that any discussion of how to define and organize work depends on the context and the participants. Job descriptions began with civil service reformers and HR directors and specialists. They evolved toward greater emphasis on managerial effectiveness (work management) and employee aspirations (career management). And they now incorporate the flexibility and focus on efficiency appropriate to market-based values and systems.

Traditional Job Analysis is a Tool for Position Management

Job analysis is the process of recording information about each employee's job. It is done by watching the employee work, talking with the employee about the job, and corroborating this information by checking it with other employees and the supervisor. It results in a product, the **job description**—a written statement of the employee's responsibilities, duties and qualifications. It may also include a **qualifications standard ("qual standard")** that specifies the minimum competencies and qualifications (education, experience, or others) an employee needs to perform the position's duties at a satisfactory level.

Traditionally, job descriptions have been used as the "building blocks" of position management. They specify the job title, occupation classification, level of responsibility, salary, and location of the job in the organizational hierarchy. **Job classification** means that similar positions can be organized into an occupational series, along with other jobs involving similar duties. Jobs in different occupations, but of comparable difficulty can be classified into a common **grade level**. Each position can be identified by an occupational and grade level code, much as a point on a graph can be located by measuring its distance from the vertical and horizontal axes.

Because each job (position) can be classified into a common occupational series as one of a number of identical positions in the agency, its grade level served to fix salary and relationship to other positions above and below it in the agency's bureaucratic hierarchy. This has had the additional benefit of identifying, in a manner similar to military rank, the status of the individual. To emphasize the power of classification systems, consider that federal government employees in Washington, D.C., have long been accustomed to identifying themselves and evaluating others based on classification system shorthand. A federal employee might describe a co-worker by saying, "She's an 11 at Agriculture, a program analyst." Both of them would immediately understand that the employee in question was a GM-305-11, that is, a classified civil service employee, pay grade 11, in the occupational specialty of program analyst. She would outrank a GM-305-9, but be subordinate to a GM-305-12. While not all classification systems are this complex, all traditional job descriptions contain the common elements shown in Figure 5–1—an occupational code and/or title, a pay grade, an organizational locator, a position in the hierarchy, job duties, and required minimum qualifications.

FIGURE 5–1   Traditional Job Description

Job Title: Secretary
Position No: 827301–2
Pay Grade: GS-322–4

Responsibilities	Works under the direction of the Supervisor, Operations Support Division
Duties	Performs a variety of clerical functions in support of the Supervisor and the mission of the Division: types correspondence and reports compiles reports maintains inventory of supplies arranges meetings and conferences answers the phone handles routine correspondence performs other duties as assigned
Qualifications	High school degree or equivalent Typing speed of 40 wpm At least six months experience as a Secretary at grade GS-322–3, or equivalent

TRADITIONAL JOB DESCRIPTIONS DO NOT HELP SUPERVISORS MANAGE WORK

The traditional job description is designed to limit patronage by facilitating external control over patronage hiring. The use of standardized job descriptions for a range of positions, with each one identified by a different position number and organizational location, reduces paperwork and streamlines position management.

But the characteristics that make the traditional job description effective against patronage also work against its usefulness as a work management tool for managers and supervisors. Conceptually, traditional job descriptions promote an artificially static view of work and organizations. Jobs change over time as an organization's goals shift; and if the goal of the personnel system is to promote rational management of work or employees, it does not make sense to "freeze" a job or an organization at one point in time. Nor does it make sense to unduly restrict the ability of the organization to move people from one job to another, as work needs change. And, with increasing emphasis on working in teams, the whole concept of an individual job may be questioned.

The traditional job description promotes a hierarchical and control-oriented relationship between the organization and its employees that works against employee involvement and "ownership" of the organization or its mission. The job description in Figure 5–1 lists the general duties performed by any number of secretaries. Because it applies to a range of positions, it is necessarily vague concerning the nature of the tasks (job elements) involved. The employee may be working in a foundry, a personnel office, or a chemical supply house. In each case, specific duties will differ. The entry "other duties as assigned" leaves the job description open to any additions the supervisor may assign but does not leave room for changes in the work caused by the employee's particular skills or abilities. Thus, this traditional job description is flexible, but only unilaterally, and in a way that assumes hierarchical and downward control over work performance by the agency.

Traditional job descriptions are ill suited to work management because they assume that work can be divided into individual units called jobs, and that these jobs can be differentiated by occupational type and arranged into hierarchies of increasing responsibility. As job analysis becomes more detailed, classification and pay systems become more complex to keep pace. After a while, this results in the creation of so many occupational categories and skill levels that people become frozen into a job. And supervisors are frequently impeded from moving employees from one type of work to another, in that their tasks are "frozen" by their original job description

Traditional job descriptions focus on the type of work to be done, not productivity or performance standards. They do discuss duties, but they do so for purposes of task analysis and job classification, not employee performance. From a manager's perspective, traditional job descriptions are deficient because they do not spell out the performance expected of the employee. Nor do they specify the linking or enabling relationship among competencies, performance standards, and minimum qualifications.

Employees and supervisors both know that a general statement of job duties must at some point be augmented by more specific information about the conditions under which the job is performed.

Is the filing system a database or a manual system using paper documents? What types of correspondence are considered "routine"? Do all duties occur continuously, or do some require more work at certain times? Are all duties equally important, or are some more important than others? What written guidelines or supervisory instructions are available to aid the employee? What conditions make task performance easier or harder? Thus, the traditional job description does not contain enough useful information to orient applicants or employees. So the supervisor must use orientation or an initial on-the-job adjustment period to teach employees how the work they do *really* fits into the organization's mission.

More critically, there are no standards for minimally acceptable employee performance of job duties. How can the supervisor, the person responsible for arranging work so as to make the employee productive, if the quantity, quality or timeliness of service required is not specified? How can supervisors establish or evaluate performance standards unless these take fluctuating conditions into account? For example, it is easier for a salesperson to increase sales 10 percent annually in an industry growing by 20 percent annually than to achieve the same rate of increase in a declining market.

Moreover, traditional job descriptions specify a general set of minimum qualifications for each position. If jobs have been classified according to the type of skill required, these minimum qualifications may also be based on the competencies needed to perform duties. In general, however, traditional methods blur the following logical sequence of relationships among **tasks**, **performance**, **standards**, **competencies** and minimum qualifications:

1. Each task must be performed at a certain minimum performance standard for the organization to function well.
2. Certain competencies are required to perform each task up to this performance standard.
3. Certain minimum qualifications ensure that the employee will have the requisite competencies.

Executives are handicapped because traditional job descriptions describe only personnel inputs, not the resultant *outputs*. That is, they do not specify how many employees would be needed for a desired level of organizational productivity. Because traditional job descriptions do not lend themselves to output analysis, they are not a useful part of the human resource planning, management, or evaluation process.

Managers are handicapped because they cannot readily use such job descriptions for recruitment, orientation, goal setting, or performance evaluation. They, not the personnel director or personnel specialists, are the ones responsible for interviewing applicants, deciding whom to hire, orienting new employees, giving them feedback on performance, and evaluating their performance formally so as to provide either discipline or positive reinforcement depending on the outcomes. For these purposes, individual jobs should each have a separate job description, in recognition of the variability of tasks, conditions, standards, and competencies they require. They should help the manager and the employee by serving as links among personnel functions such as selection, orientation, training, and performance appraisal. These two problems—the lack of evident relationship among tasks, standards, competencies, and qualifications; and the lack of clear information about the nature of the job—reduce the usefulness of job descriptions for executives, managers, and employees.

Traditional Job Descriptions Do Not Help Employees Manage their Careers

Because traditional job descriptions give only a brief outline of duties, employees must wait to find out about working conditions and performance standards until after they have been hired. Yet this may be too late; unclear or inequitable psychological contracts are a cause of much unrest between employees and organizations. Evaluating employees without giving them clear performance standards is a sure way to increase anxiety and frustration. Traditional job descriptions generally do not help employees answer the most important questions they have about their jobs.

- Which job duties are most important and why?
- What makes the job easy or hard to accomplish?
- What competencies are needed for the job and why?
- How will their job performance be measured and evaluated?
- What performance standards will they need to meet to keep their jobs?
- How will this job prepare them for possible promotions?

Thus, employees cannot use traditional job descriptions for career development because they do not specify how increases in qualifications are related to increases in skills required for satisfactory task performance. It is easiest for employees to accept the qualifications for a position and to strive to meet them if these linkages are more apparent.

Traditional Job Descriptions Limit and Stereotype the HRM Profession

But personnel managers, and the HRM function itself, are most seriously affected by the traditional job description's focus on position management rather than on the primary concerns of managers or employees. Because traditional job descriptions are unsuitable to work management, managers and employees consider them a waste of time. So if personnel managers consider job descriptions to be one of the most important personnel tools, and if managers and employees know from their own experience that job descriptions are irrelevant to their needs, then the impression may be created that other personnel activities are equally unimportant. This logic is frequently used to belittle performance evaluation, job analysis, training needs surveys, and other items from the personnel manager's stock in trade.

Consequently, the traditional job description's focus on position management makes it more difficult for contemporary HR managers to effectively establish their own professional credentials. The traditional job description has been largely responsible for the traditional view of personnel management as a series of low-level operational techniques used mainly for external control or system maintenance purposes. Position management and legislative compliance are historically respected roles for public personnel managers, but they are less important today, in a world of strategic planning, than many other objectives and values, including management efficiency and effectiveness, or employee rights.

HOW TO IMPROVE TRADITIONAL JOB DESCRIPTIONS

Job descriptions would be more useful if they clarified the organization's *expectations* of employees and the links among tasks, standards, competencies, and minimum qualifications. These improved job descriptions would contain the following information:

1. *Tasks.* What work duties are important to the job?
2. *Conditions.* What things make the job easy (such as close supervision or written guidelines explaining how to do the work) or hard (such as angry clients or difficult physical conditions)?
3. *Standards.* What objective performance levels (related to organizational objectives) can reasonably be set for each task, measured in terms of objectives such as quantity, quality, or timeliness of service?
4. *Competencies.* What knowledge, skills, and abilities are required to perform each task at the minimum standard under the above conditions?
5. *Qualifications.* What education, experience, and other qualifications are needed to ensure that employees have the necessary competencies?

These changes are all related because they clarify the enabling relationship among tasks, conditions, standards, competencies, and qualifications. In other words, they specify the qualifications needed to demonstrate that an employee has the competencies required to perform essential job functions at acceptable performance standards under a given set of conditions. Taken together, these refinements emphasize the relationship of jobs to management of work and employees, rather than of positions. They do so by focusing on outputs (what is actually produced by a job) rather than inputs (which positions are allocated to the agency).

Two examples of **results-oriented descriptions (RODs)** are shown in Figure 5–2 (page 121) and Figure 5–3 (page 122).

These examples show why results-oriented job descriptions are superior for management of work and employees. They provide clearer organizational expectations to employees. They encourage supervisors and employees to recognize that both standards and competencies can be contingent upon conditions. For example, a secretary can type neater copy more quickly with a word processor than with a manual typewriter, and different skills are required. In the second example, an increase in each probation officer's caseload from 60 to 100 clients

FIGURE 5–2   Results-Oriented Descriptions (RODS)

Word Processor/Receptionist
Operations Support Division
Position No.: 827301–2
Pay Grade: GS-322–4

TASKS	CONDITIONS	STANDARDS
Type letters	Use IBM PC, Word Perfect, and agency style manual	Letter completed in 2 hours, error-free
Greet visitors	Use appointment log provided by supervisor about waiting, provided supervisor is on time	No complaints from scheduled visitors
Maintain files	Use Excel database management software and instructions provided by supervisor	Update files weekly, with accuracy and completeness

REQUIRED COMPETENCIES

Able to type 40 wpm
Courtesy
Word Perfect, Lotus 1-2-3

MINIMUM QUALIFICATIONS

High school degree or equivalent
Two years word processing, especially Word Perfect
One year database management, especially Lotus 1-2-3

would inevitably affect the quantity, quality or timeliness of visits with probations. A probation officer preparing pre-sentence investigation reports for a new judge might be expected to have a lower level of accepted recommendations. This is the logical connection between duties and qualifications required for content validation of qualifications standards under affirmative action programs or civil service systems; and for employee productivity under personal service contracts and other alternative/flexible employment relationships.

JOB DESCRIPTIONS UNDER OTHER PUBLIC PERSONNEL SYSTEMS

All personnel systems are responsible for accomplishing common functions (PADS). Because work must be defined before employees or independent contractors can be selected, job descriptions are important under affirmative action, collective bargaining, and alternative mechanisms and flexible employment relationships.

FIGURE 5–3   Results-Oriented Descriptions (RODs)

Juvenile Probation Officer
State Department of Corrections

TASKS	CONDITIONS	STANDARDS
Meet clients to record their behavior	Caseload of not more than 60; supervisor will help with hard cases; use departmental rules and regulations	See each probationer weekly; keep accurate and complete records per DOC rules and regulations
Report criminal activity to supervisor		
Prepare pre-sentence investigation reports	Average of five per week; supervisor will review cases per court instructions;	Reports complete and accurate per judge; judge will accept recommendation in 75 percent of cases

REQUIRED COMPETENCIES

Knowledge of the factors contributing to criminal behavior
Ability to counsel probationers
Ability to write clear and concise probation reports
Knowledge of different judges' sentencing preferences for particular types of offenders and offenses
Knowledge of law and DOC regulations concerning presentencing investigations and probation

MINIMUM QUALIFICATIONS

High school degree or equivalent plus four years of experience working with juvenile offenders, or a BS degree in criminal justice, psychology, or counseling
Possess a valid driver's license

Affirmative Action

By specifying the minimum qualifications for a position, and by logically relating minimum quals to job tasks, job descriptions are the most critical element of equitable personnel practice. That is, they act affirmatively to ensure that applicants and employees are not discriminated against on the basis of non-merit factors. Moreover, they reduce the impact of the "good old boy" system that implicitly favors white males, by requiring that vacancies be identified and posted, that all qualified applicants have the opportunity to apply, and that applicants not hired be informed as to the reason for their non-selection. Of course, there are widespread abuses in recruitment and selection procedures, and the folklore of public personnel management is filled with fables confirming every suspicion: highly qualified white male applicants who were not hired because they were the "wrong gender" or the "wrong color," highly qualified minority or female applicants who were included in the interview pool only to demonstrate a "good faith effort" at recruiting a diverse workforce, yet who never had a real chance of being fairly considered for the position. But job analysis is at the heart of test validation, affirmative action compliance, and reasonable accommodation of persons with handicaps under the Americans with Disabilities Act.

Collective Bargaining

Job analysis and classification are also central to collective bargaining. First, collective bargaining starts with the identification of an appropriate bargaining unit, either occupation based or agency based. In either case, the number and identity of positions eligible for inclusion in the bargaining unit presumes that all positions, those included as well as those excluded, have been analyzed and classified in advance. Frequently, contract negotiators justify requested pay and benefits by comparing pay and benefit levels with similar jobs in other jurisdictions. Contracts stipulate pay, benefits, and working conditions applicable to covered employees, or to employees in specified occupations. Contracts may prohibit management from assigning employees work outside their classification or above their grade level. They will certainly specify that discipline can only be taken against employees who do not perform their jobs satisfactorily, for tasks assigned in their job descriptions, as measured against previously defined performance standards.

Alternative Mechanisms

In one sense, job descriptions hinder productivity. That is, they require work to write and review, without directly contributing to the outputs by which the effectiveness of the organization is measured. But in another sense, they create value by specifying the nature of the work to be done, and the rewards the organization is prepared to pay to have it done. It takes but a moment's reflection to realize that clarity with respect to performance expectations and rewards is at the heart of most alternative organizations and mechanisms for delivering public services. Outsourcing and privatization cannot be compared with in-house performance using civil service employees unless the nature of the work to be done, the performance standards, and the pay and benefits attached to the positions are clearly specified. For example, a city considering contracting out security services at public housing or transit facilities will have to define what level of service and what level of employee qualifications will be needed to do the job—whether it is eventually done in-house or contracted out.

Flexible Employment Relationships

Flexible employment relationships make it easier for management to hire, fire, and reassign workers. They also tend to remove agencies from legislative controls based on position management. But job descriptions are more important than ever under these conditions because their objective is work management and their function is to define jobs. Management needs some criteria to separate "core" and "contingent" positions—occupation, level of difficulty, or geographic location. Whatever criteria are used, jobs need to be defined and classified based on the nature of the work. And short-term performance contracts need to clearly specify the terms and conditions of employment, lest the rewards offered are not proportionate to the skills and responsibilities.

SUMMARY

Many current controversies in public personnel management center around the appropriateness of a focus on positions, work, or employees. Traditional job analysis defines the position as the unit of analysis, and it develops classification systems based on the type of work and its level of responsibility in the organizational hierarchy. More contemporary approaches focus on work management—flexible use of human resources to accomplish the mission of the agency. And employees have yet a third perspective, career development. Results-oriented job descriptions offer a way of bridging between traditional and contemporary HRM, and therefore, of linking the professional status of HR to the organizational productivity and career development that are considered more important to mature civil service systems than using position management to control patronage and enforce legislative priorities. There is no doubt that job analysis will continue to be an important personnel activity, because it is required not only for civil services systems but also for alternatives to them.

KEY TERMS

average grade-level restrictions
career development
career ladders
competencies
employee management
grade level
job analysis
job classification
job (position) description
minimum qualifications ("quals")
payroll

performance standards
personnel ceilings
position
position description (PD)
position management
qualifications standard
   ("qual standard")
results-oriented description (ROD)
staffing table (manning table)
tasks
work management

DISCUSSION QUESTIONS

1. How does the historical development of job analysis relate to the differing objectives of elected and appointed officials, merit system reformers, HR directors and specialists, supervisors and managers, and employees? How are these reflected in the concepts of position management, work management and career development?
2. Why are traditional job descriptions unsuitable for supporting personnel management as its focus has changed to human resource management and career management?
3. How do results-oriented descriptions (RODs) differ from traditional job descriptions? Why are RODs more effective from the supervisor's viewpoint? From the employee's viewpoint?
4. How can RODS be combined with traditional (position management based) job analysis?

CASE STUDY: WHO'S MOST QUALIFIED TO BE MINORITY RECRUITMENT DIRECTOR?

BACKGROUND

You have recently been appointed Personnel Director of the state police. The organization consists of about 1,000 uniformed officers and 200 civilian employees. In recent years, the state police agency has come under increasing public criticism. The major complaint: too much attention is being paid to writing traffic tickets; a more appropriate focus would be on attacking organized crime and drug trafficking. Many community activists believe that the state police routinely discriminate against blacks and Hispanics in both employment and law enforcement. Morale is low among younger officers, who see themselves as victims of societal conflicts. Turnover among recruits averages 25 percent during the first year. Reasons most often given for leaving the state police are working conditions, lack of immediate promotion opportunities, and the feeling that advancement is based on "whom you know, not what you know." Many observers consider the state police to be a highly political organization because the governor appoints its top administrative positions. Some observers believe that, as a result, top management lacks experience in law enforcement or management, and that this reduces the organization's morale and effectiveness.

As Director of Personnel, your task is to select an assistant who will be responsible for developing, administering and evaluating a minority recruitment program for the agency. An outside consulting firm has selected three candidates as the most qualified. Which one will you pick for the job?

PROCESS

Divide into discussion groups with four or five people in each group. (The instructor should designate the groups as A, B, C, etc.) Within twenty-five minutes, place all three candidates in rank order, based on their relative qualifications for the position. Their résumés are shown in Figures 5–5, 5–6, and 5–7. To do so, you will need to answer the following questions:

1. What job duties are most important to the position?
2. What competencies will successful applicants need to perform these essential job duties?
3. What objective performance standards could you use to assess whether the minority recruitment director is doing a good job?
4. What conditions make the job particularly easy or hard to perform? (Hint: think of laws, resources, organizational conditions, etc.) How do these conditions affect the performance standards that should be established, or the competencies that should be required?
5. What minimum qualifications will successful applicants need to ensure that they have these competencies? Specify education (type, level, and length), experience (type, level and length), and any other qualifications you consider essential.

FIGURE 5–4   Rank the Applicants

CANDIDATE	GROUP A	GROUP B	GROUP C	GROUP D	GROUP E
Harold Murphy					
Willie Jones					
Norma Sikorsky					

6. In what rank order should the three candidates be placed? In your group's column, write a "1," "2," or "3" opposite each candidate's name. (See Figure 5–4.)
7. Why is the applicant you chose the most qualified for the job?
8. What selection criterion was most important in making the choice?
9. Which value (political responsiveness, efficiency, or social equity) is most enhanced by your selection decision and criteria?
10. How confident are you that your selection criteria are job related?
11. How would you validate the criteria if asked to do so by a federal court or by an affirmative action compliance agency?
12. What is the appropriate definition of *merit* in this situation?
13. Was your group ever tempted to pick the "best" candidate first, and then to identify the desired competencies and minimum qualifications based on that candidate's résumé (rather than the other way around)? If so, what does this show about merit-based selection procedures?

POSTSCRIPT

The state police hired Willie Jones for the position of minority recruitment director. They were unanimously in favor of hiring Jones because his military background and demeanor led them to view him as the most likely candidate.

For almost two years after his appointment, Willie Jones gained nationwide attention for his ability to recruit black state police officers. As the only one of the three candidates with first-hand recruitment experience, he did an excellent job recruiting through schools, community organizations, and minority newspapers and radio stations.

But as strong and successful as his recruitment efforts were, within two years of his appointment it became evident that there were problems with his overall job performance. First, turnover among new recruits and trainees continued to be high. Once out of the academy, new recruits were still being assigned as trainee troopers with senior officers who were quite likely to be white males. Their view of the organization, and of the role of minorities in it, was not always consistent with Willie Jones's mission and vision for minority recruitment. So the state police personnel director ended up hiring someone with a background similar to Harold Murphy's, who could help Willie Jones institutionalize his successful minority recruitment program by designing and evaluating similar changes in other functions. These included diversity training mentoring programs for minority recruits, and increased attention to racial harassment or discrimination. And police supervisors received training in performance appraisal, promotional assessment, and other functions needed for recruits' career development.

Second, Willie Jones was well liked and respected by state police officers regardless of race. He communicated forcefully and effectively with recruits, state police officers, and the hierarchy of uniformed command. But he was not a politically adept speaker who could be trusted to deal smoothly or comfortably with the media or with federal compliance agencies. He was not an accomplished report writer or program evaluator. So the state police personnel director and media relations representative needed to cover many of these aspects of the job.

In short, the ideal candidate would have had the composite competencies of all three finalists: Willie Jones's minority recruitment experience, Harold Murphy's overall HRM expertise, and Norma Sikorsky's media relations, program evaluation, and political networking skills. And in fact the nature of the job, and the requisite competencies, did evolve over time. Initially, the critical need was to hire someone with Willie Jones's competencies. Next, to prevent minority recruitment problems from continuing as minority retention problems, the state police needed to hire someone with Harold Murphy's background. And as the program matured, it needed continual positive communication with compliance agencies, the state legislature, and the Governor's office to maintain good political relations.

Discussion Questions

After reviewing the outcome answer the following questions:

1. How does the outcome show that jobs and organizations change over time?
2. How does the outcome show that definitions of "merit" change over time, even for the same job?
3. How would you recommend that job descriptions be revised so as to accommodate these changes? How would you "sell" these recommendations to managers and employees, given their varied concerns and priorities?

FIGURE 5–5   Willie Jones's Résumé

Willie Jones
1327 W. Addison Street
Minneapolis, MN

Job Objective: A responsible professional position in minority recruitment, higher education administration, or personnel management.

Employment History:

1998–Present   Assistant Director of Admissions, Northern Minnesota State College. Responsible for minority recruitment, minority financial aid, and internship programs for a 25,000 student state university system institution. Since 1998, the percentage of minority students has increased from 7% to 11%, despite cuts in Federal loans and other financial aid programs.

1992–1998   1st Lieutenant to Captain, U.S. Army. Responsible for a variety of combat assignments in the United States and overseas. Rifle Platoon Leader responsible for the health, morale, welfare and safety of 43 men (1992–1995). Company executive officer (1995–1996). Battalion Air Operations Officer (1996–1998).

Awards and Decorations:

2001:   "Who's Who" (Outstanding Young Men in America)

1991–1998:   Silver Star, Bronze Star Medal with "V" Device for Valor (Two Oak Leaf Clusters), Air Medal, Army Commendation Medal with "V" Device for Valor, and Purple Heart (Two Oak Leaf Clusters)

1989–1990:   Medgar Evers Memorial Scholarship, Jackson State University

Education:

1991:   BA in Psychology, Jackson State University, Mississippi.

FIGURE 5–6   Harold Murphy's Résumé

Harold Murphy
3732 18th Street
Arlington, VA

Job Objective: A responsible professional job as a human resource manager.

Employment History:

1997–Present   Personnel Director, Northern Virginia Community College. Responsible for management of labor relations, recruitment and selection, training, and affirmative action compliance. Represents NVCC in negotiating session with staff union.

1993–1997:   Assistant Personnel Director, Manassas Crossroads Bank, Manassas, VA. Responsible for selection, payroll and benefits administration and staff development.

Education:

1997:   M.S. in Government (Personnel Management), the George Washington University, Washington, D.C. Master's Thesis: "Minority Recruitment Problems in Virginia State Government."

1993:   B.A. in Business Administration, George Mason University. Senior Honors thesis: "Politically Incorrect: Conflicts between Union Seniority Systems and Affirmative Action Compliance."

Honors and Awards:

1993:   Phi Beta Kappa, Pi Sigma Alpha, cum laude.

Professional Activities:

"Managing Privatization and Labor Relations Issues in State University Systems," National Association of University Personnel Administrators Conference, New Orleans, 2000.

Personal Information: married, good health

FIGURE 5–7   Norma Sikorsky's Résumé

Norma Sikorsky
P.O. Box 6597
Salem, OR

Job Objective: A responsible position in management, media relations, or affirmative action compliance.

Employment History:

1999–Present   Assistant to the Chief of Staff of the Governor of Oregon, responsible for the coordination of statewide affirmative action plans for state agencies. Made recommendations on affirmative action programs to state agency affirmative action program directors. Responsible for media relations and legislative relations between the Governor's office and affirmative action compliance agencies. Represented the state at numerous state and national affirmative action compliance conferences and news conferences.

1995–1999   Assistant Coordinator of Title IX Planning. Principal staff assistant to the Deputy Director of Education, State Board of Education. Responsible for advising the Deputy Director on design and implementation of statewide funding and curriculum changes required for compliance with federal funding guidelines for women's athletic programs under Title IX.

Education:

1999:   M.A., Education, University of Oregon
1994:   B.A., Education, University of Oregon

Honors and Awards:

2002:   "Golden Tongue Award," Oregon Media Relations Association
1994:   NCAA Finalist, Track and Field, State of Oregon

References:

The Hon. Slade Gordon
U.S. Senate Office Building
Washington, D.C.

William Groves
Director, Affirmative Action Programs
State of Oregon

6

Rewarding Work
Pay and Benefits

INTRODUCTION

Traditionally, potential employees were attracted to public jobs because civil service jobs were stable and secure. Though salaries might have been lower than those in the private sector, benefits were good and the promise of career employment meant that they would be able to stay long enough to collect them. But as public agencies move toward market-based models, both public agencies and their employees find that they need to rethink their reward systems. To be effective, the **total compensation** package—pay and benefits—must meet the needs of employee and employer under current employment conditions:

- For employees, pay and benefits must be fair compared to other employees and to the job market.
- For employers, economic rewards must be competitive, flexible, and easy to administer.

Benefits are an important aspect of total compensation. The high cost of employee benefits, the importance and expense of health care, and the need to combine flexibility and ease of administration to meet employer productivity needs and employee equity concerns mean that compensation and benefits' managers play an increasingly important role in human resource management.

By the end of this chapter, you will be able to:

1. Describe the contemporary pay and benefits environment.
2. Identify the elements included in a total compensation package.
3. Understand the laws governing compensation policy and practices.

4. Describe the comparative advantages and disadvantages of competing systems used to determine pay—job evaluation, market models, rank-in person, and broad-banding.
5. Discuss how pay-for-performance systems work, and how they differ from traditional civil service seniority and cost-of-living-adjustments (COLA).
6. Identify the issues involved in pay disparity based on race and gender.
7. Discuss how pay is set in alternative personnel systems.
8. Describe the benefits to which all employees in the United States are legally entitled.
9. Discuss discretionary benefits like pensions, health insurance, and paid vacations.
10. Discuss other emergent benefit issues and their relationship to work/family conflicts.

THE CONTEMPORARY PAY AND BENEFITS ENVIRONMENT

Traditionally, civil service compensation systems were designed with the assumption that an individual job was a basic unit of measurement and that the relationship of one job to another could be determined, and its value assessed, apart from the job incumbent. Seniority and equity were valued as products of a stable working environment. Today, the basic assumption of stability has been replaced by dynamism and change.

Siegel[1] emphasizes the trend away from civil service systems (based on their public negative image), toward increased focus on accountability, and increased emphasis on flexibility and contract management. Within civil service systems, he identifies three elements as characterizing the future of compensation policy and practices:

1. Turn away from long-term (seniority) toward shorter-term perspective
2. Performance orientation in compensation
3. Retrenchment in level and types of benefits

The impact these elements have on public-sector compensation policy and practices could be captured with the term **new pay** that is currently popular in the private sector.[2] According to Howard Risher,[3] this emerging concept is characterized by:

1. Responsibility for day-to-day salary management shifts from the human resources staff to managers and supervisors.
2. Broad-banded ranges and wide salary ranges replace traditional classification and pay systems.
3. "Paying the job" gives way to "paying the person."
4. Performance appraisal emphasizes a wider range of raters, including peers, subordinates, and clients/customers.
5. Team and group incentives replace conventional merit pay for individuals.
6. Pay plans are increasing tailored to specific work situations, not "one size fits all."

THE ELEMENTS OF A TOTAL COMPENSATION PACKAGE

Even as we move into an era where many positions may not include traditional benefits like sick leave, holidays, or pensions, the amount employers spend on pay and benefits is substantial. For example, in 1992, for public and private employers combined, the cost of employee benefits equaled about 20 percent of total compensation, excluding paid time off.[4] A different survey conducted by the U.S. Chamber of Commerce indicated that benefits totaled 41 percent of payroll costs in 1993.[5]

Usually, when employees think about their salary, they think of take-home pay. And because many employees never even see a record of some benefits, such as the employer's contribution to Social Security, workers' compensation, and unemployment insurance, they are unaware of their total compensation. Figure 6–1 shows the basic components of a total compensation package and identifies some of the indirect, or non-salary, "benefits" included in compensation.

FIGURE 6–1   Total Compensation Package (Adapted with permission from T1–Total Compensation Management, American Compensation Association (ACA), 14040 N. Northsight Blvd., Scottsdale, AZ 85260; 602–951–9191.)

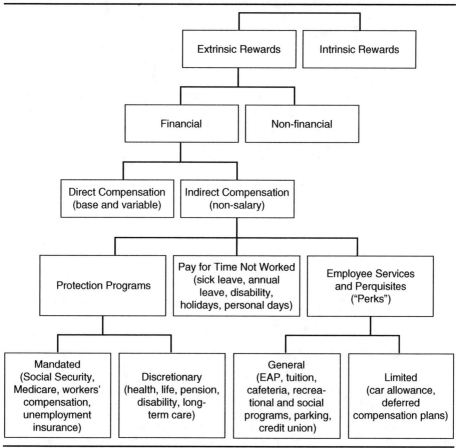

LAWS AFFECTING COMPENSATION POLICY AND PRACTICE

Pay setting in public agencies is governed by legal constraints, historical practice, and the relative power of stakeholders. Along with various state statutes, four primary federal laws apply: the **Fair Labor Standards Act** of 1938, the Equal Pay Act of 1963, the 1964 Civil Rights Act (Title VII), and Age Discrimination in Employment Act of 1967.

The Fair Labor Standards Act (FLSA) was originally passed to regulate minimum wages, overtime pay, and record-keeping requirements for private employers. In 1985, the U.S. Supreme Court's decision in **Garcia v. San Antonio Metropolitan Transit Authority** made state and local governments subject to its wage, hour, and record-keeping requirements. Employees must be paid the **minimum wage** (currently $5.25 per hour). Employees (except executives, administrative employees, and professionals) must be paid time-and-a-half for overtime, defined as more than forty hours per workweek (or given **comp time** during the same pay period). Employers are required to keep records going back two to three years of all employees' wages and hours, and to provide these records to the Department of Labor upon request. Because it is not always clear whether employees are covered by the FLSA, and because covered employees require more complex staffing patterns or considerably higher personnel costs, keeping up with FLSA provisions is critical. Many local government employees (particularly police officers and firefighters) have irregular work schedules that pose particular problems for compensation specialists.[6]

The Equal Pay Act of 1963 requires employers to provide men and women with equal pay for equal work. In order to win relief under this law, the plaintiff must demonstrate that jobs requiring equal skill, effort, and responsibility, and performed under similar working conditions, are paid differentially on the basis of sex. But "equal work" is narrowly defined under the terms of this act—it does not include dissimilar jobs, and it exempts pay differentials resulting from the impact of seniority or merit systems.

The Civil Rights Act of 1964 (Title VII) forbids discrimination in pay and benefits on the basis of non-merit factors. While it does not prohibit any sex-based pay differentials that are legal under the Equal Pay Act of 1963, it goes beyond the equal pay provisions of the EPA by allowing equal pay for comparable jobs—those not identical, but requiring equivalent skill, effort, and responsibility, and performed under similar working conditions.

The Age Discrimination in Employment Act prohibits employers from paying older workers less than younger ones for equal work. And as the workforce gets grayer, it has another important provision—prohibiting employers from using pension plan provisions to force older employees to take early retirement.

ALTERNATIVE WAYS OF SETTING PAY IN PUBLIC AGENCIES

There are two basic models for setting pay in public agencies—point-factor job evaluation and market models. And there are newer hybrids that combine the advantages of both—rank-in-person systems and broad banding.

Point-Factor Job Evaluation

The data used in analyzing a job for purposes of developing a job description also form the basis for **job evaluation**. The purpose of job evaluation is to determine the worth of the job or position (rather than the value of the work or quality of the person's performance). Although several methods of job evaluation have been used, the most prominent today is the **point-factor method**. It is popular because of its objectivity, stability, and reliability.[7] Despite its complexity and high development cost, it has largely supplanted other methods of setting pay because of its perceived internal validity (within the agency) and the ease with which objective factors can be used to validate the system in the face of attacks by employees, unions, and affirmative action compliance agencies.[8]

This is how it is done:

1. Analyze all jobs in the organization.
2. Select factors that measure job worth across all positions. Common factors include supervisory responsibility, difficulty of duties, working conditions, and budgetary discretion. It may be necessary to break jobs into broad occupational classes first, and to develop separate **compensable factors** for each class.
3. Weight job factors so that the maximum possible value is 100. (For example, there could be five factors worth 20 points each, or two worth 20 each and one worth 60).
4. Develop and define **quality levels** for each job-worth factor, and apportion points within that factor to each quality level. For example, if "working conditions" is selected as a job-worth factor with a total value of 20 points out of 100, then the following quality levels might be established for this job-worth factor:
   a. 0 points: office work
   b. 10 points: occasional outside work, some walking or standing required
   c. 20 points: constant outside work in bad weather; heavy lifting required.
5. Evaluate each job along each job-worth factor, and compute the point total.
6. Establish realistic pay ranges for **benchmark positions**—those common to many employers—based on market comparisons with similar jobs elsewhere.
7. Pay other jobs in proportion to their comparative point totals.

Figure 6–2 shows a simplified example of the point-factor method. It compares the worth of five jobs within a hypothetical city's government, each based on three job-worth factors and defined by three or more quality levels. It can immediately be seen that this initial evaluation results in some obvious pay inequities: police lieutenants make the same as the chief, and police officers more than the sergeants who supervise them! Note, however, that this is entirely due to the choice of job-worth factors and quality levels, and their relative weights. When the results defy reality or common sense, the job analyst will usually alter the choice or relative weight of the job-worth factors, or the definition and relative weight of the quality levels for each factor. These changes would probably result in alterations such as are shown in Figure 6–3. The relative value of the five jobs has been altered by changing the value of the job-worth factor "responsibility" from 40 to 60 points, and by reducing the value of the other two factors to 20 points each. And the quality factors' point values have been readjusted based on the change in point allocation to the three job-worth factors. The end result has more internal equity, meaning that it results in total job evaluation

FIGURE 6–2   Example of Point-Factor Job Evaluation

JOB-WORTH FACTORS

- competencies (30 points),
- working conditions (30 points), and
- responsibility (40 points) = 100 points total

QUALITY LEVELS

Competencies	30—professional knowledge and independent judgment
	20—technical knowledge under supervision
	10—some technical skill under close supervision
Working Conditions	30—constantly unpleasant and dangerous
	20—occasionally unpleasant or dangerous
	0—office work
Responsibility	40—makes decisions affecting a major program area
	25—makes decisions affecting a department
	15—makes decisions affecting a division
	10—makes decisions affecting individual clients

POINT-FACTOR EVALUATION AND PAY

Job	Competency	Conditions	Responsibility	Total	Salary
Mayor	30	0	40	70	$63,000
Police Chief	30	0	25	55	$49,500
Lieutenant	30	10	15	55	$49,500
Sergeant	20	10	10	40	$36,000
Police Officer	10	30	10	50	$45,000

---

scores for various departments that make more sense when compared to each other within the organization. The point is that once ratings are initially established by the job analyst, they should be reviewed by an internal committee of managers from various departments, including personnel and budget. This committee should reach consensus on adjustments to the point values and relative salaries for the various positions, reflecting both market information and their true worth to the organization.

But all job evaluation methods have a fundamental weakness—they focus on the relative worth of positions, rather than the relative importance of the work to the mission of the agency or the relative quality of employee's performance. Thus, job evaluation has increasingly come under attack as outmoded and off target.[9] Critics charge that it reinforces bureaucratic hierarchy and lack of initiative, and it discourages innovation, development of internal and external relationships, and mission orientation among employees. Employees tend to focus on internal competition for upward classification and pay increases rather than on customers and mission. Creative managers soon learn that jobs can be "upgraded" by rewriting job descriptions to gain more job evaluation points. Because supervisors can gain higher grades based on the number of resources they use and the number of employees they supervise, job evaluation provides incentives to create additional supervisory positions and thus waste resources.

FIGURE 6–3   Revised Example of Point-Factor Job Evaluation

JOB WORTH FACTORS

- competencies (20 points),
- working conditions (20 points), and
- responsibility (60 points) = 100 points total

QUALITY LEVELS

Competencies	20—professional knowledge and independent judgment
	14—technical knowledge under supervision
	7—some technical skill under close supervision
Working Conditions	20—constantly unpleasant and dangerous
	10—occasionally unpleasant or dangerous
	0—office work
Responsibility	60—in charge of a large organization
	45—in charge of a major department
	30—supervises more than ten employees
	15—supervises fewer than ten employees
	0—no supervisory responsibilities

POINT-FACTOR EVALUATION AND PAY

Job	Competency	Conditions	Responsibility	Total	Salary
Mayor	20	0	60	80	$72,000
Police Chief	20	0	45	65	$58,500
Lieutenant	20	10	30	60	$54,000
Sergeant	14	20	15	49	$44,100
Police Officer	7	20	0	27	$24,300

Market Models

Because of these drawbacks, most state and local governments combine point-factor evaluation with market-based models that are more flexible, more performance-based, and more aligned with contemporary job market conditions. Here's how the process works:[10]

1. Jobs are analyzed and classified into major categories like professional, administrative, technical, and clerical and public safety.
2. Jobs are ordered hierarchically within these major classification categories based on point-factor analysis, and tentative pay levels are assigned.
3. Benchmark positions are identified to represent these major classification categories.
4. Market-based salary ranges for these benchmark positions are established by multi-jurisdictional salary surveys, and adjusted for localized factors like cost of living, indexes.

Based on this process, each government jurisdiction determines pay ranges that reflect both **internal equity**—its own point-factor classification system, and **external equity**—the realities of the local job market. Many local government positions (like police officers or firefighters) are relatively easy to "benchmark" because most jurisdictions employ them, and salary information is readily available through wage surveys and standardized point-factor classification and pay systems. For non-benchmarked jobs, the local government will usually attempt to achieve both internal and external equity by comparing a given job title to similar benchmarked positions in the same general occupational category, or by doing a limited market comparison with neighboring jurisdictions, or some combination of the two methods.

Whatever the details, market and point-factor methods are combined to set tentative wage or salary levels. For jobs that have relatively few positions at the same level of responsibility, a single pay grade may suffice. For jobs that have a range of responsibilities and pay levels (such as engineer or manager), it will be necessary to establish a series of pay grades. And for civil service positions also covered by collective bargaining agreements, these management-determined salary ranges become the starting point for collective bargaining negotiations.

Market models are often used in the private sector, and to validate the salary levels recommended by point-factor evaluation models in civil service systems.[11] Outside of civil service systems, this means abandoning traditional job classification and evaluation altogether, and relying on managerial flexibility, performance appraisals, and the market mechanism to set salaries. In small businesses, employees and managers are hired under short-term performance contracts. Successful managers are those who hire the right employees, pay them appropriate salaries and utilize them effectively. Successful employees are those who can negotiate performance contracts, price themselves realistically in the job market and sell themselves to a succession of managers and employers. The test of the system is whether the employer survives and makes a profit.

But they do not allow for the external (executive and legislative) control of inputs that characterizes the public sector. And they raise profound equity questions.

Rank-in-Person

Rank-in-person systems are used in the military, in paramilitary organizations such as police and fire departments and the U.S. Public Health Service, in the U.S. Foreign Service, and in university faculties. They differ from traditional job classification and evaluation (**rank-in-job systems**) because they focus not on the duties of a particular position, but on the competencies of the employee. Under a rank-in-job system, all employees are classified by occupation and level of responsibility, and these factors are tied to a job analysis, classification, and evaluation system. In other words, the rank is in the job, not the person who occupies it. Employees qualify for promotion from one rank to another, based on competencies and education.[12] And the rank is carried with the employee who moves from one job to another.

When the rank attaches to the person rather than to the position, employees can be assigned or reassigned within the organization without its affecting pay or status. This reduces the immobility and status concerns generated by traditional job evaluation. Rank-in-person systems offer tremendous flexibility, and are much more effective at utilizing workforce diversity to match employee talents with agency needs. For example, assume the U.S. Public Health Service needs to respond to an increased incidence of hepatitis among hospital workers in Phoenix. Since the USPHS uses a rank-in-person system, it can search its employee data banks to come up with a list of specialists who are experienced in hepatitis-B research and education, bilingual, and living in or able to relocate to Phoenix. Once identified, individuals can quickly be put to work without worrying about whether they are in the "right" grade level or occupational specialty.

Rank-in-person systems have major disadvantages. They still must control total budget allocations for personnel by personnel ceilings and average grade levels. And employees will continue to focus on assignments perceived as developmental or as required for advancement to the next highest rank ("ticket punching"). The agency must develop relatively sophisticated human resource management information systems to match work with employees effectively. A traditional rank-in-job system requires only a match of the occupational code and grade level of the vacant position with a roster of employees who meet the minimum qualifications for that grade level. A rank-in-person system requires cataloging (and confidentiality) of a range of employee data, detailed analysis of required competencies and rapid matching of skills with needs through a user-friendly information system. Further, it requires standards and procedures to decide how a person moves from one rank to another. These systems tend to be very agency based, with employees starting at entry level and progressing through ranks rather than moving laterally from one organization to another.

Broad Banding

Grade banding (or **broad banding**) has recently emerged as a compromise that retains job evaluation yet allows flexible and performance-based management.[13] In place of complex systems, grade-banding systems arrange jobs into broad occupational classes and a few pay bands (such as "training level", "full performance level," and "expert performance level"). Managers are authorized to adjust salaries within ranges without having to gain approval from the personnel department. Employees have clearer and less restrictive career mobility ladders.[14]

Grade banding originated in the 1980s in the private sector in the United States, where it was adopted by Citicorp, General Electric, Xerox and AT&T. It was introduced in the federal government in 1981 as a research innovation authorized by the Civil Service Reform Act of 1978.[15] Examples were developed for the Pacer Share project, Naval Laboratories and the National Institute of Standards, among others. But efforts to gain Congressional approval for the general adoption of grade banding within the federal government have been thus far unsuccessful.[16]

In general, broad banding has produced favorable results: less wasted time in job analysis for reclassification purposes, a diminished importance of hierarchical levels inside the organization, improved managerial ability to use salary increases to stimulate productivity, and more flexible employee mobility. But there is one negative outcome—a tendency for average salaries to "creep" upward toward the top of authorized pay ranges.

PAY-FOR-PERFORMANCE

In the 1980s, demands that government become more businesslike led to development of **pay-for-performance systems**, based on the fundamental belief that a person's pay ought to reflect their contribution to the organization.[17] And "best practice" examples from the private and public sector suggest that flexible, performance-based incentives allow management—and employees—to use **merit pay** or **gain sharing** to work more closely together toward the maximization of both productivity *and* productivity-based pay increases. Public-sector experiments with performance-based compensation systems grew out of this movement, with the federal government leading the way. The Civil Service Reform Act of 1978 mandated performance-based pay systems for senior and middle-level federal managers.

Traditional Merit Pay, Seniority Pay, and Cost-of-Living Adjustments Under Civil Service Systems

In theory, traditional civil service pay systems maintain a separation between merit pay, pay for seniority, and cost-of-living increases. First, merit pay is given to reward superior performance on the assumption that once rewarded the performance will be repeated. Second, **seniority pay** increments (also known as **time-in-grade** increases) are given on the assumption that seniority increases an employee's skills, and hence value to the agency. Third, **cost-of-living allowances (COLA)** or market adjustments are given to employees to maintain external pay equity in the face of a competitive labor market.

But in reality there is no clearer example of the confusion between intent and effect of pay systems than the practical relationships that exist among these three factors. First, the total amount of payroll budget allocated to merit increases is usually quite small because of budget constraints and uneasiness among elected officials about voter reactions to "paying employees bonuses to do what they ought to be doing anyway," or unwillingness to trust managers to allocate bonuses fairly.

Personnel managers and supervisors are faced with bad choices—allocating relatively large bonuses to a few employees (thereby heightening conflict over the distribution of a relatively small merit pool), or spreading the merit money in small, symbolic increments among a larger group of employees, thereby diluting its effectiveness. Second, merit pay usually becomes part of the base pay upon which future increments are computed. It never is reduced, thus mitigating its motivating potential. Further, it is usually given for satisfactory performance (which almost every employee attains as a matter of attendance, not performance). Finally, despite the impact of work groups on organizational performance, merit pay is usually allocated to individuals. Thus it tends to undermine an organizational culture of teamwork regardless of how it is allocated. Under these circumstances, it is easy to see why many employees, supervisors, and managers consider merit pay not to be worth the trouble (see Figure 6–4). Last, seniority pay has also been named as a culprit in discouraging performance, turnover, and risk-taking in agencies. Just because employees have done things longer is no guar-

FIGURE 6–4 A Supervisor's View of Merit Pay and Pay-for-Performance

ONE SUPERVISOR'S VIEW

March 2001

TO: John Nalbandian

RE: Reactions to the state's merit pay system:

1. The state never funded it the way it was supposed to be funded when it was first implemented. Employees received ratings of STANDARD, ABOVE STANDARD, and EXCEPTIONAL. If employees received a STANDARD evaluation, they moved up one step on the pay scale. If they received ABOVE STANDARD, they moved up two steps, and three steps for EXCEPTIONAL. Unfortunately, the state could never fund the plan, so as long as an employee received a STANDARD or above rating, they moved only one step. There is no incentive for employees to do anything above STANDARD work. Classified workers say, "Pays the same!"

2. My second complaint is that since the state is not funding it, then they should not be requiring supervisors to justify the ABOVE STANDARD and EXCEPTIONAL ratings. For example, if an employee receives STANDARD, the supervisor is not required to make any comments. If an employee receives ABOVE STANDARD or EXCEPTIONAL, then the supervisor has to write comments under each of the critical elements being evaluated. Many supervisors are not going to take the time to rate employees accurately; it's easier to rate everyone STANDARD. I'm sure you can imagine how that affects morale!

Performance evaluations are important and have a purpose. However, I feel like I can make a much better connection with the employee if I sit down and talk with him/her about the job. So, for myself, I would rather spend more time talking with the employee than jumping through hoops to complete paperwork.

antee they do them better. Given technological change, it is equally likely that experience is an *impediment* to efficiency.

Taken together, these three types of adjustments have a questionable impact on agency efficiency and employee performance in civil service systems. If pay increases fail to keep pace with inflation or a competitive labor market, managers and personnel directors out of necessity seek to retain competent employees by inappropriately using combinations of COLA, time-in-grade increments, and merit increases. In the end, the distinctions between the purposes of these systems and their effects tend to disappear.

Different Types of Performance-Based Pay

Figure 6–5 shows various types of pay for performance. Under all pay-for-performance systems, the first critical variable is whether merit pay is added to **base pay**, or excluded from it. If the purpose of merit pay is to reward long-term performance over several years, it may be useful to add it to base pay, particularly when working with a rank-in-person job evaluation system. But if the primary purpose is to make the annual performance review more meaningful by establishing

FIGURE 6–5 Pay-for-Performance Classes (Source: Reprinted with permission from *Pay for Performance*, © 1991 by the National Academy of Sciences. Published by National Academy Press, Washington, DC.)

| | | LEVEL OF PERFORMANCE | |
		Individual	Group
CONTRIBUTION TO BASE SALARY	Added to base	(a) Merit plans	(d) Small group incentives
	Not added to base	(b) Piece rates commissions bonuses	(c) Profit sharing gainsharing bonuses

pay differentials based on employees' relative performance, then it may be better to keep merit pay separate from base pay. In this way, an employee's current pay is in fact based on current performance.

Traditionally, merit pay systems have focused on individuals because individual jobs are the historical focus of performance evaluation and pay. Individual incentives, such as piece-rate pay plans, continue to be effective where output can be quantified.[18] But as performance in teams becomes more important, managers and personnel departments may wish to focus more on the performance of individuals as members of a work team.[19] Under these circumstances, gain sharing becomes an innovative solution that everyone may find attractive—taxpayers, managers, and employees (even when they are unionized). The basis of gain sharing is team-based bonuses.[20] Implementation problems include issues defining who is to be a member of the gain-sharing team, measuring baseline productivity and productivity increases, and determining the size of the gain-sharing pool. For gain sharing to work, public sector employees and managers must be allowed the same freedom from "red tape" that characterizes the private sector—the ability to purchase goods or services on the open market without reference to a list of approved suppliers or purchasing department procedures, or exemption from specific provisions of collective bargaining agreements that may regulate employees' ability to work out of classification or at a different geographic location. Ironically, those most opposed to gain sharing are often those who gain the most from traditional adversarial collective bargaining (labor attorneys) and traditional civil service "red tape"—classification specialists, personnel directors, purchasing directors, and comptrollers!

Problems and Prospects Implementing Pay-for-Performance

Some local governments (including Charlotte and San Diego) have successfully implemented pay-for-performance plans.[21] But according to a recent comprehensive review of pay-for-performance efforts, "The reforms have by most measures fallen short of expectations. . . . Yet the belief in merit principles remains strong, as does the expectation that performance appraisal and linking compensation to performance can provide incentives for excellence."[22] Why have performance-based compensation systems' expectations not been realized? And why do employees, managers, legislators, and taxpayers continue to believe in them in spite of this?

Not much research evaluating the effectiveness of these performance-based pay plans has been conducted.[23] Several factors complicate the effective implementation of performance-based compensation systems.[24] First, not all work lends itself to pay-for-performance. For example, where goals are difficult to identify or quantify and when discrete individual contributions are hard to distinguish, such plans face severe obstacles. Second, some organizational cultures and structures do not lend themselves to performance-based compensation. For example, organizations that pride themselves on teamwork and cooperation often find the competitive and individualistic norms underlying many pay-for-performance plans contrary to their organizational culture. Third, external factors like the presence of a union or legal constraints or political forces may block successful implementation.

Given these many preconditions, it is not surprising that existing performance-based compensation systems—whether found in public or in private sectors—do not accomplish very well the several goals set out for them.[25] At the federal level, where pay-for-performance has been researched thoroughly, it has been found that not enough money is set aside to establish a motivating effect, that performance appraisals are inflated, and that employees suspect the equitable distribution of the monetary rewards. Milkovich and Wigdor found that less than one-third of the employees in the various surveys they reviewed rated their performance appraisal plan effective in tying pay to performance or communicating organizational expectations about work.[26] And Risher indicates that despite the predominance of merit pay policies in the private sector, there is little confidence that anyone has figured out how to make them work effectively.[27]

Given the overwhelming evidence suggesting at best only cautious optimism for performance-based compensation systems other than piece-rate incentive plans, why do they continue to attract advocates? Perry suggests that pay-for-performance systems have become ingrained in the institutional order of our society.[28] Bureaucracies are established as rational instruments of public policy, and nothing appears more rational than rewarding employees monetarily on the basis of their performance. According to Kellough and Lu, the professed link between performance and pay suggests control by politicians, administrators, and the public over bureaucrats and conveys to the public that government is both responsive and efficient.[29]

ISSUES INVOLVED IN PAY DISPARITY BASED ON RACE AND GENDER

Judging by its laws related to pay equity, the United States is an egalitarian society—discrimination in pay and benefits on the basis of age, sex, race, or other non-merit factors is prohibited. But judging by its history of personnel practice with respect to pay equity, ample evidence justifies the conclusion that our society has unfairly discriminated against women and minorities in particular. There are, however, two sides to this question, and one should not reach even tentative conclusions on so important an issue without examining both.[30]

Proponents of labor market mechanisms for pay setting admit that women and minorities earn less than men and that pay rates for male-dominated jobs are higher than those for female-dominated jobs. But they deny that these differences are based on sex or race discrimination as such. They attribute the difference in men's and women's salaries to traditional labor market explanations: Women have lower seniority than men because they leave the labor market to have children or move from one job to another to accompany their husbands (without commensurate increases in pay or status). Minorities tend to be clustered in low-paying, low-status service jobs.

Proponents of pay equity, on the other hand, charge that women and minorities find themselves concentrated in these occupations and employment situations because of social values and conditions.[31] As justification for this view, they compare salaries for different groups in the public and private sectors. In the private sector, where anti-discrimination laws apply but "employment at will" laws limit the power of women and minorities to protest employment conditions, the disparity between salaries of white males and other groups remains. In the public sector, where similar laws apply but are more enforceable because of merit systems and collective bargaining rights, the pay differential between white males and other groups is almost nil at entry level and only marginally different moving up the pay scale.

At the heart of this controversy is a fundamental dilemma that must be recognized and addressed, but can never be resolved. For advocates of government efficiency, it simply makes no sense to pay women and minorities more than one would have to pay them under a market model (unless required to by specific laws such as minimum wage provisions of the FLSA). The fact that women and minorities receive lower wages may be socially and ethically unfortunate, but it is the primary responsibility of the employer to provide services while meeting a payroll at the lowest possible cost, not to be an instrument for solving social problems. Advocates of comparable worth hold exactly the opposite view. For them, balancing the budgets of public agencies by maintaining lower salaries for women and minorities is morally indefensible. It violates Title VII for private employee and denies public employees the rights to equal protection and due process under the Fourteenth Amendment. At present, the judicial status of comparable worth is unclear, but the decisions of the Supreme Court in the 1990s suggest that this issue is more likely to be dealt with in legislatures and through labor relations than in the courts.[32]

SETTING PAY IN ALTERNATIVE PERSONNEL SYSTEMS

The appointing official sets political appointees' pay, though always within general limits established legislatively. Adjustments to pay are set the same way, based both on statutory limits and external and internal market comparisons. In local governments, frequent trade-offs occur between salaries and benefits, so that it is (some would say this is deliberate) hard to determine the actual rate of pay increase or to compare it meaningfully with pay paid for similar work in other jurisdictions.

Civil service employees' pay usually is established by the chief executive but authorized by the legislature. While civil service pay increases are usually justified or opposed on the basis of market comparisons, market factors are only indirectly used as the basis of setting pay. And the greater job security of civil service employees represents an intangible financial benefit that is difficult to factor into the market equation. This model applies most directly to federal civilian employees, whose pay and benefits are set directly by Congress rather than through collective bargaining.

Under a collective bargaining process (which is described more completely in Chapter 13), pay, benefits, and working conditions are set by direct negotiations between agency management and employee union representatives. But there are critical differences between collective bargaining in the public and private sectors. Public employees are usually prohibited from going on strike; and pay and benefit increases must be legislatively ratified before they take effect. In practice, this means that collective bargaining systems set wages through direct negotiations and indirect political influence on the legislature. For example, teachers' and police officers' unions frequently support local school board or city council candidates, in exchange for support for pay and benefit increases when collective bargaining agreements are ratified.

Privatization, contracting out, exempt appointments, and the use of temporary workers have proven powerful alternatives to union political influence over the contract negotiation and ratification process. Union supporters call it a threat. It offers managers and elected officials the option of approving a negotiated contract, or of deciding to provide the same services through alternative mechanisms or flexible short-term contracts. Usually contract employees without sought-after technical knowledge and skills have much lower pay and benefits than their unionized or public counterparts (because these salaries and benefits are set by a market model rather than through legislative deliberations and collective bargaining). Elected officials usually regard employees as voters and constituents and as people who can help or hinder their efforts to respond to citizen requests. Finally, they see them as employees with needs.

Affirmative action initially developed out of minority concerns over job access. But as access has increased, minorities and women have shifted their focus to pay and benefits. The impact of seniority systems on minority access to employment or promotions has been a prime target of affirmative action proponents. In most cases, courts have held that seniority systems developed with a race- or sex-neutral intent are legitimate, even if their effect is to give preference to white males. In some cases, however, courts have ordered modification of seniority systems, primarily by establishing dual seniority lists and requiring quota-based promotions until workforce comparability is achieved.

STATUTORY ENTITLEMENT BENEFITS

Employee benefit programs may be separated for analytical purposes into two categories: **entitlement or mandated benefits** and **discretionary benefits**. Entitlement benefits are those to which employees are entitled by law (Social Security, workers' compensation, and unemployment insurance). Law does not mandate discretionary benefits, but the employer may provide them to attract or retain employees. There is considerable range in the discretionary benefits offered to employees, depending not only upon the employer's budget but also upon the type of personnel system.

Social Security

Social Security is a federally administered defined benefit plan intended to supplement employer-sponsored discretionary retirement systems.[33] While coverage is compulsory for most types of employment, about seven million workers are not covered because they are members of some other state or local retirement system. Currently (1997), employees pay 7.65 percent of wages up to a maximum of $65,000. Employers are required to match this contribution. The Social Security system also provides disability, death, survivor and senior citizens' health benefits (Medicare). Federal employees do not belong to the Social Security system; they have their own defined contribution pension system or the optional federal employee retirement system (FERS).

Workers' Compensation

Workers' compensation is an employer-financed program that provides a percentage of lost wages and some medical and rehabilitation benefits to employees who are unable to work because of a job-related injury or illness. Employers pay a percentage of payrolls into a state-operated insurance pool, or a jurisdiction self-insures or can buy a private insurance contract. Because the percentage paid is based on the history of claims against the fund, employers seek to avoid payment of benefits for claims they consider fraudulent and to adopt workforce health and safety policies to reduce the incidence of job-related injuries and accidents. Workers' compensation administration is a complex topic, and those who wish to focus on it should consult more specific references.[34]

Unemployment Compensation

In 1976, state and local government employees became eligible for **unemployment compensation**. This benefit provides a portion of regular wages to employees who have been separated without misconduct and who are actively looking for work and unable to find it. There is wide variation from state to state concerning waiting periods for eligibility, length of time benefits paid, and level of benefits provided. States establish unemployment compensation funds through enabling legislation, and the system is funded through a federal tax on employers based on size of payroll.

DISCRETIONARY BENEFITS

It comes as a shock to many workers newly arrived in the United States to learn that many benefits taken for granted elsewhere are not necessarily provided employees in the United States, particularly those working outside of traditional civil service systems.[35] These include pensions, health insurance and paid leave.

Pensions

Retirement benefits, usually mandated for civil service employees, remain an important element in many other benefit systems.[36] In addition, they vary from state to state. Annual pension costs for state and local governments are estimated at some 15 percent of wages and salaries. In 1990, 90 percent of all state and local employees were covered by defined benefit pension plans.[37]

Obviously, the magnitude of public pension funds, and the value of their benefits to the individual employee mean that there are many managerial and policy issues associated with their development and administration. From the viewpoint of the individual employee, some primary issues are vesting, portability, defined benefit versus defined contribution plans, disability retirement, continuation of benefits after retirement, and the relationship between pension plan requirements and age discrimination. From the viewpoint of pension fund management policy, key issues are disclosure requirements, actuarial standards, and strategic investment potential.

Normally, employers require employees to have worked a minimum number of years (usually five) prior to vesting. **Vesting** simply means that an employee is entitled to that portion of accrued retirement benefits contributed by the employer when employment is terminated. Vesting discourages turnover. This may be an advantage or a disadvantage to the agency. Employees and some employers favor **portability**, which means that benefits earned in one agency may be transferred to another. Many state systems are already portable. For example, a recent survey by the Public Retirement Institute indicated that many state employees can transfer in or purchase retirement credits for previous service with military, in-state state and local governments, and out-of-state governments.[38] True portability involves transferring assets from one plan to another or from one jurisdiction to another (such as the TIAA-CREF system, the International City/County Management Retirement Corporation, or employer-sponsored tax-sheltered annuities authorized by the Internal Revenue Service).

State and local systems have traditionally been **defined benefit** plans. That is, employees and employers contribute a portion of salary, but the benefits are predictable based on number of years' service and salary level and some multiplier. Private pension funds are more likely to work on a defined contribution basis. That is, employees or employers contribute and thereby invest a fixed percentage of tax-deferred salary, and benefits upon retirement or withdrawal from the system will vary depending on the success of investments by the fund. In a **defined contribution** plan, like a 401(K), individual employees are able to make choices about how their tax-deferred contributions are invested. But employers need to provide flexibility and employee education for these plans to work well.[39]

Defined contribution plans are gaining popularity because they place more responsibility on employees, are easier to administer, and often cost less because an employer's contribution completely ceases once the employee leaves or retires. Many employers offer some combination of defined benefit and defined contribution plans that employees may utilize if they wish. Under so-called "cash balance" plans, many private employers seek to encourage portability and reward younger workers by decreasing pension benefits for older long-term workers.[40]

Whether employees favor defined contribution or defined benefit plans depends on their age and mobility. Older employees who expect to spend many years with one employer will favor defined benefit programs. Younger workers, or those who plan on career switches, are more apt to favor a defined contribution plan where issues of vesting and portability do not arise.

Increasingly, employees elect flexible retirement options as an alternative to either full-time employment or sitting at home in retirement. Phased retirement and deferred retirement options continue to offer employees the chance to balance work and family demands or health concerns.[41] DROP (Deferred Retirement Option Programs) offer employees otherwise entitled to retirement under a defined benefit program to continue working.[42] Instead of having the continued compensation and additional years of service taken into account for purposes of the defined benefit plan formula, the employee has a sum of money credited during each year of the continued employment in a separate account under the employer's retirement plan, in addition to whatever benefit the employee has acquired under the defined benefit plan based on earlier years of service.

At its best, **disability retirement** allows employees who are unable to work because of illness or injury and not normally eligible to retire (in terms of age or years of service) to retire with benefits. At its worst, it is a device used by employees to retire early at the employer's expense or by employers to induce an unwanted employee to retire early. Personnel directors can fulfill the intent of disability retirement programs and minimize fraud by considering alternatives such as light duty positions or early retirement programs. Long-term disability benefits are provided either by insured or self-insured long-term disability plans or with a disability retirement benefit through the pension plan.

Traditionally, pension systems interlocked with mandatory retirement policies in that employees were forced to retire by a certain age (65 or 70, earlier for public safety employees) because the employer stopped paying benefits into the pension plan when the employee reached that age. However, recent court decisions have held that such provisions represent disparate treatment of older workers, and thereby violate the Age Discrimination in Employment Act of 1967.[43] This logic was enacted into law in 1990 by the Older Workers Benefit Protection Act (PL 101–43). This law permits early retirement programs provided that they do not result in age discrimination. Early retirement incentives that provide a flat dollar amount, service-based benefits, a percentage of salary to all employees above a certain age, or that give employees who retire credit for additional years of service will be lawful. In addition, many agency managers favor the flexibility that such programs offer, as opposed to involuntary layoffs based on reduction-in-force criteria. This law was applied to state and local governments beginning in 1992. In those states where state law denies disability retirement to an individual after a certain age, modifications have to be made in the plan.[44]

In the private sector, pension systems are regulated by **ERISA (Employee Retirement Income Security Act of 1974)**. Because there is no public-sector counterpart to this law, public sector pension plans are regulated by a hodgepodge of state laws. There are no uniform standards for financial disclosure. In some cases, public pension funds managed by private investment firms during the junk bond era of the 1980s placed them at risk and gave rise to issues of disclosure and accountability for fund management.[45]

Much confusion also exists about the actuarial standards to which public pension systems should conform. These standards are assumptions about the rates of employment, death, inflation, and so on that are used to calculate the relationship between payments into the system and benefits drawn from it. Two types of systems are used—fully funded and pay-as-you-go. In a fully funded system, contributions of current employees are adjusted to meet the demands on the system by retirees, so that the system always remains solvent. Under a pay-as-you-go plan, employee contributions bear no necessary relation to payments, and funds are appropriated from general revenues to pay retirees' pensions.

Perhaps the most neglected aspect of defined benefit public pensions is their strategic investment effect. Traditionally, the administration of state and local pension systems restricted pension fund investments to low-interest, low-risk assets. During the 1980s, some pension fund managers were able to obtain higher rates of return by investing more speculatively. So states must establish some reasonable balance between security and rate of return, given the potential of public pension funds for stimulating and directing economic growth in specified geographic areas or industries.

Health Insurance

There is widespread agreement today that the system of health-care delivery in the United States is costly and inequitable. A report issued by the Institute of Medicine indicated that 30 million working Americans do not have health insurance. This leads to delayed diagnosis and treatment, ultimately causing 18,000 premature deaths each year.[46] The greater cost of medical technology and increased longevity are primarily responsible for the increase in health costs. Our present system is geared toward the development of high-technology advances that provide a longer life span for the elderly at a high price; it is driven by a third-party reimbursement system that discourages cost control or cost-benefit analysis.

In the absence of sweeping public policy reforms needed to overhaul our health system, employers have adopted what for them are reasonable strategies to contain health-care costs. These are (1) providing "permanent" employees with education, early detection, and treatment programs; (2) using temporary or contract employees to meet fluctuating employment needs; and (3) working vigorously to encourage managed care programs and competitive bidding for health-care benefit contracts. This may be working. A survey by the U.S. Chamber of Commerce shows that the cost of health-care benefits per worker declined from 1993 to 1994 for the first time in five decades. The decrease was attributed to flattened or falling health insurance premiums.[47]

Two important federal laws affect employers who choose to provide health benefits for employees. Under **COBRA (Comprehensive Budget Reconciliation Act)**, employees under some circumstances have the right to continued health coverage for a limited time period following retirement or termination. And under **HIPAA (Health Insurance Portability and Accountability Act of 1996)**, the

Department of Labor requires that employers and health insurers coordinate changes in benefit coverage resulting from personnel actions and, at the same time, maintain confidentiality of employee records.

Sick Leave, Vacations, Holiday Pay, and Discretionary Days

Employers provide sick leave so employees are not forced to work when they are sick, and so they may accrue enough sick leave to last them through a major illness or injury without loss of pay. Unused sick days are usually computed for pension purposes as part of time worked when the employee retires, but are not credited if the employee leaves prior to vesting.

Vacation days are a traditional benefit. Some jurisdictions provide discretionary days or personal days as well, and all provide some holiday leave for full-time employees. In contrast to sick leave, vacation and discretionary days are perceived to be the property of the employee. Employees are usually compensated for some unused vacation days upon termination of employment. Since the number of days provided usually increases with seniority, they may also provide an incentive against turnover.

Two elements of sick leave and vacation policy have implications for employee cost and performance. First, regardless of their differing purposes for the employer, many employees tend to treat sick leave and vacation indistinguishably. Employers can discourage this practice by clarifying the difference between the two types of leave during employee orientation, and by enforcing this distinction through disciplinary action against sick leave abuse. Second, accrued sick leave and vacation time represent an unfunded liability for the agency. While this liability is acceptable in the case of sick leave, agencies should prohibit employees from accruing large amounts of annual leave. In addition, employees not choosing to take vacations may become burned out; if supervisors are not allowing them to take vacations because of heavy workload, this indicates more fundamental HRM problems.

EMERGENT EMPLOYEE BENEFIT ISSUES

To all these items must be added some other employee benefit issues that are either continually in ferment or newly emergent.[48] These include parental leave, child care, and elder care, flexible spending accounts, tuition remission, and flexible benefit plans.

Family and Medical Leave Act of 1993 (FMLA)

The increasing number of single parents and dual-income families has focused attention on work/family conflicts.[49] Situations traditionally taken care of by "mom," like attending sick children or an elderly parent, become family challenges. **The Family and Medical Leave Act (FMLA)** of 1993 recognizes the importance of this conflict by providing twelve weeks a year of unpaid leave to an employee to cope with a family sickness, elder care, childbirth, or adoption. The leave may be taken all at once but need not be: There are provisions for intermittent leave. The law applies to employers with fifty or more employees and is estimated to cover some 50 million American workers. For some employers the FMLA represents a major departure from past practice, but for others it simply reinforces existing policy.[50]

Experts suggest the FMLA be implemented uniformly within an agency, based on coordination with existing absenteeism and leave policies, workers' compensation programs, and annual leave. Employees eligible and ineligible for FMLA should be identified in advance. Specific policies should be developed for requesting leave (including intermittent or reduced leave), along with procedures for medical certification. The personnel department should establish formal procedures for maintaining contact and monitoring the status of leave and scheduled return to work for employees granted FMLA leave. The agency should plan ways to cover the workload of an employee on leave, such as temporary replacement or distribution of workload. Policies and procedures should be clearly communicated to employees through orientation and training.[51] According to a survey conducted by the U.S. Bureau of Labor Statistics, 3 million to 6 million workers have taken leave under provisions of the act, and over 90 percent of the businesses surveyed reported little impact on operations.[52]

The U.S. Department of Labor (Wage and Hour Division) is responsible for FMLA implementation and enforcement. From August 1993 through December 1994, it received 2,065 complaints under the act and completed compliance actions on 1,967 complaints. Sixty-one percent of the complaints adjudicated were valid. Of these, 63 percent involved an employer's refusal to reinstate an employee to the same or equivalent position following FMLA leave; 20 percent involved refusal to grant FMLA leave; 8 percent involved refusal to maintain group health benefits for an employee on leave; and 8 percent involved interference or discrimination against an employee using FMLA leave.[53]

Child Care, Elder Care and Long-Term Care

While the FMLA provides some relief from intermittent work/family conflicts, the continuing problem of daily care for children and the elderly is not addressed in this law.[54] The decrease in parents staying at home during the workday has led to increases in employer-operated day-care centers, flexible spending accounts for child care, child-care referral services, and flexible scheduling for employees. At first, these actions were seen primarily as an employee benefit. But as agencies began to face shortages of qualified employees, **child care** has been demonstrated to be necessary primarily to recruit or retain qualified female employees or dual-income families.[55] The issues with employer-subsidized child care include cost, fee setting, and liability risks. But these are technical concerns rather than major impediments.

As the elderly population increases, care for elderly family members becomes a crucial work/family issue. **Elder care** involves time off, flextime, or subsidized adult care in an attempt to minimize this conflict. As the elderly population increases, this problem will become a greater challenge. According to a member survey conducted by the IPMA, 10 percent of agency respondents offered elder-care assistance, including 14 percent from state governments and 10 percent from municipalities.[56] One way of dealing with work/family conflicts is to give employees more flexibility in scheduling their work.[57] Compressed workweeks, flexible scheduling of the workday, and negotiating the location of work are all possible ways to permit employees to deal with family issues that affect their work.

With a longer life span, workers face the problem of **long-term care** for themselves and spouses as well as their parents. In a survey the National Council on Aging conducted, 59 percent of respondents indicated they already were involved in some way in providing long-term care for a friend or family member. Twenty-five percent indicated they provide some financial support.[58] Long-term care has become a key part in retirement planning, and some employers provide the opportunity for employees to purchase long-term care insurance. A recent IPMA survey of agency members showed that 26 percent offer long-term care insurance as a benefit.[59]

Tuition Remission

Many employers find that tuition remission rewards performance and helps retain desirable employees. A recent survey conducted by the International Foundation of Employee Benefit Plans indicated that nearly nine out of ten private sector employers offer educational benefits. And tuition reimbursement is by far the most common type.[60]

Flexible Benefit Programs

Flexible benefit programs are sometimes called cafeteria plans because they offer employees a menu of benefits. A full-fledged plan is developed by costing the employer's contribution to each of a variety of employer-sponsored benefit programs, and allowing employees to select alternative mixes of benefit packages depending on their needs. This has the major advantage, for the employee, of full utilization of benefits without duplication or gaps. This makes the employer's benefit package of greater value to the employee and is a tool for recruitment and retention.[61]

There are administrative and financial barriers to flexible benefit programs. First, given the wildly fluctuating cost of alternative benefits, it may be difficult for the employer constantly to calculate (and recalculate) the comparative costs of all options. Second, reconfiguring alternative benefit packages on a constant cost basis may be difficult for employees, who are unable to project benefit usage or the relative utility of alternative benefits accurately. Third, full employee utilization of benefits may increase benefit costs for the employer (who may have been able to reduce costs by relying on such overlaps as duplicate health insurance for two employees in a family). Fourth, increased benefit costs tend to force health and life insurance providers toward uniform defined benefit programs to reduce "shopping" from one program to another. In this environment, the advantages of flexible benefit programs may tend to diminish.

Rather than this full-service cafeteria approach, more typically, flexible benefit programs are isolated to a pretax premium plan for group health insurance and various flexible spending accounts. A medical flexible spending account might permit workers to direct a pretax payroll deduction that can be used for medical expenses not covered by health insurance. In another version the worker could authorize a pretax payroll deduction for child care. These medical flexible benefit programs give workers a tax break without great administrative cost. The flexible benefits employers may choose to provide, and the conditions under which they may be considered taxable income by employees, are closely regulated by the IRS (**Section 125 Cafeteria Plans**).

One interesting development is that employers are increasing the flexibility and managerial discretion attached to work/life benefit programs by making them contingent upon employee performance. In March 1999, a study conducted by the American Compensation Association indicated that 18 percent of respondents currently use some form of work life program to reward employee performance.[62] The rewards most likely to be tied to productivity are eligibility for flexible work, tuition reimbursement, or paid time off.

PAY, BENEFITS, AND CONFLICT AMONG PERSONNEL SYSTEMS

From this discussion of benefits, a conflict emerges between individual rights (pay and benefits for employees) and agency efficiency (reduced pay and benefit costs). And the outcome of this issue directly affects the conflict among competing personnel systems. For in the short term, at least, the systems that offer the lowest costs are those that provide employees with the lowest pay and least benefits—temporary and contract employment. Furthermore, a number of benefits are pegged to an employee's salary, which usually reflects longevity. High turnover reduces this cost, even for employers who offer substantial benefits.

It should be noted that despite their relatively short expected tenure in office, political appointees have frequently been able to include themselves in the benefit provisions offered public employees. The justification for this is that the relatively low salaries paid to political appointees (compared with their private-sector counterparts) necessitates attracting top candidates with a benefit package as well. Cynics would say that because legislators have the authority to approve pay and benefits for public employees, they have often also used their authority to approve pay and benefit increases for themselves.

SUMMARY

Pay and benefits are a fundamental way that employers attract, reward, and retain employees. Pay setting takes place on the basis of job evaluation and market comparisons, through different processes depending on the personnel system involved and the philosophy of the public employer. New pay advocates seek to attract individuals with valued competencies by paying a competitive market wage and benefits, but their retention strategy is to reward performance through variable pay. This does not reward longevity nor does it add to benefit costs associated with pay rates inflated by merit or time-in-grade increases or cost-of-living adjustments.

Depending on the personnel system, employee benefits are regarded as an important motivator of employee retention as well as an increasing cost to employers. Some benefits are mandated by law in the United States: Social Security (or its equivalent), workers' compensation, and unemployment compensation. At least for civil service systems that define employees as a public resource, the emphasis is on providing a range of flexible and "family friendly" benefits that enhance the performance of an increasingly diverse workforce.[63]

KEY TERMS

base pay
benchmark positions
broad banding
child care
COBRA (Comprehensive Budget
   Reconciliation Act)
compensable factors
comp time
cost-of-living-allowance (COLA)
defined benefit
defined contribution
disability retirement
discretionary benefits
elder care
Employee Retirement Income Security
   Act (ERISA)
entitlement benefits
external equity
Fair Labor Standards Act (FLSA)
Family and Medical Leave Act (FMLA)
flexible benefit programs
gain sharing
Garcia v. *San Antonio Metropolitan Transit
   Authority*

grade banding
HIPAA (Health Insurance Portability and
   Accountability Act of 1996)
internal equity
job evaluation
long-term care insurance
merit pay
minimum wage
new pay
pay-for-performance systems
point-factor method
portability
quality levels
rank-in-job systems
rank-in-person systems
Section 125 Cafeteria Plans
seniority pay
time-in-grade
total compensation
unemployment compensation
vesting
workers' compensation

DISCUSSION QUESTIONS

1. What are the characteristics of the contemporary pay and benefits environment?
2. What is new about "new pay"? How does it reflect a departure from the way pay has traditionally been viewed in civil service systems?
3. What elements are included in a total compensation package?
4. What are three laws governing public agency compensation policy and practices?
5. Describe the two competing systems—job evaluation and market models—used to determine pay, and discuss their comparative advantages and disadvantages.
6. What are the differences between merit pay, pay based on seniority, and cost-of-living allowances?
7. Identify the conditions necessary for a pay-for-performance system to work.
8. Describe the benefits to which employees in the United States are legally entitled.
9. What are some of the managerial and public policy issues associated with public pension and health benefits? If you were a benefits manager and saw the costs of these

benefits rising, what kind of recommendations might you make to account for employer and employee needs and interests?

10. If you were arguing pros and cons of wage discrimination based on race/gender, what kind of arguments would you develop?

11. Discuss other emergent benefit issues and their relationship to work/family conflicts.

12. What is the general relationship between pay and benefit systems and the conflict among public personnel systems and values?

CASE STUDY: REDUCING UNSCHEDULED ABSENTEEISM

Unscheduled absenteeism is a problem for many employers. And those employers affected by it can design flexible work-life programs that allow employees to meet goals as well as manage their time away from work to meet personal needs. They can:

- Examine if their sick-leave policy encourages unscheduled absences
- Train supervisors to be sensitive to lifestyle issues and signs of stress
- Give employees the tools to deal with personal needs
- Examine company workflows and culture to increase flexibility, and
- Get families involved in the workplace[64]

But before employers choose to become involved with this issue, they need to become aware that it is a problem, and they need to accurately estimate its cost. The following case study shows how one city might do this.

The municipality of Cityville employs 500 people. Last year, excluding vacation time, which averages two weeks per employee per year, the rate of absenteeism was calculated at 3 percent. This 3 percent loss in scheduled work time is attributed to clerical workers (55 percent), blue-collar workers (30 percent), and professional staff (15 percent). The average hourly wage for clerical workers is $5.76 with an additional 30 percent in fringe benefits; for blue-collar workers $9.62 with an additional 35 percent fringe benefits; and for professional employees $14.42 with 33 percent fringe benefits.

Twenty-five supervisors, whose average wage and fringe benefits total $12.50 per hour, handle most of the absentee worker problems; they estimate they spent about 30 minutes a day rearranging schedules and trying to organize work to compensate for the unscheduled absences. Cityville's finance director indicates that some $30,000 in incidental costs are associated with absenteeism. These include items like overtime, temporary help, and even an educated guess as to the costs attributed to lower quality of work done by the replacement workers. Problem: Using these amounts and the guide in Figure 6–6, estimate the total cost of absenteeism to the taxpayers of Cityville.

FIGURE 6–6   Total Estimated Cost of Employee Absenteeism. (Source: Wayne F. Cascio, *Costing Human Resources: The Financial Impact of Behavior in Organizations*, 3rd ed. Boston PWS-Kent Publishing Company, 1991, p. 61.)

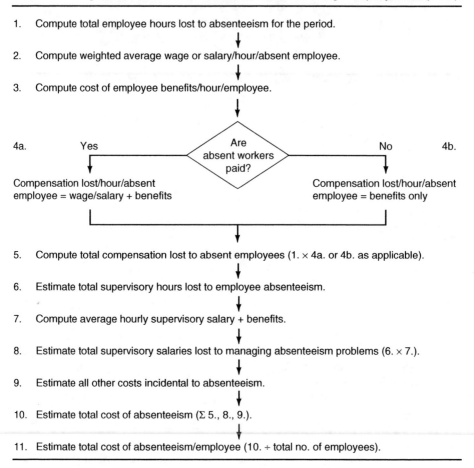

1. Compute total employee hours lost to absenteeism for the period.

2. Compute weighted average wage or salary/hour/absent employee.

3. Compute cost of employee benefits/hour/employee.

4a.   Yes   Are absent workers paid?   No   4b.

Compensation lost/hour/absent employee = wage/salary + benefits

Compensation lost/hour/absent employee = benefits only

5. Compute total compensation lost to absent employees (1. × 4a. or 4b. as applicable).

6. Estimate total supervisory hours lost to employee absenteeism.

7. Compute average hourly supervisory salary + benefits.

8. Estimate total supervisory salaries lost to managing absenteeism problems (6. × 7.).

9. Estimate all other costs incidental to absenteeism.

10. Estimate total cost of absenteeism (Σ 5., 8., 9.).

11. Estimate total cost of absenteeism/employee (10. ÷ total no. of employees).

Answers to Case Study Questions

After several years, we and our students have reached reasonable consensus on the answers to these questions:

1. 30,000 hours
2. $8.22/hour
3. $2.68/hour
4. (a) $10.90/hour
    (b) $2.68/hour
5. $327,000

6. 3,125 hours
7. $12.50/hour
8. $39,062.50
9. $30,000
10. $396,062.50
11. $792.13

NOTES

[1]Siegel, G. B. (1992). *Public employee compensation and its role in public sector strategic management.* New York: Quorum, p. 161; and Siegel, G. B. (1998). Designing and creating an effective compensation plan. In Condrey, Stephen (1998). *Handbook of human resource management in government.* San Francisco: Jossey-Bass, pp. 608–626.

[2]Schuster, J. R., and P. K. Zingheim (1992). *The new pay.* New York: Lexington Books, p. xi; and Cira, Darrell (1998). Competency-based pay: A concept in evolution, *Compensation and Benefits Review, 30* (5): 21–29.

[3]Risher, H. (Winter 1994). The emerging model for salary management in the private sector: Is it relevant to government? *Public Personnel Management, 23,* 649–665.

[4]Employee Benefit Research Institute (June 1994). *EBRI issue brief—Questions and answers on employee benefit issues.* http://www.jobweb.org/cohrma/ebri/ib150.htm.

[5]Reported in "Currents," *Compensation and Benefits Review, 27* (May-June 1995), 15.

[6]A detailed discussion of the impact of the FLSA on state and local governments is beyond the scope of this text. For more information, see *Fair labor standards handbook for states, local governments and schools,* Thompson Publishing Group, 1725 K St. NW, Washington, DC (May 1986), as updated (www.thompson.com); and Cooper, R. S. (1993). *FLSA: The public employer's guide,* Washington, DC: International City/County Management Association.

[7]Plachy, R. (April 1987). The case for effective point-factor job evaluation. *Personnel, 64,* 30–32.

[8]Barrett, G. V., and D. Doverspike (March 1989). Another defense of point-factor job evaluation. *Personnel, 66,* 33–36; Biondi, C., and J. MacMillian (November 1986). Job evaluation: Generate the numbers. *Personnel Journal, 65,* 56–63; and Sahl, R. (March 1989). How to install a job evaluation. *Personnel, 66,* 38–42.

[9]Lawler, E., III (November 1986). What's wrong with point-factor job evaluation? Management Review, 75, 44–48; and Lawler, E., III (1990). *Strategic pay: Aligning organizational strategies and pay systems.* San Francisco: Jossey-Bass, 1990.

[10]For more on salary surveys see various issues of *Compensation and Benefits Review.*

[11]Kaatz, James B., and John Morris (2000). The "overpaid bureaucrat:" Comparing public and private wages in Mississippi. *Public Personnel Management, 29* (1): 129–146.

[12]Shareef, R. (Summer 1994). Skill-based pay in the public sector. *Review of Public Personnel Administration, 14,* 60–74; Ingraham, Patricia (1993). Flexible pay systems in the United States federal government. In *Pay flexibility in the public sector.* Paris: OECD; and Risher, Howard, and Charles Fay (1997). *New strategies for public pay.* San Francisco: Jossey-Bass.

[13]Risher, H., and B. Schay (1994). Grade banding: The model for future salary programs. *Public Personnel Management, 23,* 187–199.

[14]For a thorough review of broad banding (history, strengths and weaknesses, implementation issues, and controlling costs) see: *Broadbanding: CPR Series* (1998). Washington, DC: IPMA.

[15]Risher, H., and B. W. Schay. (1994). Grade banding: The model for future salary programs? *Public Personnel Management, 23,* 487–500.

[16]U.S. Office of Personnel Management (February 1993). *Broad-banding in the Federal government.* Washington, DC: USOPM, Personnel Systems and Oversight Group, Office of Systems Innovation.

[17]Flannery, Thomas, David Hofrichter, and Paul Platten (1996). *People, performance and pay: A dynamic compensation for changing organizations.* New York: The Free Press.

[18]Huish, Gary (August 1997). Piece-rate pay plan in Clerk's office motivates quantum leap in quality production. *IPMA news,* pp. 22–23.

[19]Silverstone group. *Team-based pay programs.* http://redlandassoc.com/consujlt/projecon/compsys/teambase.htm.

[20]Thompson, M. (1995). *Teamworking and pay.* Washington, DC: The Institute for Employment Studies, No. 281.

[21]Arauz, Carlos (February 1999). Pay for performance: A reality for all San Diego County employees. *IPMA news,* p. 12; and Risher, Howard (Fall 1999). Are public employers ready for a "new pay" program? *Public Personnel Management, 28* (3): 323–343.

[22]Milkovich, G. T., and A. K. Wigdor (Eds.). (1991). *Pay for performance: Evaluating performance and merit pay.* Washington, DC: National Academy Press, p. 135.

[23]Ibid., p. 77.

[24]For a thorough discussion of PFP issues, see: *Pay for Performance, CPR Series* (1999). Washington, DC: IPMA.

[25]Kellough, J., E. and H. Lu (Spring 1993). The paradox of merit pay in the public sector. *Review of Public Personnel Administration, 13,* 46; Milkovich and Wigdor. *Pay for performance: Evaluating performance appraisal and merit pay;* Risher, H. (Winter 1994). The emerging model for salary management in the private sector: Is it relevant to government? *Public Personnel Management, 23,* 651.

[26]Milkovich and Wigdor. *Pay for performance,* p. 106.

[27]Risher. The emerging model for salary management, pp. 650–651.

[28]Perry, James L. (1991). Linking pay to performance: the controversy continues. In Ban, C., and N. M. Riccucci (Eds.). *Public personnel management: Current concerns—Future challenges.* New York: Longman, p. 80.

[29]Kellough and Lu, the paradox of merit pay, p. 55.

[30]Abraham, Y. T., and M. T. Moore (Fall 1995). Comparable worth: Is it a moot issue? *Public Personnel Management, 24,* 291–314.

[31]Joshi, Heather, and Pierella Padi (1998). *Unequal pay for women and men.* Cambridge: The MIT Press. See also: National Committee on Pay Equity (www: feminist.com/fairpay.htm); and the National Partnership for Women and Families (www.nationalpartnership.org/workandfamily/workplace/paydiscrim/payact.htm).

[32]Gardner, Susan, and Christopher Daniel (Winter 1998). Implementing comparable worth/pay equity: Experiences in cutting-edge states." *Public Personnel Management, 27* (4): 475–489.

[33]See: www.gov.ssa

[34]Little, Joseph, Thomas Eaton, and Gary Smith (2000). *Workers' compensation (4th ed.).* St. Paul, MN: Westgroup; and Thomason, Terry, Timothy Schmidle, and John Burton, Jr. (2001). *Workers' Compensation: Benefits, costs and safety under alternative insurance arrangements.* Kalamazoo, MI: The W. E. Upjohn Institute for Employment Research.

[35]Bergmann, T. J., M. A. Bergmann, and J. L. Grahn (Fall 1994). How important are employee benefits to public sector employees? *Public Personnel Management, 23,* 397–406.

[36]For more information about pension and other benefits for retirees, see: American Association of Retired Persons (www.arp.org); Employee Benefits Research Institute (www.ebri.org); International Foundation of Employee Benefit Plans (www.ifebp.org); and the Pension and Welfare Benefits Administration, U.S. Department of Labor (www.dol.gov/dol/pwba).

[37]Cranford, J. (December 1993). Providing cover: A look at public employee benefits. *Governing,* pp. 45–53.

[38]Harris, Jennifer (February 2000). Purchase of service credit: portability for public sector employees. *IPMA news,* pp. 18–19.

[39]Employers add benefits to meet boomers' retirement needs (January 2000). *IPMA news,* p. 14.

[40]Oppel, Richard (August 20, 1999). Companies cash in on new pension plan. *The New York Times,* C–1, 16.

[41]Phased retirement gradually makes its way into the workplace (June 1997). *IPMA news,* pp. 18–19.

[42]Calhoun, Carol, and Arthur H. Tepfer (August 1999). Deferred retirement option plans. *IPMA news,* pp. 13, 15; and Calhoun, Carol, and Arthur H. Tepfer (September 1999). Deferred retirement option plans. *IPMA news,* pp. 13, 15.

[43]Equal Employment Opportunity Commission v. Commonwealth of Massachusetts. November 1, 1990. Docket Nos. 90–10640–H and 90–10150–Z.

[44]Reichenberg, N. (December 1990). President signs ADEA bill. *IPMA news,* pp. 10–11.

[45]County government sues financial advisors. Out-of-court settlement reached (April 1991). *PA Times, 14* (4), 1.

[46]Wu, Ke Bin (2000). *Income, poverty and health insurance in the United States in 1998.* Washington, DC: AARP, Public Policy Institute, FS Number 79; and Connolly, Ceci (May 22, 2002). 18,000 die early among uninsured. *The Denver Post,* pp. 1A, 24A.

[47]Benefits costs decline (May-June 1996). *Compensation and Benefits Review, 28,* 11.

[48]Champion-Hughes, Ruth (January 2000). Family friendly benefits. *IPMA news,* pp. 12–13.

[49]Reed, C., and W. M. Bruch (1993). Dual-career couples in the public sector: A survey of personnel policies and practices. *Public Personnel Management, 22,* 187–200.

[50]Allred, S. (1995). An overview of the Family and Medical Leave Act. *Public Personnel Management, 24,* 67–73; Crampton, S. M., and J. M. Mishra (Fall 1995). Family and medical leave legislation: Organizational policies and structure. *Public Personnel Management, 24,* 271–290.

[51]Fortney, David, and Brian Nuterangelo (December 1998). An FMLA checklist: What can (and can't) an employer do with a returning employee? *IPMA news,* p. 10; and Kalk, Jacqueline (September 2000). What every employer should know about the Family and Medical Leave Act. *IPMA news,* pp. 7–8.

[52]Taylor, P. (May 23, 1991). Study of firms finds parental leave impact light. *The Washington Post,* p. A-9.

[53]*Daily labor report* (June 5, 1995). Washington, DC: The Bureau of National Affairs, Inc. (1995 DLR 107 d30).

[54]Kossek, E. E., B. J. DeMarr, K. Backman, and M. Kollar (1993). Assessing employees' emerging elder care needs and reactions to dependent care. *Public Personnel Management, 22,* 617–638; and Healy, M. (June 17, 1996). *Los Angeles Times,* pp. A-1, 12.

[55]Information on child-care options, laws and resources is available through: www.planetgov.com.

[56]Long-term care: Choices and knowledge (July 1996). *IPMA news,* p. 10.

[57]Ezra, M., and M. Deckman (1996). Balancing work and family responsibilities: Flextime and child-care in the federal government. *Public Administration Review, 56,* 174–179.

[58]Ibid., p. 8.

[59]Long-term care: Choices and knowledge (July 1996). *IPMA news,* p. 10.

[60]Employers believe educational benefit programs help retain employees (August 2000). *IPMA news,* p. 23.

[61]Perry, Ronald, and N. Joseph Cayer (Spring 1999). Cafeteria style health plans in municipal government. *Public Personnel Management, 28* (1): 107–117.

[62]1999 survey of performance-based work/life programs (January 2000). *IPMA news,* pp. 19, 22.

[63]Durst, Samantha (Summer 1999). Assessing the effect of family friendly programs on public organizations. *Review of Public Personnel Administration,* pp. 19–48.

[64]Checklist to reduce unscheduled absenteeism. *IPMA news* (December 1999). p. 18; and Browser, Ralph O., and Susan Kane (August 2000). A successful sick leave incentive program: St. Louis County. *IPMA news,* pp. 12–13.

7

The Saga of Social Equity
EEO, AA, and Workforce Diversity

Today, the man, or person, or corporate entity "offering the job" is, in fact, proba-bly hiring for reasons other than somebody's personal preference or qualifications or demonstrated performance. Like it or not, the present-day employer is operating under orders from the government, and the government's first priority is to main-tain the officially approved mix of genders, races, ethnic backgrounds and so on, not to hire the people best equipped to meet the stated goals of the organization.

Jim Wright, *Dallas Morning News*, September 4, 1990

This controversial editorial statement is hardly true. But it reflects the perceptions of a number of Americans, especially those who have not gotten a job they thought they were qualified for.[1] Conflict over affirmative action mirrors the larger socie-tal debate over employment criteria and preferences. "Orders" from the executive branch of government or the courts are rare, but social equity considerations at-tract attention and scrutiny and seem to challenge the belief that personnel deci-sions should be made solely on the basis of qualifications and competencies.

Ambivalent public attitudes toward affirmative action were reflected in media commentary on the 1994 Presidential candidacy of retired General Colin Powell (now Secretary of State). At the time, opinion polls showed that a large majority of Americans were opposed to **reverse discrimination**—employment quotas or prefer-ential hiring of minorities. Yet most also thought that AA was a good thing because it had allowed previously excluded minorities, as exemplified by General Powell, to rise to positions of prominence based on merit. Thus, Americans are opposed to preferential employment rules in general (because they are perceived as unfairly limiting opportunity for members of groups excluded from preferential treatment), yet favorably disposed toward them in practice (because they result in improved op-portunity for qualified individuals). That these two viewpoints are apparently con-tradictory does not stop people from believing in both simultaneously!

The critical test of affirmative action is whether the value of social equity has penetrated the core personnel functions and become a routine consideration in public personnel management, even though the political acceptability of affirmative action itself may have declined. The impact of social equity may be found in the judicial influence it has spawned over personnel decisions. EEO provisions extend to all employment decisions involving distribution of organizational resources. And workforce diversification programs are driven by economic realities as well as legal requirements. That is, the demand for productivity and effective service delivery, as well as recognition of the changing demographic composition of the labor pool in America, may overshadow the achievement of social equity through compliance with laws and regulations.

By the end of this chapter you will be able to:

1. Discuss EEO and AA laws and compliance agencies.
2. Describe voluntary and involuntary AA compliance.
3. Describe the impact of courts in interpreting and enforcing affirmative action laws.
4. Discuss how increased contracting has shifted the focus of AA compliance from employment preference to minority contractor "set-asides."
5. Discuss how workforce diversity differs from both EEO and AA, and describe how workforce diversification leads organizations to actively manage diversity by making changes in the organization's structure and processes.
6. Discuss how conflicts over the fairness of EEO, AA, and workforce diversification programs have affected the role of the public HR manager in achieving both productivity and fairness.

EEO/AA LAWS AND COMPLIANCE AGENCIES

Given that EEO and AA are often referred to in the same breath and are almost invariably enforced by the same agencies, it is understandable that people confuse them. It may help to remember that both are designed to promote social equity, though through different methods. **Equal employment opportunity (EEO)** is designed to eliminate discrimination passively by protecting fairness in employment processes and decisions. **Affirmative action (AA)** is designed to deal with the failure of passive non-discrimination to eliminate discrimination by enforcing diversity—a demographically representative workforce—through more results-oriented and operational intrusions into recruitment, selection, and other personnel functions.[2]

The first and most important social equity law is **Title VII of the Civil Rights Act of 1964**.[3] With a few exceptions, it prohibits public or private employers, labor organizations, and employment agencies from making employee or applicant personnel decisions based on race, color, religion, gender, or national origin.[4] The Equal Employment Opportunity Act of 1972 also increased the authority of the designated compliance agency, the **Equal Employment Opportunity Commission (EEOC)**.

In contrast with EEO, AA not only prohibits discrimination but also *requires* employers, unions, and employment agencies to take positive steps to reduce underrepresentation through the preparation and implementation of **affirmative**

TABLE 7–1   Federal AA/EEO Laws and Compliance Agencies[6]

Law	Practice Covered	Agencies Covered	Compliance Agency
Age Discrimination in Employment Act of 1967, as amended in 1974 (29.U.S.C. Sec. 631 and 630B)	Age discrimination against employees over 39	Virtually all employers	Equal Employment Opportunity Commission
Americans with Disabilities Act of 1990 (P.L. 101–336)	Discrimination against qualified individuals with handicaps	Employers with 15 or more employees	EEOC
Civil Rights Act of 1964 as amended by the Equal Employment Opportunity Act of 1972 (40 U.S.C. Sec. 2000e) as amended by the Civil Rights Act of 1991 (P.L. 102–166)	Discrimination based on race, color, religion, gender, or national origin	Employers with 15 or more employees	EEOC
Equal Pay Act of 1963 (29 U.S.C. Sec. 206d)	Discrimination in pay based on gender	Employees covered by the Fair Labor Standards Act	EEOC
Executive Order 11246	Discrimination based on race, color, religion, gender, or national origin	Employers with federal contracts and their subcontractors	U.S. Department of Labor
14th Amendment to the U.S. Constitution	Prohibits application of law unequally	All public employers	Various federal courts
Vietnam Era Veterans' Readjustment Act of 1974 (38 U.S.C. Sec. 2012, 2014)	Promotion of employment opportunity for disabled and other Vietnam-era veterans	Federal government and employers with federal contracts and their subcontractors	U.S. Department of Labor
Vocational Rehabilitation Act of 1973 (29 U.S.C. Sec. 701)	Prohibits discrimination against qualified individuals with handicaps	Federal agencies, grant recipients, and contractors	U.S. Department of Labor

action plans (AAPs). The two most critical governmental acts enforcing the value of social equity, through the achievement of proportional representation, are **Executive Order 11246** and the **Equal Employment Opportunity Act (1972)** (which really concerns AA rather than EEO). Table 7–1 summarizes several EEO/AA laws and compliance agencies.

Executive Order 11246 prohibited **discrimination** by most employers providing goods or services to the federal government. Furthermore, it required those with fifty or more employees and government contracts of $10,000 or more annually to prepare a written plan identifying any **underutilization** of women and minorities and establishing goals and timetables to correct it. This executive order has had great impact, since all subcontractors of covered contractors must also comply—regardless of the size of their contracts or number of employees. By 1990, this executive order covered some 27 million workers and over $194 billion in federal contracts.[5] The **Office of Federal Contract Compliance Programs (OFCCP)**, located within the U.S. Department of Labor, prepares regulations and enforces this order. Under the 1972 Equal Employment Opportunity Act, state and local governments were also required to file AA plans and to take the same types of remedial action required of federal contractors. In addition, this act granted the courts broad power to remedy the effects of employer discrimination.

VOLUNTARY AND INVOLUNTARY AFFIRMATIVE ACTION COMPLIANCE

Despite the rhetoric about "forced" compliance and "mandatory hiring quotas," it is important to remember that most affirmative action compliance is voluntary, and mandatory measures are only used as a last resort when agencies will not otherwise comply with the law.

Voluntary Affirmative Action Compliance

Voluntary AA compliance occurs when a public employer recognizes a compensatory need to diversify its workforce and complies through the preparation of an AA plan that (1) identifies underutilization of qualified women and minorities compared to their presence in a relevant labor market; (2) establishes full utilization as a goal; (3) develops concrete plans for achieving full utilization; and (4) makes reasonable progress toward full utilization.

Involuntary Compliance

Involuntary AA compliance occurs when an employer alters its personnel practices, as the result of investigation by a compliance agency, that ends in a negotiated settlement, consent decree, or court order. Understanding these three involuntary compliance mechanisms requires some background knowledge of the process by which compliance agencies investigate employers. An applicant or employee who believes he or she has been discriminated against usually seeks redress through administrative channels within the organization where the alleged discrimination occurred. This may involve an appeal, informal and then formal, to the personnel office, affirmative action officer, or through union channels if available. If dissatisfied, the employee may file a formal complaint with the appropriate compliance agency.

Filing a complaint results in a formal investigation in which the investigating officer contacts the employer asking for a written response to the applicant's or employee's charge of discrimination. The investigation may result in the complaint being rejected or the compliance agency filing a formal complaint against the employer.

Once a complaint is filed by the compliance agency, the employer may agree to the changes in its employment practices plus whatever specific remedies will "make whole" the injury to the aggrieved employee or applicant. This acknowledgement is called a **conciliation agreement**. The employer usually enters into it primarily to avoid costly litigation.

A **consent decree** results when an employer and a compliance agency negotiate an agreement subject to the approval of a court and judicial oversight. It is usually entered into by an employer in litigation who "smells" defeat. In such cases, the employer may consider it beneficial not to admit guilt, but to agree to terms that may be more advantageous than those resulting from a guilty verdict.

In situations where a compliance agency or individual has taken an employer to court over alleged AA violations, and neither a conciliation agreement nor a consent decree can be agreed upon, a guilty verdict against the employer will result in remedies being imposed by a **court order**. Cases involving "egregious" and "pervasive" discrimination may result in mandatory hiring quotas, changes in personnel policies, and back pay for the victims of discrimination. Public officials will generally do their best to avoid this outcome because of the cost and unfavorable publicity associated with it.

With declining budgets and increased workloads, it is understandable that compliance agencies such as the OFCCP and the EEOC are under continual pressure to resolve cases administratively rather than resorting to court action. And they are also targeting complaints of multiple abuses by large employers.

IMPACT OF FEDERAL COURTS ON PUBLIC AGENCY EEO/AA COMPLIANCE

Given the confusion and conflict over whether EEO or AA is the best way to achieve social equity, the federal court system, and particularly the Supreme Court, have played a major role in interpreting and enforcing social equity through case law. The earliest opinions strongly endorsed EEO and traditional merit system values. But as the Court encountered systemic and pervasive employment discrimination, it became more sympathetic to social equity, reinforcing AA programs and race-based remedies in the 1980s. Now, it has swung back toward EEO principles.

The Court's initial approach in interpreting the Civil Rights Act of 1964 was contained in its unanimous opinion in *Griggs v. Duke Power Company*.[7] Willie Griggs was a laborer at the Duke Power Company in North Carolina, where for years the workforce was segregated, with African Americans doing manual labor. In the early 1960s Duke Power Company acknowledged that it had discriminated in the past but argued that it had recently instituted objective testing of applicants for selection and promotion. Griggs sued on the grounds that the tests unfairly discriminated against African Americans and were unrelated to job performance. In a unanimous opinion, the Court established several points that prevailed until 1989. First, regarding Congress's intent, the act was interpreted to have remedial as well as prospective intent.[8] That is, an employer could not simply say, "We discriminated in the past, but no longer do so." Second, the Court said that if an employer's personnel practices resulted in discrimination, lack of intent to discriminate would not constitute a valid defense. In other words, the consequences of employment practices were more important than their intent. Third, the Court said that once an inference of discrimination could be drawn, the burden of proof shifted to the employer to show that the personnel practices that had the discriminatory effect were in fact job related. Each of these findings sent a significant message to employers, and the case is viewed as a landmark employment discrimination decision.

The Court's opinion in *Griggs* emphasized traditional merit system values of individual rights and efficiency. The Court would protect *individuals* from discrimination and would allow them to compete on the basis of competencies. It would not sacrifice job qualifications in favor of minority origins. In fact, writing for a unanimous court in 1971, Chief Justice Burger observed:

> Congress has not commanded that the less qualified be preferred over the better qualified simply because of minority origins. Far from disparaging job qualifications as such, Congress has made such qualifications the controlling factor, so that race, religion, nationality and sex become irrelevant. What Congress has commanded is that any tests used must measure the person for the job and not the person in the abstract.[9]

But from 1971 to 1987 the Court faced challenges of systemic or institutionalized discrimination that Congress had not anticipated when it passed the Civil Rights Act of 1964 and the Equal Employment Opportunity Act of 1972:

- What should the Court do about pervasive racism or gender discrimination?
- What should the Court do in cases where employers voluntarily showed racial preference to resolve a discrimination problem that had not been litigated or formally alleged?
- How should the Court evaluate seniority systems that routinely discriminated against minorities, but that were not originally conceived with that purpose?
- What balance should it draw between compensation for those discriminated against and inadvertent injury to innocent non-minorities who might have to bear some of the cost in delayed promotions or loss of training or advancement opportunities for minorities who had historically been discriminated against?

Answers to these questions could not be found in the wording of civil rights legislation or the Constitution. Further, the legislative debates leading up to the Civil Rights Act of 1964 and the EEO Act of 1972 were so entangled that *any* answer to these questions could be justified with reference to legislative intent. The Court had to use the letter of the law, its intent as interpreted by the Court, and its own precedents in deliberating and reaching answers to these and other questions. *Griggs* was the last unanimous vote the Court recorded on an affirmative action case. By 1987 the Court had moved away from its color-blind interpretation in *Griggs* and embraced the value of social equity, struggling to find a balance between social equity, individual rights, and to a lesser extent, efficiency.

Sixteen years after *Griggs*, the Court confronted two very different cases. Litigation leading to a Supreme Court review in **United States v. Paradise**[10] began in 1972 when a district court found pervasive, systemic, and obstinate exclusion of African Americans from employment with the Alabama Department of Public Safety. Continued failure to comply with consent decrees led the district court in 1983 to order the state to promote to the rank of corporal African-American troopers at a 1–1 ratio with Caucasian troopers. This order would be enforced until at least 25 percent of the corporals were black or the department could produce a valid promotional examination—that is, one that had no adverse effect on qualified minority candidates. Supporting the state of Alabama, the federal government appealed to the Supreme Court, claiming it violated the individual rights of innocent non-minorities (the Anglo troopers who may have benefited from the discrimination, but could not be shown to be party to it).

Also in 1987 the Court reviewed the reverse discrimination case of *Johnson v. Transportation Agency*.[11] The transportation agency in Santa Clara County, California, noting a substantial underutilization of women working in the agency, voluntarily developed an AA plan that considered gender as one factor in employment decisions. After adopting the plan, the agency promoted Diane Joyce to the position of road dispatcher over Paul Johnson, who had achieved a nominally higher score than Joyce in a promotional interview. Johnson claimed reverse discrimination based on Title VII of the Civil Rights Act and the case eventually reached the Supreme Court. Joyce's promotion was upheld.

To decide whether the use of race and gender preference were lawful in *Paradise* and *Johnson*, the Court employed a two pronged analytical framework it had developed since *Griggs* in 1971. First, employing the **strict scrutiny** standard for evaluating the use of AA, the Court asked: "Is there a compelling justification for the employer to take race into consideration in its AA program?" In *Paradise*, all the justices answered this question in the affirmative, agreeing that the "Alabama Department of Public Safety had undertaken a course of action that amounted to 'pervasive, systematic, and obstinate discriminatory conduct.'"[12] Therefore, the use of race to remedy the effect of this conduct was justified. In *Johnson*, a majority of the Court answered in the affirmative as well. The majority inferred discrimination based on gender from a comparison of the number of women working in several of the transportation agency's job classifications compared to their numbers in the county's total labor pool. Thus, they found justification for the use of gender in the county's AA plan.

In both cases, the Court then turned to the second and usually more important question involved in the strict scrutiny standard: Is the AA plan narrowly tailored to solve the discrimination problem, or does it create additional, unacceptable problems? In *Paradise*, a majority noted that the order was "narrowly tailored" and minimally intrusive because the promotion quota was limited in scope and duration. The remedy imposed a *diffuse* burden on the Caucasian troopers, and no individual non-minority employee must bear the entire cost of the remedy. In *Johnson*, a majority of the Court found the county's plan was narrowly tailored, and it did not "trammel" the rights of male employees. The plan did not set aside any positions for women; it did authorize consideration of gender as one factor in promotion decisions. The Court found that the county's plan was intended to "attain" a racial balance, not "maintain" one, which would have been illegal.

In both *Paradise* and *Johnson*, the Court showed its willingness to support social equity with remedies benefiting those who had not been the specific or identifiable victims of discrimination. None of the troopers who might benefit from the court's order in *Paradise* claimed to have been specifically discriminated against; and Diane Joyce did not claim gender discrimination. Nevertheless, they were members of a class who had been discriminated against. But in both 1987 cases the Court was unwilling to dismiss the value of individual rights, as it considered the effects the AA in both cases would have on the lives of the innocent non-minorities. Further, the Court acknowledged the value of efficiency by requiring that the minority troopers in Alabama be qualified and by noting that Diane Joyce was qualified.

FROM EMPLOYMENT PREFERENCES TO CONTRACT "SET-ASIDES"

As governments increasingly implement programs through contracts for goods and services, AA advocates—and opponents—increasingly recognize that the focus of compliance efforts has shifted from government employment to the personnel policies and practices of government contractors and subcontractors. Initially, efforts to improve the "mix" of contractors were thwarted because contractors were overwhelmingly white males. This led to the elaboration of procedures making it easier for **minority business enterprises (MBEs)** to qualify as bidders, to post performance bonds, and to respond to **requests for proposals (RFPs)** issued by government agencies. In some cases, this included formal or informal quotas—minimum percentages of contract funds (or **minority set-asides**, as they are sometimes called) that had to be awarded to minority contractors or subcontractors.

Naturally, these revised criteria led to abuses, such as the creation of so-called MBEs that showed minorities or females as corporate directors, but were actually covertly created and financed by white-owned firms as a mechanism for winning set-aside contracts. And awarding contracts to MBEs that in some cases were not the lowest or best-qualified bidders provoked opposition among white-owned contractors and advocates of efficiency or cost reduction as the dominant criterion for awarding contracts.

In resolving conflicts between EEO and preferential (AA) treatment of contractors, the Supreme Court faced the same issues underlying similar conflicts for employees and tended to resolve these conflicts based on prevailing political weight of the two opposing values. By 1989, with the inclusion of President Reagan's appointees, the value of individual rights grew and the value of social equity declined. This reversal was seen in *Richmond v. Croson* in 1989 and then reinforced in *Adarand v. Peña* in 1995. In **Richmond v. Croson**[13] the Court ruled 6 to 3 against the city of Richmond's voluntary plan that required at least 30 percent of each city contract to be sublet to minority contractors. While recognizing that the city's population was 50 percent black and less than 1 percent of the city's prime contracts had gone to minority business enterprises, and despite substantial anecdotal evidence of widespread discrimination against minority contractors, the Court ruled that the city had shown no direct evidence establishing discrimination *by the city* against minority contractors. Thus, the city of Richmond's plan failed to establish a compelling reason for AA by the city in minority contracting, and failed to meet the narrowly tailored test because it could not tie the 30 percent figure to the actual degree of discrimination attributed to the city's actions.

In *Adarand v. Peña*, a white-owned contractor sued the secretary of transportation over the constitutionality of minority set-asides in federally funded highway projects.[14] In resolving this case, the Court extended its ruling in *Croson* to the federal government. In so doing, it firmly established that the use of race as a preferential category in an employment context would be subject to the strictest judicial scrutiny. In essence, the court reaffirmed and anchored its guidance in *Croson* that whether used for "benign" purposes or not, racial preferences must be justified by a compelling government reason and be narrowly tailored as a solution.

Since *Croson* and *Adarand*, Californians passed an amendment to their state Constitution prohibiting affirmative action by state actors, and the U.S. Supreme Court has agreed to hear another case brought by Adarand. So it seems that the general trend away from social equity and toward individual rights and efficiency that is reflected in legislation and case law concerning AA is paralleled by case law affirming the right of corporations to compete for contracts without minority set-asides. Whether this shift reflects recognition that equality of opportunity has already been achieved for minority contractors, or simply a turning away from social equity as a dominant value because of changes in the political climate, depends upon one's point of view.

FROM AFFIRMATIVE ACTION TO WORKFORCE DIVERSITY

Workforce diversity, for our purposes, includes differences in employee and applicant characteristics (race, gender, ethnicity, national origin, language, religion, age, education, intelligence, and disabilities) that constitute the range of variation among human beings in the workforce.

Immigration and Cultural Diversity

The workforce in modern industrialized nations is becoming socially more diverse. In the United States, it is comprised increasingly of immigrants whose primary language is not English, and whose primary norms are not those of "mainstream" American culture. Whites currently account for 74 percent of the population, blacks 12 percent, Hispanics 10 percent and Asians 3 percent.[15] Preliminary 2000 census data indicate that Hispanics are virtually tied with blacks, and will surpass them within a few years.[16] By the year 2000, only 15 percent of new entrants to the workforce were U.S.-born white males: The others were people of color, women, and immigrants.[17] By the year 2050, demographers predict that Hispanics will account for 25 percent of the population, blacks 14 percent, Asians 8 percent, with whites hovering somewhere around 53 percent.[18]

Nearly one in ten U.S. residents was born abroad, a high rate for industrialized nations. In 1960, foreign born Americans came mostly from Europe. Today this new wave of immigration is coming mainly from Latin America and Asia— Mexico, the Philippines, China, Cuba, Vietnam, and El Salvador. It results from economic globalization, interminable ethnic and political conflicts in developing countries, and an intense desire among migrants to find a better life for themselves and their families in the United States.

The current wave of immigration is different from others in that increased residential segregation and cultural isolation make it possible for large immigrant communities to thrive as foreign enclaves in this country. For example, 75 percent of Miamians speak a language other than English in their homes, and two-thirds of these say they do not speak English well. In New York, the corresponding figures are 40 percent speaking a language other than English at home, and half of these not speaking English well. In short, we have increased **cultural diversity** in a nation that was formerly considered to be linguistically and culturally homogeneous. In brief, our image of America has changed from a "melting pot" to a salad bowl. This has not occurred without considerable unrest among native-born U.S. residents. White conservatives frequently voice appeals for "English-only," or seek stricter controls over immigration in an effort to keep out those who might become a burden to health, education, and criminal justice systems. And American-born African Americans, already embittered at being economically disadvantaged compared to whites, are newly embittered about being excluded from the burgeoning Latin economy if they are not bilingual. As one said at a university "career day" in Miami several years ago, "Why do I have to learn Spanish to get a job in the country where I was born?" The honest answer, "Because people who are bilingual have better job prospects in a bilingual economy," does not respond adequately to the underlying sense of anger and dispossession that impelled the question.

Workforce Diversity

In the private sector, workforce diversity can be attributed to increasing economic pressures for organizations to remain competitive in the new global economy. The general argument that workforce diversity makes good business sense grows out of a fundamental premise—that businesses whose employees "can speak the same language" as their customers/clients will be more successful than those that cannot. The market will sort out the successful from unsuccessful firms in diverse markets, and those that succeed will probably be the ones whose workforce matches the customer base in diversity.

While governments may not face economic pressures to diversify since they may operate as monopolies within a geographic area, they do face continued political pressure to do so. The values of representation and equity are articulated by demands for recruitment and selection of minority group members, especially for administrators in influential public contact positions. For example, over half of the students in the Los Angeles school district are Latinos. In 1996, the announced departure of the first black superintendent was met by rallies endorsing the appointment, without a search, of the second-in-charge, a Latino. In fact, newspaper reports cited threats of a recall election for board members who did not support the Latino candidate.

The process by which diverse minorities have been incorporated into the workforce varies dependent upon state and local conditions and laws, and overgeneralizations should be avoided. Nonetheless, examining the evolution of minority groups through several stages of empowerment and protection can show the relationship among economics, politics, and workforce diversity. In the beginning, members of diverse groups were almost automatically excluded from the workforce, except for unskilled positions, because they were outside the "mainstream" culture. This exclusion was based in law as well as custom. Second, as economic development and labor shortages increased (such as in the United States during World War II), these groups were admitted into the labor market (particularly if they possessed job skills in short supply), though they faced continued economic and legal discrimination and were excluded from consideration for desirable professional and technical positions. Third, as economic development and labor shortages continued, and as their political power continued to increase, group members were accepted for a range of positions, and their employment rights were protected by laws guaranteeing equal employment access (EEO). In the United States, for example, applicants' equal employment rights have been protected by Title VII of the Civil Rights Act (1964) and by the Americans with Disabilities Act (1990). Fourth, as these groups became increasingly powerful politically, efforts to reduce the considerable informal discrimination that continued in recruitment, promotion, pay, and benefits led to establishment of workplace policies, such as salary equality and employment proportionate with their representation in the labor market. Voluntary AA programs encouraged achievement of these goals. If voluntary achievement efforts were unsuccessful, conformance was sometimes mandated by AA compliance agencies or court orders. Fifth, continued social and political changes are now leading to the welcoming of diversity as a desirable political and social condition, and continued economic pressures lead to the development of **workforce diversification programs** for organizations that desire to remain economically competitive or politically responsive.

These stages in the evolution of political power and legal protection for diverse groups in the workforce are shown in Table 7–2.

Difference between EEO, AA, and Workforce Diversity

Because the workforce diversification programs found in the contemporary workplace are the current stage of an evolutionary process defined by increased social participation, political power, and legal protection for minorities, it is understandable that some people consider workforce diversification programs to be simply "old wine in new bottles"—a contemporary variant on the EEO or AA that have characterized HRM in the United States for the past thirty years. However, workforce diversification differs from EEO or AA programs in five important respects.[19]

TABLE 7–2 Political Power and Legal Protection for Diverse Groups in the Workforce

Stage	Employment Status	Legal Protection
1	excluded from the workforce	none
2	admitted to the workforce, but excluded from desirable jobs	none
3	accepted into the workforce	EEO
4	recruited into the workforce	AA
5	welcomed into the workforce	diversity management

First, their purposes are different. EEO is based on organizational efforts to avoid violating employees' or applicants' legal or constitutional rights. AA is based on organizational efforts to achieve proportional representation of selected groups. But workforce diversification programs originate from managers' objective of increasing productivity and effectiveness.[20]

Second, AA laws protect only the employment rights of designated categories of persons (in the United States, such groups as blacks, Hispanics, native Americans, Asian-Americans, workers over 40, women, and Americans with disabilities). Workforce diversification programs are based on recognition not only of these protected groups but also of the entire spectrum of characteristics (knowledge, skills, and abilities) that managers and personnel directors need to recognize and factor into personnel decisions in order to acquire and develop a productive workforce.

Third, AA programs emphasize recruitment, selection, and sometimes promotion because those personnel functions are most closely tied to proportional representation of protected groups. However, workforce diversification programs include all personnel functions related to organizational effectiveness (including recruitment, promotion and retention, job design, pay and benefits, education and training, and performance measurement and improvement).

Fourth, workforce diversification programs have a different locus of control. AA and EEO programs are based on managerial responses to outside compliance agencies' requirements. However, workforce diversification programs originate as internal organizational responses to managerial demands for enhanced productivity and effectiveness (although this response is itself a reaction to demographic changes in overall population).

Fifth, AA programs tend to be viewed negatively by managers and employees, because they are based on a negative premise ("what changes must we make in recruitment and selection procedures to demonstrate a good faith effort to achieve a representative workforce, and thereby avoid sanctions by AA compliance agencies or courts?"). In contrast, the most successful workforce diversification programs tend to be viewed as positive by managers and employees, because they are based on a different question ("What changes can we make in our organization's mission, culture, policies, and programs in order to become more effective and more competitive?").[21]

MANAGING DIVERSITY IN ORGANIZATIONS

Acceptance of workforce diversity can be passive or active. Passively, it means accepting demographic trends and their implications for a diverse workforce. Actively, it means **managing diversity**—seeking to change the structures and processes that effectively utilize diversity, and creating an equitable and fair work environment for all employees. Workforce diversification starts from a recognition that human resources are increasingly vital to organizational survival and effectiveness;[22] and diversification programs are the best way to effectively use human resources.[23]

Mission, Organization Culture, and Personnel Policy and Practice

Workforce diversification requires changes in **organizational culture**—the values, assumptions, and communication patterns that characterize interaction among employees. These patterns are invented, discovered, or developed by members of the organization as responses to problems or sensitivity to client needs; they become part of the culture as they are taught to new members as the correct way to perceive, think, and feel in relation to these problems or needs.[24] Viewed from this perspective, diversification is changes in the way organizations do business, rather than just an adaptation of existing personnel policies and programs to meet the specialized needs of minorities and women.

An organization's decision to use workforce diversity to increase effectiveness causes changes in its human resource management policy and practice.[25] Policies and practices are the rules and procedures that implement organizational objectives, and they are management's strategic plan for accomplishing its mission. Workforce diversification programs affect five specific areas of human resource management policy and practice: recruitment and retention, job design, education and training, benefits and rewards, and performance measurement and improvement.

Recruitment and retention policies and programs include those strategies already commonplace in AA programs: increasing the applicant pool of underrepresented groups, increasing their selection rate by developing valid alternatives for tests that have a disparate impact, and developing **mentoring** systems to encourage retention. Yet their purpose is productivity enhancement through a diverse workforce rather than legal compliance through recruitment or selection quotas; they apply to a broader spectrum of applicant and employee characteristics; they include a broader range of personnel activities; their locus of control is internal rather than external, and their tone is positive rather than negative.

To attract and retain women with child- and elder-care responsibilities into the workforce, job design options that offer flexibility of work locations and schedules need to be considered.[26] To attract and retain persons with **disabilities**, reasonable accommodation must be offered to make the workplace physically accessible and to make jobs available to persons who are otherwise qualified to perform the primary duties.[27]

Education and training programs are influenced in two ways. First, there is a need for supervisory training on policies and compliance procedures, as well as identifying harassment. Second, employer concerns with the educational preparation of future workers have led employers to include basic skills unrelated to specific job tasks (such as literacy and English as a second language).[28] And there is increasing interest in strengthening federal- and state-sponsored job training programs, and in sponsoring joint business-government policy initiatives such as tax incentives for costs associated with business training programs.[29] *Pay and benefit policies* often become more flexible and innovative: flexible benefits, benefits for part-time positions, parental leave, child- and elder-care support programs, and phased retirement. Employee assistance programs (EAPs) are an effective response to diversity in the workplace.[30]

Performance measurement and productivity improvement programs often change, in that managers and supervisors now need to consider the differing values and motivational perspectives of a diverse workforce.[31] Workforce diversity has also brought about changing definitions of productivity, based on the need for variation in managerial styles and resultant dramatic increases in organizational effectiveness.[32]

The common threads linking these five areas of personnel policy and practice are their common objective of increased organizational effectiveness, and their cumulative impact on organizational culture. Organizations that wish to attract and keep a diversified workforce must change the culture of the organization to create a climate in which persons from diverse groups feel accepted, comfortable, and productive. And this is why the tone of workforce diversification programs differs from their affirmative compliance program predecessors—affirming diversity is different from tolerating or accepting it.[33]

Characteristics of Effective and Ineffective Diversity Management Programs

Diversity management programs typically encounter two types of implementation issues—systemic and situational. Systemic issues arise when AA opponents have succeeded in forcing a premature transition from "forced" compliance to diversity management on the grounds that "we have had too much legalistic, quota-based diversification; it's time to do away with affirmative action and replace it with diversity management"—even though informal but strongly entrenched racism or gender discrimination still exist within the culture of the organization. Operational issues arise when systemic discrimination is not part of the dominant culture, yet minorities and women still confront invisible barriers—a **glass ceiling** that inhibits success almost imperceptibly at each step of the promotional ladder, but with substantial cumulative effect.[34]

To avoid both negative outcomes, experts have proposed a relatively uniform set of criteria for assessing the effectiveness of workforce diversity policies and programs.[35] These include:

1. A broad definition of diversity that includes a range of characteristics, rather than only those used to define "protected classes" under existing AA;
2. A systematic assessment of the existing culture to determine how members at all levels view the present organization;

3. Top-level initiation of, commitment to, and visibility of workforce diversity as an essential organizational policy rather than as a legal compliance issue or staff function;
4. Establishment of specific objectives;
5. Integration into the managerial performance evaluation and reward structure;
6. Coordination with other activities such as employee development, job design, and TQM; and
7. Continual evaluation and improvement.

Insufficient top-level commitment or organizational visibility generally renders diversification efforts unsuccessful because the program's long-term impact on organization mission or culture is inadequate.

Workforce Diversification and Other Management Trends

Workforce diversification programs are consistent with other contemporaneous trends such as employee involvement and participation, employee development, TQM, and non-adversarial dispute resolution. Employee involvement and participation are considered essential for maintaining high productivity (at least among employees in key professional and technical positions). Even in the absence of significant financial rewards, employees tend to work happily and effectively when they have the necessary skills, see their work as meaningful, feel personally responsible for productivity, and have firsthand knowledge of the actual results of their labor. As teamwork becomes more important—or recognized as being important—managers are increasingly called upon to demonstrate multicultural competence utilizing a diverse workforce. Employee development is related to diversification, at least for key professional and technical employees, because it (1) focuses planning and budget analysis on human resources; (2) facilitates cost-benefit analysis of current training and development activities; and (3) fosters communication and commitment of organizational goals through employee participation and involvement.

Total quality management (TQM) is an organizational change process that involves a combination of top-down and bottom-up activities: assessment of problems, identification of solutions, and designation of responsibilities for resolving them. It focuses on the connection between the quality of the work environment and the quality of individual, team, and organizational performance. It is congruent with workforce diversification efforts because it focuses on a transformation of organizational culture, policies, and programs so as to enhance productivity.

Alternative dispute resolution (ADR) is a philosophy and practice of settling organizational differences by means other than formal and quasi-legal adversarial procedures. It has several specific HR applications, and it will be further discussed as an alternative to traditional employee civil service grievance procedures in Chapter 13, and collective bargaining contract administration procedures in Chapter 14. The challenge of channeling diversity into productivity is complicated by the breadth of expectations that members of diverse cultures bring to their work. Without a method of settling disputes that models the organization's commitment to tolerance and respect, differences lead only to divisiveness that consumes organizational resources without positive results. Traditional adversarial dispute resolution techniques are not particularly effective at resolving organizational conflicts: They build acrimony, harden bargaining positions, and delay the resolution of the original conflict. Therefore, innovative conflict resolution techniques such as "win-win" negotiation and group problem solving are often more effective and have the additional advantage of modeling the organization's commitment to respect, tolerance, and dignity.[36]

THE ROLE OF THE HR MANAGER IN ACHIEVING PRODUCTIVITY AND FAIRNESS

Conflict over the relative importance of social equity and the appropriateness of alternative strategies for achieving it has caused concern in some specific areas. What has been the actual impact of all these programs on the employment of minorities and women? How can the positive and negative impacts of diversification programs on productivity and fairness be measured and assessed? What changes does diversification force them to make in how they view their jobs and how they do them?

Impact of AA on Employment of Minorities and Women

Has civil rights legislation and employment discrimination litigation reduced discrimination and opened doors for minorities and women? The answer appears to be "yes": between 1980 and 1995 the composition of state and local workforce changed as follows:

- The percentage of males decreased from 59 percent to 55 percent.
- The percentage of whites decreased from 81 percent to 77 percent.
- The percentage of white males decreased from 49 percent to 44 percent.
- The percentage of Black women increased from 7 to 9 percent.[37]

The *kinds* of discrimination reported in cases that came before the Court in the 1970s have decreased. It is difficult to conceive today of a case of intentional racial discrimination in employment like that reported in *Griggs* (1971) or *Paradise* (1987). The value of social equity has challenged merit systems to demonstrate that personnel practices once assumed to be job related are, in fact. In this way, AA has benefited all employees, regardless of race or gender. Jobs are advertised publicly and widely; interview questions and tests are tailored to specific jobs, performance appraisal instruments have become more job related, and pay systems have become more equitable and sensitive to gender differences—even if they have not erased them.

On the other hand, it seems equally clear that acceptance of diversity is not yet a part of the value structure of all Americans. While women have joined management ranks in large numbers, a "glass ceiling" inhibits their advancement to top corporate ranks. Currently, women hold only 3 percent of top management jobs.[38] Despite the "graying" of the workforce, implicit discrimination against older workers continues.[39] A *USA Today* poll, taken after the O.J. Simpson trial in 1995, shows significant differences in the beliefs of Anglos and African Americans regarding the prevalence of discrimination.[40] And **gender orientation** (status as a heterosexual, lesbian, or gay person) remains unprotected by law—it is specifically excluded as a protected class under Title VII. Public and private sector employers in most places can and do discriminate on the basis of sexual orientation with impunity.[41]

On the other hand, a backlash against AA has developed for thirty years among white males. First, they state that AA is unfair to blacks because, while it has helped the best-off blacks enhance their jobs status, it has done nothing to alleviate the employment crisis among a black urban underclass increasingly plagued by poor education, drug abuse, and crime. Second, they state that AA is the opening wedge of a comprehensive ideology that threatens the basic American value of equality under the law. They fear it will lead to the "Balkanization" of American society, the creation of a culture in which all public policy decisions are made on the basis of social equity.[42]

In addition to its specific impact on the public personnel manager, AA has a more general impact. Conflicts between social equity and merit result in the application of confusing and contradictory decision rules regulating acquisition. During periods of growth, managers overcome these conflicts by hiring more people from all groups—as long as the pie gets larger, everyone can get a bigger piece. But in periods of decline, conflicts between social equity and other values result in heightened conflict.

What can we expect in the future? This same tension among conflicting values is likely to continue. On the one hand, political pressures for representativeness and economic pressures for enhanced productivity will result in increased workforce diversification efforts. On the other hand, reactions against these pressures will result in either administrative formalism in the implementation of diversification programs, or resistance to them by particular groups that perceive them as threatening to their job prospects. To the extent that economic markets can influence personnel policies and practices, the forecast connecting workforce diversity and productivity seems on target. But the strength of the marketplace contains its weakness as well; it is driven by the value of efficiency, not by concerns of equity, fairness, or justice. While the connection between productivity and diversity may increase representation of minorities in the workplace, history suggests that if it does so fairly, it will be coincidental. In the new millennium, the value of social equity is being carried into the political arena more by demographic reality than by legislation, litigation, and conscience. While the courts will continue to orient themselves to the protection of individual rights, demographic realities will force legislatures and administrative agencies to respond to representation and the broader political concern of workforce diversity. Further, increasing emphasis on customer satisfaction in multiethnic communities may very well connect workforce diversity to productivity.[43]

Changing Role Expectations

Societal disagreement over the relative importance of social equity as an underlying value, and over the appropriateness of alternative strategies for achieving it (EEO, AA, or diversification programs), have changed role expectations for all groups in public agencies.[44]

For elected officials, it means making difficult choices among policy options that often conflict. While it is possible to influence the personnel practices of contractors through minority business programs and set-asides (contracting quotas), the use of alternative methods of service delivery reduces the ability of the public sector to directly shape agency mission, culture, policies, and procedures so as to achieve workforce diversity.

Managers and supervisors are faced with the need to maintain productive organizations in the face of two contradictory truths: It is usually easier to make decisions and resolve conflicts in a homogeneous organization, at least in the short run; and organizations must be adaptable to heterogeneous and shifting environments in order to survive in the long run. This means that managers will continue to be evaluated along two criteria—short-term productivity and changes in organizational culture that enable the organization to enhance long-term effectiveness.[45]

Employees face the need to communicate, interact, form work teams, resolve conflicts, and make decisions with other employees who may be unlike them in many ways. And they will do so in a climate of increased workplace tension due to the transformation of labor markets and increased employment opportunity for skilled and unskilled foreign workers. These changes pit workers against each other and pit new applicants against current employees.

As always, human resource managers face the need to manage human resources efficiently and effectively. With respect to workforce diversity, this means the need to develop and apply two apparently contradictory human resource strategies: policies for temporary employees designed to control costs, and policies for permanent employees designed to ensure loyalty, participation, and asset development as human resources. And because effective human resource management depends upon the communication of clear and consistent messages, public personnel managers find it increasingly difficult when they must send different messages to different employees. In general, therefore, workforce diversity is consistent with demands on public officials and administrators for more innovation. But cultivating innovation among public managers requires characteristics usually not present in the culture of contemporary organizations—reward systems that reinforce risk taking and do not penalize failure.[46]

The transition from AA compliance to workforce diversification presents AA compliance specialists with a difficult dilemma. Traditionally, AA specialists have relied upon their authority as interfaces between the organization and external compliance agencies. Given the five critical differences between AA compliance and workforce diversification, these specialists need to redefine their own role and culture in the organization.[47]

SUMMARY

EEO, AA, and workforce diversification programs have greatly affected all personnel functions. They are all based on the value of social equity and individual rights, and on the AA laws and procedures used to implement these values. Despite the current eclipse of social equity due to the renewed emphasis on other values, AA will continue to have a profound impact on public administration because of its control over the acquisition process and the increasing role of the judicial system in regulating employment decisions and ensuring procedural due process.

In the long run, it may be helpful to view the struggle over social equity as a continual conflict with many possible solutions. If discrimination is individual, then EEO is the answer. If there is systemic racism or gender discrimination, then AA is required as a political stage America needs to go through on its way to accepting increasing cultural and, therefore, workforce diversity. This demographic diversity is accompanied by economic pressures, as technological change and globalization of the economy increase public and private employers' demands for a highly trained workforce. And political pressures by women, minorities, older workers, immigrants, and persons with disabilities have resulted in legal changes in the employment rights of groups formerly excluded by law or custom from desirable professional and technical jobs.

Predictably, conflict over the relative importance of social equity and the best ways of achieving it have led public administrators and officials to reexamine the impact of diversification programs on productivity and fairness, and on how they do their jobs.

KEY TERMS

Adarand v. Peña
affirmative action (AA)
affirmative action plan (AAP)
affirmative action program
alternative dispute resolution (ADR)
Civil Rights Act of 1991
conciliation agreement
consent decree
court order
cultural diversity
disability
discrimination
equal employment opportunity (EEO)
Equal Employment Opportunity Act
    (1972)
Equal Employment Opportunity
    Commission (EEOC)
Equal Pay Act (EPA)
Executive Order (EO) 11246
gender orientation

glass ceiling
Griggs v. Duke Power Company
Johnson v. Transportation Agency
managing diversity
mentoring
minority business enterprises (MBEs)
minority set-aside
Office of Federal Contract Compliance
    Programs (OFCCP)
organizational culture
requests for proposals (RFP)
reverse discrimination
Richmond v. Croson
strict scrutiny
Title VII (Civil Rights Act of 1964)
total quality management (TQM)
underutilization
United States v. Paradise
workforce diversity
workforce diversification program

DISCUSSION QUESTIONS

1. What is EEO, what is AA, and what is the difference between them?
2. What federal agencies are responsible for compliance with EEO/AA laws?
3. What mechanisms are associated with voluntary and involuntary AA compliance?

4. Why is the role of federal courts so significant in interpreting social equity legislation?
5. With respect to the fundamental conflict between EEO and AA, how has the Supreme Court endorsed and interpreted social equity legislation from 1971 to the present?
6. Why has service contracting increased conflict between minority businesses and other contractors?
7. Have we had too much affirmative action in the past thirty years, or not enough? Why?
8. How does workforce diversity differ from both EEO and AA?
9. What do you believe is the relationship among AA, workforce diversity, and productivity in a culturally diverse community?
10. How do workforce diversification programs affect organizational culture, mission, policies and programs? Why do some work and others fail?
11. What role do you think the public HR manager should take in advancing AA and workforce diversity in an environment of conflicting values over how best to achieve social equity?

CASE STUDY 1: EQUAL EMPLOYMENT OPPORTUNITY OR AFFIRMATIVE ACTION?

Read the following passages from Supreme Court opinions, and then answer the questions:

It is plainly true that in our society blacks have suffered discrimination immeasurably greater than any directed at other racial groups. But those who believe that racial preferences can help to "even the score" display, and reinforce, a manner of thinking by race that was the source of the injustice and that will, if it endures within our society, be the source of more injustice still. The relevant proposition is not that it was blacks, or Jews, or Irish who were discriminated against, but that it was individual men and women, "created equal," who were discriminated against. And the relevant resolve is that it should never happen again. Racial preferences appear to "even the score" (in some small degree) only if one embraces the proposition that our society is appropriately viewed as divided into races, making it right that an injustice rendered in the past to a black man should be compensated for by discriminating against a white. Nothing is worth that embrace.

Justice Scalia, *Richmond v. Croson*, 57 LW 4132, 4148 (1989)

A profound difference separates governmental actions that themselves are racist, and governmental actions that seek to remedy the effects of prior racism or to prevent neutral governmental activity from perpetuating the effects of such racism. . . . Racial classifications "drawn on the presumption that one race is inferior to another or because they put the weight of government behind racial hatred and separatism" warrant the strictest judicial scrutiny because of the very irrelevance of these rationales. . . . By contrast . . . [b]ecause the consideration of race is relevant to remedying the continuing effects of past racial discrimination, and because governmental programs employing racial classifications for remedial purposes can be crafted to avoid stigmatization, . . . such programs should not be subjected to conventional "scrutiny"—scrutiny that is strict in theory, but fatal in fact.

Justice Marshall, *Richmond v. Croson*, 57 LW 4132, 4155 (1989)

Congress has not commanded that the less qualified be preferred over the better qualified simply because of minority origins. Far from disparaging job qualifications as such, Congress has made such qualifications the controlling factor, so that race, religion, nationality and sex become irrelevant.

Chief Justice Burger, *Griggs v. Duke Power Company*, 401 L Ed 2d, 158, 167 (1971)

Questions

1. Identify the values in each of the passages.
2. Which passages do you agree with most/disagree with most?

CASE STUDY 2: SOCIAL EQUITY VS. EMPLOYEE RIGHTS

Read the following scenario and complete the assignment in the last paragraph.

In 1992 a group of Hispanic-Americans sued the city government for discrimination in employment practices in the police and fire departments. The court encouraged the parties to enter a consent decree, which they did. The consent decree called for the city to cease its discrimination, to identify the victims of discrimination, to make the hiring of the qualified victims a priority, and to establish hiring and promotion goals that would bring the percentage of Hispanic-Americans in the public safety departments on par with the number of qualified potential Hispanic-American applicants in the surrounding labor market.

By 1994, although the city had hired a few of the plaintiffs who had not already found other jobs, the city had shown little effort to comply with the consent decree, and the racial imbalances were hardly affected. The Hispanics complained that those who were hired had been kept in lower-paying job classifications longer than their Anglo peers and were subjected to racial jokes; they were paired with each other in the police department and assigned to Hispanic-American high-crime areas. In the fire department they were isolated in the day-to-day informal activities of the department. It was rumored about city hall that the mayor had encouraged the personnel director to "do as little as possible" in complying with the consent decree.

In 1995 the Hispanic advocates went back to the court, requesting judicial intervention. The court summoned the parties, and a revised consent decree was entered. It provided for a court-ordered trustee to monitor the consent decree. In 1996 the city halted all hiring, citing budgetary problems. By 1998, the city began to hire on a case-by-case basis in other departments, but not in public safety, citing the lack of need for additional officers and fire fighters.

The Hispanic plaintiffs returned again to the court, seeking relief. After consulting with the trustee, the judge, citing the court's exasperation and failure to note good faith on the part of the city, was determined to craft a solution that would make a difference. At this point, the mayor announced the hiring of a chief administrative officer and assigned the CAO the responsibility of coming up with a plan to "deal with this mess." The city successfully persuaded the judge to give it six more months to rectify the problems. The judge reluctantly agreed.

You are the CAO. Develop a plan, recognizing that it will have to be approved by a judge who will tolerate no more delays. At the same time, you must understand that the judge is bound to analyze the plan according to the strict scrutiny standard. Thus, you must remedy the effects of the discrimination, but your plan must not place too much of a burden for the remedy on innocent nonminority workers.

CASE STUDY 3: FROM AA TO WORKFORCE DIVERSIFICATION PROGRAMS

You are a big-city HR director. For years, you and other city administrators have emphasized AA compliance by (1) making it a key organizational objective; (2) taking steps to reduce underutilization of protected classes by targeted programs for recruitment, testing, selection, training, and career development; and (3) establishing separate grievance systems to protect against sexual harassment, racial and ethnic discrimination, and other violations of employee rights.

Now, you hear increasing complaints about the adequacy of these AA compliance policies and programs from managers and employees. Managers ask, "Isn't there a way that we can create a climate of ethnic harmony without resorting to slow and costly administrative proceedings?" Employees in protected categories are unhappy: "Why don't you treat us as employees and human beings, rather than focusing only on gender, race, disability, or ethnicity? Aren't our skills and performance more important than these?" Other employees also dislike AA: "I can't get ahead in this organization because I'm a white male. We're discriminated against all the time, but we don't have any legal protection because we're not members of a protected class."

You decide that the best way to deal with these unsatisfactory conditions is by developing workforce diversification policies and programs. You prepare a formal presentation to the city manager and other department directors explaining how these policies and programs will help the city run better. They listen to your presentation, and then ask questions. How do you answer them?

Questions

1. How does workforce diversification differ from EEO or AA? Isn't this just "old wine in new bottles"?
2. Why does this diversification require changes in our mission, culture, or values? It's just a personnel issue, right? Can't we just say we value diversity, and let it go at that?
3. How will workforce diversification programs affect these specific areas of human resource management policy and practice: recruitment and retention, job design, education and training, benefits and rewards, and performance measurement and improvement?
4. Won't this put the AA office out of business? How will you ever sell it to them?
5. Has anyone else done this before? What results did they see?
6. If we're going to do it right, what are the characteristics of a successful diversification program? Of an unsuccessful one?

NOTES

[1] Sugrue, Thomas J. (1998). The tangled roots of affirmative action. *American Behavioral Management, 41* (7): 886–897.

[2] Miller, Fayneese, Xae Alicia Reyes, and Elizabeth Shaffer (1997). The contextualization of affirmative action. *American Behavioral Scientist, 41* (7): 223–231.

[3] The Civil Rights Act of 1964, P.L. 88–352, 78 Stat. 241, 28 USC ss. 1147 [1976].

[4] The Equal Employment Opportunity Act of 1972, P.L. 93–380, 88 Stat. 514, 2–0 USC 1228 [1976].

[5] Employment Standards Administration, U.S. Department of Labor, *Office of Federal Contract Compliance Programs: Director's Report Fiscal Year 1989* (Washington, DC, undated).

[6]U.S. Equal Employment Opportunity Commission (993). *Laws Enforced by the U.S. Equal Employment Opportunity Commission.* Washington, D.C.: U.S. EEOC.

[7]*Griggs v. Duke Power Company,* 28 L Ed 2d 158 (1971).

[8]Ibid.

[9]Ibid.

[10]*United States v. Paradise,* 94 L Ed 2d 203 (1987).

[11]*Johnson v. Transportation Agency,* 94 L Ed 2d 615 (1987).

[12]*United States v. Paradise.*

[13]*Richmond v. Croson,* 102 L Ed 2d 854 (1989).

[14]*Adarand v. Peña,* 115 S. Ct. 2097 (1995).

[15]Booth, William (March 2, 1998). Diversity and division. *The Washington Post (National Weekly Edition),* pp. 6–8.

[16]Booth, Ibid.

[17]Strenski, J. (1994). Stress diversity in employee communications. *Public Relations Journal, 50,* 32–35.

[18]Booth, Ibid.

[19]Kelly, Erin, and Frank Dobbin (1998). How affirmative action became diversity management, *American Behavioral Scientist, 41* (7): 960–984; and Agocs, Carol, and Catherine Burr (1996). Employment equity, affirmative action and managing diversity: assessing the differences. *International Journal of Manpower, 17* (4/5): 30–45.

[20]Wallsten, Kevin (1998). Diversity pays off in big sales for Toyota dealership. *Workforce (77)* 9: 91–92.

[21]Roosevelt, T.R. (1990). From affirmative action to affirming diversity. *Harvard Business Review, 68,* 107–117.

[22]The Hudson Institute (1988). *Opportunity 2000: Creating affirmative action strategies for a changing workforce.* Indianapolis: The Hudson Institute.

[23]National Performance Review (1993). *Reinventing human resource management.* Washington, DC: National Performance Review, Office of the Vice President.

[24]Schein, E. (1981). *Organizational culture and leadership.* San Francisco: Jossey-Bass.

[25]Jamieson, D., and J. O'Mara (1991). *Managing workforce 2000.* San Francisco: Jossey-Bass.

[26]Morgan, H., and K. Tucker (1991). *Companies that care.* New York: Fireside.

[27]U.S. Equal Employment Opportunity Commission (1991). *Americans with Disabilities Act handbook.* Washington, DC: U.S. Department of Justice, Equal Employment Opportunity Commission.

[28]Solomon, C. (1993). Managing today's immigrants. *Personnel Journal, 72,* 57–65.

[29]Rosow, J., and R. Zager (1988). *Training—the corporate edge.* San Francisco: Jossey-Bass.

[30]———(February 2000). EAPs: an effective response to diversity in the workplace. *IPMA News.* Alexandria, VA: International Personnel Management Association, p. 15.

[31]Rubaii-Barrett, N., and A. Beck (1993). Minorities in the majority: Implications for managing cultural diversity. *Public Personnel Management, 22,* 503–522.

[32]Loden, M., and J. Rosener (1991). *Workforce America! Managing employee diversity as a vital resource.* Homewood, IL: Business One Irwin.

[33]Soni, Vidu (2000). A twenty-first-century reception for diversity in the public sector: A case study. *Public Administration Review (60)* 5: 395–408.

[34]Grolsch, Stephan, and Liz Doherty (1999). Diversity management in practice. *International Journal of Contemporary Hospitality Management, 11* (6): 262–268.

[35]Denison, D. (1990). *Corporate culture and organizational effectiveness.* New York: John Wiley.

[36]Jahn, Karen A. (Summer 2000). Benefits and detriments of workplace conflict. *Public Manager,* pp. 24–26; Allison, John R. (2000). Five ways to keep disputes out of court. *Harvard Business Review, 78* (1): 166–176; and Carver, Todd B., and Albert Vondra (2000). Alternative dispute resolution: Why it doesn't work and why it does. *Harvard Business Review, 78* (3): 120–130.

[37]McCabe, Barbara Coyle, and Christopher Stream (Spring 2000). Diversity by the numbers: Government workforces 1980–1995. *Public Personnel Management (29)* 1: 93–106.

[38]Hale, Mary (1999). He says, She says: Gender and work life. *Public Administration Review (59)* 5: 410–424; and Miller, Will, Brinck Kerr, and Margaret Reid (1999). A national study of gender-based occupational segregation in municipal bureaucracies: Persistence of glass walls? *Public Administration Review (59)* 3: 219–230; and Crampton, Suzanne, and Jitendra M. Mishra (Spring 1999). Women in management. *Public Personnel Management (28)* 1: 87–106;

[39]Judy, Richard W., and Carol D'Amico (1997). *Workforce 2020: Work and Workers in the 20th Century.* Indianapolis: Hudson institute; and Fyock Catherine Dorton and Anne Marrs Dorton (February 1995). Welcome to the unretirement generation. *HR Focus (72)* 2: 22–24.

[40]———. (February 23, 1995). *USA Today,* p. 8A.

[41]Riccucci, Norma, and Charles Gossett (June 1996). Employment discrimination in state and local government: the lesbian and gay male experience. *American Review of Public Administration (26)* 2: 175–200.

[42]Lemann, N. (June 11, 1995). What happened to the case for affirmative action? *The New York Times Magazine,* pp. 36–43.

[43]Cox, T. H., and S. Blake (1991). Managing cultural diversity: Implications for organizational competitiveness. *Academy of Management Executive,* 5 (3), 45–56; Coleman, T. (October 1990). Managing diversity at work: The new American dilemma. *Public Management,* 72, 2–6.

[44]Ivancevich, John, and Jacqueline Gilbert (Spring 2000). Diversity management: Time for a new approach. *Public Personnel Management (29)* 1: 75–92.

[45]Naff, Katherine (Summer 1998). Progress toward achieving a representative federal bureaucracy: the impact of supervisors and their beliefs. *Public Personnel Management (27)* 2: 135–150.

[46]Gullett, Carlos Ray (Spring 2000). Reverse discrimination and remedial affirmative action in employment: Dealing with the paradox of nondiscrimination. *Public Personnel Management (20)* 1: 107–118.

[47]Mathews, Audrey (Summer 1998). Diversity: a principle of human resource management. *Public Personnel Management (27)* 2: 175–185.

8

Recruitment, Selection, and Promotion

On December 13, 2000, seven inmates escaped from a maximum-security prison near San Antonio. A nationwide manhunt with rewards totaling $500,000 for information leading to their capture was offered. Public attention and fear heightened after a police officer was slain on Christmas Eve, as the escapees held up a sporting goods store and obtained an arsenal of weapons. The Texas Board of Criminal Justice report cited a handful of prison staff who violated security procedures as responsible for the escape. Ryan Olsen, Executive Director of the American Federation of State, County and Municipal Employees blamed the escape on low salaries, resulting in understaffing and a 20 percent turnover in prison staff. When the escape at the Connally Prison occurred, nearly one-fourth of the correctional positions at the facility were not staffed. At a Texas State Senate Finance Committee Hearing, Senator John Whitmire expressed his concern for the safety of the guards and public in that the 116 prisons housing over 150,000 inmates had 2,500 vacant guard positions out of the total 26,000 statewide.[1]

This problem is not isolated to corrections. It can be found in other occupations, such as teachers, nurses, engineers, and those related to information technology.

The public sector is faced with many responsibilities that distinguish it from the private sector. Insuring public safety, justice, and environmental quality are just a few areas that go beyond the demands placed on private organizations. Recruiting and retaining highly qualified employees to provide the services citizens take for granted is becoming increasingly difficult in a competitive labor market because even though the responsibilities may differ, the private and public sectors are in direct competition for the same scarce qualified applicants. Even when the economy starts to weaken and the unemployment rate increases, the demand for labor in skilled and knowledge-based professions will remain.

Dynamism in the economy has forced many adaptations in the recruitment, selection, and retention of public employees. But much remains the same, anchored by conflicts that frequently characterize debate over the appropriate criteria to use in the recruitment and selection of job applicants and the promotion of employees. In addition to describing some of the technical aspects of recruitment and selection, this chapter reviews the value conflicts and the compromises that take place over the criteria used in these acquisition and planning functions. It discusses how the contemporary labor market impacts the view of work and how organizations of the future affect the acquisition function.

By the end of this chapter, you will be able to:

1. Define the acquisition function.
2. Describe the influence different values have on the objectives of the acquisition function.
3. Describe how characteristics of the workforce and the nature of contemporary work influence the acquisition function.
4. Describe ten steps in the recruitment and selection process.
5. Identify six practices that are likely to produce timely and valid hiring processes.
6. Discuss the comparative characteristics of centralized, decentralized, and electronic staffing techniques, and outsourcing.
7. Describe the concept of test validation and three validation strategies.
8. Describe the main provisions of the Americans with Disabilities Act and how the ADA affects recruitment and selection.

THE ACQUISITION FUNCTION

The second of the four functions every comprehensive personnel system must fulfill, **the acquisition function**, involves the acquisition of competencies that will enable an organization to fulfill its mission. It may seem impersonal to talk about the recruitment and hiring of people in terms of acquisition. But traditionally, the impersonality of merit systems—the most comprehensive and pervasive personnel systems in government—has been a virtue. In merit systems, personnel decisions are supposed to be made on the basis of an applicant's competencies and the performance that results from the employee's application of his or her competencies to the agency's work, not on the basis of whom an applicant or employee knows. Competencies traditionally have been seen in terms of knowledge, skills, and abilities (KSAs). The knowledge portion deals with the information that allows a person to perform from an informed perspective, e.g., theories, facts, and principles. The skills piece addresses the demonstrated abilities or proficiencies, which are developed and learned from past work and life experience. Recently, the concept of these qualifications has been expanded to include **personal attributes** reflected in a person's past effectiveness, e.g., attitudes, habits, traits, and behaviors.[2]

VALUE CONFLICTS AND THE ACQUISITION FUNCTION

President George W. Bush faced a sensitive political task once elected by a slim electoral margin in 2000. He pledged to reach out to a divided country, and one of his first opportunities to demonstrate that commitment came with his choice of cabinet appointees. To be sure every key appointment had solid Republican credentials. But in addition, virtually all represented a commitment to policy and/or managerial competence, and the cabinet comprised as diverse a group as anyone could remember.

Rod Paige, a long-time Republican partisan, joined the cabinet as Secretary of Education from his post as superintendent of the Houston school district, where he was credited for numerous successful reforms as well as building a sense of inclusion. For Secretary of Agriculture, the President turned to California, a key state in the national economy, instead of the traditional farm belt. Secretary Ann Veneman, a stalwart Republican, served as California's secretary of food and agriculture under Republican Governor Pete Wilson. Her experience was not lost on the senators that would have to confirm her appointment.

Most recruitment, selection, and promotion decisions are not made within a politicized environment. Yet it would be naive to argue that all are conducted according to routine procedures designed only to reward competence. Tension occurs when the elected leadership believes it could accomplish more to advance its political platform—legitimized through an election—if it had more influence over top-level classified positions. In these cases, partisan pressures crop up either formally or informally to influence career appointments. Over time, if these attempts are successful, the response is that the competencies necessary for informed public policy formulation and implementation are eroded. If the inroads result in notoriety or scandal involving political appointees, counter pressure is felt to strengthen the merit system.

Not only must merit systems respond to political pressures to accommodate the value of responsiveness, they also must adapt to public policy initiatives and political pressure stemming from the values of social equity and individual rights.[3] Arvey and Sackett write, "Most organizations value productivity; a great many also value cultural diversity. When selection systems known to contribute to the first detract from the second, as in the case of valid selection systems with adverse impact on protected groups, conflict arises. No clear solution has emerged, although what is surfacing is a clear sense that **fairness is a social issue** *rather than a scientific one* [emphasis added]."[4]

The most direct way of realizing social equity is through the establishment of selection quotas—for veterans, women, or racial and ethnic minorities. But the historic strength of merit systems and the ongoing appreciation of the need to bring expert knowledge to bear on public policy formulation and implementation decreases the availability of this solution. In fact, even though quotas are commonly associated with affirmative action, they are rarely part of formal affirmative action programs. It is useful to remind ourselves that where hiring or promotion ratios do exist, they have resulted from a court order that usually follows convincing evidence of egregious and systemic discrimination attributed to a specific employer. Even when hiring ratios are present, they are usually tempered by the phrase "qualified minorities," and they are not enforced if legitimate budgetary constraints place limits on hiring.

So far, we have talked about issues of political responsiveness, efficiency, and equity in the staffing process. The value of individual rights enters as protection from partisan political influence. Thus, acquisition routines that include open access and selection criteria based on competencies derived from the job to be performed have the effect of protecting the rights of individual job applicants to fair treatment.

The value of individual rights is also expressed significantly in the promotion process where upward mobility is allocated, or in layoffs, where jobs themselves are allocated through the planning and sanction functions. Collective bargaining systems, seeking to protect the rights and treatment of their members, are particularly oriented toward these kinds of allocation decisions rather than acquisition—recruitment and selection—decisions.

Even though a union may not seek to influence recruitment and selection decisions in non-apprenticeship positions, it will make every effort to convince newly appointed employees to join the union if the job falls within the union's bargaining unit. In Kansas City, Missouri, every newly appointed firefighter joins the union, even though Missouri is a right-to-work state. During the initial training period, peer pressure is applied to accomplish this goal.

One of the ways unions protect their members from management favoritism is by insisting that seniority play a major role in allocation decisions like promotion and layoffs. Similarly, they argue against contracting out of city services if unionized city employees currently perform those services. Again, where merit systems exist alongside collective bargaining systems, compromises are commonly reached. For example, it would not be unusual to see promotion scores calculated according to a formula that includes credit for an examination score and for years of service.

A major thesis of this book is that these value conflicts, whether between responsiveness and efficiency, efficiency and equity, or responsiveness and individual rights, cannot be avoided because the values themselves are fundamental to the political culture. As long as public jobs are considered scarce resources, these values will be brought to bear on acquisition and planning or allocation in personnel decisions. This results in merit systems under continual pressure from advocates of values other than efficiency, and public policy compromises that eventually are reflected in personnel routines, techniques, and regulations.

What complicates human resource management tremendously is that advocates of individual rights rely on legislation, civil service review boards, and judicial tools to constrain managers, while organization theorists and commentators are arguing for flexibility, consideration of contextual factors, and personal attributes in selection decisions. Advocates of these two views rarely have to confront each other. And, in the absence of an authoritative, legal reconciliation of these perspectives, managers dealing daily with personnel issues must find their own solutions.

EXTERNAL INFLUENCES AND CONTEMPORARY CHALLENGES

In addition to the conflict over values in the allocation of public jobs as scarce resources, other factors like demographics of the workforce and the nature of contemporary work also influence the acquisition function.

Workforce Demographics

Judy and Amico identify several characteristics of the future workforce:[5]

- If birthrates and immigration policy remain similar to today, immigration will be the chief cause of population and workforce growth in the decades ahead.
- Regional growth rates will vary appreciably with most growth occurring in the west and south. California, Texas, and Florida will account for 45 percent of the growth between 1995 and 2020.
- The average age will rise significantly including significant retirement of today's workforce, although many older Americans may continue working in various capacities. The number of younger people entering the workforce will not match those retiring, especially in the public sector.
- Women will constitute half the workforce in 2020—with a greater percent in the public sector, according to Smith.[6]
- Educational levels of immigrants and educational attainment of American born students will constitute significant obstacles to economic productivity.
- Additionally, 30 percent of American workers are in non-standard work arrangements: part-time, contract employees, temporary employees, and employees on call. Non-standard arrangements are increasing.

In light of these trends, Smith[7] concludes that public employers need to:

- Develop a strategy for attracting younger workers
- Investigate work/life benefits, child-care options, and transitional work for mothers
- Promote open and fair recruitment and selection procedures
- Open positions to non-traditional work arrangements

Nature of Work

In addition to strategic considerations resulting from workforce composition, the way work is performed requires rethinking of recruitment and selection functions as well. Most prominently, the increasing reliance on teams and teamwork emphasizes what traditionally are seen as important but non-task-related factors connected to productivity in the work environment. Borman and Motowidlo call them **contextual factors** and include:

- Volunteering to carry out task activities that are not formally a part of the job
- Persisting with extra enthusiasm or effort when necessary to complete task activities successfully
- Helping and cooperating with others
- Following organizational rules and procedures even when personally inconvenient
- Endorsing, supporting, and defending organizational objectives[8]

To these factors one might add conflict resolution skills and working within a demographically diverse environment. According to Borman and Motowidlo, these activities "do not support the technical core itself as much as they support the organizational, social, and psychological environment in which the technical core must function."[9] Their research shows that the contextual parts of manage-

ment jobs are substantial, and they should be considered in recruitment and selection processes. Along this line, Guion's literature review shows that social skills
and motivation are as important as knowledge in predicting job performance.[10]
The challenge is that these and other contextual factors relate to *personal attributes*,
complicating recruitment and selection processes which in the last few decades
have increasingly become more formalized and impersonal in order to avoid the
risk of civil rights violations in employment decisions. Guion asks, "What are decision makers to do if the people predicted to perform tasks well are not predicted to do very well contextually—or vice versa?"[11]

It seems reasonable to conclude that some of these contextual factors may be
more important in some situations than others. In his discussion of privatization of government services, Mintzberg has identified five models for managing government.[12]
Each has implications for recruitment and selection. In the normative-control model,
attitudes, values, and beliefs significantly influence task accomplishment, and he argues that they should be considered as part of the recruitment and selection process.
This is probably truer with regard to social service delivery than other government
work, but traditionally the virtue of public service has been found in the dedication
of public servants to the collective good.

In their edited volume, Hesselbein, Goldsmith, and Beckhard describe leadership and organizations of the future. The essence of their message is that traditional hierarchical structures will have limited utility because they are best suited
to operating in stable environments. In dynamic environments, more loosely structured organizations, composed of individuals with the capacity and willingness to
learn continually, are more effective.[13]

Competencies

Of the many changes in human resources management that have occurred
in the last several years is the addition of the term **competencies** to our vocabu-
lary. The state of Kansas defines competencies as, "the knowledge, skills and personal attributes that facilitate exceptional job performance and organizational
success." The state defines core competencies for three leadership levels: lead
workers, supervisors, and managers. In addition to these core competencies, they
identify those that are "global"—common to all classified positions; and those that
are "flexible"—unique to specific jobs.

The emphasis on competencies can be found in every progressive public
agency.[14] The state of Kansas identifies its competencies as:

- Achievement orientation
- Analytical thinking
- Business systems thinking
- Building relationships
- Communication
- Decision making
- Employee development
- Innovation

- Integrity
- Performance management
- Personal effectiveness
- Persuasion
- Problem resolution
- Project management
- Resource management
- Strategic planning
- Teamwork
- Values diversity

A review will find few common definitions of the term *competencies* and few common lists of what is included as a competency, thus complicating a discussion of the concept. But, the thrust is clear. The emphasis on strategic thinking has produced a direct emphasis in selection processes to determine what exactly should a job applicant be able to do and has the job applicant demonstrated that he/she is competent to do what is required. Interviewing has become more interactive as employers probe to identify candidates who have demonstrated valued competencies in the past. Training, the development function, is becoming more targeted towards competencies. And performance appraisal is being geared in that direction as well.

What is not clear in this movement is whether something truly new in human resources management is emerging or whether *competencies* is simply a synonym for the traditional terms: knowledge, skills, and abilities.

STEPS IN THE STAFFING PROCESS

Before proceeding with a discussion of recruitment and selection methods, it will be useful to identify various steps and responsibilities in the staffing process, which includes both planning and acquisition functions:

1. Identify human resource needs
2. Seek budgetary approval to create and/or fill the position
3. Develop valid selection criteria
4. Recruit
5. Test or otherwise screen applicants with questions unique to each position
6. Prepare a list of qualified applicants
7. Interview the most highly qualified applicants
8. Conduct background and reference checks where appropriate
9. Select the most qualified applicant
10. Extensive new hire orientation and training

Different jurisdictions or agencies will carry out these steps in different ways. The important point to be made here is that the line manager—the person the potential hire will actually be working for—is most heavily involved in steps 1, 2, 3, 7, 9 and 10. The personnel department's job is to assist the line manager in finding and hiring the best applicant (a staffing role) and to ensure that the staffing process takes place without the undue influence of politics or favoritism (a regulatory role).

Every step in this process is important, but in many cases the first step has become undervalued. It is easy to overlook this step when faced with the replacement of many positions that are embedded in organizational routines and services that go unquestioned. For example, replacing a secretary rarely triggers an examination of unit goals.

But, consider a different situation. Those of you reading this book probably are taking a university level course in human resources management. Let's say the department offering the course has a faculty vacancy. Here are some of the questions the department will ask itself:

- What will student demand be in the future and in what kinds of areas?
- How are present faculty prepared to meet future demands?
- Does the department possess the faculty competencies to teach in technology-supported formats anticipated for the future?
- To give it flexibility, should the department hire one full-time replacement or one or more part-time faculty as needs arise?

These questions require the strategic thinking outlined in Chapter 3. Without answering these questions, the remaining steps in the staffing process are tools with narrow purpose.

The next step is establishing the minimum qualifications for a position through job analysis. Then, the hiring authority must determine the appropriate method(s) to measure the extent to which applicants or employees possess these qualifications. In a tight labor market standard qualifications may be called into question. For example, should elimination from the applicant pool of those with criminal records be revisited when public services cannot be adequately provided because of labor shortages?

Nine methods are commonly used to assess qualifications: review of biographical data, aptitude tests, ability tests, performance exams, references, performance evaluation (for promotional assessment of current employees only), interviews, assessment centers, and a probationary period.

A review of an applicant's education and experience, through a standardized application form, is fundamental to the selection process.[15] Levine and Flory estimated that in 1976 over *one billion* résumés and job applications were completed and reviewed annually. One can imagine what that number is today! Even if education and experience are not important selection criteria, they do serve other important purposes: They are a tally of the number and the qualifications of applicants for research and record-keeping purposes; they provide a basis for interviewing; and they serve as a component of the personnel record of selected applicants. Research suggests that the data provided through job applications are more valid and reliable than information provided during interviews.[16]

Four types of written tests are commonly used for selection purposes although the use of written tests has decreased significantly in the past decade: aptitude, characteristics or traits, ability, and performance. Aptitude tests measure general intelligence or cognitive ability (for example, the federal government's now-discontinued Professional, Administrative Career Entrance (PACE) examination, or the Otis-Lennon). Aptitude tests are both relatively inexpensive to administer and score, and highly reliable. Some commentators are wary of the ease with which responses to psychological tests can be "faked" to match the presumed desired responses to the set of test scores. However, interim reliability checks can reduce the likelihood of this happening. The validity of such tests, however, can range from minimal to moderate, depending on the quality of the job analysis and the resulting **construct validation** of the aptitude as a predictor.

A second type of paper-and-pencil test measures personality traits or characteristics. The resulting personality profiles are then compared against profiles of current employees considered successful in the position or against traits judged as job related through construct validation. Examples are the Edwards Personality Preference Scale (EPPS) and the Minnesota Multiphasic Personality Inventory (MMPI).

Ability tests measure the extent to which applicants possess generalized abilities or skills related to job performance through empirical or construct validation. Examples would be verbal or mathematical ability, such as the Scholastic Aptitude Test (SAT) or the Graduate Record Examination (GRE). The more closely an ability test simulates actual job tasks and context, the more it becomes a performance test. A realistic typing or word processing test would be a good example. A performance test would be position-specific in that it would measure an applicant's ability to type a given kind of material on the specific machine used on the job. Research studies generally confirm that ability tests, which result from job analysis, are logically related to subsequent job performance.[17]

Interviews are a popular selection or promotion method.[18] Most organizations will not hire an employee without one because they believe the interview gives them the opportunity to observe an applicant's appearance and interpersonal skills and to ask questions about subjects not adequately covered on the application form. However, interviews are not recommended as a primary selection method. Not only do they take a good deal of the supervisor's time, but they also require interviewing skills on the part of the supervisor or interviewing panel. Since interviews are a prime method of rejecting candidates who look good on paper but might not fit into an organization, they are subject to close scrutiny as potentially invalid selection criteria.

What, then, are some good guidelines to follow concerning interviews? Behavioral interviewing is a method starting to become popular in achieving the desire to understand an applicant's competencies including personal attributes. Interview questions are open-ended and request that the applicant provide actual occurrences of past employment that address the topic of the question. As an example, "provide a time when you found yourself confronted with an angry customer and explain how you handled this situation." These types of questions allow the reviewer to see how the applicant views a situation, what priorities were held, and what they consider to be effective actions. Behavioral interviewing relies on predefined questions, but is less structured in that questions may be expanded upon based on the response given by the applicant. Panel interviews (those involving more than one interviewer) are more reliable than individual interviews, and can use either style, structured or less structured, though they also increase the cost of this already expensive selection method.

Rodger M. Matthews, Kansas Division of Personnel Services states, "The State of Kansas has improved its recruitment and selection process by eliminating testing and enhancing the registration process with a qualitative approach to measuring competencies. The emphasis has shifted to assessing the level, quality, complexity, and behavioral descriptors performed rather than on the amount of time spent performing a skill or the testing ability of applicants. The qualitative approach allows the state to de-emphasize 'minimum qualifications' and concentrate on the 'competencies' of an outstanding employee throughout the applicant process" (February 2001). In essence, the goal is to identify well-rounded applicants who posses the knowledge, skills/abilities, and personal attributes needed to be successful. Lets say an engineer has outstanding competencies within the field of engineering, but is unable to personally interact, contribute, and cooperate with others. This person may be viewed as a liability rather than an asset in an organization needing projects completed under a team approach versus individually. Organizations bear responsibility in becoming familiar with their own work culture, workflow structures and demands before recruiting, to ensure a proper match and to allow success to both the new employee and organization.

The open-ended and probing nature of some interviewing has replaced the strict, by the book, stick to a specific list of questions approach that prevailed a decade ago. In part, the reason has to do with increased emphasis on finding the right candidate, more acceptability of practices that promote fairness in selection processes, and less prominence of the law as the dominating force in human resources management.

References are another selection tool. They are usually used to verify educational and employment records or to obtain information about the applicant's skills or personality. Their validity depends upon the opportunity that the writer has had to observe the applicant and upon the relatedness of this relationship to the prospective job. Because recommendation letters are overwhelmingly positive, readers frequently fall into the trap of looking for the smallest of differences as they attempt to distinguish one applicant from another. A better use of reference letters is to stimulate questions that can be asked in an interview.

Reference checks pose challenging legal problems in today's society. If employers fail to reveal damaging yet relevant information about a former employee or if they give out the damaging information but it unfairly harms the employee's chances of obtaining employment, they may become involved in litigation.

Previous performance evaluations are often used to assess potential for reassignment or promotion. They are valid to the extent that the ratings are based on job performance and this performance involves the same skills or abilities required in the prospective job. Their reliability is based on the extent of inter-rater agreement among previous supervisory evaluations.

Assessment centers may be used to stress performance on job-related tasks. They are used in both the public and the private sectors; in the public sector, their use is most prevalent among law enforcement organizations. If performance criteria are validated, they can be useful in selection, promotion, and career development. Candidates may be given an "in-basket" full of documents that an employee might confront in a typical day and be asked how the various items should be dealt with. A panel would then judge the candidates' responses.

The last selection or promotion method is the probationary appointment. This technique possesses the highest possible validity and reliability factors because it measures actual performance on the job. However, it also carries the highest cost and greatest risk to the organization, since a potentially unqualified employee may occupy a critical position until he or she makes enough serious mistakes to be considered unfit. The use of the probationary period places upon supervisors the responsibility of weeding out unsatisfactory or marginal employees before they attain career status (and hence the right to grievance hearings to protest a discharge after they have attained a "property interest" in their jobs); it places upon personnel managers the responsibility of developing valid probationary period evaluation systems. After an employee is no longer on probationary status, their "property right" makes it extremely difficult to dismiss the employee. The "property right" representing individual rights appears to have greater value than efficiency. An employer must show that an employee has been given substantial "due process" before a permanent employee may be dismissed.

Because each of these methods differs in value orientation, cost validity, and reliability, organizations must compare them.[19] Table 8–1 summarizes their comparative advantages.

In this section, we have described steps involved in the staffing process. We have made it sound logical, rational, and uniform. The fact of the matter is that in today's competitive labor market, the most rational and valid recruitment and selection procedures may take the longest time to implement. In a competitive environment, this may mean the loss of good candidates to other employers. Government can no more afford the loss of qualified candidates than can the private sector.

TABLE 8–1   Comparison of Selection Methods

Method	Validity	Reliability	Cost
1. Biodata	moderate	high	low
2. References (letters of recommendation)	low	low	low
3. Aptitude tests	moderate	moderate	low
4. Characteristics of trait tests	moderate	moderate	low
5. Ability tests	moderate	moderate	moderate
6. Performance tests	high	moderate	moderate
7. Interviews	low	low	high
8. Assessment centers	moderate	high	high
9. Probationary appointment	very high	very high	very high

TIMELY HIRING PRACTICES

Acknowledging tight labor markets, the International Personnel Management Association and NAPSE Human Resources Benchmarking Project asked human resources professionals about their hiring habits.[20] Several best or promising practices were identified to foster timely yet valid hiring:

- Decentralization that gives more latitude, authority, and responsibility to hiring managers
- Flexibility, for example, in the number of applicants that must be interviewed
- Technology, especially in the submission of applications and development of data bases to select list of qualified applicants
- Tracking and monitoring practices to determine if they are meeting the dual criteria of timeliness and validity
- Use of alternatives to written exams such as skill inventories and résumé screens
- Continuously recruiting for hard-to-fill and high volume job classifications

While these steps will increase the timeliness of the hiring process, Kellough raises the possibility that decentralization and flexibility could undermine merit principles.[21] The fundamental question here is whether merit values and operating principles have anchored themselves strongly enough in human resources management's thinking that decentralization and flexibility pose minor risk.

RECRUITMENT AND SELECTION MODELS

Because both the number of positions agencies need to fill and the conditions under which staffing is conducted may vary, staffing models differ with circumstances. Generally, four types are possible: centralized, decentralized, electronic models, and outsourcing.

Centralized Recruitment

If the agency has several thousand employees, and if different departments recruit large numbers of clerical or technical employees for the same types of positions, **centralized recruitment and selection** will frequently be used because it is more efficient.

If recruitment is centralized, the central personnel agency will be responsible for requesting from agency personnel managers periodic estimates of the number and type of new employees needed in the future (the next quarter or fiscal year). The staffing needs of all agencies are entered into a computer, after being classified by occupational code and salary level, and a summary listing of all projected new hiring needs is produced.

In reality, producing an accurate projection of new hiring needs is rarely this simple. To begin with, it is not always possible for agencies to predict their needs a year ahead of time. A political crisis or budget cut can drastically affect recruitment needs, and hence the quality of the estimate. Central personnel agency recruiters also realize that agency personnel managers will tend to overestimate the number of employees they require, just because from their point of view it is better to have too many applicants than too few. Naturally this conflicts with the need of the central personnel agency to reduce selection costs by reducing the number of applicants to the minimum number needed to ensure that all available positions are filled with qualified applicants. In addition, specialized positions require a greater ratio of applicants to projected vacancies, because a higher percentage of applicants are likely to be rejected by the selecting agency as not meeting the specialized requirements of the position.

While there are many drawbacks to centralized human resources management, two factors argue in its favor. First, the amount of variation in the recruitment and selection process in individual agencies is reduced, thus benefiting the values of social equity and individual rights. Second, it may be easier to advance systemwide human resources management policy—like emphasizing the recruitment and selection of minorities.

Decentralized Recruitment

Decentralized recruitment and selection is traditionally likely to occur in agencies that are relatively small, for which recruitment needs are limited, and where each agency employs different types of workers. Increasingly, it is used in larger units.[22] It is almost always used for professional, scientific, or administrative positions peculiar to a particular agency. For example, smaller municipalities may not have enough vacancies to utilize the services of a central personnel department. Or the department heads may have successfully argued that their particular employees are unique and that it is more appropriate to handle recruitment and selection on a departmental level. Police and fire departments are likely to make this argument at the municipal level.

If recruitment is decentralized, individual public agencies will go through essentially the same steps required for centralized recruitment, except that dealings with the central personnel agency are limited. Agency personnel managers will work directly with the supervisors in their agencies to make periodic estimates of hiring needs. Then agency recruiters will meet with agency affirmative action specialists to determine whether recruitment efforts should be targeted toward specific minority groups. After evaluating both the need for new employees and the diversity goals of the agency, the agency personnel director will determine what recruitment efforts are required. The job announcement process is exactly the same as that of a central personnel agency, except that applicants are requested to send their applications to the specific agency.

The trend in human resources management is towards decentralization. In response to criticisms that personnel practices are burdensome, time-consuming, and unresponsive to sister agencies, the federal government has increasingly decentralized recruitment and selection over the past decade. Presently, over 80 percent of federal jobs in the executive branch are filled through decentralized agency processes. Kellough has expressed concern that decentralized personnel processes could lead to more violations of merit principles.[23] On the other hand, a recent

U.S. Merit Systems Protection Board report concluded that the decentralization has occurred with no corruption linked to "spoils," no decline in the quality of federal employees, and increases in diversity.[24]

"I have authority now that I only dreamed of five years ago" is a comment by John Martello, Human Resources Director at the Kansas State School for the Blind, about the decentralization underway within the State of Kansas. He gives the following example of how "Classification Authority" was issued to the agency by the central Division of Personnel Services, for the first time in its history. This allows the Kansas State School for the Blind to directly administer FTE and position management in a more responsive manner, with regular audits by the central Division of Personnel Services for compliance within established classification standards.

Some agencies utilize a combination of centralized and decentralized recruitment. For example, a central personnel agency may authorize individual agencies to recruit and test applicants independently, subject to audit by the central personnel agency once they have been hired. This compromise will provide for a greater degree of centralized control than is possible with a decentralized system, while simultaneously providing agencies with timelier and more flexible recruitment available from a central personnel agency.

Electronic Recruitment

For twenty-five years, touch-tone dedicated phone lines have allowed agencies to advertise current vacancies, and to refer applicants to agencies with hiring needs. Now, the development of the Internet allows agencies and associations to advertise current vacancies through on-line **job banks** and various websites, including an agency's own website; and permits applicants to submit résumés and have their qualifications evaluated through the establishment of a "virtual" electronic "hiring hall."[25] Among the available job banks is the federal government's central website (www.usajobs.opm.gov) and America's Job Bank (www.ajb.dni.us/), a cooperative effort between the U.S. Department of Labor and some 2,000 state employment service offices, and free commercial websites, such as www.monster.com. Jobs are listed by category, by state, and in other ways as well.

Job Bank includes links to many other websites, including those of the states. Organizations can even target recruitment efforts to specific vocations and professions. An example, posting a vacancy on www.spedex.com allows for a convenient, comprehensive, and cost effective means of targeting blind education specialists within special education profession. A net search is guaranteed to produce numerous other sites of interest to job seekers and employers. Applicants are able to leave their employment history and qualifications electronically on file for employers to categorize and then prioritize through massive database searches.[26] Interviews can even be arranged and conducted via Internet through various communication applications, and the transfer of electronic applications with encrypted signatures is considered valid in some states.

Outsourcing

Outsourcing and the elimination of personnel services historically provided by government have increased over the last decade. This increased use of contracting to achieve economies of scale without sacrificing core organizational competencies has meant that agencies are increasingly choosing to use outsourcing as a recruitment device. In particular, they are likely to use employment services for hiring temporary employees, or executive search firms ("headhunters") for professional and managerial recruitment.

The efficiency in time of outsourcing for temporary workers is evident. The process is shortened noticeably with responsibility for recruitment and selection resting with the temporary employment agency. And while this type of outsourcing seems to make sense, it raises a larger issue: Is it necessary for a government jurisdiction itself to recruit and select for other positions or can these activities be performed just as effectively by private employment agencies under contract? Searches for chief administrative officers and some department heads now are conducted by executive search firms. Why not other positions?

Initially the goal of outsourcing was to save money. Temporary employment agencies are used to aid in locating qualified candidates in a tight labor market to augment the recruitment efforts of the agency. But it also allows an organization to concentrate on its mission, that which it can do uniquely. Why not contract with a private employment agency for recruitment and selection with the stipulation that all applicant pools will contain individuals with required competencies and will reflect demographically the appropriate labor market?

In some ways, the real challenge here is first to identify what the agency or government jurisdiction considers its core mission and values. Tom Lewinsohn, former personnel director in Kansas City, Missouri, and past president of the International Personnel Management Association, suggests that recruitment and selection are so integrally connected to the concept of merit, a core governmental value, that outsourcing these activities undermines the concept of the public service.[27]

Seven Recruitment and Selection Models

The availability of centralized, decentralized, electronic recruitment methods, and outsourcing means that the actual staffing process followed by public agencies is complex, and varies with the nature and context of the agency. Table 8–2 depicts seven recruitment and selection routines that take place in Lawrence, Kansas, a council-manager city with a permanent population of some 80,000. By reviewing the information, one can find a number of the steps and methods already discussed as well as the influence of the values of efficiency, social equity, responsiveness, and individual rights. Knowledge, skills/abilities, and personal attributes are weighted very heavily in each of the selection processes. For both the non-public-safety and public-safety entry-level positions, usually the city administers a test of knowledge or skill supplemented by interviews and reference checks. For all positions in the city, a preemployment physical includes a drug-screening test. Oral interview boards have replaced interviews with individual supervisors, in order to get a broader range of opinion on the suitability of applicants. Interview boards also protect the individual rights of applicants to fair and equal treatment. A review of licenses and certificates is particularly important in screening applicants for technical positions. In the last few years, electronic mail bulletin boards and a dedicated information phone line have expanded recruitment efforts.

No paper-and-pencil testing takes place for department heads or for the city manager, but the national recruitment procedure indicates a desire to secure professionally trained talent. In addition, the interview board usually includes a professional in a related field, one who is not a member of the city staff. For example, selection of a new finance director might include a banker or the city's auditor as a member of the interview board.

Social equity is particularly noticeable in the public-safety positions, where special efforts are made in the recruitment process. Recent *recruitment* efforts for police and firefighters featured a poster advertising the positions and showing minority and female officers and firefighters; special booths at a shopping mall in the metropolitan Kansas City area with concentrations of minority populations; special visits to a junior college with a large minority population; and special outreach in the Topeka, Kansas area working with the YWCA to identify female candidates. No special efforts were made to show preference to women and minorities in any of the four *selection* processes.

The value of responsiveness is apparent only in the selection for city manager. The manager serves at the pleasure of the governing body, and elected officials are heavily involved in all phases of the selection process, whether they hire an executive search consultant or handle the process through their own personnel department. They employ criteria designed to determine whether the manager will work well with the governing body and will fit in with the political and social culture of the city.

While Table 8–2 shows the value of responsiveness isolated to selection of the city manager that is not an entirely accurate portrayal. In many jurisdictions, even though the chief administrative officer legally can hire and fire department heads, it often is wise to consult with the governing body or mayor before doing so. For example, hiring and firing a police chief in most communities is fraught with potential political problems; the same often is true of the planning director.

Finally, the table shows that recruitment for temporary and part-time positions is not nearly as time consuming when compared to other categories of employees. Efficiency is the dominant value with little attention paid to individual rights.

Table 8–2 was developed in 1997. In 2001, we asked the director of administrative services for the City of Lawrence to review the table for accuracy. His comments are entirely consistent with other comments in this chapter that staffing has become a more challenging management function as the supply of labor has shrunk. He said, "I found little has changed from the basic processes found in the table. However, because of the extremely tight labor market and with rapid changes in technology, I found several elements within the model have changed."[28] These changes include:

- Speeding up the hiring process so as not to lose good applicants to competing employers
- Becoming more aggressive in retention of current employees

TABLE 8-2 Recruitment and Selection Process in Lawrence, Kansas

Entry-Level Positions (Non-Public-Safety)	Public-Safety Positions	Department Director	City Manager (Chief Administrative Officer)	Temporary Employment Agency	Part-Time Positions	Technical Positions
RECRUITMENT						
• Local newspaper • Announcements to 80 local agencies including Jobs Service Center, NAACP, Haskell Indian Nations University • E-Mail Bulletin Boards • Dedicated information telephone line	• Local and regional newspapers • Announcements to 80 local agencies and law enforcement and fire agencies • Special effort to recruit women and minorities • E-Mail Bulletin Boards • Dedicated information telephone line	• Local and regional newspapers • Professional associations (national) • Announcements to 80 local agencies • Dedicated information telephone line • E-mail bulletin boards	• Local and regional newspapers • Professional associations • Announcements to 80 local agencies • E-mail bulletin boards • Dedicated information telephone line	Bid process on key positions	• Local newspaper • Announcements to 80 local agencies • E-mail bulletin boards • Dedicated information telephone line	• Local and regional newspapers • Professional associations national and/or state/regional • Announcements to 80 local agencies • E-mail bulletin boards • Dedicated information telephone line
SELECTION						
• Applications screened by personnel office	• Written test • Physical fitness evaluation	• Applicants screened by personnel/office	• Applications screened by consultant/	Order position as needed for specified time needed	• Applications screened by department	• Applicants screened by personnel office and department

•Reduced applicant pool reviewed by hiring authority •Test where appropriate •Interview with board •Reference checks •Post-offer physical, including drug screening •Appointment by personnel director	•Interview with board •Interview by chief •Reference checks •Post-offer physical, including drug screening and physiological test for police officers •Appointment by department director	selection committee/ city manager •Reduced pool reviewed by city manager •Assessment lab •Committee interview •Interview with city manager •Reference checks •Post-offer physical, including drug screening •Appointment by city manager	personnel department/committee of the governing body/entire governing body •Reference checks •Interview with governing body (may also include visits with department heads) •Post-offer physical including drug screening •Appointment by governing body		•Interview by supervisor •Reference checks •Appointment by supervisor	•Reduce pool reviewed by division manager •Assessment lab •Interview with committee •Interview with department director •Reference checks •Test on technical data •Review of certificates •Appointment by supervisor/ department director

LENGTH OF TOTAL PROCESS

4–8 weeks	3–4 months	2–3 months	3–5 months	1–5 days	3–5 weeks	2–3 months

TRAINING

On the job	•Law enforcement academy •Fire training program	On the job	On the job	On the job	On the job	•On the job •Technical training as needed to retain certifications

- Conducting special recruitment to hire experienced police officers with special rate of pay as opposed to everyone starting at the bottom
- Coordinating with the state employment office
- Enhancing our presence on the internet including on-line applications
- Expanding outreach for recruitment with an additional recruiter position

TEST VALIDATION AND THE ACQUISITION FUNCTION

A test is any device used to separate qualified from unqualified applicants for selection or promotion. Included are written examinations as well as selection methods not normally thought of as tests, including interviews, medical examinations, drug tests, background investigations, and physical requirements.

To be valid, a test must separate qualified from unqualified applicants on the basis of knowledge, skills, or ability related to job performance.

Social equity advocates are often associated with promoting preferential treatment of minorities and women. But their greatest and most lasting contribution to personnel management may prove to be in the area of **test validation**. For in seeking to remove barriers to equal opportunity based on discriminatory hiring criteria (those based on race, religion, or other non-merit factors), social equity advocates have been responsible for general acceptance of the merit system principle that job applicants are to be chosen on the basis of job-related criteria.

What is a job-related test or selection device? The answer is simple to state but difficult to put into practice. It is a test that does a good job of predicting job performance. For example, an interview process is valid if those who do well on the interview do well on the job and if those who do not do well in the interview, do not do well on the job (or would not do well if hired). To simplify our discussion, we will talk in terms of valid and invalid when in reality we are talking in degrees. No selection device can predict with 100 percent accuracy who will and will not do well on the job. Are undergraduate grades a good predictor of subsequent performance in graduate school? For those who enter graduate school right after their undergraduate education, the answer is probably yes—but it is not foolproof. But, for those who have been out of school for a long time, they tend to be less reliable, except at the extremes. Then, there is a subsequent question: Are good grades in graduate school a good predictor of good career performance?

Figure 8–1 shows in matrix form the possible relationships between test scores or other selection devices and job performance.

The more valid a test, the more **true positives** and **true negatives** it will produce. In other words, those who do well on the test in fact will do well on the

FIGURE 8–1   Relationships between Test Scores and Job Performance

		Job Performance	
		High	**Low**
	High	True Positive	False Positive
Test Score			
	Low	False Negative	True Negative

job, and those who do poorly on the test will do poorly on the job. The less valid a selection method, the more likely it will produce **false positives** and **false negatives**. A false positive is a person who does well on the test, but does not turn out to do well on the job. The test falsely predicted a good job performance. A false negative occurs where a person fails to do well on the test but does (or would do well) on the job. Social equity advocates are mostly concerned with selection methods that produce false negatives when those clustered in that quadrant are members of disadvantaged classes. An example would be an arbitrary height requirement for firefighters in an area that has a high Asian population. It is likely that women in general and Asian men will be discriminated against with this requirement. The burden is on the employer to show that the height requirement produces a minimum number of false negatives and that those that are produced are not systematically drawn from a disadvantaged population— unless, of course, the test is valid; that is, the height requirement is indeed related to job performance.

TEST VALIDATION METHODS

Three established validation strategies are acceptable: empirical, construct, and content validation. *Empirical validation*, also known as **criterion validation**, requires that a test score be significantly correlated, in a statistical sense, with important elements of job performance. The expectation is that those who perform well on the job will have done well on the preemployment test.

Construct validation involves both identifying psychological traits and aptitudes that relate to successful job performance and devising a test that measures these traits. For example, most insurance companies give psychological tests to applicants for sales positions. These tests purport to measure the applicant's congeniality, outgoing nature, liking for people, and other traits supposedly related to ability to sell. Police departments require a psychological profile on new recruits. In the sales example, tests have been developed by identifying the best salespeople in the organization, giving them a psychological test measuring a variety of traits, and establishing a personality profile of the "ideal salesperson." Police professionals are trying to eliminate individuals with unacceptable traits—overly aggressive, inflexible—from the applicant pool. Profiles are then used as a yardstick against which the characteristics of applicants are measured. Those who approximate this yardstick move on in the selection process; those who do not are more carefully screened.

Content validation requires that the job be analyzed to determine its duties; the particular conditions that make work easy or difficult; realistic performance standards; the competencies required to perform these tasks up to these standards under these conditions; and the minimum qualifications required to ensure that an applicant would have these competencies. For example, it is logical to assume that a prison guard, responsible for transporting prisoners by car from one location to another, would need to know how to drive. An example of the application of the relationship between content validation and job analysis is given in the section on results-oriented job descriptions (RODs), in Chapter 4.

Content validation, therefore, links the functions of affirmative action and job analysis. In addition, it connects them with a third function, productivity. This is because the establishment of a logical relationship between duties and qualifications is not only a defense of validity, it is also a justification for discriminating between qualified and unqualified applicants on the basis of their anticipated performance. It would follow from this that a content-valid job description (such as an ROD) could be used to assess the validity of a selection or promotion criterion by measuring the performance of an employee hired on the basis of that criterion.

AMERICANS WITH DISABILITIES ACT (ADA)[29]

While civil rights legislation and judicial action have had significant impact on recruitment, selection, and test validation, those effects now have been felt, and public employers have incorporated the legislative intent, judicial rulings, and administrative regulations into human resource policy and routine practices. In other words, it is no big deal anymore when interview questions are connected to a specific job. In fact, the surprise comes when they are not.

The Americans with Disabilities Act may do for the disabled what the Civil Rights Act of 1964 did for racial minorities and women. The Americans with Disabilities Act (ADA) of 1990 prohibits discrimination against the disabled in areas including public and private employment, availability of public services, and access to public accommodations, transportation, and telecommunications. The employment provisions of the act have been applied to employers with more than twenty-five employees since July 26, 1992, and to employers with fifteen or more employees after July 26, 1994. They prohibit discrimination against *qualified* individuals with disabilities, defined as an individual with a disability who meets the skill, experience, education, and other job-related requirements of a position held or desired, and who, with or without reasonable accommodation, can perform the essential functions of a job. What constitutes a reasonable accommodation and an undue hardship on an employer obligated to make the accommodation are dealt with in Chapter 12. Here, we will focus on the recruitment and selection issues more directly.

Who Is Protected?

The definition of individuals with a disability is quite broad—some estimates place the number of qualified individuals at 43 million! A person with a disability is someone who (1) has a physical or mental impairment that substantially limits one or more of his or her major life activities; (2) has a record of such an impairment; or (3) is regarded as having such an impairment.

Recent Supreme Court cases have clarified the term "disabled."[30] The court ruled that a disability should be considered in its treated rather than untreated state. In other words, a person who wears eye glasses that mitigates a vision condition is not considered disabled even if without the glasses the person would be considered disabled. A second ruling is that all cases must be viewed on an individualized basis. In other words, an employer need not presume that everyone with a condition that might be considered a disability in fact is disabled according to the ADA. The ADA specifically states that certain individuals are not protected by its provisions. Persons who currently use drugs illegally are not individuals protected under the ADA when an employer takes action because of their continued use of drugs. However, people who have been rehabilitated and do not currently use drugs illegally, or who are in the process of completing a rehabilitation program may be protected by the ADA. The act also states that homosexuality and bisexuality are not impairments and therefore are not disabilities under the ADA.

What Practices Are Prohibited?

Employers cannot discriminate against people with disabilities in regard to any employment practice. This includes application, testing, hiring, assignments, evaluation, disciplinary action, training, promotion, medical examinations, layoff/recall, termination, compensation, leave, or benefits.

Applicants may be asked about their ability to perform specific job functions. But an employer may not ask a job applicant about the existence, nature, or severity of a disability. An employer may not make medical inquiries or conduct a medical examination until after a job offer has been made. A job offer may be conditioned on the results of a medical examination or inquiry, but only if this is required for all entering employees in similar jobs. Medical examinations of employees must be job-related and consistent with the employer's business needs.

It is not a violation of the ADA for employers to use drug tests to find out if applicants or employees are currently using drugs illegally. Tests for illegal use of drugs are not subject to the ADA's restrictions on medical examinations. Employers may hold illegal users of drugs and alcoholics to the same performance and conduct standards as other employees.[31]

The ADA's Implications for Public Personnel Managers

Because the employer must demonstrate that a requested accommodation is unreasonable, or that the employee could not in any case perform the essential functions of the job, employers now may have the burden of proof shifted to them to demonstrate a rational basis for employment decisions. At a minimum, the ADA reinforces requirements in existing civil rights laws that personnel policies be rational, and that selection and evaluation criteria be job related. Job analysis criteria and procedures may need to be clarified, so that each position includes information on essential functions and requisite competencies. This requirement comes at a time when human resource specialists and academicians are questioning the formality and utility of existing job analysis techniques, which tend to reinforce existing ways of thinking about work and organizations rather than incorporate futuristic thinking. This is another of many examples where individual rights and managerial flexibility associated with efficiency can create tension in human resources management. These inevitable tensions add to the challenges of supervision and management.

SUMMARY

The acquisition function reflects conflict among the competing values of responsiveness, efficiency, individual rights, and social equity as the basis of allocating public jobs. The goal of most public employers is to hire and promote those with the best knowledge, skills/abilities, and personal attributes to perform the job. But other interests—represented by politics, collective bargaining, and diversity—frequently challenge this goal. Ultimately, the differences in value and policy orientations must be transformed into workable recruitment, selection, and promotion procedures that permit routine, cost-effective application and promise fair treatment for applicants.

As the workforce continues to change and the availability of qualified labor becomes scarcer, the public sector will need to become more responsive and resilient to compete with the private sector for the same resources. The acquisition of resources will become less bureaucratic and more in-line with the private sector. The changing nature of work and organizations affects recruitment and selection processes as well. As organizations become less hierarchical, more is demanded of employees than traditional competencies connected to a narrowly defined job. As the context within which public agencies operate becomes more heterogeneous and unstable, job analyses become less dependable, recruitment is expanded to include situational skills and personal traits, such as the ability to contribute to a work group. And selection decisions become more tentative as loyalty between employee and employer is weakened by contemporary trends toward downsizing and privatization.

While contemporary trends question traditional approaches to job analysis, recruitment, and selection, legal requirements imposed by the Civil Rights Act of 1964 and the Americans with Disabilities Act are built on traditional assumptions about work and reinforce the status quo of personnel management.

KEY TERMS

acquisition function	decentralized recruitment and selection
centralized recruitment and selection	fairness as a social issue
competencies	job bank
construct validity	personal attributes
content validity	test validation
contextual factors	true and false positives and negatives
criterion validity	

DISCUSSION QUESTIONS

1. How does one's value perspective influence the objectives of the recruitment and selection process?
2. What does it mean to say that fairness is a social judgment rather than a scientific calculation? What are the implications for the tension between efficiency and diversity?
3. Describe how workforce demographics and the nature of contemporary work influence the acquisition of public employees.
4. What kind of flexible personnel policies are needed to accommodate the caregiving needs of the modern family where both mother and father work? Or where the family consists of children with a single parent?

5. What is meant by contextual factors that influence how well a person performs as an organizational member? How easy do you think it is to recruit and select for these factors? Does an emphasis on contextual factors conflict with an emphasis on recruiting for diversity?
6. Identify ten steps in the recruitment and selection process. In an organization you are familiar with, which steps are the most difficult to perform? Why?
7. Identify six timely hiring practices and describe how several might be employed to recruit and select for a job category you are familiar with where demand exceeds supply of applicants and service is suffering from staffing shortages.
8. Compare and contrast centralized and decentralized recruitment techniques.
9. Outsourcing or privatization of government services displaces value issues governments deal with in recruitment and selection processes. Which values do you think will be emphasized by private employment agencies? Can the benefits of outsourcing be realized if vendors are required to incorporate the values of responsiveness, efficiency, social equity, and individual rights into their practices?
10. Review the recruitment and selection processes in Table 8–2 and identify the values emphasized in each model. How would you improve these processes?
11. Describe the concept and importance of test validation and three validation strategies. How have affirmative action and advocates of social equity and individual rights advanced the importance of test validation, and therefore the value of efficiency?
12. How might the Americans with Disabilities Act become as important as the Civil Rights Act of 1964? How do the legal requirements for job analysis implied in two acts conflict with modern theories about future organizations?

EXERCISE: DRIVING FORCES OF CHANGE IN RECRUITMENT AND SELECTION

This exercise is best conducted with mid-career students in class.
Depending upon the size of the class, divide into discussion groups.

- Each group should make two lists. First, make a list of how recruitment and selection processes have changed over the last decade. Then, make a list of recruitment and selection processes that have remained the same.
- Share the lists and come up with one agreed-upon list of what has changed and one list of what has remained the same.
- Identify the driving forces behind the changes that have occurred. Are these forces internal organizational forces or forces external to organizations? If external, what conclusions would you draw about the relationship between internal organizational change and external organizational environments?
- Regarding those aspects that have remained the same, which of the four values— responsiveness/representation, efficiency, social equity, and individual rights—seems evident in them? How do the values you have identified compare to the values that underlie the merit principles listed in Chapter 1? We often talk about organizational values that provide anchors for organizations in times of change. Would you say that the values that underpin merit systems qualify as anchor values?

CASE STUDY: INFORMATION TECHNOLOGY RECRUITMENT

Recruiting in information technology and related fields poses a significant challenge to many public sector organizations that do not pay at market rates; and where recruitment and selection procedures take so much time qualified candidates may find jobs with other employers.

Let's look at what it takes to recruit and hire employees skilled in IT. One of the nation's leading economists, Federal Reserve Chairman Alan Greenspan, told a business audience in North Carolina, "The United States is currently confronting what can best be described as another industrial revolution. The rapid acceleration of computer and telecommunications technologies is a major reason for the appreciable increase in our productivity in this expansion, and is likely to continue to be a significant force in expanding standards of living into the twenty-first century."[32] Groups such as the Information Technology Association of America and the U.S. Department of Commerce's Office of Technology Policy identified what they considered "substantial evidence that the United States is having trouble keeping up with the demand for new information technology workers."[33]

Even when the economy starts to weaken and companies start downsizing, demand for labor in knowledge-based professions will remain. Unfortunately, an economic downturn hinders governments' ability to attract and retain needed labor. "In a recession, taxes don't necessarily decline, but if they stop growing and your expenses grow, you have a problem," said Donald Boyd, Director of the Fiscal Studies Program at the Rockefeller Institute of Government in Albany, New York.[34]

When budget pressures are combined with a labor shortage, delaying IT capital projects, outsourcing and contracting out more technology is usually the solution. Some government organizations have resorted to simply hiring minimally qualified people with the aptitude and motivation to learn, or identifying motivated staff internally, and then investing in appropriate training for these select employees. Unfortunately, these newly skilled and trained employees are prime candidates for targeted recruitment efforts by the private sector, with more lucrative compensation and benefit packages. To illustrate, the president of an Arizona IT company said, "I am afraid as an employer of getting people who would require an awful lot of training. We have eight hours to learn a new system. We don't have three months or six months." In this environment, many companies have concluded that they cannot afford the time penalty and the uncertainty associated with "making" the employees they need (through training or retraining). Many employers are, instead, pursuing a "buy" strategy, seeking the exact skills and experience they need for a particular project and paying a premium for that.[35] This lack of IT personnel could "pose problems with the increasing number of governments rolling out electronic government applications. Without adequate safeguards, the public likely won't trust electronic government applications."[36]

In response, governments have attempted to become competitive by becoming creative in obtaining and retaining employees with coveted skills, even within the structured Civil Service System. A perfect example of this, is reflected in a letter submitted to the Kansas Senate Ways and Means Committee by Charles E. Simmons, Secretary of Corrections, requesting that Senate Bill 96 remove key information technology positions from the classified Civil Service System and place them in the unclassified service. Here's an excerpt of the letter:

> By placing these positions in the unclassified service, the Department will have the flexibility to offer compensation levels needed to retain qualified personnel in these positions. The existing personnel performing these functions do so through designation as temporary project positions, while the authorized FTE are being held vacant. SB 96 would allow the Department to place these individuals into authorized FTE positions.[37]

Secretary Simmons is pointing out that the compensation structure of the classified Civil Service System (merit system) within the State of Kansas is inadequate
to appoint needed personnel, resulting in the classified positions remaining vacant.
The use of temporary project positions, with flexible compensation provisions, is
the method the Department of Corrections utilized to retain these individuals.
Temporary project positions are not considered by the Kansas Division of Budget
under the FTE funding structure and can have an unfavorable long-term impact
on the agency and incumbents, which is why Secretary Simmons is proposing
counting the positions as FTE under the unclassified service. This bypass of the
classified Civil Service System is an example of just one creative method used by
a government organization to meet critical needs while confronted with limited
options.

A number of bonuses have been devised to specifically compensate IT incumbents, beyond the rigid salary structure of a merit system. These include signing bonuses for accepting a position, project bonuses for working on a project, skill
bonuses for learning new skills, referral bonuses paid to an employee when an IT
applicant they referred accepts an IT position, and longevity bonuses for remaining
with the agency for a set period of time.[38] Additionally, some states and regions have
undertaken efforts to lure people away from other regions of the country.

> For example, the State of Michigan launched its "Come Home to Michigan" cam-
> paign to attract IT workers who grew up in Michigan or were educated there. The
> Minnesota High Technology Association, in partnership with the Minnesota De-
> partment of Economic Security, conducted a five month "Upgrade to Minnesota"
> ad campaign in Silicon Valley to introduce workers there to the advantages of Min-
> nesota living. The campaign reportedly generated thousands of résumés of techni-
> cal and scientific workers for the sponsoring companies. The loss of skilled IT workers
> to others is also a concern of economic development officials. For example, the Hud-
> son Valley, New York area is losing IT professionals to contract work for employers
> in other areas. It was noted at the Hudson Valley town meeting that the northern New
> Jersey market pays IT professionals 10 percent more and the New York City market
> pays 25 percent more. Others see information technology as a tool to keep the resi-
> dents from moving to other states for job opportunities. U.S. Senator Kent Conrad
> expressed his concern about the isolation of small towns around the country stating,
> "There is a need to keep the best and brightest in North Dakota. This is the biggest
> concern of parents. IT is an opportunity to provide these jobs."[39]

In this type of aggressive environment, from both the private and public sectors,
governments must be creative and resourceful to ensure that they obtain and retain the necessary skilled workforce to serve their citizens.

Who are these information technology applicants that everyone wishes to employ? They are mainly younger workers (nearly 75–80 percent under the age of 45)
who do not remain with the same employer more than four years.[40] Their education and background does not fit the traditional mold, with extensive prepara-
tory training and education in the specific vocational area. "Many people who
work in skilled information technology jobs come from educational backgrounds
other than computer science and engineering. According to 1993 data from the
National Science Foundation, about one-third of people working in computer
programmer employment hold degrees in computer science, and about one-
quarter of those in computer and information sciences employment hold computer

and information science degrees. Other workers in these fields hold degrees in areas such as business, social sciences, mathematics, engineering, psychology, economics, and education."[41] A growing number are not U.S. citizens. Larger numbers of foreigners with H-1B visas are employed to help supply this competitive labor market. The challenges in recruiting and employing staff with H-1B visas adds to the complexity and cost for an employer, in that Immigration and Naturalization documents, timelines, and processes are jointly the responsibility of the employee with a H-1B "non-immigrant" visa and the employer. "In 1995, only about a quarter of temporary skilled foreign workers were in IT-related fields; by 1997 about half were in IT fields. Largely due to the increased use by the IT industry, the H-1B cap was reached for the first time in August 1997. In 1998, the cap was reached in May."[42]

The use of temporary workers and consultants is increasing to help fill voids in staffing, or by-pass merit systems that provide inadequate compensation. The benefit of such relationships is that an employer obtains specific skills needed for a short-term project, without the need for training or for a lengthy (time-consuming) recruitment process. The trade-off is that the employer does not retain the talents and skills of temporary worker or consultant beyond the length of the project, the level of compensation paid is higher than that of regular staff, and the level of continuity and commitment on a project is always suspect. "Staffing firms are ideally situated to provide flexibility to employees and companies as the workforce adapts within an increasingly high-tech, service-oriented, knowledge-based economy."[43] As a result, compensation equity among the workforce is a difficult goal to achieve when there are significant external forces requiring competitive responses on a number of fronts.

Discussion Questions

1. What factors make recruiting for IT skills a challenge?
2. If your organization recruits for IT professionals, what steps has it had to take to get the best-qualified candidates?
3. Are merit principles compromised with hiring practices that short-circuit traditional merit systems administrative routine?
4. While the acquisition function clearly is affected by the shortage of IT professionals, what other functions are affected? How?

NOTES

[1]Heimlich, J. (January 18, 2001). Texas Prison System. National Public Radio, Morning Edition report.

[2]Kansas Division of Personnel Services. "Leadership Focus Group Discussion Guide." State of Kansas Competency Project; http://da.state.ks.us/ps/subject/comp.

[3]Mosher, F. C. (1982). *Democracy and the Public Service.* (2nd ed.). New York: Oxford University Press.

[4]Arvey, R. D., and P. R. Sackett (1993). Fairness in selection: Current developments and perspectives. In N. Schmitt, W. C. Borman, and Associates (Eds.). *Personnel Selection in Organizations.* San Francisco: Jossey-Bass, pp. 199–200.

[5]Judy, Richard W., and C. D'Amico (1997). *Workforce 2020.* Indianapolis: Hudson Institute; see also Smith, M. (March 2000). Innovative personnel management: Changing workforce demographics. *International Personnel Management Association News,* pp. 12–14.

[6]Smith, M. (March 2000). Innovative personnel management.

[7]Ibid.

[8]Borman, W. C., and S. J. Motowidlo (1993). Expanding the criterion domain to include elements of contextual performance. In Schmitt, Borman, and Associates (Eds.). *Personnel Selection in Organizations*, p. 73.

[9]Ibid., p. 73.

[10]Guion, R. M. (1993). The need for change: Six persistent themes. In Schmitt, Borman, and Associates (Eds.). *Personnel Selection in Organizations*, p. 491.

[11]Ibid., p. 493.

[12]Mintzberg, H. (May-June 1996). Managing government and governing management. *Harvard Business Review, 74*, 75–80.

[13]Hesselbein, F., M. Goldsmith, and R. Beckhard (1996). *The Leader of the Future*. San Francisco: Jossey Bass.

[14]State of Kansas, http://da.state.ks.us/ps/subject/comp; the Canadian Civil Service, http://learnet.gc.ca.eng/comcentr/manage/building/summary e.htm; the International City/County Management Association, www.icma.org; the U.S. Office of Personnel Management, www.opm.gov/ses/ecq1.html.

[15]Brown, B. K., and M. A. Campion (1994). Biodata phenomenology: Recruiters' perceptions and use of biographic information in résumé screening. *Journal of Applied Psychology, 79*, 897–908.

[16]Levine, E. L., and A. Flory, III (1976). Evaluation of job applications—A conceptual framework. *Public Personnel Management, 5*, 378–385.

[17]Arvey, R. D., and R. H. Faley (1988). *Fairness in Selecting Employees* (2nd ed.). Reading, MA: Addison-Wesley.

[18]Dipboye, R. L., and B. B. Gaugler (1993). Cognitive and behavioral processes in the selection interview. In Schmitt, Borman, and Associates (Eds.). *Personnel Selection in Organizations*, pp. 135–170; Whetzel, D. L., F. L. Schmitt, and S. D. Maurer (1994). The validity of employment interviews: A comprehensive review and meta-analysis. *Journal of Applied Psychology, 79*, 599–616.

[19]Arvey and Faley (1988). Fairness in Selecting Employees.

[20]Trice, E. (June 1999). Timely hiring. *International Personnel Management Association News*, pp. 10–11. Also see Sullivan, J. (June 1999). Gaining a competitive advantage. *International Personnel Management Association News*, pp. 14–15; and Greene, T. (November 1999). City of Hampton's innovative recruitment efforts. *International Personnel Management Association News*, p. 19.

[21]Kellough, J. E. (1999). Reinventing public personnel management: Ethical implications for managers and public personnel systems. *Public Personnel Management, 28*, 4, pp. 655–671.

[22]———— (1993). Award winning programs–interviews with the winners. *Public Personnel Management, 22*, 1–5.

[23]Kellough, J. E. (1999). Reinventing public personnel management. Ethical implications for managers and public personnel systems.

[24]United States Merit Systems Protection Board (1994). *Entering Professional Positions in the Federal Government*. Washington, DC: U.S. Merit Systems Protection Board, p. xii.

[25]Hutchinson, B. (May 2001). Webifying the employment process. *International Personnel Management Association News*, pp. 12–14; Smith, M. (April 2000). Internet recruiting: The next best thing since? *International Personnel Management Association News*, p. 13.

[26]Wheeler, K. (June 1999). The big decision: Buy a tracking system or buy a service. *International Personnel Management Association News*, pp. 15–16. Also see www.ipma-hr.org, web site of the International Personnel Management Association.

[27]Personal correspondence with the author, July 5, 1996.

[28]Hummert, R. (April 18, 2001). Letter to the authors.

[29]For information available electronically about the Americans with Disabilities Act (P.L. 101–336, July 26, 1990), see http://janweb.icdi.wvu.edu.

[30]*Sutton v. United Airlines Inc.*, (97–1943) 130 F .3d 893 (1999); *Murphy v. United Parcel Service, Inc.* (97–1992) 141 F. 3d 1185 (1999); *Albertsons Inc. v. Hallie Kirkingburg* (98–591) 143 F .3d 1228 (1999).

[31]Segal, J. A. (1992). Drugs, alcohol, and the ADA. *HR Magazine, 37*, 73–76.

[32]Alan Greenspan July 10, 1998. The Implications of Technological Changes, remarks at the Charlotte Chamber of Commerce, Charlotte, North Carolina.

[33]U.S. Department of Commerce (March 1998). *America's New Deficit: The Shortage of Information Technology Workers.* Office of Technology Policy, p. 3.

[34]Dizard III, W. (January 2001). Economic downturn imperils IT funding. *State & Local Government Computer News,* pp. 1, 6.

[35]U.S. Department of Commerce (June 1999). *The Digital Work Force: Building Infotech Skills at the Speed of Innovation.* Office of Technology Policy, p. 11.

[36]Peterson, S. (February 2001). Security Lapse. *The Government Technology,* p. 14.

[37]Charles E. Simmons, Secretary of Corrections, Memorandum to Senate Ways and Means Committee. SB96, February 5, 2001.

[38]———— (September 1999). Talent deficit: No relief for employers in new millennium; and Recruiting techniques. *International Personnel Management Association News,* pp. 16–17.

[39]U.S. Department of Commerce (June 1999). *The Digital Work Force: Building Infotect Skills at the Speed of Innovation.* Office of Technology Policy, p. 15.

[40]Based on the Department of Labor's Current Population Survey data, 1996.

[41]U.S. Department of Commerce (January 1998). *Update: America's New Deficit.* Office of Technology Policy, p. 4.

[42]U.S. Department of Commerce (June 1999). *The Digital Work Force: Building Infotech Skills at the Speed of Innovation.* Office of Technology Policy, p. 16.

[43]Brogan, T. (1999). "Staffing Services Annual Update." National Association of Temporary and Staffing Services. http://www.staffingtoday.net/memberserv/9901ct/staffingservicesupdate.html.

9
Leadership and Employee Performance in Turbulent Times

In Chapters 3 to 5 we showed how public employers plan and organize around the human resources needs of their agencies. These efforts result from policy planning and decisions that elected officials, agency executives, managers and supervisors take. Depending upon their role, some of these plans are made legislatively and others administratively. Some are made in consultation with interest groups and citizens, and others with unions and employees.

Also, we have seen how agencies target recruitment and acquire staff, sorting out priorities among conflicting values. Having looked at the planning and acquisition functions, we now turn to the **development function**. It involves the challenge of applying employee competencies to organizational problems, building those competencies in light of future problems, and then assessing employee performance in light of specific job descriptions. In this chapter, we will address issues of leadership and motivation.

In the 1990s, the focus of personnel systems changed from defending abstract merit system principles to a concern for maximizing productivity and measurable outcomes. Personnel systems are under pressure to become increasingly responsive to external pressures for productivity, work measurement, and political accountability. Effective human resource management is assessed by how well employees are doing tasks that match the overall objectives of the work unit and the organization. The focus is changing from management of positions—with primary concern for staying within a budget and following civil service laws, rules, and regulations—to more directly facilitating accomplishment of the agency's mission. In other words, there is more emphasis on human resources management as a means to an end rather than ends in themselves.

By the end of this chapter, you will be able to:

1. Describe the differences between political and administrative viewpoints.
2. Describe how a market-based perspective differs from that of elected officials and public administrators.

213

3. Describe the concept of the psychological contract and how it can be used to clarify relationships.
4. Describe the basic components of equity and expectancy theory.
5. Describe the ways that elected officials, managers, and personnel specialists affect an employee's motivation to perform.
6. Describe the ways that elected officials, managers, and personnel specialists affect an employee's ability to perform.
7. Identify four innovations to enhance productivity: total quality management, job enrichment, work-life balance, and teamwork.

DIFFERENCES BETWEEN POLITICAL AND ADMINISTRATIVE VIEWPOINTS

We can think strategically as well as practically about leadership and motivation—the development function. Thinking strategically requires that agency managers understand the broad demographic trends outlined in Chapter 8 that affect the present and future workforce. It also involves understanding and respecting different perspectives that elected officials and administrative specialists bring to their work. Finally, thinking strategically requires that agency managers have an understanding of theories of motivation as a building block for the competence needed to understand and influence employee performance. Let's start with the different perspectives that elected officials and technically trained civil servants bring to their work.[1] Then, we will add a third dimension, how a market perspective differs from those helped by elected officials and public administrators.[2]

One of the ways to understand the differences between politics and administration is simply to look at them as alternative perspectives, as **political** and **administrative logic**, rather than as behavioral differences. Figure 9–1 attempts to chart those differences in broad terms.[3]

For a politician, the primary value is responsiveness to the will of the people. This means sometimes acting to promote efficiency, social equity, or individual rights; sometimes representing the interests of a few; and sometimes doing what is good for the majority over the long run. The elected official's focus is primarily outside of the organization and into the community or environment of political interests that rally for and against specific policies and solutions to problems. Even when elected officials "meddle" internally, it can be justified in terms of an external role like "oversight," or helping citizens find their way through an administrative agency's labyrinthine procedures.

To some extent politics differentiates itself from administration in that part of it can only be understood as a game, with its own rules and strategy and tactics. We even refer to the game of politics. Partially, it is a game because the boundaries are so broad and vague. Elected officials must manage their own careers. They cannot count merely on hard work and conscientiousness to keep them in office, and they operate in a world of values where compromise and negotiation are valued more than right answers. They come to their office with no special expertise and often without much relevant experience. They are chosen because they represent something their constituents believe will serve them well.

FIGURE 9-1 Characteristics of Politics and Administration

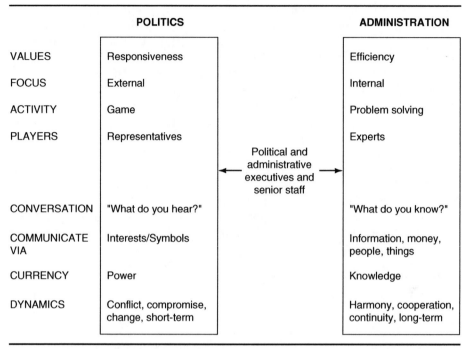

	POLITICS		ADMINISTRATION
VALUES	Responsiveness		Efficiency
FOCUS	External		Internal
ACTIVITY	Game		Problem solving
PLAYERS	Representatives		Experts
		Political and administrative executives and senior staff	
CONVERSATION	"What do you hear?"		"What do you know?"
COMMUNICATE VIA	Interests/Symbols		Information, money, people, things
CURRENCY	Power		Knowledge
DYNAMICS	Conflict, compromise, change, short-term		Harmony, cooperation, continuity, long-term

Because the world of politics is a world of conflicting values, communication is often through symbols that reveal those values. Politicians love to tell stories and, in return, constituents tell them stories—stories about the (in)efficiency of government, about fairness, about the special needs they want represented. The currency is power. The bottom line for an elected official is the ability to influence other elected officials and build community consensus in order to get things done, and there is no formula for success.

Hierarchy removes so much uncertainty from the lives of administrative officials that it is difficult for them to imagine the uncertainty that elected officials work with. It is hard for the outsider to identify how power is acquired and who is powerful, again because in most legislative bodies there is no hierarchy. In addition, in some governing bodies there is no specialization. The elected official's time perspective is shorter than an administrator's because, for most elected officials, elected office is not intended to be a career. Even when it is, managing that career requires making short-term, noticeable achievements in an environment of conflicting values.

The administrative world is very different, especially at the level of the personnel specialist, the planner, the engineer, the water plant operator, the scientist at the Environmental Protection Agency, the systems analyst at the Department of Defense, the agronomist at the Department of Agriculture, the budget analyst, and so on. To these people, administration is not a game; it is about the rational, analytical application of knowledge to solve problems. While the problems may have an external origin, the focus is internal; the work is largely internal. The water plant operator may never interact with a citizen unless it's on a tour of the water treatment plant; the same for the budget analyst and the personnel specialist. Their professional/technical knowledge and the hierarchy they work in bind their world. They are experts whose knowledge has been acquired over years of education and experience. They were selected for their work on the basis of their knowledge, skills/abilities, and personal attributes, and not because they appealed in some abstract way to a group of voters.

"What do you know?" invites a very different response than "What do you hear?" It suggests a factual exchange where those with the most knowledge are the most valued. Usually, this is reflected in a report. Problem solving requires cooperation, and fairness in the implementation of public policy relies on continuity. The administrative specialist thinks in terms of a career, and knowing that he or she is going to be around for the long haul, the vicissitudes of electoral politics are likely to be shunned rather than respected. For every elected official who has bashed a bureaucrat, there are ten public employees who have returned the favor.

The following example illustrates different perceptions of administrators and elected officials.

August 30, 1996

TO: Journal Entry

FR: John Nalbandian, Mayor

RE: Differences in thinking between professionals and elected officials

Last night I was struck by the continuing differences I notice between the ways that staff and the council think about issues. The city and the county are considering a merger between the city's fire department and the county's emergency ambulance service. They would join to form a new city department. Now, the county provides emergency medical service for city residents as well as for residents of the unincorporated parts of the county. The city fire department provides fire service only within the city's boundaries. Townships and other smaller cities in the county provide their own fire protection.

It is clear that the merger would benefit city residents who have first-class fire service, but second-rate ambulance service because the ambulance stations are not co-located with the fire stations, which are strategically placed within the city. Both fire and ambulance personnel are highly trained, and the new proposal would require all personnel to become cross-trained within a designated period of time.

The chiefs of the fire and emergency medical service initiated the idea of the merger. The governing bodies of the city and county encouraged the effort and left it to staff to work up a proposal and work through the details of merging two personnel systems. The sticking point seems to be the differences in rank. In order to retain their pay and seniority, EMS personnel would have to enter the new organization at a higher rank than some of the firefighters. The firefighters have expressed their concern at having to follow direction from EMS personnel who aren't qualified to fight fires. Most of the firefighters have some level of emergency medical skills. When the issue finally came to the city commission, I asked whether the proposal had been formally agreed to by the three smaller incorporated cities in the county. It hadn't been, although the city administrator of one city said his council would favor it because it would increase accessibility to emergency medical service.

But the issue for me is whether residents of the unincorporated parts of the county and of these smaller cities, really will be satisfied with the biggest city in the county deciding about kinds and levels of emergency medical service for their residents without any provision for them to be represented.

The way I approach the rank question is simply to think to myself, "You (staff) get this straightened out or we'll just mandate something because it is clear this is in the best interest of the residents even if it causes problems for employees."

Well, we will get all this worked out because it really is clear that the public interest would be served by this merger, but we sure do come at it from different directions.

The insert describes an incident involving the merging of an ambulance service with a fire department. It shows clearly the different perspective the elected official and staff brought to this problem. One was looking externally at a broader range of values; the other internally. The elected official was concerned about issues of representation and how the agreement would be seen by the smaller cities in the county. The appointed officials were concerned about how to integrate two personnel systems—the furthest thing from the elected official's mind.

As another example in the human resource area, the police department continually operates under pressure from elected officials who want to know immediately about that incident last night in their district. The elected official is trying to do the best he or she can for the district; to the police department staff, this is just another request that gets in the way of real police work. Also, the police department draws districts and allocates personnel based on a rational analysis of crime statistics. Downtown interests to increase police presence to "manage" the homeless approach the city council. The mayor needs the support of downtown for a major suburban economic development initiative. The mayor urges the council to act on the homeless problem. The police department regards the "homeless problem" as minimal compared to their other responsibilities and shows little enthusiasm for the mayor's initiative, angering the mayor and his supporters on the council. Again, the perspectives are very different; and without adequate interpretation, these worlds grow farther apart as communities become more politically diverse and problems become more technically complex.

These perspectives differ, but successful governance, including the survival of administrative agencies, requires a blend or at least some understanding of the other perspective. It is too much to expect the politician to understand the world of the budget analyst; nor can the wastewater treatment plan operator be expected to know what it is like to see the world from the council chambers. Those who speak both languages understand both technical and political rationality; they occupy the middle ground. This is one of the crucial roles of the chief administrative officer and other senior administrative officials and political executives or their senior staff. In effect, they are called upon to interpret—to translate the world of administration into value questions and to transform value issues into problems subject to administrative expertise. For example, at an orientation of new county commissioners, the purchasing officer was going over purchasing procedures. She said that staff was authorized to accept bids over the phone for purchases of not more than $5,000. Unnoticed by the purchasing director, the commissioners squirmed. After she had finished, the county administrator said, "I would like to clarify something. Staff exercises little discretion in this process. The commission has authorized and scrutinized all of these proposed expenditures during its budget process." In adding this policy clarification, the administrator understood that the new commissioners were very concerned about their oversight role and about government spending. He spoke to their unspoken concern that went unnoticed by the purchasing agent, who was more interested in removing responsibility for "minor" requisitions from the hands of elected officials in the mistaken belief that they would welcome this outcome.

While traditionally public administrators have looked at their work in relationship to that of elected officials—the politics/administration dichotomy—the recent emphasis on **market-based values** adds a third element—politics, administration, and markets. In the privatization case at the end of Chapter 4 we saw not only our four familiar political values come into play, but the option of contracting out for the trash services introduced another very important element into the policy-making and administrative process.

We have suggested that thinking politically and administratively involve different mindsets. Thinking from a market perspective involves yet another. Administering a contract with a private vendor involves more than a straightforward contractual arrangement. It involves different ways of thinking. The private sector is not likely to place as much emphasis on individual rights and equity as the elected official or public administrator. Similarly, there is less likely to be much appreciation for the need to conduct business in the open. The need for profit as a driving force is unlikely to be fully appreciated by the public administrator.

PSYCHOLOGICAL CONTRACTS

We have identified perspectives held by elected officials, public administrators, and decision makers in market driven organizations. In Chapter 3 we contrasted perspectives held by public executives, managers, and line employees. And, based on the workforce characteristics described in previous chapters we can see how diversity will challenge agency managers. Since no organization can operate effectively without competent communication among those who view matters from different perspectives, we need a concept that will help one group understand and work with another. That concept is the **psychological contract**.

A psychological contract is similar to a legal contract but with some important differences. First, let's look at the similarities. A legal contract between two parties sets out what each expects from the other and what each is willing to give to the other. These terms can be referred to as expectations and obligations. The parties will negotiate these terms, and when they agree, they can sign the contract.

The relationship between any two people or groups can be seen in similar terms. A supervisor has expectations of employees and employees have expectations of their supervisor. Also, each party is willing to obligate itself to the other in various ways. For example, the supervisor may expect a lot of initiative from employees and is willing to give employees the freedom needed to express that initiative.

The same logic holds when we look at the relationship between governing body members and civil servants who find themselves in a working relationship. For example, the elected officials may expect the civil servants to point out problems that need legislative attention. In turn, they may obligate themselves not to criticize the civil servants when they bring bad news to the elected officials. Obviously, this quid pro quo is not always present. If the elected officials "punish" the civil servants when they deliver bad news, they are less likely to have their expectation fulfilled because the civil servants will not feel committed to the obligation. In this case, the contract is not working very well and needs to be discussed among the parties.

While we can use the same terms to describe a psychological contract as we do a legal contract, there are important differences. First, in a psychological contract, many times the terms are not spelled out even though they are the basis for action. In our examples above, the elected officials have said one thing but have acted in ways that send mixed messages. But, rarely is the discrepancy articulated in a forum that can lead to some positive action. Second, the terms can change over time, again without spelling out the changes. An employee, when new, will expect more guidance from a supervisor than when experienced. If the supervisor does not realize this, what is seen as helpful behavior to the new employee will be seen as oversupervision as the employee gains expertise.

One way a supervisor or manager can develop a relationship with a group of employees is with discussion that centers on the psychological contract and its terms. The same is true of a public administrator who is managing a contract with a vendor or department heads who are frustrated with a new governing body. At the end of this chapter, we have an exercise that will take you through this kind of discussion. Earlier in this chapter we described some demographic characteristics of the workforce of the future. We can expect to see the diversity in the workforce reflected in different expectations and obligations. Younger workers and older workers are at different places in their lives, and the expectations they have of themselves and others will reflect that. The same can be said of obligations. This can be as simple a matter as how much time each is willing to spend at work.

When expectations and obligations go unfulfilled—whether they are made explicit or not—people can feel like they are being treated unfairly, and their motivation to work may be affected. For all the discussion in books, magazines, and newsletters extolling the need for leadership, there is no area more important for the exercise of leadership than clarifying psychological contracts, starting with supervisors and subordinates. Because mismatches in expectations and obligations can influence perceptions of fairness, we will look more analytically at how people come to the conclusion that they are being treated fairly or not. Then, we will examine a framework to look at motivation.

THE FOUNDATION THEORIES: EXPLAINING
EMPLOYEE PERFORMANCE WITH EQUITY
AND EXPECTANCY THEORIES

Equity Theory[4]

Equity theory helps us understand how a worker reaches the conclusion that he or she is being treated fairly or unfairly. It is crucial to an understanding of the "burned-out" worker, the worker who feels mistreated or feels he or she is being asked to do too much, the worker who feels his/her job is threatened but has no alternatives, the employee who is trying to balance family and work and weighing the consequences. Furthermore, equitable treatment of employees is shown to directly affect employee loyalty, expressions of good will, organizational citizenship, and "going the extra mile" (see Chapter 13).

The feeling of being treated equitably is an internal state of mind resulting from a subjective calculation of what one puts into a job and what one gets out of it, in comparison to some other relevant person. Inputs can include anything of value the employee brings that he or she thinks deserves special recognition in comparison with others—seniority, expertise, type of work, difficulty of work, level of responsibility, and education. Inputs can also include the less formally recognized but still frequently claimed credit for age, sex, race, political influence, and other non-merit factors like ability to get along with others and demands that family life places on the employee. Outcome credits have an equally wide range: job security, pay, future opportunity, promotion, recognition, organizational climate, work schedule and flexible work arrangements, autonomy, a reserved parking space, a certain size and location of office.

Equity calculations involve two types of subjective comparisons: input to output and comparison with other employees. The comparison is important. You make less than you think your education warrants, but if friends of yours with similar educational backgrounds are out of work, you may be thankful just to have a job. If they are working and make more than you, your reaction will be very different.

The theory can be illustrated with the following formula, where one Person compares what he or she puts into a job with what he or she gets out of that job measured against another person—the Other.

$$\frac{\text{Person}}{\text{Inputs}} = \frac{\text{Other}}{\text{Inputs}}$$
$$\frac{\text{Person Inputs}}{\text{Outcomes}} = \frac{\text{Other Inputs}}{\text{Outcomes}}$$

Equity does not require that all employees receive equal outputs, only that outputs be proportional to inputs, and that employees with comparable inputs receive comparable outputs. For example, managers earn more money (outcomes) than employees, but generally employees find that equitable because of the added responsibility (inputs) managers have.

There are several ways to deal with an employee's feeling of being treated unfairly. First, the supervisor must recognize that reaching a conclusion that one has been treated unfairly is the product of someone's unique internal logical processes, driven in many cases by a gnawing sense of injustice. Also impending simple resolution of equity issues is the tendency to distort input-output ratios to justify feeling ill-treated. The supervisor may feel that dealing with an employee's perception of unfair treatment is hopeless because the sense of injustice is part of the employee's character rather than a rational response to the situation. Nonetheless, the supervisor should try to find out what the employee perceives his or her rewards and contributions to be and who an appropriate person for purposes of comparison might be, in order to clarify the source of perceived injustice. In effect, the supervisor can try to elicit the terms of the psychological contract that up to that time have either not been articulated or are not being lived up to. Finally, the supervisor can attempt to forestall equity claims by making clear what inputs justify organizational rewards, consistently applying rewards and punishments, and specifying the reasons behind the actions. Supervisors who establish expectations and provide timely feedback on performance can also prevent unrealistic assessments of the individual's inputs and outputs.

Expectancy Theory

Expectancy theory attempts to reconstruct the mental processes that lead an employee to expend a certain amount of effort toward meeting a work objective. Its premise is that "motivation depends on how much an individual wants something (the strength of the valence) relative to other things, and the perceived effort-reward probability (expectancy) that they will get it."[5] It also augments equity theory in part by showing how employees' feelings of job satisfaction are translated into performance. It assumes that effort results from three factors:

- The extent to which an employee believes that he or she can do the job at the expected level
- The employee's assessment that identifiable rewards or consequences will occur as a result of doing (or not doing) the job at the expected level
- The value the employee places on these rewards or punishments

In reality, employees do not make these calculations explicitly or formally. Rather, they adjust their level of effort (or change focus from one task to another) based on implicit and intuitive responses to these issues. For example, if an employee is given a task with an indication that a promotion is possible for performing the task well, she will probably do the task well provided that she believes she has the ability to do so and wants a promotion. Given the same circumstances, another employee who wants to spend more time with his family may turn down the promotion because it means more work (an undesirable consequence), even though he believes he could do the job and might get the promotion.

Expectancy theory helps explain employee reactions to many situations at work including burnout, for example. Burnout results when an employee has challenging work (moderate to high confidence in one's ability to perform the work) but few valued outcomes are associated with doing a good job. Performing the job does not lead to rewarding outcomes. In fact, doing a good job just leads to more work or to punishing consequences without offsetting rewards. The consequences usually are a combination of *extrinsic* and *intrinsic* factors. For example, there maybe little positive recognition of the work's value (providing **extrinsic motivation**) by the lay public or elected officials and high-ranking administrators. Successes are so infrequent that self-satisfaction or a sense of achievement (**intrinsic motivation**) is hard to come by. At some point, the person becomes burned-out—the effort just doesn't produce rewarding outcomes.

A temporary employee may expend a lot of effort believing that good performance could lead to a permanent job. If there are no positive outcomes associated with performing well, it is doubtful that over time the employee would do so. An employee who is trying to balance work and family may determine that the outcomes associated with expending effort on family life are more rewarding than overtime. Of course, the difficulty comes when this employee wants to be with the family, but the family needs the money the overtime can earn.

Expectancy theory and equity theory help us understand why the satisfied worker may not be productive. People at work can be satisfied for a variety of reasons that may have nothing to do with their performance. For example, an employee may be very satisfied because pay is good, the social environment at work is lively and rewarding, the working conditions are good, and the workload is not unduly taxing. There is nothing in these elements that would lead one necessarily to expect this person to be a productive worker. The worker may lack some knowledge, skills, or ability or maybe enjoys the work environment so much that it detracts from work.

In order for the productive worker to be satisfied, high performance must lead to satisfying outcomes. In addition, the recognition or rewards for high performance must be perceived to be distributed equitably. Furthermore, it is easy for a productive worker not to be satisfied. The worker could be very productive and be paid well, but hate the job, be overworked, see no value in the work, and so on. This is why the relationship between satisfaction and performance is not a direct one—that is, all satisfied workers are not productive and all productive workers are not satisfied.[6]

Using These Theories in Management

The expectancy model provides an excellent diagnostic tool for analyzing an employee's work behavior because it focuses attention on how the organization affects employee effort and performance in several ways. First, the probability that effort will result in task performance is low if the task is difficult and high if the task is easy. But since easy jobs are usually boring, supervisors must delegate responsibility appropriately by striking a balance between setting a performance level so high as to be perceived as unattainable, or so low as to be seen as attainable but boring. Second, the perceived equity and adequacy of performance evaluation and reward systems have a major influence on the employee's perception that performance will lead to rewards (or punishment). Performance appraisal systems that do not distinguish high and low performers, or that do not result in differential rewards (or punishments) for them, will lead to a downward adjustment of inputs to meet outputs by all workers. Finally, consequences must be desirable to result in effort. A detective, who is rewarded for solving cases quickly and well by the assignment of more cases and more difficult ones, will soon learn to work more slowly, unless other rewards are available to adjust the balance or the cases turn out to be interesting and intrinsically rewarding to work on.

Let's take a look at how equity theory helps explain one segment in the life of the modern worker. Bill (the Other in the formula above) works very hard and has done work over and above the call of duty (Other's input). One day the nurse at school calls him and says his child is sick and needs to be taken home. He talks to the supervisor who, wanting to be flexible in order to accommodate the family needs of employees, says to him, "You've been working extra hard (supervisor recognizes Other's input), go ahead and take some time off (Other's outcome) and we won't count it against your vacation time." Other says to himself, "I worked extra hard, it's OK if I take the time off without leave." Bill feels that he has balanced inputs and outcomes and feels no discomfort in what he has done. Meanwhile Sally (Person) feels like she works just as hard as Other. Sally is young and single, and whenever she has to run an errand or go to the doctor or take care of her pet she is told either to do it during lunch or take leave. She feels like she is being treated unfairly while having done nothing wrong.

Sally now has some choices to make depending on how strongly she feels the perceived injustice. A very important contribution of equity theory is its proposition that Sally's goal is to get the ratio back into balance. That is, equity theory is based on the concept of cognitive balance. People seek cognitive balance, and when inputs and outcomes are imbalanced, workers will feel motivated to rectify the imbalance. Sally feels like she is putting more into the job than she is getting out of it, at least compared to Bill, her comparison Other. She can voice her displeasure to the supervisor and hope that the supervisor will change the policy or treat everyone equally (different sometimes from equitably). Or, she can simply acknowledge a difference between her situation and Bill's and say something like, "Bill really does work hard, as hard as I do, and he has a special situation that deserves the special consideration." If Sally comes to this conclusion, from an equity theory standpoint she has given Bill extra input credit to match the outcome, and now the ratio between Sally and Bill, Person and Other, has been restored.

But if Sally does not acknowledge that Bill deserves special consideration, she will still feel mistreated. Her ratio of inputs to outcomes is out of balance when compared to Bill's, so she just might cut back on her own inputs saying, "If they won't reward me for working as hard as Bill, I'm not going to work as hard." This will work for Sally psychologically, as long as she is willing to accept the consequences of not performing at her former level. If she is working in an organization where she feels her job is in some jeopardy, Sally may not say anything to her supervisor about her displeasure, not cut back on her work, and simply internalize the displeasure. She can become a disgruntled employee if the injustice is felt strongly enough. From her view the supervisor acted unfairly; from Bill's point of view the supervisor acted justly; and from the supervisor's view he acted with consideration for Bill's special needs. If none of the parties talks about this, it simply gets pushed into an interpersonal underworld where it will affect their relationship, but in ways that will not be easily understood.

Equity theory and expectancy theory lead thoughtful supervisors away from more prescriptive, universal theories of human motivation and performance (such as Maslow's hierarchy of needs or Herzberg's motivator-hygiene theory). In reality, employees are individuals with subjective perceptions of their own needs and abilities. No employee is an unmotivated person. Everyone is motivated to certain behaviors. For example, the employee who expends little effort at work may play his/her heart out for the softball team. The failure of an employee to expend desired effort at work can be attributed to factors identified through equity and expectancy theory. These theories provide useful starting points. Effective human resource managers are those who can develop personnel functions that recognize the impact of organizational climate on employee performance, and good supervisors are those who can use these systems to develop relationships based on open communication and trust.

INFLUENCES ON EMPLOYEES' MOTIVATION TO PERFORM

Both equity and expectancy theories speak to our understanding of employee performance by focusing our attention in part on the willingness of employees to perform and their ability to perform. In this section we will explore several factors that influence motivation and ability. In addition, we will suggest techniques and alternative work systems that would strengthen motivation and ability. Throughout this discussion, it should be evident that we are discussing the shared roles of personnel managers, supervisors, and appointed and elected officials in promoting effective employee performance.

Increasing Employee Motivation

There is an array of organizational and environmental factors which affect employee motivation or effort. Political leaders, agency managers, and human resource directors are responsible for creating and funding human resource programs that provide incentives for superior performance. With regard to pay for performance, will sufficient money be appropriated so that it actually serves as a reward, or will the amount merely symbolize an effort to make government more like a business? Politicians and agency executives are so engaged externally that sound internal human resource practices often fall beyond their attention span, even though the decisions they might make can have crucial impact on the ability of managers to manage. David Blumenthal, a highly successful private sector executive, said about his term as secretary of the treasury, "A Secretary often tends to ignore administrative things because it is not worth his time, it's not where he should put his emphasis. That doesn't mean you neglect administrative matters, but it does mean that you do far less than you might wish."[7]

Political considerations may require compromises on staffing levels, wages, benefit packages, the availability of incentives, privatization, and contracting out. For most politicians, these compromises are ends in themselves. Their primary goal is to get something done amidst conflicting political objectives, and their work is done when the policy compromise is reached. Many of the nitty-gritty consequences of these decisions are simply left to managers to deal with. Managers trying to promote progressive and comprehensive changes internally face uphill battles in this environment, and their primary task must be to make elected officials and political executives aware of the consequences of the political compromises on their agency's day-to-day operations.

At the departmental level, linking incentives to desired performance will critically affect the employee's belief that high performance will be rewarded and poor performance dealt with. The creation of challenging jobs will tap the intrinsic desire people have to master their work and avoid boring, fatiguing activities that hold few positive outcomes. Moreover, establishing career paths allows employees to look ahead to a future with their employer. Endorsement of fair but streamlined disciplinary procedures will carry the message to managers as well as employees that unsatisfactory performance will not be overlooked.

Perhaps the greatest influence on employee effort involves the fairness with which employees feel they are being treated. The day-to-day interactions between supervisor and subordinate, the small seemingly inconsequential matters of doing one's job daily, and the cordial relationships between co-workers are the foundation on which employees build trust that they will be treated fairly by those applying the organization's policies and procedures. Thus, the organizational climate in the work unit as guided by the manager will be the main determinant of the perception of fairness for the entire organization.[8] The personnel office, in turn, can influence this climate indirectly by training supervisors on how to motivate employees and how to enhance perceptions of equity in the workplace. They can monitor pay and evaluation processes to ensure no obvious abuses are occurring. They can assist departments in the design of challenging jobs and can work toward developing classification and compensation plans that foster innovative work design and work assignments, and the availability of monetary incentives.

Public Service Motive

One way to influence employee motivation is to acknowledge what research is beginning to show—there is something that can be called a *public service motive.* That is, people are drawn to public service, in varying degrees of course, by a desire to serve.[9] Brewer, Coleman Selden, and Facer have shown that this desire can be divided into four more specific motives: Samaritans—guardians of the underprivileged; communitarians—motivated by sentiments of civic duty and public service; patriots—acting for the good of the public; and humanitarians—those motivated by a strong sense of social justice.[10]

Huddleston's interview project with Senior Executive Service award winners corroborates the presence of a public service motive.[11] While he questions whether the younger generation is similarly motivated, he finds that those he interviewed referred to the attraction to public service as a "calling."

To the extent that a public service motive exists, its implications for human resources management are clear. The work itself can be motivating, and making a difference can increase employee commitment. Too much emphasis on making government run like a business, with focus on financial incentives to the exclusion of rewards that recognize the public service motivation, could have a negative effect on these members of the workforce.

Increasing Employee Commitment[12]

Employee motivation and effort is demonstrated by **employee commitment** to the organization and its goals. If all a manager had to worry about was increasing employee commitment, the task would be fairly simple—provide incentives, challenge, security, and meaningful work. However, conflicting forces in today's public organizations make securing commitment a difficult task. On the one hand, managers are encouraged to promote teamwork and participative decision making to give employees more voice in determining how their work life will proceed. They encourage commitment to the work group and its goals, and they provide incentives to work together well. On the other hand, employees see the rising trend for privatization of any and all governmental services and the downsizing of the public workforce in the interests of cutting costs. They see full-time jobs being divided into part-time jobs in order to avoid benefit payments.

Employees become quite cynical about team building and commitment if they believe their efforts will not stave off the possible loss of their jobs. They may feel the conflict within themselves between loyalty to the work unit and colleagues and the necessity to "look out for yourself" in uncertain times. Nevertheless, managers need to continue to try innovations to build that commitment while being honest with employees about the current status of the organization's plans because external political influences on government continue to demand more for less, and one can never be sure whether this is just rhetoric or a real call to action.

Flexible Work Locations and Schedules[13]

There are several common innovations in working conditions that serve to increase employee commitment. In the past all employees were expected to have identical working hours and a fixed job location, but this is no longer true or necessary. Changes in technology (primarily telecommunications and computers) have meant that employees can work productively at decentralized workstations, or even at home.[14] The need for broader service delivery to clients and the complex child-care and elder-care arrangements necessitated by two-career families have resulted in the development of part-time and flexible work schedules. And the focus on employees as resources has led to the development of variable models of resource use that have proved effective at achieving improved performance.

Under **flextime**, all employees are expected to work during core hours (such as 9:30 to 3:00). Depending on agency needs and personal preferences, each employee is free to negotiate a fixed work schedule with different start and end times. Some agencies have flextime programs that enable employees to work longer days in order to have fewer workdays in a week or month (such as ten hours per day, four days a week). Research on flextime experiments in both the public and private sectors generally reveals positive results in employee attitudes and in the reduction of absenteeism, tardiness, and, in some cases, increases in productivity.

Job sharing, is the splitting of one job between two part-time employees on a regular basis. There are obvious advantages for employees (part-time work rather than having to choose between full-time work or no work at all) and the agency (lower costs, more skill sets for the job). Job sharing requires clear expectations and precise coordination between the employees, with their supervisor, and with clients/customers inside and outside the agency. And the agency must develop policies for contributions to and division of pensions, health care, and other benefits.

Under flexi place, employees may work away from the office provided a suitable outside workstation is available. This works best for professionals who can work independently and yet remain in contact with the agency through a variety of electronic media (such as, e-mail, voice mail, fax). The advantage to the agency is that it may be able to attract competent individuals who value independence and flexibility as well as to save on overcrowded workspace. The downsides, of course, are predictable things like communication and control, and unpredictable ones like workplace health and safety and workers' compensation claims.

INFLUENCES ON EMPLOYEES' ABILITY TO PERFORM

In addition to motivation, employees must have the necessary competencies in order to perform well. Legislatures and personnel experts have the most significant effect on the ability of the worker through the wage-setting process. The more money allocated to salaries, the more competitive a governmental employer will become in the labor market and the more talent it will attract. For example, some attributed the problems in the yearlong troublesome effort to change a pay system at the University of Kansas to a vendor's failure to attract and hold onto the needed computer programming talent. Similarly, salary level and working conditions affect an employee's intention to stay with an employer. Unfortunately, public agencies often serve as training grounds for the private sector by paying relatively low salaries for experienced employees. For example, social workers hired by a state human service agency are usually paid competitive entry-level salaries, but if they are not given pay increases as they gain experience, they may choose to leave state employment for nonprofit or private-sector jobs. This turnover of experienced employees can reduce productivity by making case tracking more difficult, by hampering management development, and by diminishing organizational memory.

Department managers and personnel directors affect productivity significantly through employee selection. If a market wage will attract talented applicants to the public employer, then the hiring process must be able to select the candidates with the best potential to perform current responsibilities as well as learn new skills and possess personal attributes necessary to work in tomorrow's organizations. Other important departmental influences on the employee's ability to perform include the quality of on-the-job training and coaching and the quality and timeliness of feedback regarding performance.

It is in the area of training (covered in more detail in the next chapter) that the human resource department has significant effect on the ability factor by conducting training needs assessments and by locating or offering training opportunities. In addition, the department can support managers by emphasizing and researching the validity of selection methods, by working with supervisors and employees to develop performance-based appraisal methods, and by increasing supervisory skill in communicating constructive feedback to employees. In some cases, personnel departments will track labor market conditions and gather data on prevailing wage rates for input into legislative decisions regarding allocation or collective bargaining positions.

ORGANIZING FOR PRODUCTIVITY

Total Quality Management[15]

Total quality management is a management philosophy that combines scientific methods for experimentation and continuous improvement of processes with teamwork and participative decision making as the approach for implementing improvement changes. The central theme is the improvement of quality and the gaining of customer satisfaction. While the total quality movement has lost some of its luster over the past few years, there are four key ingredients that warrant enduring attention. They are:

- a customer focus
- data-driven decisions
- participative decision making
- and continuous improvement.

The organization is seen as a complex of systems, with each system made up of interrelated processes that deliver services or goods to "customers." Identifying and understanding these processes is often the starting point of developing a TQM approach in an organization. Finding root causes of quality problems and collecting data before and after implementing solutions to track the success of such solutions are often the mundane and difficult aspects of TQM. In addition, defining quality for the organization, clarifying the values and mission of the organization, and identifying who are the customers and their wants are basic activities that TQM organizations engage in to provide direction for their quality efforts. TQM organizations often reorganize themselves into cross-functional teams to better reflect core processes and improve responsiveness to customer needs.

Critics of TQM in public organizations cite a number of concerns of the applicability of TQM. Among them, they caution against the view that TQM advocates fail to distinguish between customers and citizens. Second, they claim that ambiguous and conflicting political policy goals make TQM in the public sector unrealistic.

As to the first concern, there is validity in cautioning that citizens are not always customers. Traditionally, customers who are dissatisfied with something they buy simply choose another brand. This is not very often an option in government.

Furthermore, customers have no obligations to make their dissatisfaction known (other than switching to another product), nor do they have any obligations to help improve the service. In addition, the private-sector stories of companies going out of their way to satisfy individual customers would be seen as favoritism and inequitable treatment and would be severely criticized in the public sector.

The criticism regarding ambiguous and conflicting goals cannot be disregarded. James Q. Wilson premises his book, *Bureaucracy*, on the idea that public organizations are fundamentally different from private ones because they are prone to have conflicting or ambiguous objectives that are the result of political compromises.[16] TQM works best where objectives can be clarified.

Job Enrichment

The effort to identify conditions conducive to high performance led in the 1970s and 1980s to research into **job enrichment**. "Enriched jobs" are those where performance of the work itself is rewarding. Figure 9–2 illustrates this approach to designing work that leads to high job satisfaction and effectiveness. High internal work motivation, "growth" satisfaction, general job satisfaction, and work effectiveness result when people experience their work as meaningful, when they feel responsible for the quality and quantity of work produced, and when they have firsthand knowledge of the actual results of their labor. These psychological states are likely to result from work designed to incorporate the characteristics of variety, work with a beginning and identifiable end, work of significance, and work characterized by autonomy and feedback.[17]

Jobs that are high in these characteristics are said to be enriched and to have a high motivating potential. Whether high internal motivation, satisfaction, and productivity actually do come about as outcomes for employees depend on their knowledge and skill, their growth needs strength (such as the need for self-esteem or the esteem of others), and their satisfaction with working conditions (such as pay, supervision, and co-workers).

Results of research into this model have been generally supportive. Personnel policy innovations have been adopted first as experiments, and then as options in the "tool kit" the supervisor and personnel director use to match employees with work and to generate good individual and team performance. The design of jobs to enrich them assumes that employees are long-term assets. Once again, we find a technique employed to promote high performance is challenged by contemporary working conditions in many organizations.[18]

Work/Life Balance

Results from a national survey sponsored in part by the *Washington Post*, show that 75 percent of both men and women believe that in recent years there has been "a great deal" or "quite a lot" of change in the relationship between men and women in families, at work, and in society in general.[19] In that same survey, 80 percent believe that because of the changes, it has become harder to raise children and for marriages to succeed. Based on census data for 1998, Tamar Lewin reports that

FIGURE 9–2   Job Characteristics Model. (Source: Richard Hackman/Greg Oldham, *Work Design*, © 1980 by Addison-Wesley Publishing Company. Reprinted with permission of the publisher.)

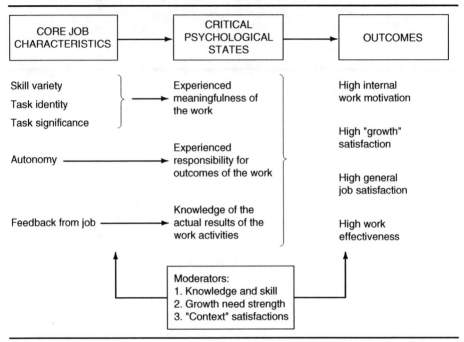

in 51 percent of marriages both spouses are working, compared to 33 percent in 1976.[20] Fifty-nine percent of married or single women with babies younger than a year old were working. Of those whose children are older than a year, 73 percent of mothers were working in 1998. Furthermore, people are working longer hours, and for many the effort is required to keep up with basic living expenses.[21]

The combination of more women entering the workforce and a shortage of labor has required innovative responses from employers in tight labor markets. For example, the Kansas Department of Insurance allows a parent to bring a baby to work regularly.[22] Others see telecommuting as an adaptation to this solution. Providing family-friendly benefits like those outlined in Chapter 6—child care, elder care, flexi work, long-term care—and providing job security also are responses to balancing the work/life tension.[23]

These responses make good sense. Family issues are the most cited (26 percent) reasons for last minute absences from work. In 1998 personal illness accounted for 22 percent of unscheduled absences. Given these figures, it may be that traditional sick-leave plans do not address the real issues driving employee absenteeism, according to Paul Gibson reporting on a CCH, Incorporated, survey.[24] Survey results show that the most effective employer responses to reducing unscheduled absenteeism were: flexible scheduling, on-site child care, and emergency child care.

Teamwork

Organizing employees into groups to work together on certain projects or on everyday tasks is increasingly the structure that public and private organizations are choosing.[25] There are several reasons for the popularity of **teamwork** as the preferred approach. Organizational problems and issues are so complex today that no one person can grasp all of the information nor have all the skills to adequately and thoroughly analyze and choose the best solutions. The complexity of problems also requires innovativeness and diversity of viewpoints to see all of the options and consequences involved. Finally, today's most serious problems do not fall neatly into our traditional functional departments. For example, to promote economic development a local government must coordinate financial incentives, zoning and site plan issues, infrastructure issues, and code enforcement. In the usual organizational structure, this would involve several different departments: finance, planning, engineering, and public works.

In terms of employee performance, the team concept addresses both the motivational and ability aspects of performance. Because teamwork usually involves participation by team members in decision making, commitment to work tasks and organizational goals are enhanced. When teams work together well, team members learn from one another, thus increasing each individual member's ability to perform. If the combined efforts of the team are directed well, the results can be innovative solutions, highly motivated employees, and efficient use of resources.

The challenge for managers and supervisors is to be able to direct and guide the team toward these results while allowing time for team cohesion to develop, for conflicts to be faced and resolved, for diverse opinions to be heard, and for learning from mistakes.

Much has been written recently about teams in both academic journals and management books. Following are several factors that appear to be most important for team leaders to understand if they are to succeed in team building.

A Stable Workforce That Values Organizational Goals. For teams to work effectively, their members must be able to get to know and trust one another. Furthermore, the team members must value the team goals as worthy of their collective effort.

Agreement That Teams Are Useful and Needed. Before the team approach can be used, group members must realize that there are some problems and tasks that teams can do better than individuals, that the time invested in building a team is worthwhile, and that priorities have to be negotiated with the understanding that their individual (or departmental) concerns may not always receive the highest priority.

Clear Expectations and Goals. Teams need to spend time, especially in the beginning, clarifying why they are there. Often teams are given broad general goals that they must then understand and accept as well as translate into concrete objectives they want to achieve with recognizable outcomes.

Understanding and Training in Communication and Group Dynamics. Team members need to recognize what is happening interpersonally among them. They must realize that not everyone expresses teamwork and commitment to the team in the same way. They must be comfortable in talking about "process" matters, such as conflicts between different factions on the team, competition for leadership, power struggles, hidden agendas, fight/flight behavior and other symptoms of anxiety and stress experienced by team members. They must be able to talk productively about these matters that require communication skills such as giving and receiving feedback, listening, responding to feelings, and interpreting nonverbal communication. It is unlikely that these skills will develop through on-the-job training without some kind of developmental skill-building program.

Much of what is written in this chapter applies to team performance as it does to individual performance. However, teamwork is complicated by the fact that another goal is to enhance group performance and build synergistic group effort. The leader of the team must balance fair treatment of each individual with flexibility to encourage diversity of contribution by those individual members along with the idea that the team and its goals may have to come first.

SUMMARY

Elected officials, managers, supervisors, and human resource specialists have a significant influence on employee performance. Within the parameters set by legislators and chief executives, human resource systems must be developed that make the fullest use of employee motivation and capabilities. This requires an understanding of what employees need to perform well (such as adequate skills, clear instructions, feedback, and rewards). The external focus of political leaders often deflects their concern for the impact of policy compromises on human resource management within public organizations. Equity theory and expectancy theory provide a useful framework to understand the links between performance and motivation and job satisfaction, as well as diagnostic tools for implementing techniques and methods and also for understanding how and why organizational members are responding as they do to higher-level policy and managerial decisions. Those responsible for improving employee effort and performance must be willing to experiment with new approaches and to know how to evaluate their effectiveness in employee performance. The psychological contract is a concept that can be used to help explore differences that may be affecting the performance of an employee or work group.

Tomorrow's organization with increased specialization, downsizing, teamwork, and pay for performance all add challenges and anxiety to the work of elected and appointed executives, managers, supervisors, and employees. Organizing work in this type of environment of change highlights the importance of an organization and its members who are capable of dealing with the resultant ambiguity and who are willing and able to learn from their organizational experiences and make personal and organizational changes based on that learning.

KEY TERMS

administrative logic
development function
employee commitment
equity theory
expectancy theory
extrinsic motivation
flextime
intrinsic motivation

job enrichment
job sharing
market-based values
political logic
psychological contract
teamwork
total quality management (TQM)

DISCUSSION QUESTIONS

1. Identify the differences between political and administrative logic and give examples of each. How important do you think these differences are when it comes to understanding the ways that elected and appointed officials act? What do you think is the most significant difference between market-based logic and political and administrative logic?
2. Describe the concept of the psychological contract and identify a situation you are familiar with where it might be employed to help clarify and resolve differences.
3. Describe the basic components of equity and expectancy theory. How do they help to explain employee performance? Identify an example from your own life where equity theory or expectancy theory helps you understand why you did what you did.
4. Describe the ways that elected officials, managers, and personnel specialists affect an employee's motivation to perform.
5. Describe the ways that elected officials, managers, and personnel specialists affect an employee's ability to perform.
6. Describe four types of innovations that may improve work performance: total quality management, job enrichment, work/life balance, and teamwork.

CASE STUDY 1: REQUIEM FOR A GOOD SOLDIER

"How about Rachel Fowlkes?" Gordon asked. "She's certainly in line for the job. Rachel has had all the requisite training and experience to become an assistant director." Harold Nash, manager of the Department of Health and Welfare, rolled a ballpoint pen between his fingers and rocked slowly in his executive desk chair. "I don't know," he said softly. "I really don't know. Give me another rundown on her experience."

Clifton Gordon opened the manila personnel folder and laid it on Nash's desk. "Six years with this bureau, but she'd been with the old Vocational Rehabilitation Department for almost nine years before the reorganization. She started as a clerk, was in line for assistant director at the time we reorganized."

"We had too many chiefs as a result of that merger," Nash said. "As I recall, a few people were bumped."

Gordon smiled. "I remember that, all right. She was one that was bumped and I was the one who took over as assistant director."

"How did she take it?" Nash asked.

"No problem," Gordon said. "She was a good soldier."

"A good soldier," Nash echoed.

"She was very capable and versatile," Gordon said. "In fact I relied on her heavily for new personnel training. Many of those green young men she trained are now directors and assistant directors." Gordon pointed to the personnel folder.

"Rachel was made acting assistant director of the information and public assistance section four years ago and apparently was seriously considered for the position of assistant director when Tom Walters retired."

Nash shook his head. "Regrettably, I had a difficult choice then as well. I had to choose between a capable career woman and an equally talented young man. Both were on the cert as bests qualified. In the end I felt Manpower Research was not the right place in which to place our first female assistant director."

"Now would be a perfect time," Gordon said, "especially in view of the governor's recent order on the EEO Act and the stress on the utilization of minorities and women. I think that's what all this talk of affirmative action is all about. Wouldn't promoting Rachel be an affirmative action?"

Nash winced. "Don't remind me. That report to the governor is due shortly! But back to Rachel; promotions must ultimately be based on merit and not on sex or color of skin."

"I agree completely," Gordon replied quickly, "but with all other things being equal, why not select a woman?"

"If that were true, I just might. But all other things are not equal. Not only do I again have several capable candidates along with Rachel on the cert, but there have been problems with Rachel lately."

"I wasn't aware of that. What's happened to Rachel, the good soldier? I can't imagine her causing problems for anybody."

"That's what I'd like to know," Nash said. "For the past six months I've given her several responsibilities and she just hasn't responded the way she used to. Her work output is definitely deteriorating and her attitude is, too."

"What's her complaint?"

"No one seems to be able to put his finger on the problem: I even had her in the office once for a casual chat, but she claimed there was nothing causing her any concern. I mentioned her slipping work performance and she promised to improve."

"And?"

"Oh, she's improved. I guess her work is O.K., but that old spark is gone."

"That's a shame," Gordon said. "Rachel has done so well . . . for a woman."

Nash nodded, "Yes, it is a shame. I'm afraid we'll have to look elsewhere to fill that assistant director position."

Source: U.S. Civil Service Commission Bureau of Training, *The Equal Employment Opportunity Act: Implications for Public Employers.* Washington, DC: U.S. Government Printing Office, 1973.

Questions

1. Using equity theory, analyze how and why Rachel's behavior has changed during the time period of the case.
2. What are the important inputs and outcomes from Rachel's point of view? Who is the focus of her social comparison?
3. What factor(s) has Harold Nash given input credit for that Rachel may have overlooked?
4. Utilizing expectancy theory, analyze how Rachel's behavior has changed during the time period in the case.

5. How has Rachel's estimation of her ability to perform as assistant director changed? Has the value she places on different outcomes associated with being assistant director changed? Has her expectation changed that good performance in her current job will lead to a promotion?
6. How would you define "old spark" in terms of a performance goal or job standard? How would you feel as an employee if someone failed to promote you justifying it, in part, by your loss of the "old spark"?
7. How do you think Rachel feels at this point in her job? How do you think you might feel? How common do you think the case of Rachel is in modern organizations?
8. Who is responsible for the changes in Rachel's behavior in this case? Who is accountable for them? What is the difference?
9. If you were Harold Nash, would you promote Rachel, given the deterioration of her morale and her apparent competent but lackluster performance?

CASE STUDY 2: RECRUITING A WATER PLANT TECHNICIAN

The city of Valdez is recruiting for a water plant technician. Shelly Wong appears to be head and shoulders more qualified than the other candidates. Her knowledge is up to date; she has had enough experience to establish a reliable work record; and she comes with great recommendations as a solid organizational citizen by her present employer. She has outgrown her present job.

Everything seems to be going well with the recruitment and selection process. When Ms. Wong is asked if she has any questions she responds, "This looks like a great place to work, but we take care of an elderly parent in our home, and we have day-care needs for our children." She continues, "I am looking for an employer who can offer a flexible work schedule. Will I need to take leave each time I have to pick up a sick child from day care? And on occasion my mother, who lives with us, needs transportation to the doctor's, and I like to be there when she talks with the doctor because she doesn't speak English very well."

The personnel officer responds, "I'm sorry, we run a pretty tight ship around here, and the water treatment plant technicians are mostly men who don't seem to have these kinds of needs. We'll try to work something out; we really want you to work for us. But I don't want to mislead you—maybe we aren't where we should be in this area."

Questions

1. Could the personnel director have approached this situation differently?
2. If the city wanted to "get where it should be in this area," what should it do?
3. What possible problems might this organization encounter in "getting where it should be," and how might it overcome them?

EXERCISE: PSYCHOLOGICAL CONTRACTS

Assume you are working to improve a supervisor-subordinate relationship. (If you like you may substitute another relationship.) Divide into two groups. One group will act as the supervisor, the other as the employees. Each group should list the expectations it has of the other. The supervisory group should list the expectations that supervisors ideally have of subordinates. The subordinate group should list the expectations they would ideally have of supervisors. Do the same for obligations. Do not include simplistic items on your lists like "honesty" or "open communication." Try to be more specific.

Share your lists. Put the subordinates' obligations next to the supervisors' expectations and the supervisors' obligations next to the subordinates' expectations. Compare the lists. See if what one group expects, the other is willing to give. Can you tell from your lists whether you have the basis for a good relationship? If not, what needs to be altered, added, or subtracted?

Is the ideal relationship you have described oriented towards traditional hierarchy or is it more team oriented? How would you alter your lists to make them more team oriented?

Could you do this exercise at work? If not, what is holding you back? What kind of responsibility could YOU take to help promote this kind of discussion in your work group?

NOTES

[1]Nalbandian, J. (1994). Reflections of a "pracademic" on the logic of politics and administration. *Public Administration Review, 54*, 531.

[2]Klingner, D. E., J. Nalbandian, and B. S. Romzek (forthcoming). Politics, administration, and markets. *American Review of Public Administration.*

[3]Nalbandian, J. (1994). Reflections of a "pracademic" on the logic of politics and administration.

[4]Adams, J. S. (1965). Inequity in social exchange. In L. Berkowitz (Ed.). *Advances in Experimental Social Psychology* (Vol. 2). New York: Academic Press.

[5]Vroom, V. H. (1964). *Work and motivation.* New York: John Wiley.

[6]Iaffaldana, M. T., and P. M. Muchinsky (1985). Job satisfaction and job performance: A meta-analysis. *Psychological Bulletin, 97*, 251–273.

[7]Blumenthal, D. (January 1979). Candid reflections of a businessman in Washington. *Fortune,* p. 40.

[8]Moorman, R. H. (1991). Relationship between organizational justice and organizational citizenship behaviors: Do fairness perceptions influence employee citizenship? *Journal of Applied Psychology, 76*, 845–855.

[9]Perry, J. L. (1997). Antecedents of public service motivation. *Journal of Public Administration Research and Theory, 7*, 2, 181–197; Rainey, H. G. (1996). *Understanding and Managing Public Organizations.* San Francisco: Jossey-Bass.

[10]Brewer, G. A., S. Coleman Selden, and R. L. Facer, II (2000). Individual conceptions of public service motivation. *Public Administration Review, 60*, 3, 254–264.

[11]Huddleston, M. W. (1999). *Profiles in Excellence: Conversations with the Best of America's Career Executive Service.* The PricewaterhouseCoopers Endowment for the Business of Government.

[12]Balfour, D. L., and B. Weschler (1996). Organizational commitment: Antecedents and outcomes in public organizations. *Public Productivity and Management Review, 19*, 256–277; Romzek, B. S. (1990). Employment investment and commitments: The ties that bind. *Public Administration Review, 50*, 374–382.

[13]Nelton, S. (December 1993). A flexible style of management. *Nation's Business, 81*, 24; Olen, H. (February 1996). Getting a handle on flextime. *Working Woman, 21*, 55.

[14]Brown, J. (February 2000). Teleworking/Telecommuting: A potential solution to the work/life balancing act. *International Personnel Management Association News,* pp. 20–21; Hafner, K. (November 2, 2000). Working at home today? *New York Times,* p. D–1; Harris, B. (December 28, 2000). Companies turning cool to telecommuting. *Los Angeles Times,* p. A–1.

[15]Deming, W. E. (1982). *Out of the crisis.* Cambridge, MA: MIT Press; Hackman, J. R., and R. Wageman (1995). Total quality management: empirical, conceptual, and practical issues. *Administrative Science Quarterly, 40*, 2, 309–343.

[16]Wilson, J. Q. (1989). *Bureaucracy.* New York: Basic Books.

[17]Hackman, J. R. (1986). *Psychology and Work.* Washington, DC: American Psychological Association; J. R. Hackman, and G. R. Oldham. (1980). *Work Redesign.* Reading, MA: Addison Wesley.

[18]Niehoff, B. P., R. H. Moorman, G. Blakely, and J. Fuller (March 2001). The influence of empowerment and job enrichment on employee loyalty in a downsizing environment. *Group & Organization Management, 26,* 93–114.

[19]Rosenfield, M., and R. Morin. (April 20, 1998). The politics of fatigue. *The Washington Post National Weekly Edition,* pp. 6–10.

[20]Lewin, T. (October 24, 2000). Now a majority: Families with 2 parents who work. *New York Times,* p. A–14.

[21]Bluestone, B., and S. Rose (March-April 1997). Overworked and underemployed. *The American Prospect,* pp. 58–69.

[22]Belluck, P. (December 4, 2000). A little bit of burping is OK if it keeps parents on the job. *New York Times,* p. A–1.

[23]Durst, Samantha (Summer 1999). Assessing the effect of family friendly programs on public organizations. *Review of Public Personnel Administration,* pp. 19–48.

[24]———— (June 1998). 1998 CCH unscheduled absenteeism survey. *International Personnel Management Association News,* pp. 18–20.

[25]Hesselbein, F., M. Goldsmith, and R. Beckhard. (Eds.). (1994). *The Leader of the Future.* San Francisco: Jossey-Bass; International City Management Association (1994). *Building Teams and Teamwork.* Washington, DC: International City Management Association; Katzenback, J. R., and D. K. Smith (1993). *The Wisdom of Teams.* Cambridge, MA: Harvard Business School; Senge, P. M. (1990). *The Fifth Discipline.* New York: Doubleday.

10
Training, Education, and Staff Development

The need for greater investment in the training and development of public employees in this decade and beyond is widely recognized and is part of the strategic thinking explored in Chapter 3. Several factors are responsible for projected shortages in valued competencies and the resultant need for training. Demographic projections of the future workforce coupled with heightened demand for professional and technical skills suggest critical gaps. Rapid technological change suggests that the knowledge, skills, and abilities of workers today will be obsolete tomorrow. The mismatch is between the education and training received, and the changing knowledge and skills—both in quantity and kind—demanded by organizations.

A common way of equipping organizations with valued competencies that will position an employer to respond to present and future challenges is to hire new employees, acquiring their competencies. Alternatively, an organization can negotiate with other organizations to purchase or lease required competence. As we have seen in other chapters, it is becoming increasingly common for public employers to contract with other employers—private and public—for both service delivery and staff work. In this chapter, we explore a third way of renewing human resources—working with new and existing employees to tailor, update, and develop new competencies.

The American Society for Training and Development's 2001 State of the Industry Report shows that the average American company is training more of its employees than ever. Overall, in 1999 training expenditures averaged about 2 percent of payroll. The biggest share of training focused on technical processes and procedures. E-learning constituted about 5 percent of training. And, more training in 1999 was conducted in-house than outsourced, in order to save money and to tailor the training to specific organizational needs.[1]

Every organization must invest time and money developing employees. Different organizations fulfill this function to varying degrees and with varying priority. Most organizations provide new employee orientation, on-the-job training, and mandated training such as training in safety procedures and preventing sexual harassment. Others have a comprehensive human resources development plan that includes formal and informal instruction, internal and external programs, organizational development, and sophisticated tracking systems connected to organizational goals and objectives for every employee. The **development function** is seen as more important in organizations where employees are considered assets than in organizations where it is simply a cost of production, and training is viewed as integral to mission accomplishment and for preparation to meet tomorrow's challenges.

By the end of this chapter, you will be able to:

1. Identify the relationship between training and strategic planning.
2. Distinguish between training, education, and staff development as part of the development function.
3. Identify issues and methods associated with developing the organization as a whole, new employees, and existing employees.
4. Identify and briefly describe the three roles of the human resources development specialist.
5. Briefly describe training needs assessment, design, and evaluation.
6. Discuss the way the development function is viewed from the perspective of alternative personnel systems.

TRAINING AS PART OF STRATEGIC PLANNING

Training as strategic planning, planned change, and total quality management broadens the development focus to encompass individuals, groups, and the organization as a whole. Bernhard and Ingols, a human resources development executive and an academician, have commented that in many organizations the development function produces "pleasant but basically irrelevant" activities resulting from corrective but not strategic goals.[2] According to Rosow and Zager, "Today a new notion has begun to take hold—that the sole objective test of relevance for a training program is whether the corporation's business strategy requires it."[3] A U.S. Merit Systems Protection Board report found that, in the federal government, one of the main characteristics was the absence of a connection between training and strategic planning. The study found that training budgets were more likely to be supported when the costs were included as part of the cost of funding a particular program.[4]

Aligning a development strategy with agency goals has several advantages.[5] First, it helps to clarify budget options in the human resources development area. It provides guidance for determining how much money an agency is going to invest in development. Also, alternative investments can be evaluated in terms of how well they advance agency goals. Second, the alignment provides a framework to evaluate whether or not the development activity has actually produced a cost-effective result. Finally, it provides additional resources and mechanisms to advance agency goals. It facilitates communication about agency goals and can advance commitment to agency goals through participative and team-based discussion, design, and implementation of development activities.

Linking training objectives to strategic agency goals presumes consensus among political executives, legislators, senior administrative staff, and union officials regarding agency purposes and objectives. The field of education provides an example where this external environment impacts on the training of schoolteachers. School districts face the political reality of low teacher pay and high demands for increased quality of teaching. Building a training plan to address the strategic goal of upgrading the subject matter knowledge of teachers as well as their teaching skills, without acknowledging how the rate of pay affects the quality of the applicant pool, is a political reality that undermines the linkage between training goals and agency goals. Similarly, a teachers' union's failure to acknowledge skill deficiencies among teachers limits ability to connect training objectives and strategic goals. Both of these issues, essentially involving personnel functions such as acquisition and development, relate closely to broader issues of conflict among values and systems.

OBJECTIVES OF THE DEVELOPMENT FUNCTION: TRAINING, EDUCATION, AND STAFF DEVELOPMENT

Nadler and Nadler have identified three categories of development activities—training, education, and staff development.[6] Most often the **development function** is associated with training employees to perform existing jobs more efficiently, effectively, and responsively. But in many organizations the development function includes more than training for short-term improvement. It is not uncommon for organizations to **educate** employees for the longer term, to build the competencies they will need for promotions to specific jobs in the career ladder. For example, some agencies offer supervisory training for non-supervisory employees who might be in line for a promotion to a supervisory position. **Staff development** is designed to open the organization to broader vistas and new ways of thinking. Staff development aims to build the competencies of employees and teams, to enhance the general knowledge base of the organization, and to prepare a cadre of people to think strategically even if strategic thinking is not required in their present jobs.

The primary distinguishing feature among these three development functions is time. **Training** provides learning for current responsibilities and tasks. Much of this learning focuses on skill building but also can include understanding concepts and theories and increasing self-awareness of one's own personal attributes, perceptions, attitudes, and ways of thinking. For example, supervisory training often includes performance management as a main topic, which can include skills such as setting goals and performance standards, assessing performance, and giving feedback. It can also include learning theories of motivation and understanding one's own communication style and its impact on others. All of this learning is directed toward improving the supervisor's current responsibilities and enhancing managerial competence.

Education is more future-oriented. It can include skill building but may put more emphasis on learning that can be generalized to different situations and on preparing the individual for new responsibilities and challenges. A supervisor who aspires to a managerial position may be encouraged to continue his or her formal education by obtaining a college degree at the bachelor's or master's level. A literacy program offered by an organization has specific benefits currently for the employee, but its benefits are more to enhance the overall functioning of that individual once his or her reading skills are improved.

Staff development is also future-oriented, but the future is less clear and less defined. The focus is to prepare employees for changes that are not specifically anticipated or clearly known. Employees are being asked to prepare themselves to meet unknown problems and to be ready to face a changing, uncertain future. While skill building may still be a component of this type of development, the emphasis is much more on building attitudes and knowledge that are consistent with the organization's values and changing requirements. The emphasis is also on developing the competencies that will enhance the individual's ability to lead. For example, the U.S. Senior Executive Service has identified key competencies as: leading change, leading people, being results driven, having business acumen, and building coalitions/communications. Many leadership programs fall into this category of development in which self-awareness, change management, strategic planning, visioning the future, and becoming a leader who will inspire and build confidence in others are taught.

The distinction between training, education and staff development is mirrored in public agencies that have developed comprehensive sets of competencies for first-line supervisors, managers, and administrative executives.[7] In addition to work by the U.S. Office of Personnel Management,[8] the Canadian public service has similarly developed competencies for middle managers and also for Assistant Deputy Ministers—senior managers.[9]

This emphasis on competencies, whether in training, education, or staff development, promises to connect the development function more directly to managerial goals for service delivery by focusing on what employees actually are capable of doing and what they will need to be able to do in the future, as opposed to time in grade and what they have been exposed to through experience and training.

TRAINING, EDUCATION, AND STAFF DEVELOPMENT AS STRATEGIC HUMAN RESOURCES MANAGEMENT— CURRENT ISSUES AND METHODS

We can look at current issues and methods of training, education, and staff development from three perspectives—the organization as a whole, new employees, and existing employees. What methods exist to build the capacity of the organization as a whole? What methods and issues focus on new and existing employees?

BUILDING ORGANIZATIONAL CAPACITY

Organizations are like individuals in some respects. Just as individuals seek feedback to improve, organizations and organizational units must undergo their own self-assessments. There are many ways to do this, and we identify and discuss some of them in this section.

Organization Development and Planned Change

Managers and supervisors are responsible not only for training individual employees to improve their work skills, but also for helping to make changes in the work environment so that skills are used most effectively. This process is called **organization development (OD)**. It developed in the 1960s as a combination of sensitivity training, a focus on the emotional side of interpersonal work relationships, and **action research**. Action research is based on gathering data about practical problems and feeding the data back to employee participants for interpretation and assessment. An employee-centered problem-solving process follows these phases. OD is similar to training in that both are change oriented. However, OD is usually participant focused rather than trainer oriented; it seeks to increase productivity by increasing employee identification with the objectives of the organization rather than by increasing employee job skills; it focuses on the process variables that comprise human interaction rather than the work product itself; and it tends to be systems- and group-oriented rather than aimed at building the knowledge and skills of individual employees.[10]

One widely used method of organization development is **team building**. Team building activities are designed to assist members of a work group to increase their productivity as a group. Typically, team building begins when a consultant is called into an organization to diagnose and correct a problem in the relationships within a department or between departments. Rather than define the problem alone, the consultant will invite members of the work group(s) to engage in diagnostic exercises aimed at assessing how well the group is working together and where the problem areas might be. Data are collected through questionnaire or discussion, then summarized and fed back to the participants. Work group members are asked to help the consultant interpret the results. The consultant might ask, "What do these data tell you about how well you are working as a group?" What do you need to be doing more of/less of to increase your team effectiveness?" If this group were operating at a high performance level, what would we see that now is missing?" Problems are identified, discussed, given a priority, and then a process for dealing with them is devised by the group with the help of the consultant.

Team building is gaining more notice currently because of the emphasis on teamwork, as discussed in the previous chapter. It focuses on training individuals to work together in teams as well as enhancing the job skills of individual members because the capacity of teams is what will enhance productivity in many agencies. Thus, it is closely tied to a number of related trends, such as diversity training, 360-degree evaluation, team-based performance pay, and strategic human resource management.

Training on Appreciating Diversity

The composition of the workforce is changing both demographically and in terms of the number of temporary and part-time workers, and these trends pose several challenges to the human resources development specialist. One of the biggest development challenges for public employers in the 1990s and beyond will be accommodating administrative processes and human relations to differences in culture and ethnicity. America's minorities will be entering the workforce at a faster rate than ever before; immigrants will constitute a larger proportion of the workforce than at any time since World War I; and women will make up 60 percent or more of the new entrants into the workforce.[11] A generalized tolerance for differences and adherence to procedural rules simply cannot be expected to absorb the organizational shocks these demographic changes are bringing.

The nature of bureaucracy itself may mitigate some of the differences. That is, job descriptions, work goals, performance standards, and the general impersonality of bureaucracy can be expected to have a homogenizing effect on the workforce. Nevertheless, the remarks of Bellah and associates provide words of caution. They observe: "Americans, it would seem, feel most comfortable in thinking about politics in terms of a consensual community of autonomous, but essentially similar, individuals. For all the lip service given to respect for cultural differences, Americans seem to lack the resources to think about the relationships between groups that are culturally, socially, or economically quite different."[12]

It seems reasonable to think that investments will be needed in training and educating employees to understand, deal with, and even appreciate diversity. But training and education will not be enough. In some cases, organizations will have to come to grips with prejudice not only among Anglos but also among the minorities. In such cases, organizational expectations will need to be clarified, and rewards and discipline may be required to make the point that, at a minimum, differences are to be tolerated if not valued. Training in team building and in creativity and innovation may serve to reinforce and add to specific diversity training. See for example, the training program outline that follows.

OUTLINE FOR A ONE-DAY DIVERSITY TRAINING PROGRAM

1. *Appreciating Differences*
   Introductions and overview
   What is diversity? Why is it important?
   Differences that matter in your organization
2. *Identifying Our Uniqueness*
   Influences on our attitudes and behaviors
   Issues around being seen as "different"
   Impact of family background
3. *Understanding Diversity in Others*
   Assumptions and stereotypes
   Cultural and ethnic differences
   Gender differences
4. *Managing Conflict Productively*
   Types of conflict
   Negotiating strategies
5. *Constructing a Professional Work Environment*
   Norms and practices
   Activities and programs
   Developing effective working relationships
6. *Summary*
   Personal plan for improvement
   Evaluation

Training in workforce diversity (see appendix at end of chapter) should include several components:[13]

- Skilled instructors sensitive to multicultural awareness
- Experiential learning, including role playing, exercises, discussions, and group experiences
- Flexibility and latitude for tailoring to specific work group circumstances
- Clearly identified goals that connect to a larger organizational philosophy and effort
- Evaluative instruments to assess effectiveness
- Follow-up programs and other activities because increasing awareness may occur in a half-day training session, but long-term change of attitudes and behavior takes much longer

Commitment to Continuous Learning

Underpinning many innovations in the development area is the overriding precept that organizations increasingly must prepare themselves to adapt to change. They can do this by seeing themselves as learning systems, with employees serving as both learners and teachers.[14] **Continuous learning** requires that the organization teach its employees new skills, new technology, and new knowledge. It assumes that the more employees know about their equipment and work processes, the better prepared they will be to discover problems and ideas for solutions. The commitment to continuous learning also requires that employees use their knowledge and skills to proactively discover administrative and production problems they can then help to solve. It also requires developing the attitudes of the learner—curiosity, creativity, open-mindedness, willingness to take risks, willingness to learn from mistakes, and willingness to teach others.

At first, the concept of continuous learning seems simple. No one consciously would oppose continuous learning, yet many resisting forces exist. Argyris identifies organizational norms like avoiding conflict and "straight talk" that work against questioning an agency's basic assumptions and operating procedures.[15] Managers are more likely to reward workers who solve problems rather than discover them. Further, in a hierarchical system, workers are often reminded that management has the upper hand, and improvements in work methods may threaten job security. In the face of today's external environmental pressures which require organizations to make rapid changes in the least costly way, organizational norms often do not allow for mistakes much less pressures that require organizations to make rapid changes in the least costly way; organizational norms often do not allow for mistakes much less for learning from them.

Finally, history would suggest that organizations are more likely to make technical work simple; they mask its complexity in order to accommodate basic employee skills rather than investing in an upgrade of basic skills so that employees could learn more about their equipment. Rosow and Zager observe, "The amount of training required to profit from a new technology varies directly with the amount of diversity of new knowledge embodied in it."[16] In sum, a commitment to continuous learning takes more than a slogan on the wall or a phrase in a mission statement; it requires a philosophical orientation that challenges many of the ways Americans are used to conducting business and government.

Development Programs for Executives

This type of staff development activity takes on critical importance if an organization is to build a cadre of effective and responsive leaders who will guide the organization in the uncertain future. Often entire levels of managers are required to participate in a particular seminar or series of seminars and activities as condition of their current position or to be considered for higher-level promotion. There are several advantages to this **executive development** approach: (1) Managers develop a common language and foundation by which to communicate with one another; (2) when a critical mass of managers share common experiences, organizational culture changes will more likely occur; (3) when managers attend a seminar together, they can use the time to face difficult team work issues; and (4) when the experience involves some emotional intensity and involvement, a sense of camaraderie can develop among the participants. Typical activities include formal presentations by leadership experts, problem-solving simulations, outdoor experiences or "challenge courses," group interactions facilitated by a consultant, and individual skill and attitude assessments with group feedback.

DEVELOPING NEW EMPLOYEES

New Employee Orientation

Easily one of the most neglected areas of training, the new employee orientation can have several valuable purposes.[17] It can:

- Reduce start up costs by providing the employee with basic information in an efficient manner
- Relieve supervisors and co-workers of basic orientation tasks
- Reduce anxiety by familiarizing new employee with information and reducing need to "bother" supervisors and co-workers to obtain basic information
- Reduce employee turnover by showing that the organization values the employee
- Develop realistic job expectations and introducing organizational values and culture

Training for Basic Skill Development

Public employers are no different from private employers in their need for job applicants with increasingly sophisticated basic skills. Estimates of the number of Americans whose reading, writing, and computing skills limit their employment opportunities are frightening. A Department of Labor Report comments that more than 20 percent of adults read at or below the fifth-grade level.[18] That same report shows that in 1979 the average college graduate earned 38 percent more than the average high school graduate. Today that number is 71 percent!

According to the Hudson Institute, while disadvantaged minorities will be entering the workforce in larger numbers, it is not clear whether their economic outlook will improve: "Unskilled and poorly educated workers will face multiple threats on tomorrow's labor markets. Modern technology—especially IT—tends to reduce the demand for unskilled labor. Globalization will increase U.S. consumption of imported goods and services produced by low-skilled workers. As a result, there will be less demand for low-skilled workers who produce comparable goods and services here. A rapidly changing economy will harm low-skilled and poorly educated workers who cannot adapt to changes in the workplace."[19] They continue, "The average earnings of whites significantly exceed those of blacks and Hispanics. But blacks are increasing their earnings more rapidly than whites. Gains in Hispanic earnings, on the other hand, are lagging, because Hispanics are not improving their overall levels of educational attainment."[20]

The Hudson Institute's report *Workforce 2020* paints a challenging picture, and one that makes training and education not only an organizational problem, but more importantly a public policy problem of significant proportions. Just as many have assumed that government employers should take the lead in affirmative action, it may be that public agencies will be seen as primary agents of public policy initiatives emphasizing **basic skill development** in the workplace.

In today's work environment, the knowledge of computer operations, especially of word processing and database management, can be considered a basic skill not unlike those of reading and writing. In this area, it is the younger workers, who have been schooled early on in computer technology and are more comfortable with electronic media, who will have the advantage over older workers. Unfortunately some older employees are reluctant to admit their limited skill in this area and will not seek the necessary training. Their advantage of work experience will not benefit them in an era of rapidly changing technological conditions. However, it is also amazing how some older workers want to learn new technology that builds on what they already know.

Integrating On-the-Job Training (OJT) with Other Training

Sometimes **on-the-job training (OJT)** is carried out simply by directing an experienced worker to "teach Sam your job" or "break Jan in." It is often overlooked as an integral part of the development function, especially since it is directed in each unit idiosyncratically. For this reason, there is wide variability in the effectiveness of on-the-job training. It is among the best and poorest of development activities. It is done informally at all levels most often including new employee orientation and training in job tasks, policies, and procedures. Formal programs include apprenticeships and internships. A good example of a formal progression of skill training on the job is found in many police and fire departments.

OJT can be a highly successful and highly motivating form of training because the individual puts into practice right away what he or she has learned. There is immediate feedback on the level of proficiency attained, and it often occurs at the moment when the individual needs and wants to learn a particular skill. For example, a new employee is using the computer and gets stuck because he or she doesn't know how to perform a particular function. The employee may ask a co-worker who then spends a half hour instructing him or her on that particular function.

One problem associated with OJT activities is that it is not planned in any systematic way to provide a progression of skill development at regular intervals. If conducted haphazardly, there is no way of tracking who has received what kind of training. In addition, often OJT is not seen as a part of the responsibilities of supervisors and other employees and, therefore, they are not given credit or training for performing this function. It may be seen more as an imposition by the co-worker selected to "break in" the new employee.

Besides tracking and recognition as part of a systematic approach to OJT, evaluation procedures must be incorporated so that individuals will see their progress. Human resource development (HRD) specialists can provide assistance by developing tracking and evaluation procedures, by identifying skill sets which are appropriate for OJT, and by training staff to be OJT trainers. If certain competencies can be well defined, if instructional materials are developed, and if individuals can evaluate their progress, OJT can also be a self-paced, individualized activity with minimal supervision.

DEVELOPING CURRENT EMPLOYEES

Training for Temporary and Part-time Employees

With the increased use of temporary and part-time employees, organizations face the practical question of how much training to offer these workers. Since these employees may constitute a significant portion of the workforce, the financial investment could be considerable. Because these employees often are not considered as part of the "regular" workforce, their training needs are forgotten. It is not unusual for someone to be a "temporary" worker for two to three years and not have received any training. If there are too many of these forgotten workers in an agency, productivity will eventually be affected. There will be serious gaps between the competency of full-time personnel and temporary and part-time employees. There will also be a "class" distinction made which can affect teamwork and feelings of commitment and loyalty.

Coaching and Counseling: Whose Job Is It?

Coaching and counseling are often overlooked as training activities—yet they are done by every manager, supervisor, and HRD specialist at one time or another. Coaching involves a situation or behavior-specific characteristic that has been identified as needing improvement. Coaching is conducted in one-to-one sessions with either an outside consultant, an HRD specialist, or with one's own supervisor. The latter option has the advantage of being conducted by someone who has seen the behavior in context and who can provide immediate feedback and reinforcement for improved progress. However, because of the inherent authority of the supervisor, the individual may resist exploring the causes of the situation and be unwilling to be honest with him- or herself and thereby too defensive to make any improvements. The solution may be to have individual confidential sessions with someone outside the reporting hierarchy but enlisting the individual's boss and peers to provide support, reinforcement, and feedback in day-to-day interactions.

A development activity related to coaching is counseling, a more general approach to helping the employee. It may involve correcting a particular behavior or attitude that is more person-centered than situational. It may involve career counseling to help the individual develop a plan for building that worker's career. It may involve helping a person deal with a personal crisis that is adversely affecting his or her work performance. While no one should engage in doing therapy without the clinical training and knowledge, managers and supervisors are often called upon to work with employees on a personal level. There are several points that should be considered.

Managers and HRD specialists should know their own limits and comfort in this area. A manager may refer a person to the human resource department or specialist for counseling without ever personally attempting it because it is a terribly uncomfortable situation. While it is true that referral in this case to HR or an outside referral may be appropriate, the manager will also need to increase his or her comfort level and skill in this area.

Managers and supervisors should know when and how to make referrals for outside professional help. Whether the referral is to an employee assistance program, to an outside consultant, or to another type of professional, it is important that they recognize what is appropriate and how to suggest this alternative in a way that will not increase the employee's resistance.

Department managers and supervisors should understand the human resources policies when providing coaching and counseling assistance. What is available? For which type of matters? Is training for managers and supervisors offered?

Coaching and counseling sessions should be conducted in private and, to the extent possible, confidentially. A climate of support will enable the individual to more honestly and willingly examine the behavior and issues in question.

On-Line Interactive and Self-Paced Training

With the proliferation of the internet into many organizations and individual's homes, new, innovative computer applications allow training to occur wherever a portable laptop computer can be connected and whenever an individual chooses.[21] In Chapter 2 we emphasized the Internet as providing access to continuing education opportunities for human resources professionals, and that extends to all managers. Every professional association has a web site and most post newsletters, documents, publications, and training and education opportunities. The availability of on-line journal databases promises to make research easier for students and professionals alike.

Distance learning between people geographically dispersed, allows organizations the ability to provide timely training with minimal interruption to each person's professional and personal life, by eliminating the need to travel to and from a physical training site.[22] At a Training 2001 Conference and Expo in Atlanta, Mr. Tom Kelly, Vice President, Internet Learning Solutions Group, Cisco Systems stated, "E-learning will not put trainer out of business. On-site learning is still a good way to learn, but it's not the only way anymore."[23] Additionally, extensive and elaborate training packages for individual study can be contained on a CD-ROM, providing an individual a comprehensive and self-paced training session. For example, Microsoft Corporation provides step-by-step interactive tutorials on the configuration and application of a wide number of software applications, allowing a user to master timesaving features. E-learning is often more efficient than traditional training because it allows trainers to divide a program into smaller pieces; users can go directly to a specific part of the course they're interested in and bypass the rest, thereby saving time.

THREE ROLES FOR THE HUMAN RESOURCE DEVELOPMENT SPECIALIST

Trends in the development function impact the way the role of the human resource development specialist is envisioned, independent of fluctuations in funding for training, education, and staff development. The trend away from canned training packages to training designs tailored to strategic agency goals places the HRD trainer in a more essential organizational position.

Nadler and Nadler have conceptualized the HRD specialist's role in three ways.[24]

- *Learning Specialist*: facilitator of learning, designer of learning programs, developer of instructional strategies
- *Manager of HRD*: supervisor of HRD programs, developer of HRD personnel, arranger of facilities and finance, maintainer of relations
- *Consultant*: expert, advocate, stimulator, change agent

Although all roles must be filled if the development function is to operate comprehensively and effectively, they can be merged, and one is not necessarily exclusive of the others. The list roughly approximates the historical evolution of the human resource development function. In addition, it is clear that for development to be tied to the agency's goals and mission, the HRD specialist must be well versed in strategic planning theories and processes.

In general, human resource development staff must demonstrate several competencies to fulfill these roles: knowledge of the organization, its purposes, and structure; knowledge of adult learning; knowledge of the relationship between an organization's culture and its learning environment; and knowledge of organizational, group, and individual change.

These competencies and the trends in the development function create a career track for the HRD specialist that requires formal management education and a consultant orientation. It is no longer adequate for the HRD specialist oriented to organizational productivity simply to receive vendors and decide which training packages to buy.

Perhaps as important as the human resources department enhancing their competence as development specialists is the heightened awareness that an essential generic managerial competence relates to facilitating learning and managing change. Specific competencies include: building teams and teamwork, valuing diversity, supporting innovation, facilitative leadership, and empowering employees. Thus, while the human resources department may have a specialist role to play in the development function, the bulk of the daily responsibility for developing employee competencies rests with every manager.

TRAINING NEEDS ASSESSMENT, DESIGN, AND EVALUATION

There are a number of practical issues connected to training that HRD specialists face. For example, when is training appropriate? And how does one design and evaluate training development programs? Even though we will concentrate in this section specifically on training programs as opposed to education and development, much of the information will be applicable to all three categories of development interventions.[25]

Assessment Function

When Is Training Appropriate?   Training is frequently used as a solution to a performance problem without considering alternatives. Table 10–1 summarizes the causes of performance problems, the preferred organizational responses to them, and the personnel activity involved.

Many organizations ignore performance problems if they are insignificant or if there is no readily apparent solution. The second response to a performance problem involves examining selection criteria to determine if they really reflect the competencies needed to perform the job; and if not, then raising the standards or

TABLE 10–1 Organizational Responses to Performance Problems

Situation	Organizational Response	Personnel Activity
1. Problem is insignificant	Ignore it	None
2. Selection criteria are inadequate	Increase attention to selection criteria	Job analysis
3. Employees are unaware of performance standards	Set goals and standards and provide feedback	Orientation, performance evaluation
4. Employees have inadequate skills	Provide training	Training
5. Good performance is not rewarded; poor performance is not punished	Provide rewards or punishments and connect them to performance	Performance evaluation, disciplinary action

reexamining the criteria themselves. This involves a trade-off between the higher salaries that must be paid to attract more qualified people and the higher cost of on-the-job training after they are hired, plus the greater risk of losing them to a competitor once they are trained. The third response is deceptively simple, for it involves merely clarifying standards by providing orientation or feedback to employees. This assumes, of course, that performance standards have already been established for the job—a big assumption in many cases. The fourth possible solution is to train employees by giving them the job-related skills needed to meet current performance standards. Finally, supervisors may offer greater rewards to employees who meet performance standards, or initiate disciplinary action against those who do not.

Some of these options are more difficult to implement than others. Changing selection criteria or rewards and punishments may be difficult, since these involve changes in job evaluation and flexible compensation plans. Because training is one of the easiest options to implement, the probability is relatively high that it will be used regardless of its appropriateness to the situation and, even though it is problematic, it will produce the desired results. Employers can train their employees and increase their ability to perform the work, but generally they are in for a disappointment if they think one can *train* people to expend more energy on the job. If the person could perform up to standard if his or her life depended upon it, low performance is not a training problem![26]

Before designing a training program or a series of training programs, the HRD specialist should conduct some kind of assessment. What problems exist? Are they suitable to a training solution? Then the content of the program is designed. Once the program is completed, an evaluation should be conducted to measure the reactions of the trainees and, where appropriate, the objective impact of the training on the original problem area.

Assessing Training Needs. Management may require training for all employees in a job classification without regard for data concerning a particular employee's performance. For example, all newly appointed supervisors may be required to take training in supervisory methods and delegation; or employees whose jobs require extensive public contact may be required to take communications training. This type of **training needs** assessment may be called a *general treatment need.*

A second type of training needs assessment is based on *observable performance discrepancies.* These are indicated by problems such as standards of work performance not being met, accidents, frequent need for equipment repair, several low ratings on employee evaluation reports, high rate of turnover, the use of many methods to do the same job, and deadlines not being met. In this case, management's job is to observe the jobs and workers in question and uncover the difficulties. This may be done through observation, interviews, questionnaires, performance appraisal, and by requiring employees to keep track of their own work output.

A third type of development assessment is related not to present performance discrepancies but to future human resource needs. Nadler and Nadler would call these educational and staff development needs. For example, an organization contemplating the networking of personal computers with linkage to a central computer will need to account for the training necessary for the employees. This type of needs assessment is based on the anticipation of a future discrepancy caused by technological advances and changes in mission and strategic goals.

Planning, Delivering, and Evaluating Training Programs

Designing a Training Program.   Once a problem area is identified, an intervention can be planned. Often sending someone to training is a naively simple solution. To reiterate, training can only benefit an employee who does not know how to work effectively; it should not be used in cases where employees know how to perform effectively, but for other reasons do not perform up to standard.

If training is an appropriate intervention, the appropriateness of a particular **training design** depends upon the target of the change. The simplest distinction in training objectives is whether or not the change will involve an interpersonal dimension. Traditional training methods, which are more directive, teacher-oriented, and have as their objective transferring knowledge, work best where the trainees are motivated to change, see the value in the change, and where the change can be readily incorporated into the way the employee currently performs the job.[27]

The more significant the change anticipated, the more likely it will involve rejection of something the employee already knows and relies upon. Training techniques appropriate to these situations must be trainee oriented, with the trainer taking a more facilitative role. If the anticipated change is tangible and involves technical training, the trainer must maintain a delicate balance between getting the material across and recognizing that not all the trainees may be eager to reject what they already know and what may still serve them well.

Supervisory training is probably as difficult as any other because it involves a degree of new knowledge, but knowledge that has to be filtered through an interpersonal and cognitive screen unique to each individual. Further, there is no one best way to be an effective supervisor. Mass production supervisory training falls victim to the charge that it is activity oriented rather than results oriented. Results-oriented supervisory training must at some point be tailored to individual supervisors. Regardless of the goal of the intervention, group discussion, case studies, and role play are techniques commonly used to get trainees involved and invested in the learning process. By encouraging the trainee to integrate material presented with his or her own knowledge, and by reinforcing the integration through performance at the training session, the likelihood increases that training will result in the learning of new behaviors.

The steps involved in tailoring a training intervention to a specific agency or work group move through five phases.[28]

- *Problem perception*: sensing that a problem exists because previous work methods or relationships are no longer effective.
- *Diagnosis*: defining the nature of the problem(s).
- "*Unfreezing*": reducing reliance on unsuccessful methods and exploring reasons why standard operating procedures are not working.

- *"Movement" or increased experimentation*: committing time and money to testing alternatives and working to reduce the forces resisting change.
- *"Refreezing"*: integrating changes into the organization's natural work processes and anchoring them to reward and other administrative systems.

The likelihood of change occurring depends upon several factors like the nature of the change expected. Does it present a relative advantage to the person who is supposed to adopt the change? Can the person see what the change will produce or is the proposed result vague? Is the change compatible with past practice, competencies, and values? And can the change be adopted gradually and incrementally, or does it need to be adopted whole?[29]

Evaluating Training Programs

To be effective, training must be an appropriate solution to an organizational problem; that is, it must be intended to correct a skill deficiency. For optimum learning, the employee must recognize the need and want to acquire new information or skills. Whatever performance standards are set, the employee should not be frustrated by a trainer who requires too much or too little.

Many learning theories resolve around the idea of reinforcement. It is natural for people to repeat behavior that is followed by rewards and to avoid actions they associate with negative outcomes. If employees in a training situation are given no feedback, there is no opportunity to guide the desired learning. It is extremely important that supervisors understand the value of positive reinforcement. Supervisors are in the best position to observe performance problems, show employees the correct work method, provide feedback, and connect subsequent rewards or punishments to performance. Most organizational training is informal and occurs on the job, through precisely this process.

To justify itself, training must demonstrate an impact on the performance of the employee. By determining how well employees have learned, management can make decisions about the training and its effectiveness. The mere existence of a training staff, an array of courses, and trainees do not ensure that learning is taking place. Because development activities consume both time and money, evaluation should be built into any program.

Training can be evaluated at five levels: reaction, learning, behavior, results, and cost effectiveness.[30]

Reaction	How well did the trainees like the training? Do they feel they benefited from the training?
Learning	To what extent did the trainees learn the facts, principles, and approaches that were included in the training?
Behavior	To what extent did the trainee's job behavior change because of the program?
Results	What increases in productivity or decreases in cost were achieved? To what extent were unit or organizational goals advanced?
Cost effectiveness	Assuming the training is effective, is it the least expensive method of solving the problem?

Perhaps the greatest challenge facing those who evaluate training is to recognize that while most development activities are delivered to individual employees, the goal is to get the organization as a whole learning, growing, and pulling together. Modest individual changes directed uniformly toward organizational goals may be highly desired yet difficult to achieve and measure.

DIFFERENT PERSPECTIVES FROM ALTERNATIVE PERSONNEL SYSTEMS

The development function is viewed differently from the perspective of alternative personnel systems. Political executives are selected for their partisan loyalty and partisan policy orientations. Usually, they receive little training prior to or following their appointment, despite the fact that many have little public policy-making experience and few of the skills required to manage complex public organizations. Because training, education, and staff development represent time-consuming investments in the future, political executives, who frequently spend a short time in government, have little interest in the development function, either for themselves or for those who work for them. The function takes on a special significance, however, if political executives are able to influence the selection of training consultants.

As the permanent bureaucracy, members of the civil service value the development function more than do political executives. In fact, many professionals working for public employers, like those in health-related professions, are required to enroll in a minimum number of continuing education hours annually in order to maintain various certifications or licenses.

By its very nature, the civil service houses an abundance of public-policy-related knowledge as well as the competencies needed to translate public policy goals into service delivery and regulatory actions. The quality of public policy making depends on the knowledge of a government's civil servants. Without the ability to acquire and enhance the valued knowledge, expertise, and experience of government employees, civil service systems lose their credibility and focus as the reservoir of society's knowledge about its own problems. One could argue that as a result of major cost-cutting measures, the knowledge base of civil service systems has been seriously eroding since the late 1970s.

As we have seen during the discussion of training for basic needs, the development function is of vital importance in advancing the goals of affirmative action. The danger in the next decade is that equity gains for minorities will be lost if disadvantaged minorities enter the workforce without advanced competencies in reading, writing, and computing or if they cannot obtain these skills once hired.

The development function meets with mixed reaction in the collective bargaining personnel subsystem. On the one hand, union members value the continuous development of knowledge, skills, and abilities needed to maintain timely competencies and to involve union members in organizational decisions about work processes. For example, the National Treasury Employees Union has given a positive reception to total quality management initiatives that promise to involve union members in decision-making processes previously off limits to them. Further, the development function is connected to a long-standing apprenticeship tradition involving structured experiences designed to transform the apprentice into a skilled craftsperson. As a counterexample, because of perceived threats to job security, union members often have resisted organizational development efforts designed to improve the quality and efficiency of work processes. Training is rarely seen as an organizational priority for temporary workers or when a service is being contracted out. Temporary workers are seen as either sole proprietors, responsible for their own level of knowledge, skills, and abilities and personal attributes, or as referrals from employment agencies that are accountable for their expertise. The competence of employees of private contractors is accounted for through a bidding process where the contract itself specifies expected levels of services.

SUMMARY

Even though training budgets seem the first to be cut in times of fiscal stress, ample evidence suggests that the development function will increase in importance in the coming decade. Seeking quality requires an employer investment in the competences of a workforce that must become intimately acquainted with service delivery systems and committed to a customer orientation. The value of efficiency that is captured in the basic concept of civil service systems provides the foundation for government to face these challenges. However, investments in the development function go beyond traditional training and extend into the areas of education and staff development, where employers indicate their willingness to make long-term investments in their employees. In part, this depends upon whether public employers are able to view their employees as assets rather than costs and whether citizens are willing to do the same.

Strategic thinking in human resources management depends in large part on being able to connect the development function to the organization's short- and longer-term goals and objectives—identifying the competencies needed and then preparing to develop them. In this effort, every manager becomes a development specialist practicing facilitative leadership, developing employees, and managing change.

KEY TERMS

action research	on-the-job training (OJT)
basic skill development	organization development (OD)
coaching and counseling	staff development
continuous learning	team building
development function	training
education	training design
executive development	training needs

DISCUSSION QUESTIONS

1. Identify the relationship between training and strategic planning. Can you give an example from an organization you are familiar with that illustrates how training is or should be connected to strategic thinking about agency goals?

2. Of the issues and methods associated with developing the organization and training new and existing employees, which should be paid more attention to in an organization you are familiar with? Why? How would doing a better job on the issue/method you selected make the organization more effective?
3. Distinguish between training, education, and staff development as part of the development function.
4. Identify and briefly describe the three roles of the human resource development specialist. Which of these roles or activities do you think general managers should be able to perform?
5. Briefly describe training needs assessment, design, and evaluation.
6. Discuss the way the development function is viewed from the perspectives of alternative personnel systems.

APPENDIX: A PERSONAL VIEW OF DIVERSITY TRAINING

TO: John Nalbandian
FROM: Carol Nalbandian
RE: Diversity Training

Diversity training is often referred to as cultural sensitivity training. When the emphasis is on teaching the diversity of cultures or ethnic groups, the assumption is that if one knows more about a different culture (for example, the behaviors, values, communication styles, concept of time, individuality versus group identity) one will be better able to interact appropriately with individuals of that particular culture. One will be more sensitive and aware of the differences between one's culture and someone else's, and will hopefully be less inclined to make judgmental and insensitive remarks to that person. I think for the most part this is true. The more a person knows about the differences that exist between cultures, ethnic groups, religions, and so forth, the less likely the person will be to unintentionally offend; and the more a person believes that these differences are just different, not good or bad, the more likely the person will be able to work with a variety of people.

However, the difficulty lies in providing information about cultures and ethnic groups. In training situations with its time constraints, information is necessarily condensed and generalized. What happens is that we are presenting information that is stereotypical—the very thing we are so adamant about not doing. In diversity training, we talk about the damaging effects of stereotyping individuals and of acting on assumptions we make about categories of people. But when we talk about Asians having a high need for preserving family name and honor, aren't we doing the exact same thing?

I have tried to approach this dilemma in two ways. One, I don't refer to cultural traits too often in my training. For example, I have presented a case study in which one person does not make eye contact with another. I say that cultural differences could be one reason, but I do not refer to any specific culture. In fact, I say that there are several cultures in different parts of the world where making eye contact would be considered impolite. Secondly, my approach is to emphasize that each person is an individual and that even individuals within the same culture will behave differently. My main point is that each person wants to be treated as an individual.

The value of diversity training is not so much to increase knowledge of different cultural or ethnic groups, but to increase one's tolerance and, eventually, one's appreciation for diversity in thought, action, and ideas. To me that is the ultimate value to the organization and to the employees. It is not just because diversity is a reality of our workforce, but because organizations need different ways of thinking and a variety of ideas to be efficient and effective. In addition, an appreciation of diversity develops open-mindedness, flexibility, and a wider comfort zone which all employees will need to survive in a rapidly changing environment.

Diversity training is really about changing attitudes more than skill building, so that it might be better considered as a development activity than strictly training. Yet, we all know that attitudes are very difficult to change; we can only hope to succeed in changing behaviors. So diversity training cannot succeed by itself. There really have to be other activities to support and enhance that appreciation of diversity. These can be social activities such as potlucks with ethnic dishes or community service projects; specific mention in team-building activities, performance evaluations, and staff meetings; informative articles in newsletters. All of these can support the attitude of appreciating diversity.

There is one type of skill building that, I believe, should be part of diversity training—conflict management. Whenever there is a diversity of people, opinions, ideas, values, there is bound to be conflict. Employees need to know how to confront issues which may be blocking the effective discussion of solutions to problems. They need to know how to deal with interpersonal issues which may be blocking effective working relationships.

CASE STUDY 1: DEVELOP A DIVERSITY TRAINING PROGRAM

You are the director of the human resource development department of a city with a population of 105,000. Your city provides its citizens with a full array of services, including police, fire, water, sanitation, roads, parks, and recreation. Your city employs some 750 employees, including 150 police officers.

Over the years there has been an influx of recent Asian immigrants and Spanish-speaking people into this city, which used to be predominantly Anglo, with about a 5 percent African-American population. Some of the immigrants are joining the city's workforce and racial/ethnic cliques are developing. Over the years, the African Americans have complained that the police treat them differently than other citizens, and they are being joined by spokespersons for the other minorities.

The values of tolerance, dignity, and fairness were underlying issues in the most recent election for city council. The new council has requested that the chief administrative officer develop a program of diversity training to heighten awareness of the value of differences in the workforce and the community. The CAO calls you into the office and asks you to work on a proposal.

Develop a proposal that includes a plan for assessing the need, designing the program, and evaluating it. What problems do you anticipate with the training program?

CASE STUDY 2: TRAINING VIGNETTES

What factors would you consider to make a decision in the following situations? Identify these factors from the manager or supervisor's perspective, as well as from the perspective of the HRD specialist who is called in for assistance.

1. Focus on your present work or work you are familiar with. You have an employee temporarily assigned to your area. What kind of training would you have the person go through if the person is assigned for three months? What if the time frame is uncertain, but you know it will be at least six months?
2. It has come to your attention that an employee who is going through a divorce is having performance problems (lower productivity, absenteeism, and tardiness). What would you do?
3. You suspect an employee may have an alcohol problem. What would you do?
4. You are considering promoting a very capable manager to an upper level position, but his abrasive style is causing problems in his working relationships with peers and subordinates. What should you do?

CASE STUDY 3: "HOW SHOULD THIS MANAGEMENT TEAM WORK TOGETHER?"

The city manager of a suburban midwestern metropolitan city decided to embark on an ambitious change plan. Hired two-and-a-half years ago, he has committed himself to decentralizing power and to encouraging more initiative and decision making from department heads and their division directors. At about the same time two other initiatives were occurring. First, a strategic plan, developed from a survey of citizens and focus groups and identifying several priority areas, needed to move forward to implementation. Second, upon its return from a national meeting, the governing body—led by the mayor—expressed interest in John Carver's policy governance model. This model structures the council-staff relationship in ways designed to keep the council focused on policy issues while providing broad discretionary responsibilities to staff.

The overriding picture emerging from these three initiatives is that, along with its other work, the council would focus on the policy issues outlined in the strategic plan. The staff would develop policy questions that needed council resolution in order to provide the boundaries within which staff could operate. Work committees that cut across departments would develop the policy statements for the council thus reinforcing the manager's desire to decentralize authority.

Attempts to blend these three initiatives have proven easier in theory than in practice. Several factors have combined in unanticipated ways to create obstacles. No single factor appears unmanageable, but in combination they have created a lot of uncertainty.

- With a change in mayor, the council's commitment to the policy governance model appears somewhat uncertain.
- The organizational culture historically has oriented itself around hierarchy with considerable focus on the manager's office for overall direction and decisions. This orientation has created a range of commitment from the department heads for the new initiatives.

- A scandal involving a previous city manager has led to relative instability in the city manager position. Reacting to the relatively short tenure and different styles of the previous city managers, some department heads have decided to go their own way. They believe that they have been fulfilling their responsibilities quite well without the new initiatives. Some may even believe that these initiatives are just the latest in a series that stretch back over many years and see them as a diversion from the real work the departments must perform day to day.

- A few years ago one department, exercising its initiative, invested heavily and apparently successfully in modern management techniques and philosophies; it views the new organizationwide initiative with mixed feelings.

- Lastly, the manager himself is an experimenter, quick to act, and unafraid of bold action. He espouses a desire to decentralize power, but sometimes in practice his assertive style contradicts the message.

Several division directors, department heads, and members of the city manager's office have gathered to discuss the situation. You are among that group. Here are your tasks:

1. Divide into three groups: division directors, department heads, and the city manager's office.

2. Within your group come to some agreement on a definition of the problem that now exists.

3. Once you have described the problem, each group should identify the responsibilities that its members should fulfill as well as the responsibilities it expects the other groups to fulfill if the problem is going to be addressed effectively.

NOTES

[1]IPMA (May 2001). ASTD releases its 2001 state of industry report. *International Personnel Management Association News,* p. 3.

[2]Bernhard, H. B., and C. A. Ingols (September-October 1988). Six lessons for the corporate classroom. *Harvard Business Review, 88,* 40–48.

[3]Rosow, J. M., and R. Zager (1988). *Training—The Competitive Edge: Introducing New Technology into the Workplace.* San Francisco: Jossey-Bass, p. 9.

[4]United States Merit Systems Protection Board. (1995). *Leadership for Change: Human Resource Development in the Federal Government.* Washington, DC: U.S. Merit Systems Protection Board.

[5]Casner-Lotto, J., and Associates (1988). *Successful Training Strategies: Twenty-Six Innovative Corporate Models.* San Francisco: Jossey-Bass, pp. 5–6.

[6]Nadler, L., and Z. Nadler (1989). Developing Human Resources (3rd ed.) San Francisco: Jossey-Bass.

[7]State of Kansas, http://da.state.ks.us/ps/subject/comp.

[8]U.S. Office of Personnel Management, http://www.opm.gov/ses/handbook.html.

[9]Learning Resource Network, http://learnet.gc.ca/eng/comcentr/manage/building/summary_e.htm.

[10]Cunningham, J. B. (1995). Strategic considerations in using action research for improving personnel practices. *Public Personnel Management, 24,* 515–530; Gardner, N. (1974). Action training and research: Something old and something new. *Public Administration Review, 34,* 106–115.

[11]Smith, M. (March 2000). Innovative personnel management: Changing workforce demographics. *International Personnel Management News,* pp. 12–14.

[12]Bellah, R. N., R. Madsen, W. M. Sullivan, A. Swidler, and S. M. Tipton (1985). Habits of the Heart: Individualism and Commitment in American Life. Berkeley: University of California Press, p. 206.

[13]Smith, M. (February 2000). The impact of diversity training on workforce discrimination. *International Personnel Management Association News,* pp. 13–14.

[14]Willingham, R. (October 2000). The redefinition of training. *International Personnel Management Association News*, p. 16.

[15]Argyris, C. (1980). Making the undiscussable and its undiscussability discussable. *Public Administration Review, 40*, 205–213.

[16]Rosow and Zager. Training—The competitive edge, p. 4.

[17]Brown, J. (April 2000). Employee orientation. *International Personnel Management Association News*, pp. 10–11; IPMA (April 2000). New employee orientation programs key to starting employees off right. *International Personnel Management Association News*, p. 12.

[18]U.S. Department of Labor (1999). *Futurework: Trends and Challenges for Work in the 21st Century*. Washington, DC: U.S. Department of Labor, p. 6.

[19]Judy, R. W. and C. D'Amico (1997). *Workforce 2020*. Indianapolis, IN: Hudson Institute, p. 49.

[20]Ibid., p. 85.

[21]Hurdy, J. J. (March 2001). E-learning: A new tool for government in the new economy. *International Personnel Management Association News*, pp. 9, 11; Smith, M. (March 2001). E-learning in the 21st century. *International Personnel Management Association News*, pp. 10–11.

[22]Smith, M. (May 2000). Distance learning as a future workplace trend. *International Personnel Management Association News*, p. 21.

[23]McIlvaine, A. (May 1, 2001). Training 2001: An e-Learning Odyssey. *Human Resource Executive*, p. 8 and 24.

[24]Nadler and Nadler. *Developing Human Resources*.

[25]IPMA (June 2001). Competency based training. *International Personnel Management Association News*, pp. 1, 4–5, 8.

[26]Mager, P., and P. Pipe (1980). *Analyzing Performance Problems*. Belmont, CA: Wadsworth.

[27]Nalbandian, J. (1985). Human relations and organizational change: Responding to loss. *Review of Public Personnel Administration, 6*, 29–43.

[28]French, W. L., and C. H. Bell, Jr. (1990). *Organizational Development* (4th ed.). Upper Saddle River, NJ: Prentice Hall.

[29]Rogers, E. M. (1995). *Diffusion of Innovations* (4th ed.). New York: Free Press.

[30]Trice, E. (September 1999). Exercise training evaluation efforts. *International Personnel Management Association News*, pp. 10–11.

11
Performance Appraisal

One of the most challenging aspects of human resources management is the switch in emphasis from managing positions to managing performance. Position management, including analyzing jobs, establishing essential duties and responsibilities, determining necessary knowledge, skills, and abilities, classifying jobs, setting a pay scale and using the "position" as a critical feature of financial management could all be done without a single reference to a real live person. As public agencies have come to view human resources management in more of a strategic light—looking for the connections between human resources policies and management and agencies goals and objectives, performance management has become at least as important as position management. Whereas the components of position management are fairly clear-cut, the components of performance management range from legislation that creates authority for an agency and its employees and thus channels their performance to supervisory coaching and counseling of employees. Any deliberate act intended to affect employee performance falls under the category of performance management. The goal of the contemporary organization is to orient these acts towards unit and agency goal accomplishment.

Performance appraisal is supposed to play a key role in the development of employees and their productivity. Theoretically, the appraisal of performance provides employees with feedback on their work, leading to greater clarity regarding organizational expectations and to a more effective channeling of employee ability and effort. In these ways, performance appraisal is a crucial aspect of performance management.

When a formal performance appraisal leads to organizational decisions regarding promotion and pay-allocational decisions, the process becomes more complicated; it is accompanied by heightened legal scrutiny for civil rights violations and employee demands for reasons behind the decisions. Where the results of an unsatisfactory appraisal lead to disciplinary action or denial of an organizational reward, due process guarantees are invoked through union contracts, merit-system rules, or possibly even through the United States Constitution. Often these legal, accountability, and due process considerations overshadow the feedback purpose of appraisal systems, forcing a formalism better suited to litigation than to management and employee development.

Even though the appraisal function is related to employee productivity and employees' desire to know how well they are doing, rarely are supervisors or employees satisfied with the process. On the one hand, in some organizations it is not taken very seriously and is viewed as a waste of time. In others, it plays a major role in the distribution of organizational rewards, and then it frequently becomes the source of considerable tension in the employee-employer relationship. For example, in 1994 the federal government ended its sixteen-year experiment with pay for performance for civil service employees, on the grounds that it had contributed to organizational conflict without increasing employee motivation or performance.

By the end of this chapter, you will be able to:

1. Clarify the goals of performance appraisal.
2. Describe the role of appraisal in different personnel systems.
3. Identify contemporary work trends and their challenges to the appraisal function.
4. Differentiate between performance-based and person-based performance evaluation criteria.
5. Distinguish among seven performance appraisal methods; and discuss the comparative validity, reliability, and cost.
6. Discuss the controversy between traditional supervisory evaluation and alternatives (self-, peer, and 360-degree evaluation).
7. Describe the characteristics of an effective rating system.
8. Describe the human dynamics of the appraisal process, including the supervisor's motivation to assess the performance of subordinates.
9. Describe the relationship of performance appraisal to the sanctions function and particularly its role in creating a sense of fairness in an organization.

WHY EVALUATE PERFORMANCE?

Performance appraisal is directed toward technical and management goals but rarely toward employee aspirations. The technical part focuses on developing an instrument that accurately measures individual performance in order to identify an individual's strengths and weaknesses and to differentiate one employee from another. Because personnel decisions like promotions and merit-pay increases are connected to individual performance, the instrument used to evaluate performance must withstand serious scrutiny by employees and managers.

Management hopes to achieve several objectives through the performance appraisal process:

1. Communicate management goals and objectives to employees. It is clear that performance appraisal reinforces managerial expectations. After instructing employees

what to do, it is management's responsibility to follow through by providing feedback on how performance matches the stated criteria.

2. Motivate employees to improve their performance. The purpose of providing feedback, or constructive criticism, is to improve performance. Appraisal, then, should encourage employees to maintain or improve job performance.

3. Distribute organizational rewards such as salary increases and promotions equitably. One of the primary criteria of organizational justice and quality of employee work life is whether rewards are distributed fairly.

4. Conduct personnel management research. Logic suggests that if jobs have been analyzed accurately, and if people have been selected for those jobs based on job-related skills, knowledge, and abilities, their subsequent on-the-job performance should be satisfactory or better. If not, one might suspect defects in the job analysis, selection, or promotion criteria—or in the performance appraisal system itself.

From the employee's standpoint, the issue is fairness. Title VII of the 1964 Civil Rights Act, as amended (1972), requires employers to validate any personnel technique that affects an employee's chances for promotion. This includes performance appraisal. For this reason it is strongly suggested that personnel managers adopt one of the performance-oriented techniques discussed later in this chapter. Latham and Wexley[1] cite the Civil Service Reform Act of 1978 as providing the model for a sound, straightforward approach to performance appraisal. The act requires most federal agencies to:

1. Develop an appraisal system that encourages employee participation in establishing performance standards
2. Develop standards based on critical job elements
3. Assess employees against performance standards rather than each other or some statistical guide like a bell curve

It is interesting to note the parallel between these requirements and those applying to techniques for the selection of employees. The common ground is found in the overall mandate that personnel decisions be based on job-related criteria.

PERFORMANCE APPRAISAL AND ALTERNATIVE PERSONNEL SYSTEMS

Much of the discussion in this chapter focuses on civil service systems. Civil service personnel systems often are called merit systems, frequently confusing even government employees. Personnel systems based on merit are those where a variety of personnel decisions are based on competencies and performance rather than seniority or politics. Merit-pay plans are those that attempt to tie compensation to performance. Performance appraisal and civil service systems go hand in hand, and to the extent they can help distinguish and document employee performance, they advance the goals of personnel systems based on merit.

Affirmative action personnel systems also have a significant investment in reliable and valid appraisal systems. This interest parallels a similar interest in the development of selection devices free of inappropriate or irrelevant judgments.

This interest has thrust performance appraisal systems into the judicial arena, subjecting them to standards of validity and reliability that they may not be able to meet when preserving the essential subjectivity involved in one person evaluating another's work.

Performance appraisal systems are largely irrelevant to political personnel systems. Political executives rarely remain on the job long enough to benefit from or suffer formal appraisals. Their superiors are other political executives, often elected officials whose subjective criteria for effective job performance make formal assessments like those in civil service systems difficult to implement. Further, the higher up in an organizational hierarchy one travels, the more likely that the substance of an individual's job will be determined by that individual, with only limited guidance by superiors or the previous incumbent's job description.

Collective bargaining personnel systems generally oppose pay for individual performance and appraisal plans developed as a part of performance-based compensation. Unions prefer to negotiate wages for their workers and see individual incentive or merit plans as ways of pitting one union member against another and introducing conditions where managers can favor one employee over another.

Performance-evaluation systems have some applicability to the emergent personnel systems (alternative organizations and mechanisms for providing public services and contingent employment). First, where contractors or other organizations provide public services, contract negotiation, administration, and compliance replace traditional supervisory practices (setting performance standards, providing feedback, and arranging consequences). While this process involves many of the same elements as performance appraisal, it has a different basis in law, administrative procedure, and managerial practice.

From the public employer and employee's standpoint, formal performance appraisals for part-time or temporary workers seem much less relevant than for career employees, except for those looking for a permanent, full-time job. In those cases, the employer's interests may differ from the employee's. The employer sees little gain from investing time in performance appraisal. But the employee may see the appraisal as essential to the search for a permanent, full-time position, in that it results in documentation of performance relative to job standards or other employees in similar positions.

There is one exception. In some cases, it may be desirable for supervisors to evaluate *volunteers'* performance. Sometimes, this is done to "weed out" volunteers who are incompetent, or those whose behavior creates legal or financial risks for the agency.

CONTEMPORARY CHALLENGES
TO PERFORMANCE APPRAISAL

Traditionally, performance appraisal has been regarded as a necessary and basic technical personnel function, even though it has never quite lived up to its expectations.[2] It is not difficult to understand why its stature has remained secure among human resource management advocates over the years. It is difficult to imagine behavior changing without feedback. So, it stands to reason that formalizing feedback from supervisor to employee would lead employees to behave in ways their employer valued.

Even though in practice an employee's behavior is influenced by feedback from a variety of sources (most significantly from peers and colleagues), performance appraisal has usually been associated with communication from supervisor to employee. This tradition coincides with the view that organizations are hierarchies of command and control, and the premises upon which employees make decisions should be hierarchically determined.

While formal appraisal systems are comfortably nested in routinized administrative procedures and hierarchical structures, several contemporary work trends challenge the utility of the traditional appraisal. These trends are:

- The changing nature of work means less commitment between organization and employee, and therefore less possibility of influencing employee behavior through feedback and rewards.
- Part-time or temporary work makes performance appraisal less important for the employer, but more important for the employee seeking a permanent, full-time job.
- Privatization eliminates the need for appraisal of individual performance, but substitutes the importance of contract compliance monitoring.
- Flatter organizational hierarchies challenge traditional superior-subordinate appraisals.
- Greater spans of control hinder supervisory observation of employee work.
- The shift from individual positions to work teams necessitates multirater evaluations, which run counter to many supervisors' notions of control, and evaluations are technically more difficult to perform.
- Limited organizational rewards and punishments make evaluation ineffective at linking pay or disciplinary action to performance, particularly in personnel systems governed by civil service rules or collective bargaining agreements.

These factors combine to diminish the value of performance evaluation in all but traditional civil service systems, where evaluation systems are legally required to demonstrate the job relatedness of promotion or disciplinary action. Because supervisors must exercise discretion in the allocation of organizational rewards and discipline, the demand for fairness requires organizational focus on the criteria used to make these decisions, the processes used to reach them, and the outcomes or sanctions they produce.[3] In other words, procedural and substantive fairness argue for formalized appraisal systems which encourage rational judgments.

However, even in civil service systems, performance evaluation is widely regarded (in private) as irrelevant by employees and supervisors. The ambivalent status of the performance appraisal function in essence parallels the tension that exists more generally in human resource management between the values of efficiency (the flexibility to manage and control employees) and political responsiveness on the one hand, and individual rights and equity on the other. The future of the appraisal function will evolve out of this tension as well as the way we organize ourselves to work—whether in teams or individually; whether relatively permanently or temporarily; whether publicly or privately.

PERFORMANCE-BASED AND PERSON-BASED EVALUATION CRITERIA

If we assume that the appraisal function will not disappear, if only because organizational justice demands some formalization of the criteria used to allocate rewards and punishments (as it does in the allocation of jobs through the staffing function), the fundamental question is: What factors should be evaluated? There are two basic sets of criteria, person-based and performance-based, though some appraisal methods employ a mixture of the two types.

In the **person-based rating system**, the rater compares employees against other employees or against some absolute standard. **Performance-based rating systems** measure each employee's behaviors against previously established behaviors and standards. Each criterion has advantages. Person-based systems are, beyond a doubt, the easiest and cheapest to design, administer, and interpret. Many organizations evaluate employees on the extent to which they possess desirable personality traits—initiative, dependability, intelligence, or adaptability. Ratings are easily quantified and compared with past appraisals or ratings of other people or units through computerization so that frequently overburdened supervisors in a minimum of time can complete the appraisal process. However, person-oriented appraisal systems share the same drawbacks as trait-oriented job appraisal and classification systems—they have low validity, have low reliability, and are of dubious value in improving performance.

First, such systems are invalid to the extent that personality characteristics are unrelated to job performance. For example, organizational and environmental characteristics heavily influence the nature of a given position and, by implication, the kinds of skills or characteristics needed for successful performance. It is impossible to specify for all positions in an organization, a uniform set of desirable personality characteristics that can be demonstrably related to successful job performance. Second, the reliability of trait ratings are frequently marginal at best; two supervisors may have very different definitions of loyalty, depending on their views of the job or their level of expectation for their employees. Third, comparative trait appraisals are not useful for counseling employees because they neither identify areas of satisfactory or unsatisfactory performance nor suggest areas where improvement is needed. Since an employee's personality characteristics are central to his or her self-concept, it is difficult for supervisors and employees to discuss them without lapsing into amateur psychology and defensiveness. As a result of their low validity and reliability, person-oriented systems are not very useful for personnel management research aimed at validating selection or promotion criteria.

For these reasons, most performance specialists advocate the use of performance-based systems that evaluate job-related behaviors. In fact, person-based systems can rarely stand the test of legal scrutiny that examines their reliability and validity in relation to actual job performance. In contrast to person-based systems, performance criteria communicate managerial objectives clearly, are both relevant to job performance and reasonably reliable, and better fulfill the purposes of reward allocation, performance improvement, and personnel management research. If objective performance standards are established between employees and supervisors through some process of participative goal setting, the employee becomes clearly aware of the specific behavioral expectations attached to his or her position.

The fact that desired behaviors are specified makes the evaluative criteria more valid. That is, the job behaviors or expected competencies themselves provide the basis for evaluation, rather than personality characteristics believed to be related to performance.[4] Performance-based appraisals are more reliable because the use of objective standards enables raters, employees, and observers to determine whether or not predetermined performance standards have been met. As a result, changes in salary levels, promotions, or firings can be amply justified by reference to employee productivity. Reward allocation decisions can be explained to employees by discussing their performance objectively, rather than by arguing about the desirability of changing certain negative personality traits. Areas where performance improvement is needed can be identified for counseling, training, or job assignment purposes. The performance-based system increases job-related communication between employees and supervisors, primarily because performance standards must be altered periodically to meet changes in organizational objectives, resource allocation, or environmental constraints. In short, performance-based appraisal systems are fairer than person-based systems, even though personal qualities of employees are highly valued.

Tziner and colleagues found that performance-based rating systems produced higher levels of goal clarity, goal acceptance, and goal commitment; resulted in greater levels of employee satisfaction with the appraisal process; and were associated with greater improvements in individual performance over time.[5] Taylor and associates found that perceived fairness in appraisal systems results in more loyalty and organizational commitment to and satisfaction with the appraisal process even when employees receive lower evaluations.[6]

However, performance-based systems are considerably harder to develop than person-based systems. In a 1994 survey of federal managers and supervisors, some 44 percent noted that it was difficult to identify job-related performance standards, and 62 percent said it was difficult to describe the standards in objective terms.[7] Because performance standards will vary (depending on the characteristics of the employee, the objectives of the organization, available resources, and external conditions), separate performance standards must be developed for each employee, or for each class of similar positions. Second, the organization may wish to specify desired methods of task performance as well as objectives. Third, the changing nature of organizations and environments means that employee performance standards may also change, and seldom at regularly scheduled or administratively convenient intervals. As a result, supervisors will need to spend more time working with employees to develop performance standards and subsequent appraisal interviews. Since supervisors are rewarded primarily for improving their work unit's short-term productivity, they may view developmental counseling as an inefficient use of their time.

Fourth, it is difficult to develop objective performance standards for many staff people or for positions that are complex or interrelated in a job series. Job-related, objective measures are more suited to simple jobs with tangible output that can be attributed to employee performance. Attempts to measure performance in complex jobs objectively can focus attention on concrete but trivial factors. Further, an employee's performance is also subject to other influences: the quality of the performance standards-setting process, the relationship with others in the work unit, and environmental factors. An example would be when teachers point out that, in addition to teacher performance, student accomplishments are influenced by home environment, peers, level of ability, class size, and other factors that complicate the assessment of teachers based on student performance. Since evaluative standards are individualized, computerized scoring or interpretation of results is difficult.

Last, it is difficult to compare the performance of employees with different standards. If each of three employees has met previously established performance standards, how does a supervisor decide which of them should be recommended for a promotion?

APPRAISAL METHODS

The criterion question concerns whether personality characteristics or behavior will be the object of appraisal and the difficulty of separating the two; the methods question concerns the format or technique by which the criterion will be evaluated. Seven methods are commonly used:

- Graphic rating (or adjectival scaling)
- Ranking
- Forced-choice
- Essay
- Objective
- Critical incident (or work sampling)
- Behaviorally anchored rating scales (BARS)

Some of these techniques, primarily the first three, are more adaptable to person-oriented systems. Others are utilized primarily in performance-based systems.

1. **Graphic-rating scales** are the most easily developed, administered, and scored format. They consist of a listing of desirable or undesirable personality traits in one column and beside each trait a scale (or box) which the rater marks to indicate the extent to which the rated employee demonstrates the trait. An example of a graphic-rating scale appears in Figure 11–1.
2. **Ranking techniques** are similar to graphic-rating scales in that they are also based on traits. However, they require the rater to rank-order each employee on each of the listed traits. While they overcome one fault of graphic-rating scales, the tendency of raters to rate all employees high on all characteristics, it is difficult for raters to rank more than ten employees against one another.
3. **Forced-choice techniques** are the most valid trait-rating method. Based on a previous analysis of the position, job analysts have determined which traits or behaviors are most related to successful job performance. Several positive traits or behaviors are given in the form of a multiple-choice question, and the rater is asked to indicate the

FIGURE 11–1 Employee Rating

Date of Rating _____   White—Personnel; Canary—Dept./Div; Pink—Employee

Rating Period: From _____ To _____

Soc. Sec. No.	Activity	Class	Obj.	Employee Name

_____ Probationary
_____ Annual
_____ Special
_____ Final

INSTRUCTIONS

Evaluate employee's performance and behavior to the degree he or she meets job requirements, taking into consideration all factors in the employee's performance. Individual factors under each trait should be designated, where applicable, as (+) high; (✓) average; (−) low. The overall mark for each trait should be indicated by placing an (×) in the applicable columns labeled Outstanding, Above Average, Average, Below Average, and Unsatisfactory. BEFORE RATING EMPLOYEE, PLEASE REVIEW YOUR RATING MANUAL.

TRAIT		Outsdg.	Above Average	Average	Below Average	Unsat.
Quality of Work	_____ Accuracy _____ Completeness _____ Oral expression _____ Written expression _____ Soundness of judgment in decisions _____ Reliability of work results					
Work Output	_____ Amount of work performed _____ Completion of work on schedule _____ Physical fitness _____ Learning ability					

269

TRAIT	Outsdg.	Above Average	Average	Below Average	Unsat.
Work Habits Organization and planning of assignments — Job interest — Attendance	— Compliance with work instructions — Observance of work hours — Conscientious use of work time				
Safety Care of equipment, property, and materials	— Personal safety habits				
Personal Relations Cooperation with fellow employees — Personal appearance and habits	— Dealing with the public — Ability to get along with others				
Adaptability Performance in emergencies — Performance with minimum of instruction	— Performance under changing conditions — Self-reliance, initiative, and problem solving				
Supervisory Skills FOR USE IN RATING SUPERVISORS ONLY: — Leadership — Acceptance by others — Decision making — Effectiveness and skill in — Planning and laying out work	— Fairness and impartiality — Communicating problems to others — Training-Safety				

TRAIT	Outsdg.	Above Average	Average	Below Average	Unsat.
General Evaluation — Indicate by an (×) in the appropriate column your own general evaluation of the employee's rating, taking all the above and other pertinent factors into consideration. A written statement must be made on the reverse side of this form if the ratings is OUTSTANDING or UNSATISFACTORY on this item				*	*#

Signature of
Rater: _____

Title: _____

Signature of
Rater's Supervisor: _____

Title: _____

*An (×) here indicates loss of annual salary increase
#An (×) here indicates employee must be rated again in 90 days.
TO EMPLOYEE: Your signature is required, however, it does not imply that you agree with the rating.

Date _____ Employee Signature _____

one that corresponds most closely with the employee's job performance or personality. Because supervisors are unsure which item is the "best" response according to the person who designed the test, forced-choice techniques reduce supervisory bias. Naturally, they are disliked by supervisors, who want to know how they are rating their employees. An example of the forced-choice format appears in Figure 11–2.

4. The fourth appraisal technique, the **essay format**, is among the oldest and most widely used forms of appraisal. The rater simply makes narrative comments about the employee. Since these may relate to personality or performance, the essay method is suitable for person- or performance-oriented systems. However, it has the disadvantages of being time consuming, biased in favor of employees with supervisors who can write well, and impossible to standardize. It is frequently used in conjunction with graphic-rating or ranking techniques to clarify extremely low or high ratings. But the burden on supervisors is so great that when essay elaboration is required to justify high or low ratings, supervisors have a tendency to rate employees toward the middle of a normal curve.

5. The objective method is a measure of work performance—quality, quantity, or timeliness—against previously established standards. It is used most often in private industry by companies with piece-rate pay plans; however, public-sector organizations are adopting a variant of this approach by measuring workload indicators. For example, employment counselors may be evaluated on the number of jobs they fill or on the percentage of placements who remain on the job after three months. An example is provided in Figure 11–3.

FIGURE 11–2   Forced-Choice Performance Evaluation Format

Person Evaluated _____

Position _____

Organization Unit _____

Date _____

Instructions: Please place a check on the line to the left of the statement that best describes this employee.

1. This employee
   ___ a. always looks presentable
   ___ b. shows initiative and independence
   ___ c. works well with others in groups
   ___ d. produces work of high quality

2. This employee
   ___ a. completes work promptly and on time
   ___ b. pays much attention to detail
   ___ c. works well under pressure
   ___ d. works well without supervisory guidance

3. This employee
   ___ a. is loyal to his or her supervisor
   ___ b. uses imagination and creativity
   ___ c. is thorough and dependable
   ___ d. accepts responsibility willingly

FIGURE 11–3 Health Center

HEALTH CENTER

JOB DESCRIPTION

JOB TITLE _____ Primary Nurse _____ Department _____ Nursing Service _____ Date _____

Job Code No _____

Job Title of Person
to Whom Reporting _____ Head Nurse _____ Pay Grade _____

Date _____
Revised _____

Job Summary: A professional nurse, who has responsibility, authority, and accountability for quality nursing care for an assigned group of patients.

PERFORMANCE EVALUATION

Probationary Review [ ]

Merit Review [ ]   Special [ ]

Present Grade _____ Step _____

Name _____

Date of Hire _____

Evaluation Due Date _____

RESPONSIBILITIES	PERFORMANCE STANDARDS	ATTAINED YES/NO	IF NO, HOW CAN SUCH BE ATTAINED
ASSESSMENT:			
1. Complete the admission procedure to include	Within one hour of patient's admission to the unit, introduces self and identifies the primary nurse's role to the patient and/or the family.		
Orientation	Orients patient/family to the unit.		
Assesses the patient needs	Tentative assessment and nursing judgment, based on the patient's immediate needs at the time of admission to the unit, will be reflected in the initial notation on the nurse's progress notes and/or the nursing history summary		

273

RESPONSIBILITIES	PERFORMANCE STANDARDS	ATTAINED YES/NO	IF NO, HOW CAN SUCH BE ATTAINED

	Performs assessment within 24 hours of admission to the unit. Assessment is based on subjective and objective data which may include records, consultation, and test data.
	Physical:
	  breath and bowel sounds
	  peripheral pulses
	  level of consciousness
	  general skin condition and color
	  physical abnormalities		

Completes a nursing history	Completes nursing history within 24 hours of admission to the unit and enters notation on Patient Care Guide.		
PLANNING:			
1. Initiates a patient care guide	Assures that a 24 hour patient care guide is completed within 24 hours of patient admission to the unit. This will define patient/family problems and formulate plan of care that attempts to modify or eliminate each nursing problem.		
2. Includes the patient and family in the planning of the patient's care.	Includes the patient and the family in the planning of the patient's care both initially and throughout the hospitalization and reflects this action via documentation on the patient care guide and verbal feedback from the patient and/or family.		
3. Initiates discharge planning	Describe short and long term goals, as identified by the patient and/or family, beginning at time of admission.		

RESPONSIBILITIES	PERFORMANCE STANDARDS	ATTAINED YES/NO	IF NO, HOW CAN SUCH BE ATTAINED
INTERVENTION:			
1. Performs all independent nursing functions and performs dependent nursing functions as ordered by the physician and documents all nursing assessment, plans, and interventions.	Within the framework of the health center policies and procedures, and documents accordingly on the patient chart.		
2. Communicates patient's status to other health care and family members.	Communicates daily with patient and/or family regarding events of the day and current status. Provides time for questions. Communicates to personnel on her tour of duty verbal and written assignments with deadlines for completion. Communicates patient data to oncoming shift via organized, pertinent, factual walking report and updates Kardex accordingly. Attends doctors' rounds, and communicates with physicians.		
3. Utilizes social service department and resources in order to promote, restore, and maintain optimal health care for patient/family	Initiates utilization of community health resources with the cooperation of the physicians and communicates these actions.		
4. Utilizes team members appropriately; according to their abilities and position description	Establishes priorities of nursing care based on assessment of patient needs, reflected on the daily primary nursing assignment worksheet.		

275

RESPONSIBILITIES	PERFORMANCE STANDARDS	ATTAINED YES/NO	IF NO, HOW CAN SUCH BE ATTAINED
	Assures that delegated assignments have been completed before the end of the shift. Schedules break and meal times for team members.		
5. Coordinates patient/family teaching, based upon assessment of patient readiness.	Patient/family teaching will be reflected in the chart at the time of discharge.		

JOB SPECIFICATIONS

Comments on Work Habits: _____

Supervisor _____ Date _____   Department Head _____

My supervisor has reviewed my Job Description and Performance Evaluation with me. My signature does not necessarily mean that I agree.

Comments _____

_____ Signature _____ Date _____

6. The sixth technique has been termed **critical incident** or **work sampling**. This objective technique records representative examples of good (or bad) performance in relation to agreed-upon employee objectives. It has the same advantages and disadvantages of performance-oriented systems generally. One cautionary note, however: To the extent that the selected incidents are not representative of employee performance over time, the method is open to distortion and bias. Figure 11–4 presents an example of a critical incident appraisal form.

7. The **behaviorally anchored rating scale (BARS)** is a technique that employs objective performance criteria in a standardized appraisal format. The personnel manager who wishes to use BARS develops a range of possible standards for each task and then translates these statements into numerical scores. To be job related, these performance-oriented statements must be validated by job analysis.

BARS are handy because they make use of objective appraisal criteria and are easy to employ. But they are time consuming to develop, and they have not lived up to expectations because the distinction between behavior and traits is not as salient as once thought.[8] Figure 11–5 presents an example of a behaviorally anchored rating form for a primary nurse.

So far our discussion has emphasized that the purpose of an employee appraisal system must be clearly stated and that evaluation methods must be suitable to the evaluative criteria chosen. Table 11–1 summarizes these relationships.

FIGURE 11–4 Critical Incident Performance Evaluation Format

Person Evaluated _____

Position _____

Organization Unit _____

Time Period _____ to _____

Employee Objectives	*Examples of Successful or Unsuccessful Performance*
1.	a.
	b.
	c.
	d.
2.	a.
	b.
	c.
	d.
3.	a.
	b.
	c.
	d.

FIGURE 11–5 Behaviorally Anchored Rating Scales (BARS) Evaluation Format

Student evaluated _____ Course: _____ Dates: _____ to _____

COURSE GRADE

EVALUATIVE CRITERIA	A	B	C	D
1. Term paper (75 percent of course grade)	Meet criteria for a grade of B and in addition: Develop new insights, theories, or solutions	Meet criteria for a grade of C and in addition: Analyze and critically evaluate existing knowledge presented in lectures, discussion, and outside reading	Completed by date scheduled in course outline; repeat existing knowledge from lectures and outside reading Follow proper style (grammar, organization, footnotes, and bibliography)	Not completed by date scheduled; not meeting minimum criteria for a grade of C
2. Class participation (25 percent of course grade)	Meet criteria for a grade of B and in addition: 1. Listen to and evaluate the class participation of other students 2. Show ability to analyze and evaluate material presented in lecture and discussion	Meet criteria for a grade of C and in addition: 1. Participate in class discussions 2. Demonstrate correct factual knowledge of concepts and theories from lectures and reading	Attend class as scheduled or notify professor in advance of absences	Not meet criteria for a grade of C

TABLE 11-1 Performance Evaluation Systems

Purpose	Criteria	Methods
Communication of objectives	Performance-oriented	Critical incident (work sampling), objective measures, BARS
Reward allocation	Person- or performance-oriented	Graphic rating, ranking, forced-choice, BARS
Performance improvement	Performance-oriented	Critical incident (work sampling), objective measures, BARS
Personnel research	Performance-oriented	Essay, work sampling (critical incident), objective measures, BARS

While Table 11-1 points out the uses of each appraisal method, judicial reviews of discrimination cases involving appraisal instruments will be forcing more uniformity in future appraisal systems. Feild and Holley[9] report that, on the basis of their research examining employment discrimination court decisions involving appraisal systems, the following characteristics clearly contributed to verdicts for the defending organizations: A job analysis was used to develop the appraisal system; a behavior-oriented versus person-oriented system was used; evaluators were given specific written instructions on how to use the rating instrument; the appraisal results were reviewed with employees; and the defending organizations tended to be nonindustrial in nature. A recent survey of 3,052 firms suggested that successful appraisal systems included written goals, supervisory instructions, senior management training, training in objective setting, and providing feedback, and integration with the pay system.[10]

WHO SHOULD EVALUATE EMPLOYEE PERFORMANCE?

An employee's performance may be rated by a number of people. The immediate supervisor most commonly assesses the performance of subordinates, and this is the way most employees prefer it.[11] Supervisory assessments reinforce authority relationships in an organization and are frequently seen as the primary function distinguishing a superior from a subordinate. Because the superior-subordinate relationship itself is affected by so many factors, supervisory ratings are easily biased. Self-ratings can be employed to promote an honest discussion between superior and subordinate about the subordinate's performance. But self-ratings receive mixed support: Some studies find them inflated; others see them deflated in comparison with supervisory ratings.

While alternatives to traditional superior-subordinate appraisals have received much discussion recently, a 1989 study of Fortune 100 companies found only two organizations using self-appraisals, less than 3 percent of the appraisals were conducted by peers, and no subordinate appraisal systems were reported.[12,13] In a federal employee survey, 67 percent surveyed indicated that they should have a "considerable/great" input into their performance rating.[14] In the same group, 84 percent indicated their supervisor should have "considerable/great" input into their performance rating. Peer ratings, while infrequently utilized, have proved acceptable both in terms of reliability and validity. Peer ratings solve several problems associated with traditional superior-subordinate evaluations. They offer multiple raters who have more access to the ratee's (employee's) behavior, including a more comprehensive view of the ratee, and they are able to assess collegiality or teamwork, an increasingly salient behavior in today's work environment.

But peer ratings are difficult to sell to employers and employees. Fifty-six percent of the federal sample indicated they felt peers should have "little or no" input into their rating. Subordinate ratings are equally rare, and their main function is to provide data to begin discussion of the superior-subordinate relationship in a work group.

One of the challenges these findings on peer and subordinate ratings pose for human resource management is that future trends in the design and philosophy of work point toward the necessity of peer and self-ratings. Working in teams and seeking quality through an organizational philosophy of continuous improvement suggest less emphasis on methods of human resource management that grow out of current assessment techniques. More emphasis on teamwork requires greater emphasis on "getting along with others" and a host of other specific team-related, personal behaviors. Any appraisal system must fit into an organization's larger system of command, control, and coordination. And if an organization retains a hierarchical orientation, anything other than superior-subordinate ratings are going to cause friction. One reconciliation is the possibility of retaining allocational decisions and formal evaluative judgments in the superior, while emphasizing the developmental role of appraisals with peer and subordinate ratings.

Nevertheless, it would appear difficult to reconcile the goals of continuous self-improvement with hierarchical control and authority. This observation, frequently made in normative statements during the human relations movement of the 1960s and 1970s, is becoming more relevant in the 1990s as technological changes and pressures for quality and productivity challenge traditional methods of organizational command and control. Table 11–2 summarizes perhaps the most important factor in credible appraisal systems—access to information about the ratee. Peer ratings stand out as the most useful in this regard.

TABLE 11–2 Access to information about Task and Interpersonal Behaviors and Results

	SOURCE				
	Sub-ordinates	Self	Peers	Next Level (Supervisor)	Higher Level (Upper Management)
TASK					
Behaviors	Rare	Always	Frequent	Occasional	Rare
Results	Occasional	Frequent	Frequent	Frequent	Occasional
INTERPERSONAL					
Behaviors	Frequent	Always	Frequent	Occasional	Rare
Results	Frequent	Frequent	Frequent	Occasional	Rare

Source: Reprinted with permission from *Understanding performance appraisal,* © 1995 by Kevin R. Murphy and Jeannette N. Cleveland. Published by Sage Publications, Thousand Oaks, Ca.

A significant amount of effort has gone into creating accurate appraisal instruments and in training supervisors to dismiss inappropriate and irrelevant considerations when making formal assessments—and one wonders if technique dominates purpose in this area. The goal is to minimize rater bias without jeopardizing the supervisory discretion necessary in making judgments about employee performance. The difficulty in eliminating rater bias is that people, including supervisors, tend to make global evaluative judgments of others.[15] The fact is that supervisors come to conclusions about employees without the help of assessment instruments. Raters tend to use the performance appraisal process to document rather than discover how well an employee is performing. This probably helps account for Milkovich and Wigdor's observation that "There is no compelling evidence that one appraisal format is significantly better than another. Global ratings do not appear to produce very different results from job-specific ratings.[16] This leads them to assign marginal value to the expenditure of more time and money developing more accurate assessment instruments.[17]

The inevitable global assessments that supervisors make acknowledge the complexities of work, the multiplicity of factors causing different levels of work performance, the difficulty of actually describing the constituent elements of a job without trivializing it, and the critical role that who a person is influences the kind of work a person does, both its quality and its quantity. In addition, supervisors know that each employee creates an environment for the work of other employees, and to separate out individual performance artificially distorts what happens in an office.

A recent effort to meet several of the traditional criteria of performance appraisal with modern emphasis on teams, clients, and customers is the 360-degree appraisal.[18] With this method the ratee is placed in the middle of a metaphorical circle, and salient members of his or her role set become potential raters, usually with the immediate supervisor either conveying a summary to the ratee or actually gathering the information and evaluating it individually. This kind of appraisal encourages communication of the ratee's goals and understanding of organizational expectations to members of the role set, and it enhances communication with "customers," whether internal or external to the organization. These multiple views give a more accurate picture of the employee's contribution to the organization than a traditional superior-subordinate appraisal would. This approach, however, is time consuming, may challenge the hierarchical nature of an organization, and may bring issues of trust, confidentiality, and anonymity to the forefront among peers. As part of a human resources management information system, there now is available software to help manage the "paperwork," data collection, and consolidation required of a 360-degree system.[19]

CHARACTERISTICS OF AN EFFECTIVE APPRAISAL SYSTEM

Even though different evaluative methods are likely to identify the same employees as high or low performers, we have already seen in Table 11–1 that different appraisal methods are suitable for different evaluative purposes. Several guidelines follow for the effective use of appraisal systems by public organizations.[20]

First, it may be wise to utilize separate systems for separate purposes. It seems clear when one looks at the purposes of appraisal systems that two fundamentally different supervisory roles can be detected. If the purpose is allocation of rewards, the supervisor or other rater becomes a judge. If the purpose is to improve employee performance, the supervisor is a counselor, coach, or facilitator. The fact is that supervisors assume both roles in their day-to-day work, but the roles are difficult to integrate successfully. It may well be that different appraisal instruments lend themselves to the different functions, just as different times should be set aside to discuss allocation decisions and developmental issues with employees. Furthermore, it may be that the developmental function can be better fulfilled with ratings by peers, subordinates, and customers than by a superior who does not have as frequent access to the ratee's behavior or, in some cases, is not as credible.

Second, raters should have the opportunity, ability, and desire to rate employees accurately. Since employee understanding and acceptance of evaluative criteria are keys to performance improvement, it follows that employees should participate jointly in the determination of goals. The performance appraisal system must be job related, must allow the opportunity for interaction and understanding between rater and ratee, and must serve the performance improvement needs of both individual and organization.

Third, job analysis and performance appraisal need to be more closely related by developing occupation-specific job descriptions that include performance standards as well as duties, responsibilities, and minimum qualifications. Such job descriptions must specify the conditions under which work is to be performed, including such factors as resources, guidelines, and interrelationships. Necessarily, they will be specific to each occupation and perhaps to each organization as well. If the organization is attempting to structure itself along team lines, traditional, individual-oriented appraisals will become questionable and, where present, will have to adapt themselves to assessing behaviors that make teams work well.

Fourth, appraisal must be tied to long-range employee objectives such as promotion and career planning and more generally capture the employee's motivation for self-improvement. Performance appraisal is not an end in itself; nor should it be driven solely by short-term consequences like pay for performance. While performance improvement is administratively separate from promotional assessment and organizational human resource planning, both employees and organizations realize that performance appraisal relates to rewards, promotional consideration, and career planning. Further, connecting pay to performance places a significant burden on performance appraisal systems.

Fifth, because appraisal systems inevitably attempt to minimize subjectivity there always will be a formalism about them that cannot capture the nuances of behavior and personal attributes that contribute to a full appreciation of employee contributions at work. Supervisors will attempt to fudge their formal ratings to reflect these informal behaviors or behaviors that add value to employee performance but are not included formally because of their subjective nature. At the same time, there are some jobs that defy objective evaluation of employees. This is another case where any formal appraisal system cannot provide a full account of employee performance. The subjectivity involved in any evaluation of employee performance means that the effectiveness of any performance appraisal system rests on a foundation of trust within an organization and open communication, particularly between the person being rated and the rater.

Finally, the last but perhaps most important characteristic of an effective appraisal system relates to the criteria used to select supervisors. In a recent report on supervision and poor performers, the U.S. Merit Systems Protection Board makes the selection to supervisory jobs of people who have an aptitude for the human relations aspects of supervisory work its number one recommendation for improving the federal performance management system.[21] In that same report (p. 21), some 37 percent of the managers and supervisors surveyed indicated that it was difficult or very difficult for them to discuss performance deficiencies with their problem performers.

THE HUMAN DYNAMICS OF THE APPRAISAL PROCESS

Despite the attention appraisal techniques have received, there is no reason to believe that Lazer and Wikstrom's observation from several decades ago is outdated. They commented that appraisal systems are "still widely regarded as a nuisance at best and a necessary evil at worst."[22] Considering that feedback is essential to goal accomplishment and productivity, why were appraisal systems regarded so lightly prior to judicial scrutiny and the emphasis on pay for performance?

One reason is that not all employees are interested in productivity. When the caseload of an income maintenance worker in a social service agency is increased because of budgetary constraints to the point where the unspoken emphasis is on *quantity* of cases processed at the expense of *quality*, the individual worker begins to value his or her welfare, working conditions, and equity of the workload more than productivity. A second reason is that multiple sources of performance feedback exist in an organization, with the formal appraisal system constituting only the most visible and tangible. People in organizations are constantly receiving and interpreting cues about others and attributing motives to their behavior. A third reason concerns the human dynamics of the appraisal process as opposed to measurement issues surrounding the reliability and validity of the appraisal instrument itself.

Douglas Cederblom has reviewed literature on the appraisal interview—the formal part of the appraisal process where the rater and the person being rated sit down to talk about performance.[23] He found three factors contributing to the success of the appraisal interview. First, goal setting during the interview seemed positively associated with employee satisfaction with both the interview and its utility. Underlying the goal-setting process is the employee's confidence in the rater's technical knowledge about the subordinate's work. Second, the encouragement of subordinate participation in the interview—"welcoming participation," "opportunity to present ideas or feelings," and "boss asked my opinion"—seemed to produce positive subordinate assessments of the interview process. Last, the support of the rater expressed in terms of encouragement, constructive guidance, and sincere, specific praise of the subordinate also results in positive feelings about the interview.

Criticism from superior to subordinate produces mixed results. On the one hand, a certain amount of criticism should lend perceived credibility to the superior's assessment. On the other hand, research rarely shows much lasting change in an employee following a supervisory critique. In part, this is because few raters know how to provide a constructive critique of an employee, and when a trait-rating form is used, employees inevitably interpret criticism in personal rather than behavioral terms. The obvious here warrants mention. Anything in the appraisal interview that produces a defensive employee reaction (regardless of the rater's intent) is likely to detract from the subordinate's satisfaction with the interview and is unlikely to have much success in altering an employee's behavior at work.

Palguta observes that while it may be statistically impossible for all employees to perform better than average, the emotional investment of employees in believing they are better than average is significant.[24] When pay is tied to performance, this investment is magnified because pay tangibly reflects supervisory judgments about employees in ways that employees cannot ignore or easily discount. And, even in the federal government where there is no evidence to suggest that the number of poor performers is large or that incompetence is a serious problem,[25] the goal of feedback on below-average performers is to encourage poor performers to quit or to improve. There is some evidence that poorer performers are more likely to leave the federal government than those who rate higher.[26] But when the results of appraisals are used for allocation decisions like pay, superiors tend to become more lenient in their ratings.[27] While some poorly rated employees may leave, most stay, harboring feelings of inequity and discontent. In the federal government less than 1 percent of employees receive a rating below "fully successful." In fact, the majority receive a rating of better than fully successful, which is 3- on a 5-point scale. A rating of fully successful puts an employee in the bottom 10 to 20 percent of many occupations in federal agencies.[28] The difficulty with inflated ratings is that the emotional investment of workers in their performance leads them to discount "satisfactory" ratings—which carry few economic rewards—and become disgruntled; they then blame their discontent on organizational factors like supervision and managerial policies and practices.[29]

In looking for reasons why appraisal systems seem to have little real effect as managerial tools despite their theoretical promise, Nalbandian has turned to expectancy theory for an explanation.[30] He argues that the appraisal tool an organization uses may increase a supervisor's ability to assess employees, but many factors affecting the willingness of supervisors to evaluate employees seem easily overlooked. From an expectancy theory perspective, raters anticipate few positive outcomes from an honest attempt to rate subordinates. Most supervisors generally know who their effective and ineffective employees are even if they cannot always articulate their reasoning to someone else's satisfaction. From the supervisor's perspective, then, the formal appraisal process duplicates an assessment the supervisor has already made. Thus, when the supervisor conducts an appraisal, it is seen as benefiting someone else. Further, research in the federal government has shown that in 1989, according to supervisory reports, in 43 percent of the cases where employees received less-than-satisfactory ratings, no difference resulted in the employee's performance, 34 percent of the supervisors said performance improved, and 20 percent said it made things worse.[31] In a 1994 survey of federal managers and supervisors, 25 percent indicated that when they notified a poor performer that he/she might be demoted or terminated, the performance of 16 percent improved, and 25 percent of those employees became more difficult to manage.[32]

In addition, many authors and practitioners have pointed to the emotionally discomforting outcomes, the ones with negative valences, that the rater associates with the appraisal interview.[33] This is where the supervisor's assessment of the employee must be communicated face to face. Behaviorally oriented rating systems are designed to make assessments more objective and thus more acceptable to employees. Unfortunately, bad news is bad news regardless of whether or not it results from an assessment a supervisor feels is objective. When employees argue, sulk, look distraught, bewildered, or disappointed, or threaten to file a grievance because they disagree with the supervisor's assessment, most supervisors will experience such behavior in negative terms. The supervisor is likely, then, to find ways of behaving in the future that will not stimulate these employee responses. Is it any wonder that supervisors are prone to assess employees similarly, with most employees rated at least satisfactory? In fact, as we have seen already, in many organizations employees take a satisfactory rating as a sign of disapproval, and the majority of ratings exceed satisfactory.

The negative experiences supervisors have when rating subordinates appear unappreciated by others. For example, in a survey where federal employees were asked which changes in the performance management system in their agency they believed would advance agency missions, 66 percent indicated that a pass/fail system might help. Fifty-five percent indicated that not using performance ratings as the basis for cash awards might help.[34] Another survey of federal employees showed that the more experience supervisors have with performance appraisal, the less complicated they want it to be.[35]

One of the goals to a successful appraisal is putting the parties at ease as they begin discussing the employee's performance. The city of Irving, Texas, asks each employee to fill out a short questionnaire to begin the process. The following questions are designed to engage the employees and to produce information that will lead to a more productive appraisal.[36]

- In appraising your performance, are there any other persons you work with or around with whom your supervisor should speak to get a more complete picture of how you do your work/get results?
- Of what accomplishments and skills acquired during the last appraisal period are you particularly proud?
- What can be done to make you more effective in your job?
- What can be done to help you provide better service to your customer?

In sum, while a considerable amount of effort goes into the seemingly endless task of producing accurate measurements of performance, the human dynamics of the appraisal process probably remain a greater challenge. Until supervisors experience the appraisal process positively, the underlying motivation to make appraisal systems work will be absent.

PERFORMANCE APPRAISAL, THE SANCTIONS PROCESS, AND FAIRNESS

Discipline is a formal way for an organization to perform the sanctions function by letting employees know they have violated an organizational expectation and by imposing negative consequences. Employees can be disciplined for poor performance or for inappropriate conduct. A performance appraisal is a critical precursor to disciplining an employee for poor performance, unless the discipline involves a performance incident that is a clear policy violation. Usually, if an employee gets into a fight, or is drinking on the job, or sleeping on the night shift, a performance appraisal is not required prior to discipline.

An employee who has been disciplined has had something taken away—a suspension involving pay, a demotion, or dismissal—or has been set on this path with a formal warning or a letter of reprimand.

With the consequences of disciplinary action as great as they can be, the issue of fairness in exercising discipline is paramount in the employee's mind. If the organization can withhold an employee's pay or take away a job for poor performance, the employee wants to know what is expected. An employee who is performing below supervisory expectations wants an opportunity to respond to these concerns (so that an alleged performance deficiency is demonstrated in fact to be valid before discipline is imposed), and a chance to improve.

A performance appraisal is essential in this process because it formally serves as a warning device, and then as documentary evidence if a third party is called upon to make a judgment about the fairness of the discipline. It is a crucial step in establishing an environment of organizational justice because a valid performance appraisal requires (1) preset expectations, (2) accurate observations of behavior, and (3) a written record that can form the basis for a discussion between employee and employer and a third party or higher up if necessary.

The struggle human resource managers face is this: How far does an organization go in establishing formal procedures, including performance appraisal, to advance fairness and organizational justice when added formality limits managerial flexibility and responsiveness? There is no set answer to this question. It is a values question that is complicated in the case of performance appraisal especially, by contemporary work trends outlined earlier in this chapter—part-time and temporary workers, privatization, organizing into teams, and promoting flatter organizational hierarchies.

SUMMARY

This chapter has identified the purposes and methods of assessing employees as well as the legal framework affecting the appraisal process. The benefits and costs of each method were described, along with the observation that while different methods may be more acceptable to subordinates, they do not seem to produce significantly different ratings of employees.

Does the appraisal process actually fulfill its various functions, or does it represent a triumph of technique over purpose? There is no doubt that the formalism of appraisal systems challenges the essentially subjective nature of one person assessing another's work or even one person assessing his or her own performance. However, as long as the distribution of organizational rewards and punishments is connected to individual performance, the formalism can be expected to remain. The desire for organizational justice and the protection of individual rights require that employees know how and why rewards are distributed and that employees be given an opportunity to appeal these judgments and question the processes. This promotes formal performance appraisal methods and processes. If the technology and design of work and the philosophy of total quality management successfully transfer the appraisal process from the individual to the work group, the formalism associated with individual performance appraisal may diminish, even if the employee's demand for fair treatment does not.

Ultimately, in order to produce effective performance appraisal, for those personnel systems for which appraisal serves a useful purpose, some groundwork needs to be laid:

1. Promoting to supervisory positions people who, among their other qualifications, want to supervise and will not look upon the appraisal of employees as a necessary evil
2. An appraisal tool that has been developed with employee participation and that focuses more on performance than traits
3. Training programs directed at supervisory use of the appraisal instrument and understanding of the human dynamics surrounding the appraisal process
4. Rewards for supervisors who competently and seriously approach the appraisal function
5. An open discussion and understanding of the superior-subordinate relationship at work
6. Consequences that mean something for good/poor performance

KEY TERMS

behaviorally anchored rating scale (BARS)
critical incident (work sampling)
essay format
forced-choice techniques

graphic-rating scale
objective method
performance-based rating system
person-based rating system
ranking techniques

DISCUSSION QUESTIONS

1. Describe four operational functions of a performance appraisal system. Do you think all four can be accomplished with one appraisal method? Are the four functions complementary?
2. Why is performance appraisal associated most closely with civil service systems? How has it contributed to public perceptions that civil service systems are inefficient or ineffective, in comparison with those systems based on employment at will?
3. Identify the contemporary challenges to performance appraisal. How is the tension between administrative efficiency and individual rights reflected in the appraisal function?
4. Draw up a list of pros and cons for person-based and performance-based rating systems.
5. Identify the six characteristics of an effective rating system. Which of the six do you believe are the more difficult to implement?
6. Utilize an expectancy theory perspective and analyze the motivation of supervisors to rate the performance of subordinates honestly and accurately.

7. Some research shows that fairness in performance appraisal leads to positive employee behavior, commitment, and satisfaction. But fairness is associated with formality, due process, rules, and procedures. Tomorrow's organizations need to be flexible and adaptable. How can you devise a fair appraisal system that is consistent with the attributes of tomorrow's organization?

CASE STUDY: EVALUATING APPRAISAL INSTRUMENTS

Figures 11–1 and 11–3 present the appraisal instruments used in two organizations. Review the figures and respond to the following questions:

1. Which of the two forms is more job-related? Which type would you rather use to evaluate employees? Which type would you rather have your supervisor use to evaluate you?
2. Discuss the two forms with regard to the following criteria:
   - Job relatedness
   - Cost and time in developing
   - Ease of completing
   - Use in counseling and developing employees
   - Use in promotion, pay, or other personnel decisions
   - Rater bias
   - Use in providing specific feedback
   - Accuracy in measuring employee performance

NOTES

[1]Latham, G.P., and K.N. Wexley (1981). *Increasing Productivity Through Performance Appraisal*. Reading, MA: Addison-Wesley, pp. 28–30.

[2]Greller, M. (1998). Participation in the performance appraisal review: Inflexible manager behavior and variable worker needs. *Human Relations, 51*, pp. 1061–1084.

[3]Freedland, M. (1993). Performance appraisal and disciplinary action: The case for control of abuses. *International Labour Review, 132*, 493.

[4]Smith, M. (August 1999). Competency-based performance appraisal systems. *International Personnel Management Association News*, p. 16.

[5]Tziner, A., R.E. Kopelman, and N. Livneh (1993). Effects of performance appraisal format on perceived goal characteristics, appraisal process satisfaction, and changes in rated job performance: A field experiment. *The Journal of Psychology, 127*, 281–291.

[6]Taylor, S.M., K.B. Tracy, M.K. Renard, J.K. Harrison, and S.J. Carroll (1995). Due process in performance appraisal: A quasi-experiment in procedural justice. *Administrative Science Quarterly, 40*, 495–523.

[7]U.S. Merit Systems Protection Board (July 1999). *Federal Supervisors and Poor Performers*. Washington, DC: U.S. Merit Systems Protection Board, p. 28.

[8]Milkovich, G.T., and A.K. Wigdor (Eds.) (1991). *Pay For Performance: Evaluating Performance Appraisal And Merit Pay*. Washington, DC: National Academy Press, p. 143.

[9]Feild, H.S., and W.H. Holley (1982). The relationship of performance appraisal system characteristics to verdicts in selected employment discrimination cases. *Academy of Management Journal, 25*, 397.

[10]The Wyatt Company (Fourth Quarter, 1989). Wyatt Communicator: Results of the 1989 Wyatt Performance Management Survey. Chicago: The Wyatt Company, pp. 7–8. Reported in Milkovich and Wigdor (Eds.). *Pay for Performance*.

[11]United States Merit Systems Protection Board (June 1990). *Working For America: A Federal Employee Survey*. Washington, DC: U.S. Merit Systems Protection Board, p. 17.

[12]Cited in Latham, G.P., K.N. Wexley (1994). *Increasing Productivity Through Performance Appraisal* (2nd ed.). Reading, MA: Addison-Wesley, p. 112.

[13]Ash, A. (1994). Participants' reactions to subordinate appraisal of managers: Results of a pilot. *Public Personnel Management, 23,* 237–256.

[14]United States Merit Systems Protection Board (June 1990). *Working for America,* p. 17.

[15]Milkovich and Wigdor. *Pay For Performance,* p. 50.

[16]Ibid., p. 149.

[17]Ibid., p. 3.

[18]Coggburn, J.D. (1998). Subordinate appraisals of managers: Lessons from a state agency. *Review of Public Personnel Administration, 18,* 1, 68–79; Milliman, J.F., R.A. Zawacki, B. Schultz, S. Wiggins, and C.A. Norman (1995). Customer service drives 360-degree goal setting. *Personnel Journal, 74,* 136–142; Milliman, J.F., R.A. Zawacki, C.A. Norman, L. Powell, and J. Kirksey, Jr. (1994). Companies evaluate employees from all perspectives. *Personnel Journal, 73,* 99–103.

[19]Fried, E. (July 1999). 360-degree feedback software roundup. *International Personnel Management Association News,* pp. 26–27.

[20]Longenecker, C.O., and N. Nykodym (1996). Public sector performance appraisal effectiveness: A case study. *Public Personnel Management, 25,* 151–164.

[21]U.S. Merit Systems Protection Board. (July 1999). *Federal Supervisors and Poor Performers.* Washington, DC: U.S. Merit Systems Protection Board, p. 31.

[22]Lazer, R.I., W.S. Wikstrom (1977). *Appraising Managerial Performance: Current Practices and Future Directions.* New York: The Conference Board.

[23]Cederblom, D. (1982). The performance appraisal interview: A review, implications, and suggestions. *Academy of Management Review, 7,* 219–27.

[24]Palguta, J. (May 6, 1991). Performance management and pay for performance. A presentation before the Pay-for-Performance Labor-Management Committee and the Performance Management and Recognition System Review Committee. Washington, DC: U.S. Merit Systems Protection Board.

[25]U.S. Merit Systems Protection Board (July 1999). *Federal Supervisors and Poor Performers.* Washington, DC: U.S. Merit Systems Protection Board, p. 12.

[26]United States Merit Systems Protection Board (July 1988). *Toward Effective Performance Management in Government.* Washington, DC: U.S. Merit Systems Protection Board, p. 6.

[27]Milkovich and Wigdor. *Pay for Performance,* p. 72.

[28]Palguta. Performance management and pay for performance.

[29]Gabris, G.T., and K. Mitchell (1988). The impact of merit raise scores on employee attitudes: The Matthew effect of performance appraisal. *Public Personnel Management, 17,* 369–386.

[30]Nalbandian, J. (1981). Performance appraisal: If only people were not involved. *Public Administration Review, 41,* 392–396.

[31]United States Merit Systems Protection Board. *Working for America,* p. 20.

[32]U.S. Merit Systems Protection Board. (July 1999). *Federal Supervisors and Poor Performers.* Washington, DC: U.S. Merit Systems Protection Board, p. 19.

[33]Kikoski, J.F. (1998). Effective communication in the performance appraisal interview: Face-to-face communication for public managers in the culturally diverse workplace. *Public Personnel Management, 27,* 4, pp. 491–514.

[34]U.S. Merit Systems Protection Board. (July 1999). Federal Supervisors and Poor Performers. Washington, DC: U.S. Merit Systems Protection Board, p. 29.

[35]Ibid., p. 17.

[36]Grote. Public sector organizations: Today's innovative leaders performance management, p. 9.

12
Safety and Health

An employer's first responsibility is to provide workers with a safe and healthy work place. Yet despite the best efforts of government and industry, the United States has one of the highest work-related injury and illness rates of any major industrialized nation. Work-related injuries account for more than 200 million lost work days annually, at a cost in excess of $25 billion.[1]

Paradoxically, society's expectations for environmental health and safety management have risen over the same period.[2] Among them are frequent job changes, decreased unionization, population expansion and technological changes. Prevention of work-related accidents is of primary concern to public personnel managers. In addition to the personal pain and suffering caused by these incidents, they are also significant because of cost containment. These include not only the direct cost of reduced productivity but also the hidden costs of sick leave, employer insurance payments (for disability and workers' compensation policies), and the costs of processing or contesting disability retirement and workers' compensation claims. Moreover, some government employees (police officers and firefighters) receive occupational injuries and disability retirements at more than three times the rate of employees in other jobs. Hospitals and other health care facilities report the highest incidence of non-fatal occupational injuries.[3]

The general topic of employee safety and health includes a variety of programs: accident prevention, compliance with occupational safety and health regulations, health insurance, health benefits, smoking cessation, stress management, drug testing, AIDS and other life-threatening diseases, workplace violence, and employee assistance programs.

These are all related, for three reasons. First, health and safety are a *sanction*-related issue. In other words, these issues have become a significant concern of the employee-employer relationship because of legal compliance responsibilities and legal liability risks. The regulations of the Occupational Safety and Health Act (OSHA), which protect employees against agency violations of health or safety standards, apply to public agencies as well as private companies. The Family and Medical Leave Act requires public and private employers to grant employees leave to meet child- or eldercare commitments. And employers who do not have programs to counter workplace violence, or drug and alcohol abuse, risk being held liable in civil lawsuits for the consequences of these problems that result in death or injury to customers or other employees. In one widely reported case, for example, Southern Pacific Railroad was found liable in a multimillion-dollar lawsuit arising from a fatal auto accident involving an employee. The employer was liable because a supervisor told an employee who showed up for work drunk to go home, rather than calling a cab and sending the employee home in it. Therefore, because the employee was following a lawful supervisory order, and because the supervisor knew the employee was drunk, the employer was responsible for damages arising out of the accident!

Second, this topic is a *development*-related issue because there is increasing evidence that healthier employees are more productive (and happier) than unhealthy ones. Considering how much money employers may have invested in training skilled technical and professional employees, it makes sense to develop employee wellness programs (EAPs) that help employees manage stress, reduce drug and alcohol abuse, stop smoking, and make other positive **lifestyle choices**.

Third, because of the increasing cost of health care for employers, health and safety are an *allocation* or *planning* issue for the employer. Workplace programs to reduce accidents and injuries are important not only for legal compliance but also to reduce health benefit costs and workers' compensation insurance rates. Healthy employees use less sick leave and have lower rates of accidents and injuries. Employer-sponsored health programs are not a "frill"—they are a calculated effort to reduce operating costs.

High health-care costs and legal liability risks offer employers a powerful incentive to "weed out" applicants and employees whom they consider unacceptably high risk. These legitimate employer objectives (legal compliance, risk management, and cost control) often conflict with employee rights. Do employers have the right to deny employment to otherwise qualified applicants based on invasive testing procedures that may indicate potential health problems, even if the employee is currently able to do the job and where there is no direct link of the risk factor to current job performance? Do employers have the right to refuse employment to smokers? To illegal drug users? To HIV positive applicants or to those with unacceptably high blood pressure or to those with a family history of heart disease? At what point do these employer objectives conflict with employee rights under the Americans with Disabilities Act (ADA)?

By the end of this chapter, you will be able to:

1. Discuss the legal framework for safety and health, including the Occupational Safety and Health Act (OSHA), workers' compensation, the Americans with Disabilities Act, the Family and Medical Leave Act, and the special safety and health issues posed by at-home workers, independent contractors and health-care professionals.

2. Review personnel policies and programs to reduce workplace accidents and injuries.
3. Explain what employers can do to reduce the problem of workplace violence.
4. Assess the impact of tobacco, alcohol, and illegal drugs on the workplace.
5. Discuss the impact of AIDS and other life-threatening diseases on personnel policy.
6. Describe the role of employee wellness programs as an organizational response to these health and safety issues.
7. Show how drug testing, ADA compliance, and AIDS illustrate the dilemma managers face in balancing employers' concerns for productivity and safety with employees' concerns for job rights, health care, and privacy.

THE LEGAL FRAMEWORK FOR WORKPLACE SAFETY AND HEALTH

The legal framework for workplace safety and health involves landmark legislation (The Occupational Safety and Health Act of 1970), a workers' compensation system for routine reimbursement of costs for injuries and lost wages, the Americans with Disabilities Act, and the Family and Medical Leave Act. It also requires concern for specialized health and safety issues posed by independent contractors and health-care professionals.

The Occupational Safety and Health Act of 1970

Organized employer concern for work-related accidents and injuries combined with public concern for their social consequences, led the federal government to pass legislation regulating private and public employers. The **Occupational Safety and Health Act (OSHA)** was passed in 1970 to ensure that working conditions for all Americans meet minimum health and safety standards.[4] Under the provisions of this act, the **Occupational Safety and Health Administration (OSHA)** in the Department of Labor is charged with setting health and safety standards, inspecting public agencies, and levying citations and penalties to enforce compliance.

While most of the OSHA regulations apply to private industry, many apply to government as well. Typical regulations for office buildings include standards for number and size of entrances, lighting, ventilation, fire protection, and first-aid facilities. While public agencies are generally not subject to fines, they are subject to administrative sanctions like letters of reprimand.

The Occupational Safety and Health Act does not establish standards for state and municipal agencies. Instead, it gives states the option of complying with established federal standards or of establishing and enforcing standards through a designated state agency. Most states have chosen the option of designating a state agency to administer the plan. If this second option is chosen, the state must develop standards at least as effective as those promulgated by the Occupational Health and Safety Administration under federal regulations, must staff the agency with qualified employees, and must submit required reports on agency compliance to the Department of Labor.

Workers' Compensation

Workers' compensation systems were developed early this century because of dissatisfaction with the previous practice of discharging injured employees without any employer responsibility for treatment or rehabilitation, or of relying on the civil litigation system to recompense employees for the costs of accidents or injuries. Workers' compensation is an insurance system with variable payment rates for employers based on the historical risks of accident or injury their employees have suffered. Employers may self-insure, buy private insurance or seek universal coverage through a publicly chartered insurance agency in each state. The agency pays death benefits, hospitalization expenses, and expenses for a caregiver if an employee is injured or permanently disabled on the job. It reimburses employees on an actual cost basis, based on decisions rendered by an administrative hearing body that decides whether the injury or illness is job related, and what compensation from the fund is to be awarded for it.

The workers' compensation system has worked fairly well in providing a routine system of treatment and rehabilitation for job-related injuries. But costs are high, though a recent survey indicated that employer costs diminished slightly between 1996 and 1997 as a percentage of total insurance costs.[5] And two types of fraud and abuse need to be controlled by constant vigilance. First, there may be **claimant fraud**—collusion among health-care providers and employees to increase reimbursable health-care costs unnecessarily, by lengthy and unnecessary treatments, and by requests to cover time away from work as compensated time. While this is a problem, **premium fraud** by employers is far more serious. The system is self-supporting, funded by employer contributions that in turn are based on the number of employees and historical data about the nature and severity of occupational hazards (illness and injury) associated with particular types of work. Because in some dangerous jobs (such as roofing) the cost to employers may be as high as the cost of wages themselves, employers often seek to reduce costs by fraudulently classifying employees in less-dangerous occupations.

Americans with Disabilities Act

The Americans with Disabilities Act (1990) prohibits employment discrimination on the basis of disability. About 20 percent of the population, or 54 million Americans, have disabilities.[6] The ADA gives employment access rights to qualified persons whose disabilities do not adversely affect their work performance, or for whom employers can make reasonable accommodations to allow them to work productively. Generally speaking, public personnel directors report that the ADA has had no significant impact on personnel practices in their agencies, particularly since the Rehabilitation Act of 1973 already covered most.[7]

However, there have been noticeable impacts on job analysis, classification, and evaluation, and on affirmative action compliance.[8] Specifically, employers continue to struggle with the question of when an employee with a disability is covered by the ADA (and thus eligible for a "light duty" position), or is subject to discharge for inability to perform the essential functions of a position.[9] Another dilemma arising under ADA is that disabled employees have a greater risk of workplace injury.

A study published in the *Journal of the American Medical Association* indicates that work disability was associated with a 36 percent increased risk of occupational injury.[10] Common disabilities such as blindness more than tripled the risk for injury, and deafness more than doubled it. While the study does not advocate excluding such workers because of elevated risk (because they are indeed protected by the ADA), it emphasizes that employers should not hesitate to deny employment—as the law allows—when the applicant's disability is a direct threat to his own health or safety. And as the mean age of workers rises to 41 in 2005, employers should also remember that older workers have higher rates of disability.

And finally, coverage for mentally ill employees is perpetually problematic.[11] While treatment of physical disabilities often requires physical modifications, treatment of mental illnesses often requires changes in the nature or context of the job that are beyond the employer's capacity. And specifically, employers may even run into ADA conflicts when they attempt to enforce provisions against bizarre or hostile employee behavior as part of a program to detect and prevent workplace violence.[12]

Family and Medical Leave Act

Congress enacted the Family and Medical Leave Act (FMLA) in 1993 to respond to growing concerns over job security for people with health problems, and to assist working parents. The Act is an attempt to promote family integrity by balancing the demands of the workplace with family needs.[13] It was originally intended to allow employees with a "serious health condition" to retain their job rights if they needed to take time off to care for themselves or a family member. But recent administrative interpretations of the FMLA have made it difficult, in many employers' opinion, to comply with the law. "Serious health conditions" may include illness such as colds or flu if they are incapacitating and require continued treatment; and the statutory 12-weeks of leave (paid or not) can be taken in increments as small as 15 minutes per week. The complexity of legal requirements and interaction among laws (such as ADA and FMLA) are compelling reasons for employers to seek expert advice or to contract out their benefits adjudication policies and procedures.[14]

Emergent Issues Posed by Independent Contractors

Two emergent and interrelated issues also affect employers' ability to manage employee health and safety—working at home and part-time work "on the side." First, "telecommuting" means employees can better balance personal and work needs and increase flexibility of work schedules or locations, by communicating through networked computers, internet, phones, and faxes. Yet at-home or distant work locations are virtually impossible to monitor for health and safety concerns. The Department of Labor recently ran into a firestorm of criticism when it attempted to "police" home office work stations by establishing and enforcing workplace regulations. Yet this issue remains: As employee preferences and employer practice encourage more work at home, how will the lack of safety standards or enforcement affect employer responsibility for the costs of accident or sickness?

A second troublesome issue is "side jobs." Americans work longer hours than their European counterparts, and still find time to do work "on the side." This can be both legal and of little concern regarding health and safety. But it may be illegal (if payments are accepted in cash and not declared as outside income), and dangerous for the moonlighting employee (such as tree trimming, house painting, etc.). The issue arises as a legal concern because moonlighting workers are technically classified as independent contractors, not as employees. They are supposed to provide their own social security, workers' compensation and other "hidden" payroll costs. This seldom happens. Those they work for may also prefer to pay in cash and thus avoid the paperwork and costs associated with being an employer. But the unintended consequence is workers' comp fraud. Employees often seek workers' compensation coverage from their "regular" employer for accidents or injuries that really happened *outside* of work, particularly if they also lack health insurance.

Also, there is increasing pressure on the system from psychological and environmental illnesses (such as depression), or from stress-related illnesses (stroke and heart attack), where it is difficult to separate the effect of job stress from other stressors. These problems have led to efforts to reform the workers' compensation system in many states. Typical reforms include substitution of light-duty positions for full-time disability, on the theory that paying an employee who can work productively in a light-duty position is better than paying temporary or permanent disability benefits to that employee, and hiring another to take his or her place. Or states may seek to tighten the laws by restricting the award of benefits to employees with stress-related or repetitive strain injuries.

Health-Care Workers

Health-care workers, whether in the public or private sector, face increased risk of job-related accidents and illnesses. Congressional hearings indicated that health-care workers experience higher accident and illness rates than those working in factories, mines, or on construction sites.[15] Risks include not only those to which other industries are susceptible (lifting, chemical hazards, and slips and falls), but also life threatening diseases like AIDS, hepatitis and tuberculosis. Because of these risks, OSHA and the Joint Commission on Accreditation for Health-care Organizations (JCAHO) work together on worker and patient safety and health issues in these organizations.[16] AIDS has received the most attention, but because it is a blood-borne pathogen it is relatively easy to control through education, training, and what health-care professionals call **universal precautions**— preventing blood-to-blood contact (either from an infected patient or worker to an uninfected one) by thorough use of gloves and other specialized clothing, and safe techniques for handling and disposing of contaminated "sharps" (needles, etc.).[17] This also effectively bypasses the troublesome legal issue of whether health-care professionals should be tested for life-threatening diseases (including AIDS), when circumstances often make it impossible to conduct the same sort of test on incoming emergency patients whom health-care professionals are routinely asked to treat without regard to their own safety.[18] Ironically, health-care professionals—and patients—are at much greater risk from the airborne tuberculosis ("TB"), staphylococcus ("staph") and streptococcus ("strep") infections, which are easily spread by closed buildings with mechanical ventilation and air conditioning systems.

IMPROVING WORKPLACE HEALTH AND SAFETY

Improving unsafe or unhealthy working conditions is a legal requirement. But it is also a desirable policy to protect employees and their continued productivity. HR directors, risk managers, and other professionals can exert great influence on occupational health and safety, including assessing risks, developing an organizational culture that supports safety, correcting unsafe facilities and workplace conditions, designing jobs to make them safer, conducting employee orientation and training programs, and providing feedback and incentive systems for employees and supervisors.

Risk Assessment

Risk assessment requires understanding federal regulatory agency policies and guidelines with respect to four types of risks that may be present in the workplace: hazardous agents, physical hazards, ergonomic hazards, and psychological hazards.[19]

- Hazardous agents include biological agents, chemicals, disinfectants, antibiotics, hormones, medications, and hazardous waste.
- Physical hazards include injuries, noise, temperature extremes (including burns caused by heat and freezing), mechanical injuries, radiation, violence, and slips and falls.
- Ergonomic hazards include lifting (strains or back injuries), standing (for long periods of time), and poor lighting (eye strain).
- Psychological hazards include boredom, discrimination, technological change, shift work, downsizing, and other adverse working conditions.

Developing a Safety-Conscious Organizational Culture

According to estimates by the National Safety Council, work injury costs totaled $125 billion in 1998.[20] This includes wage and productivity losses of $63 billion, medical costs of $20 billion, administrative expenses of $25 billion, employer costs of $12 billion (including the value of time lost by uninjured workers), $2 billion for damage to motor vehicles, and $4 billion for fire losses. The average burden per worker was $940 (the value of goods and services each worker must produce to offset the cost of injuries); and the average cost per disabling injury was $28,000.

Increased safety generally requires not only occupational safety and health programs, but also an informal organizational culture that supports safety. As Mansdorf notes (1999), "Management systems and programs can provide an effective safety framework; however, it ultimately is the worker's perception of the value of safety to himself and the importance of safety to the organization that governs safety performance."[21] Health and safety climate scales have been developed to provide useful instruments to measure organizational change related to worksite health-promotion activities. Studies indicate that "Integration of health promotion and health protection will enable employers and workers to establish a strong communication through which both can balance the responsibility of educating one another while developing a healthy work environment."[22]

Correcting Unsafe Facilities and Conditions

Together with facilities managers and safety engineers, personnel directors and risk managers can correct unsafe facilities or working conditions reported by employees or supervisors. Two types of audits are useful. "Management audits evaluate whether the occupational safety or health management system fulfills the needs of the organization, whereas compliance audits monitor the organization's compliance with regulatory provisions. An ineffective audit program can result in even the best safety and health program failing due to regulatory change and organizational disorder."[23] Typical elements included in the occupational safety and health audit are program elements (such as safety, ergonomics, and medical care) or environmental factors like resource availability, organizational structure, and accountability.[24]

Faulty Job Design

In many cases, high rates of injury and illness are due to faulty job design. For example, many nurses are physically unable to lift and move heavy patients, so hospitals have assigned this duty to male nurses' aides or orderlies. Yet hospitals are frequently understaffed, particularly on the night shift, so nurses often end up doing this themselves. The result can be a disabling back injury. This situation could be prevented by greater recognition of the costs of *not* filling nurses' aide positions, or by redesigning the nurse's job to *not* include lifting heavy patients.

Ergonomics is the design of jobs and tools to fit human physiological and psychological needs. The issue has become an important one because the incidence of so-called "repetitive strain injuries"—work-related illnesses due to repeated motion, vibration, or pressure—has increased rapidly over the past ten years, from 50,000 to 300,000 cases annually.[25] The worst jobs are in meatpacking and poultry processing plants, garment manufacturing, and automobile repair. But many injuries are caused by common office equipment such as computers and video display terminals. In response, many companies have started training programs in how to use computers so as to avoid carpal tunnel syndrome or eyestrain. But OSHA's role in measuring and preventing these types of injuries is also disputed by some business interests, who fear that implementation of regulatory standards for repetitive strain injuries would prohibitively increase the cost of doing business.[26] In the meantime, employees and supervisors can do many things on their own. Employers can provide job rotation, rest breaks, lifting support, and ergonomically correct tools. Employees can stretch, minimize reaching, use safety equipment, and promote positive lifestyle changes.[27]

Training and Orientation Programs

The growth of training and orientation programs as a means of increasing employee health and safety is an outgrowth of risk management.[28] These programs should contain information on work safety, potentially hazardous conditions that may be encountered on the job, emergency evacuation procedures, the location of fire extinguishers and alarms, and procedures for reporting job-related injuries or illnesses. This will reinforce the importance of health and safety for supervisors and employees. It will also minimize the employer's financial and legal liability for workplace injuries and accidents. If employees have read and signed policies for reporting accidents, they will be ineligible for disability benefits based on claims of accidents or injuries that were not reported at the time.

Training programs need to be comprehensive yet specific to the job.[29] It is no coincidence that employees in high-risk occupations, such as public safety and health, are required to undergo the most training. For example, firefighters who are also qualified as paramedics need technical training in both fields, and training to improve their ability to provide complex services in a multiethnic urban environment.[30] And illiterate employees cannot be expected to properly use equipment or supplies, even if they are provided with explicit written instructions for their safe use.[31]

Feedback and Incentive Programs

Training, combined with feedback and incentive programs that reward employees and supervisors for safety, can support a culture of occupational safety. Over the past twenty years, repeated results have shown that reward programs for such safety behaviors as use of seat belts and mandatory protective equipment are effective at increasing safe work practices.[32] Since most local governments are self-insured, it makes sense to pass on some of the savings from safety to responsible employees through incentive programs. For example, some cities award savings bonds to employees whose job duties require the use of a city car, who drive for a year or more without any chargeable accidents (those attributable to traffic violations).

It is important to reward not only employees for safe work habits but also their supervisors for recognizing, evaluating, and controlling occupational health and safety hazards. This means publicizing the agency's record of time lost through work-related accidents or injuries, comparing this with other work units or overtime, and using compensation and disability payouts as one measure of the supervisor's performance evaluation. Granted, supervisors cannot control all the unsafe conditions inherent in a job. But they can work with employees on safer ways of handling jobs, and with top management on ways of designing work so that it can be performed with less risk to employees.

WORKPLACE VIOLENCE

Ours is a violent society, and it is not surprising that this violence carries over into the workplace.[33] According to the Centers for Disease Control and Prevention, about

20 people are murdered and 18,000 others are attacked at work each week in the United States alone.[34] According to the U.S. Department of Justice, more than 2 million violent incidents and 1,000 murders occur each year in the U.S. workplace.[35] The annual cost of workplace violence to U.S. corporations is nearly $40 billion.[36]

The Occupational Safety and Health Administration (OSHA) and the Department of Justice classify victims of **workplace violence** in the following manner:[37]

- *Stranger Violence:* This includes cab drivers, sales clerks, gas station attendants, and police. The main motive is robbery. About 80 percent of workplace homicides are of this type.
- *Client Violence:* A current or former client, customer, or patient attacks victims. Common settings are hospitals, psychiatric facilities, mental health clinics, drug abuse centers, long-term care facilities, prisons and schools.
- *Employee violence:* Victims are current or former employers, spouses, or significant others of the perpetrators.

Workplace Violence and Public Employees

Government employees—especially health care and social service workers—are particularly at risk of client violence. They must serve all segments of the population, including many who are mentally ill, have convictions for violent crimes, or are under the influence of drugs or alcohol. Further, they must enforce laws, rules and policies that are unpopular. Nor are potentially violent "customers" particularly inclined to distinguish between levels of government or types of agencies. They can resent local government officials simply because they dislike the national government's policies.[38] A 1997 Department of Justice survey indicated that, although public employees make up only 16 percent of the U.S. workforce, 37 percent of the victims of workplace violence work in local, state, and federal government![39]

Women are likely to be victims of employee violence.[40] Homicide in the workplace was the greatest cause of death among female workers from 1980 to 1985.[41] A report done by the **National Institute for Occupational Safety and Health (NIOSH)** found that homicides accounted for 12 percent of the workplace deaths among men and 42 percent of the workplace deaths among women.[42] Some of the workplace violence can be attributed to domestic violence; husbands and boyfriends commit 13,000 acts of violence against women in the workplace every year. Abusive husbands and lovers harass 74 percent of employed battered women at work—either in person or over the telephone—causing 56 percent of them to be late at least five times a month, 28 percent to leave early at least five days a month, and 54 percent to miss at least three full days of work a month.[43] The cost for **domestic violence** alone in lost productivity, increased health-care costs, absenteeism, and workplace violence is estimated to be $3 billion to $5 billion annually.[44]

Beyond these costs, workplace violence has a less measurable impact on employee stress and organizational climate. Organizations that are already working to establish principles of objectivity and fairness as part of alternative dispute resolution procedures under a workplace-diversification program, will find these efforts undermined by workplace violence or the threat of it.

Employers' Legal Liability for Employee Violence

In spite of its prevalence, employers are reluctant to get involved with workplace violence because they fear that, if they are aware that an employee is being abused and they do nothing, they will be sued.[45] The traditional theory under which employers have been held liable is the doctrine of *respondent superior*: The employer can be held "vicariously" liable for the violent actions of its employees as long as (1) the employee is acting within the scope of his employment; (2) the employee is authorized by the employer; or (3) the employer ratified the employee's actions subsequent to the occurrence.[46] And more recently, courts have held that employers may be liable to victims under the theory of negligent hiring, retention, and referral.

Under these theories, courts have established that there is a duty that the employer owes its employees, customers, suppliers, and other individuals who come in contact with its employees. For example, an employer can be held liable for acts of violence committed by current or former employees: for (1) **negligent hiring** if it failed to verify references or employment gaps which could indicate the applicant had spent time in prison; (2) **negligent retention** if it is aware that an employee has dangerous or violent tendencies but takes no action to reclassify or discharge the employee; or (3) **negligent referral** for terminating an employee for violent behavior and then failing to disclose the violent behavior to prospective employers during reference checks, or providing a positive letter of recommendation to the employee. To establish employer liability, a victim generally must show that the employer breached the duty it owed to the victim, and the employer's breach of that duty "caused" the victim's injury.[47] The principal means of limiting or expanding employer liability for negligent hiring and retention claims is the requirement of "foreseeability." The stronger the connection between the information known or available to the employer and the harm ultimately suffered, the greater the likelihood that the employer will be found liable in negligence.[48]

Employers who attempt to screen job applicants for violent tendencies run the risk of violating applicants' civil rights. For example, Title VII of the 1964 Civil Rights Act prohibits employers from refusing employment or discharging employees based on (1) an arrest record (since an arrest is not a conviction); or (2) a criminal conviction[49] unless the prospective employer can establish that the conviction would indicate that the applicant poses "a substantial and foreseeable threat to the safety of individuals or property."[50]

Liability issues are not limited to the hiring process. Employers who attempt to discharge an employee for violent outbursts, threatening staff, or demonstrating odd and erratic behavior can also be sued under the Americans with Disabilities Act (ADA). And labor lawyers indicate that it can be difficult to distinguish bad behavior from a protected mental disability.[51]

Employer Responses to Workplace Violence

What precautions can employers take to protect themselves and their employees from workplace violence?[52] First, employers should examine hiring policies and procedures to be sure that information about gaps in employment, disciplinary action from former employers, use of illegal drugs, and previous criminal convictions is available to those making a hiring decision. Previous employment references should be checked. A criminal background check may be worthwhile depending on the position.

Second, the most important step is to prevent violence among current employees by working to create an employee culture that makes violence unthinkable. The characteristic profile of the violence-prone employee is a middle-aged white male, with five to fifteen years' seniority, who collects guns and has few social ties.[53] Yet many nonviolent employees also fit this profile. The best response, therefore, is to take verbal and physical violence seriously, and to establish a "zero tolerance" policy that establishes consequences for the perpetrator. Supervisors should be trained in how to handle verbal violence. The best form of prevention is to remain calm and decide on the best course of action, listening carefully and being interested in what the angry person is saying. The objective is to let the angry person calm down and lead him or her to focus more on facts rather than opinions or personality dynamics. Furthermore, it is almost always easier to discipline or separate an employee for misconduct than it is for poor performance. Just as threats should be taken seriously, so actual incidents of workplace violence should be reported to the police for investigation and possible criminal prosecution.[54]

Managers should be aware of the link between workplace violence and a deteriorating climate. If the management style of the company allows people to communicate freely with each other and with management, threats will be reported more readily and agency values will be transmitted more clearly. Particularly in a paternalistic agency where employees have come to expect that they will be taken care of, workplace violence is often the result of layoffs or downsizing. Yet if employees feel protected, appreciated, and respected, there is less chance that they will become violent. Potential violence can be prevented and downsizing somewhat humanized if the manager has the opportunity to explain and clarify the company's actions. For example, companies that use layoff criteria that de-emphasize recent performance in favor of long-term performance history will find that they eliminate many rationalized motives for disruptive behavior.[55]

Employers should create a plan that describes how the organization would deal with warnings from employees about other potentially violent employees.[56] They should consider establishing a "threat management team" comprising legal staff, security personnel, the personnel director, psychological experts, union representatives, and employee assistance workers to respond to threats of violence or an actual incident.[57] Special care should be taken when it is necessary to terminate an employee for threats or violence: The termination should be conducted in private with at least two supervisors present; security should be immediately available yet unobtrusive; the last paycheck should be provided by mail so that the discharged employee is not required to return to the premises after termination; and an employee should be designated to work with the employee on such post-termination issues as accrued leave benefits and unemployment compensation.[58]

TOBACCO, ALCOHOL, AND ILLEGAL DRUGS

Tobacco, alcohol, and other drugs are widely used in our society. Because workplace policies on drug use involve basic conflicts between individual rights to privacy and employer concerns with productivity and health-care costs, it is important to examine three critical areas of research: effects of these drugs in the workplace, legal requirements for employers, and recommended workplace policies and practice.

Effects on Health, Safety and Productivity

Thirty years ago, smoking was considered a personal habit rather than a workplace policy issue. Today, most public employers ban smoking in the workplace because it is considered a violation of employees' right to a safe and healthy workplace.[59] Research has shown that smoking is linked to increased risk of cancer, heart attacks, and strokes. Smoking costs employers $25.8 billion in productivity each year, including costs for medical care, absenteeism, premature retirement, and early death.[60] According to a 1982 study, excess insurance costs for each smoker average $247 to $347 annually.[61]

The National Institute on Alcohol Abuse and Alcoholism estimates **alcohol abuse** results in a yearly $117 billion loss in productivity along with $13 billion in employee rehabilitation expenses.[62] The Institute concluded that alcoholism accounts for about 105,000 deaths each year, and an estimated $136 billion in lost employment, reduced productivity and health-care costs in 1990.[63] Alcohol abuse increases liability risks for employers. Also, employees do not like to work with alcohol abusers because this tends to reduce their own morale and productivity.

Drug abuse is a serious public health problem, and the workplace is obviously not immune from its effects.[64] The National Clearinghouse for Drug and Alcohol Abuse estimates that drug abuse costs U.S. employers $7.2 billion per year in productivity losses. A large-scale longitudinal study of 5,465 postal employees found higher rates of absenteeism and turnover for employees who tested positive for drugs (59.3 percent and 47 percent, respectively).[65] One Fortune 500 company released profiles of the typical drug abuser indicating that, in comparison with the typical employee, this person functions at about 67 percent of potential, is 3.6 times as likely to be involved in an accident, receives three times the average level of health-care benefits, is five times as likely to file a compensation claim and more likely to file grievances, and misses more than ten times as many workdays.[66] Substance abuse also results in higher health insurance costs for employers—as much as 170 percent in three years for several major plans.[67]

However, because general population drug use estimates are not valid indicators of employee drug use, there is also considerable controversy over the nature and severity of employee drug abuse. Alcohol is the drug of choice at the workplace, followed by marijuana.[68] A large sample of high school graduates indicated that in 1991, 8 percent of women and 5 percent of men have used alcohol on the job. The next most abused drug is marijuana with 5 percent of the men and 1 percent of the women reporting using marijuana while at work. All other drugs (amphetamines, barbiturates, and cocaine) are used by less than 1 percent of the surveyed employees.[69] Men have higher rates of drug and alcohol use than women; and drug use is highest for young adults. Therefore, there is little support for concluding that drug and alcohol abuse is rampant in the workplace.[70] A large survey conducted by the National Institute of Mental Health found that casual drug use does not normally influence work performance.[71] However, there is likely to be significant underreporting of drug-related accidents as twenty states deny any workers' compensation claim if drug or alcohol use is present.[72]

Legal Requirements for Employers

Tobacco and alcohol are legal drugs. However, most employers ban smoking in the workplace because of the health and liability issues raised by secondhand smoke. Intoxication by alcohol or illegal drugs is illegal for federal agencies or contractors under Executive Order 12564 (Drug Free Federal Work Place).

Enforcement of policies banning alcohol and illegal drugs in public agencies raises legal questions, primarily constitutional rights to privacy and against self-incrimination. Employers may run into difficulties if employees are hurt or cause injury to others at organizational functions where alcohol is served. In such cases, the issue comes down to the extent of the employer's knowledge of, or control over, things like "happy hour" receptions as part of conferences or training seminars.[73]

In the past, courts have routinely upheld **drug testing** for cause, when there was evidence of impaired performance or misconduct. In deciding whether drug testing of employees without such evidence represents an unreasonable search, courts must balance the degree to which the search is an intrusion upon the individual's privacy rights, and the degree to which the search reflects a legitimate government interest. Several Supreme Court decisions clarify its thinking concerning this balance. In *National Treasury Employees Union v. von Raab* (1988), it upheld the government's right to require drug testing for customs agents carrying guns and seizing drugs because of the policy-sensitive nature of their positions. In *Samuel Skinner v. Railway Labor Executives' Association* (1988), the Court upheld mandatory post-accident testing of railroad workers on grounds that this was a closely regulated industry where the government had a responsibility to protect public safety. Subsequent federal court decisions have clarified, but not substantially changed, these two landmark cases.[74] For example, *Connelly v. Newman* (753 F. Supp. 293, 1990) addressing the privacy rights of federal employees with respect to the drug testing policy of the U.S. Office of Personnel Management (OPM), declared that mandatory post-accident testing was authorized only for employees for whom there was a reasonable suspicion of drug use. The majority of public employers have instituted some form of pre-employment drug testing policy for job applicants. In the absence of a legally defined mandate, employers are generally reluctant to institute random drug testing.

The **Omnibus Transportation Employee Testing Act of 1991** requires drug and alcohol testing of employees required to have commercial driver's licenses (including drivers of trash trucks, dump trucks, buses, and street sweepers), among others. Several types of testing are required under guidelines issued by the U.S.

Department of Transportation: pre-employment testing of all applicants, post-accident ("critical incident") testing for all employees involved in an accident, random testing of a specified percentage of the workforce annually, and "reasonable suspicion" testing of employees who appear to be under the influence of alcohol or drugs.

Workplace Policies and Programs

Many states and localities restrict smoking in private businesses; thirty-two states regulate smoking by public employees in the workplace.[75] For example, many municipal fire departments are refusing to hire smokers as firefighters because smoking increases the likelihood that firefighters will subsequently be eligible for workers' compensation or disability retirement based on heart or lung disease. Usually, an exploratory survey by the personnel department to assess employee attitudes toward smoking will show that relatively few people smoke, and that many who do are willing to limit their use of tobacco on the job. In fact, the pendulum has swung so completely against workplace smoking that some researchers are concerned that the objectivity of smokers' performance appraisals may be affected by this stigma.[76] Employee cooperation with smoking policies can best be achieved by managerial compliance with the policies, union involvement, the availability of **smoking cessation programs** offered by the employer, and passing some of the savings along to nonsmoking employees in the form of lower health-insurance premiums or health-benefit costs.

Given the lack of consensus on the magnitude of illegal drug and alcohol use as a workplace problem, there is considerable disagreement on the appropriateness of drug testing as a workplace policy response.[77] Critics argue that drug testing is costly, requires elaborate and complex procedures to ensure integrity, violates employee privacy, and has not been causally linked to a reduction in drug use.[78] In addition, drugs do not necessarily have an adverse effect on job performance—the only drug for which a correlation between presence and impairment has been conclusively demonstrated is alcohol.[79] Given the privacy and self-incrimination issues raised by random drug testing, it may be useful to consider alternatives that more directly assess employee performance. Written tests are more effective and reliable than urinalysis testing, particularly at revealing information about drug history or employee involvement in drug sales.[80] Computer tests that measure hand-eye coordination are indicators of employee impairment, which is the critical variable in terms of the effects of drugs on job performance. Skills testing is another technique that can detect drug abuse.[81]

The ultimate solution in the eyes of many authorities is education and changing the norms and values of the workplace. The elements of an effective program include cultivating a shared responsibility between labor and management for reducing drug and alcohol abuse, a comprehensive drug education and awareness program, supervisor training on identifying drug use, clear employee policies on drug and alcohol abuse, a fully functioning employee wellness program, and a focused and limited drug and alcohol testing program.

AIDS AND OTHER LIFE-THREATENING DISEASES

AIDS and other life-threatening diseases pose a risk for employers and employees in general, and especially for those in the public sector. **Acquired Immune Deficiency Syndrome (AIDS)** was first reported in the United States in 1981. It is currently estimated that 1.5 million people are **HIV positive (HIV+)** (they carry the human immunodeficiency virus that causes AIDS). AIDS is a progressive disease. Infected individuals fall into four categories: (1) those who have been exposed to the virus but display no physical symptoms beyond testing HIV positive (HIV+); (2) those who experience some AIDS-related symptoms (such as night sweats, weight loss, swollen lymph nodes, or fatigue); (3) those who have developed opportunistic infections but do not require hospitalization and are physically able to work; and (4) those who are weakened by multiple infections (and are thus unable to work and may require hospitalization).

The health-care costs of AIDS are enormous. Early studies estimated a cost of $61,000 to $94,000 per person from onset to death, but these figures were based on a brief life span from onset to death (one to three years), and extensive use of volunteer patient care providers. As HIV is detected earlier, and patients survive longer, life span estimates have now increased far beyond the abilities of volunteer social service agencies to provide treatment. This means that health-care providers must be increasingly used at a far greater cost.[82]

The group that runs the greatest risk of contracting HIV is the health-care workers (doctors, dentists, nurses, dental hygienists, laboratory technicians, paramedics) whose jobs involve working with the body fluids of HIV+ patients. There is a *very slight* chance that these workers can become infected through an accidental needle stick from a syringe containing blood from an infected person, or by a cut. There is no evidence that the AIDS virus can be transmitted *if* the employee is following universal precautions.

Other workers—those whose jobs do not involve the risk of blood-to-blood contact—are in no danger of contracting HIV from a co-worker under normal working conditions. However, the fear and denial that AIDS generates among employees and their families can cause the issue to give rise to serious personnel problems.[83] Thus, AIDS generates increased concern among employers about liability risks and employee productivity. But these are relatively simple issues to address, at least in theory. Liability issues can be dealt with by educating employees about the remote possibility of contracting the HIV virus in the workplace. Concerns for productivity can be met by developing clear policies designed to determine whether an HIV carrier can perform the duties of the position. The desired outcome is a balanced approach reflecting the employer's desire to make reasonable accommodation to the HIV+ employee while this person is still healthy enough to perform the primary duties of the position, and to clarify policies with respect to sick leave, **disability retirement**, and dependent benefits once the person is forced by failing health to leave the workforce.

But tremendous pressure is being exerted on employers by the health-insurance industry. Obviously, although this is a clear violation of the ADA, it is in their best interest to identify carriers of the virus that causes AIDS prior to employment, and to have AIDS or AIDS-related diseases excluded from coverage as preexisting conditions. Some employers who would want to treat AIDS as an exclusionary precondition may also discriminate against homosexuals in hiring on the basis that they are members of a high-risk group. These pressures cause a fundamental conflict between the values of individual rights (for AIDS victims, homosexuals, and their co-workers) and efficiency (defined as reduced health-care costs and employee productivity).[84]

AIDS is important as a workplace issue because of its implications for productivity and liability. Most of all, the potentially huge losses it threatens for health-insurance carriers or self-insured employers means that it brings two fundamental values into open conflict. Under penalty of lawsuit for violation of the Americans with Disabilities Act, applicants and employees who carry the AIDS virus have the right to a job as long as they can perform its primary duties with **reasonable accommodation** by the employer.[85] But no employer or health insurance carrier would make a voluntary, rational decision to employ an applicant knowing that this person would live only a few more years and would cost the employer $100,000 to $250,000 in health care from onset until death. And it is worthwhile to remember that AIDS is only one of many life-threatening diseases that employers confront. Hepatitis B and staphylococcus are blood-borne pathogens that afflict health-care workers; and many virulent strains of tuberculosis are an increasing hazard for all employers because they are airborne.

EMPLOYEE WELLNESS PROGRAMS

Consider the following statistics, and you will begin to believe why employers have adopted **employee wellness programs** (or **employee assistance programs—EAPs**, as they are also called) to deal with a range of employee issues that can interfere with work performance.[86]

- In 1997, 6.8 percent of Americans employed full-time reported heavy drinking in the past month.
- Of the 11.2 million heavy drinkers in 1997, 30 percent were current illicit drug users.
- By the year 2005, individuals aged 50 or over will make up 25 percent of the work force. The population 65 and over consumes more prescription and over-the-counter medications than any other age group.
- One-fourth of American households are providing care for an older friend or relative, a three-fold increase over a decade ago.
- At any one time, one employee in 20 is experiencing depression.
- More than a million episodes of workplace violence occur annually.

Employee wellness programs are designed to diagnose, treat and rehabilitate employees whose personal problems are interfering with work performance. From the employee's viewpoint, the objective is to treat personal problems before they have an irreparable effect on job status. From the employer's viewpoint, the objective is to rehabilitate employees whose personal problems are a threat to productivity, health-care costs, or legal liability; and to lay the groundwork for possible disciplinary action and discharge (if the employee cannot be rehabilitated) before these threats become a reality.

Over time, both the functions of wellness programs and the role of the supervisor have changed substantially and rapidly. While the traditional program was charged almost exclusively with confronting the problem of alcohol abuse, the contemporary program also addresses drug abuse, AIDS education, and other personal problems that may affect job performance.[87] Because the wellness program deals with personal problems that may affect job performance, it is directly concerned with treating employee stress caused by increased economic pressure, increased family responsibilities, and the weakening of the social safety net of institutions.[88] Stress is a leading cause of absenteeism. A recent Commerce Clearinghouse study reported that 2 of every 5 unscheduled absences were the result of worker stress and time-off policy abuse.[89] Stress leads to physical disabilities such as high blood pressure, stroke, and heart disease. It leads to increased alcoholism and drug abuse, because employees as stress reduction mechanisms often use both of these.[90] Finally, stress increases the possibility of poor or erratic work performance.

Managers can help employees reduce stress by several simple strategies:[91]

- Allow them to talk freely with one another
- Reduce personal conflicts on the job
- Give employees adequate control over how they do their work
- Ensure that staffing and expense budgets are adequate
- Talk openly with employees.
- Support employees' efforts
- Provide competitive personal leave and vacation benefits, maintain current levels of employee benefits, reduce the amount of red tape for employees
- Recognize and reward employees for their accomplishments and contributions.

Managers can use the wellness program to help employees recognize and manage stress by developing good health habits (such as meditation, exercise, or work breaks), and providing health counseling. They can also recognize ways the organization causes stress: downsizing, inadequate training and feedback, or management pressures for unreasonable productivity increases or mandatory overtime to cope with economic competition. Today the supervisor is expected to observe and record changes in employee behavior and job performance. This is the **documentation** that can be used to discipline employees and to refer them to the program for professional diagnosis and treatment. And it poses a final ethical issue. Have employers endorsed wellness programs for their value in **rehabilitation** and productivity, or as a sort of legal insurance policy against employee grievances and lawsuits arising out of disciplinary action?

Traditionally, wellness programs were delivered either directly by the employer or referral by the employer to an outside contractor. Now the development of the Internet has increased the popularity of Web-based employee self-service, under which employers may purchase software that enables employees to enter their own program transactions, connect directly to providers, and track the services they receive.[92] And as an unexpected dividend, program providers find that many employees feel that email is more confidential than talking face-to-face about a personal problem.

While they may seem frivolous to old-timers, hard evidence supports wellness programs. They result in improved morale, positive lifestyle changes, improved medical claims and insurance rates, and reduced turnover.[93]

BALANCING ORGANIZATIONAL EFFECTIVENESS AND EMPLOYEE RIGHTS

The ability to predict long-term health risks by evaluating employee health profiles was originally developed as a component of employee wellness programs. But "permanent" employees incur higher benefit costs than temporary workers.[94] Whenever possible, given the limits of available technology and the applicability of handicap laws protecting applicant rights, employers have sought to reduce benefit costs by excluding high-risk applicants (including drug abusers and HIV carriers) from permanent employment.[95]

With respect to drug testing, the primary practical issue for personnel directors is whether rejecting applicants and disciplining employees who test positive is a useful way of stopping employee drug abuse. The primary legal issue is whether personnel policies or practices should distinguish between legal drugs (alcohol and prescription drugs) and illegal ones. Ethically sensitive personnel directors may also wonder if **substance abuse** has a greater effect on employee job performance than other issues. Agencies that do **substance abuse testing** of current employees do so primarily based upon incidents or reasonable suspicion, as defined by the supervisor. But because the use of drugs is not clearly and directly related to work performance, in the absence of clear guidelines and rewards, they are more likely to avoid these risks by declining to identify suspected substance abusers or to refer them for testing and treatment.

Employers have always used job-related medical criteria (such as a history of back injuries in an applicant for a job requiring heavy lifting) to exclude applicants who cannot perform the essential functions of a job, and for which no reasonable accommodation exists. And such exclusion is legal under the ADA. But employers are under considerable pressure from insurance carriers and risk managers to illegally exclude otherwise qualified applicants by using more generalized health indicators.[96]

AIDS is a more frightening issue to employees, and it raises fundamental questions about protecting the rights of victims, while at the same time educating the workforce. On the risk-management side, it means treating AIDS like any other life-threatening illness, while recognizing that insurance carriers will have a vested interest in excluding AIDS carriers from the workplace. But in reality, the lengthy incubation period for AIDS means that screening applicants (which is illegal under the ADA) is not an effective technique for excluding them from the workforce.

The Supreme Court recently (1991) overturned selection standards under which chemical companies refused to employ females of childbearing age in positions in which there was risk of exposure to chemical toxins that could cause birth defects in unborn children. In the first example, courts have held that the risk to the employer outweighs the right of the individual applicant to be considered for jobs for which they are interested and qualified. In the second example, the Supreme Court has ruled that the risk of birth defects and subsequent lawsuits is relatively slight compared to the employment rights of the affected individuals.

SUMMARY

Employee health and safety are important for maintaining human resources as an asset and reducing the health-care costs and liability risks generated by unsafe or unhealthy workplace conditions. Personnel directors have a critical role to play in providing a positive work environment to appropriately accommodate qualified persons with disabilities, where such practice does not compromise health, productivity, and safety. Personnel directors are also responsible for providing employees with a safe and healthy workplace by addressing such concerns as occupational safety and health, smoking, drug and alcohol abuse, and life-threatening diseases.

Many public personnel directors justifiably view controversial topics such as AIDS education or substance abuse policy as *risks* because these issues confront them with unavoidable conflicts among key human resource management values— responsiveness to elected officials, administrative efficiency, and protection of employee rights. But these issues also present personnel directors with *opportunities* to play a critical role in the resolution of emergent public policy.

KEY TERMS

Acquired Immune Deficiency Syndrome (AIDS)
alcohol abuse
claimant fraud
disability retirement
documentation
domestic violence
drug abuse
drug testing
employee wellness program (employee assistance program—EAP)
ergonomics
HIV positive (HIV+)
lifestyle choices
National Institute of Occupational Safety and Health (NIOSH)
National Treasury Employees Union v. von Raab (1988)

negligent hiring, retention and referral
Occupational Safety and Health Act (OSHA)
Occupational Safety and Health Administration (OSHA)
Omnibus Transportation Employee Testing Act of 1991
premium fraud
reasonable accommodation
rehabilitation
Samuel Skinner v. Railway Labor Executives' Association (1988)
smoking cessation program
substance abuse
substance abuse testing
universal precautions
workers' compensation
workplace violence

DISCUSSION QUESTIONS

1. What is the relationship between employee health and productivity?
2. What is the Occupational Safety and Health Act (OSHA)? What does it require of employers?

3. What can personnel directors can do to improve workplace health and safety?
4. How does employee substance abuse affect productivity, liability, and risk management?
5. What policies and programs have employers adopted to combat workplace substance abuse?
6. Why is AIDS a workplace health issue for public agencies? For health-care employers?
7. What are employee wellness programs (EAPs)? What is their role with respect to workplace substance abuse and AIDS?
8. What dilemmas do public personnel directors face in designing selection, development, and disciplinary action policies and procedures that balance agency concerns for productivity with employee concerns for privacy and individual rights? How should they resolve these dilemmas?

CASE STUDY 1: DEVELOPING A WORKPLACE AIDS POLICY

You are the personnel director of a state government agency. Top management and employees have both been putting pressure on you to develop a comprehensive agency policy for AIDS and other life-threatening diseases. Because the agency does not provide health-care services, there is no risk of blood-to-blood contact in the course of employees' job duties.

1. What would be the major components of your policy?
2. How would you "sell" it to employees and management?
3. What would be the role of the employee assistance program? How would you evaluate the effectiveness of its services?

CASE STUDY 2: WORKPLACE VIOLENCE: "IN HINDSIGHT, WE COULD SEE IT COMING"

THE EVENT

In the predawn hours on February 9, 1996, a disgruntled former park and recreation department employee, Clifton McCree, burst into the maintenance trailer where six of his former co-workers were starting their day's work. In five minutes, six people were dead of gunshot wounds: Clifton McCree had killed five of the six co-workers, and then had turned the gun upon himself; one co-worker escaped to tell the story of horror and death.

THE BACKGROUND

After eighteen years of employment, Clifton McCree had been discharged from the city of Ft. Lauderdale in October of 1994 after failing a drug test. After this, he had been unable to find steady work, and he had grown increasingly depressed and angry over what he saw as racial discrimination and retaliation by white employees and supervisors.

Mr. McCree had a history of workplace confrontations with co-workers. In the past, other employees had complained about his occasional threats to kill them. His supervisors had counseled him informally about the need to control his temper. Although he frequently went into rages, and co-workers were afraid of him, his supervisors and other employees had avoided formal complaints and tried to handle the problem internally because they didn't want him to lose his job. Despite his temper, he continued to receive satisfactory performance evaluations for nine years, and there was no formal record of his problems. Finally, in 1993, after a screaming match with a white co-worker, McCree's supervisor counseled him formally.

PERSONNEL POLICIES AND PROCEDURES

The problem came to a head just days after the city issued a new policy on workplace violence in 1994. This policy grew out of another tragedy—the murder of two lawyers in a downtown office building earlier that year. The city's policy was designed to raise awareness of what a potentially violent worker might do, and it set up a procedure for handling such incidents.

Immediately after the policy was issued, the supervisor came to the park and recreation department director, who had just come on the job a few weeks before, and told her about Clifton McCree. Within days, she had interviewed other workers, and prepared a chilling memo detailing McCree's threats and racial slurs against his co-workers. The memo indicated that McCree exhibited at least five of the warning signs of potential trouble, including threats, paranoid behavior, and a fascination with workplace violence.

City officials acted quickly, ordering a psychiatric evaluation and a drug test within days. By the end of the month, McCree had been suspended without pay, he flunked the drug test, and his firing was in the works. Until the day of the murders, eighteen months to the day after his discharge, he never returned to his workplace.

THE POSTMORTEM: SHOULD THE CITY HAVE DONE ANYTHING DIFFERENTLY?

In hindsight, it is difficult to find fault with anyone's actions. Most co-workers and supervisors would initially attempt to counsel a troubled employee informally because they were his friends and they knew he needed the job. With no formal counseling taking place, there would be no written record of previous performance incidents upon which to base a negative performance evaluation. When formal counseling finally occurred in 1993, it was only because co-workers had exerted pressure on management to do something. The city developed a clear and responsible policy on workplace violence in 1994. It was this policy that led to a strong and immediate response by the park and recreation department, and it was the department director's memo that led the city to take action. Appropriately, Clifton McCree was removed from work pending psychiatric evaluation and drug testing. He tested positive and was discharged.

Yet six people died. In addition to the human tragedy, the city faced civil charges from the victims' families, alleging that the city knew that Clifton McCree was violent but did not take adequate precautions to protect co-workers against violence.

1. In hindsight, what do you think the city could have done differently (if anything)?
2. Under the standard of "foreseeability," do you think the city can be held liable for failure to take more timely action against Clifton McCree?

3. Did the city's prompt and responsible action (to discharge Clifton McCree under its new workplace violence policy) in fact increase the chance of workplace violence?

4. Personnel management often takes place in communities where racial or ethnic unrest are part of the culture, and where disgruntled employees find it easy to get firearms. Is there anything personnel managers can do to lessen the chances of these factors resulting in workplace tragedies such as this one?

NOTES

[1]Wax, Nina (1994). *Occupational Safety and Health Management.* New York: McGraw-Hill, p. 14.

[2]Webb, D. A. (1994). The bathtub effect: Why safety programs fail. *Management Review, 83,* 51–54.

[3]U.S. Bureau of Labor Statistics (1996). *Occupational Injuries and Illnesses (BLS Bulletin 2512).* Available online: http://www.osha.gov/oshstats/bls/serv7html.

[4]Sand, R. H. (1991). Current developments in safety and health. *Employee Relations Law Journal, 17,* 145–148.

[5]——— (March 1999). Workers' comp still leads insurance costs. *IPMA News.* Alexandria, VA: International Personnel Management Association, p. 3.

[6]Trice, Eleanor (July 1998). Opening doors to ability: ADA and disabilities. *IPMA News.* Alexandria, VA: The International Personnel Management Association, p. 15.

[7]Kellough, J. Edward (2000). The Americans with Disabilities Act: A note on personnel policy impacts in state government. *Public Personnel Management, 29* (2): 211–224.

[8]Ibid.

[9]——— (February 1999). No permanent light duty for injured corrections officers. *IPMA News.* Alexandria, VA: International Personnel Management Association, p. 8.

[10]——— (July 1998). Disabled employees have greater risk of injury in the workplace. *IPMA News.* Alexandria, VA: The International Personnel Management Association, p. 15.

[11]Schott, Richard L. (Summer 1999). Managers and mental health: Mental illness and the workplace. *Public Personnel Management, 28* (2): 161–183.

[12]Seaman, James, and Taryn Goldstein (June 1999). Recent court and regulatory decisions make it harder for companies to manage their human resources. *IPMA News.* Alexandria, VA: The International Personnel Management Association, pp. 21, 22.

[13]Kalk, Jacqueline (September 2000). What every employer should know about the Family and Medical Leave Act. *IPMA News.* Alexandria, VA: International Personnel Management Association, pp. 7–8.

[14]Center for Personnel Research (CPR) (October 1998). *FMLA.* Alexandria, VA: International Personnel Management Association. Available online to agency members at: cpr@ipma-hr.org.

[15]Borwegen, B. (1999). "March 23, 1999 Testimony of the Service Employees International Union, AFL-CIO CLC Before the Subcommittee on Workforce Protections of the Committee on Education and the Workforce of the U.S. House of Representatives." Available online at: www.house.gov/ed_workforce/hearings/106th/wp/osha32399/borwegen.htm.

[16]Orr, G. (1999). JCAHO and OSHA partner to protect health care workers. *Job and Health Safety Quarterly, 10* (3): 36–40.

[17]Schottmuller, G., and J. Rover (1999). Managing employee exposure. *Surgical Services Management, 5* (9): 37–42.

[18]Oswald, E. M. (April 22, 1996). Why all employers should manage AIDS-HIV risk. *National Underwriter (Property & Casualty/Risk & Benefits Management Edition), 100:* 16–18.

[19]NIOSH (1996). Federal Register notice/Health care workers guidelines. *Federal Register: December 17, 1996, Volume 61 (243) Notices:* pp. 66281–66282. Available online: www.cdc.gov/niosh/hcw-fr.html.

[20]*Injury Facts (1999).* Work injury costs. Available online: www.nsc.org/lrs/statinfo/99051.htm.

[21]Mansdorf, Z. (1999). Organizational culture and safety performance. *Occupational Hazards, 61* (5): 109–110.

[22]McMahon, S., and J. Kuang (1999). Merging health promotion and protection: A unified philosophy toward employee health. *Professional Safety, 44* (7): 38–39.

[23]Blotzer, M.J. (1998). Safety and health program audits. *Occupational Hazards, 60* (5): 27–28.

[24]Mitchell, C.S. (1998). Evaluating occupational health and safety programs in the public sector. *American Journal of Industrial Medicine, 34*: 600–606.

[25]Lohr, S. (April 16, 1995). Waving goodbye to ergonomics. *The New York Times*, pp. 3–1, 14.

[26]Koutsandreas, Zachary (March 1998). HR managers, ergonomics and the ADA dilemma: 5 tips to avoid litigation. *IPMA News.* Alexandria, VA: The International Personnel Management Association, pp. 25–26.

[27]———— (December 1997). Opening doors to ability: ACOEM checklist outlines. *IPMA News.* Alexandria, VA: The International Personnel Management Association, pp. 24–25.

[28]———— (September 2000). From injury prevention to increased productivity. *IPMA News.* Alexandria, VA: International Personnel Management Association, p. 16.

[29]Bielous, G. A. (March 1995). Promoting safety in the workplace. *Supervisory Management*, p. 6.

[30]Garza, N. (1992). Riots, fires tax L.A. EMS resources. *Journal of Emergency Medical Services, 17*: 6.

[31]Tompkins, N. (April 1995). Overcoming language barriers for effective safety training. *Supervisory Management*, pp. 12–13.

[32]Streff, F.M., M.J. Kalsher, and E.S. Geller (1993). Developing efficient workplace safety programs: Observations of response covariation. *Journal of Organizational Behavior Management, 13* (2): 3–14.

[33]Chenier, Errol (Winter 1998). The workplace: A battleground for violence. *Public Personnel Management, 27*(4): 557–568.

[34]Rosenstock, Linda (2000). *Violence in the Workplace.* Available on-line at: www.cdc.gov/niosh/violfwd.html.

[35]Occupational Safety and Health Administration. *Workplace Violence.* Available on-line at: www.osha.gov/oshinfo/priorities/violence.html.

[36]———— (November 1999). Workplace violence costs U.S. employers nearly $40 billion annually! *IPMA News.* Alexandria, VA: International Personnel Management Association, p. 25.

[37]*Workplace Violence Defined.* Available on-line at: www.osha.gov/oshinfo/priorities/violence.html.

[38]Burnett, Stephen (May 1997). Protecting against workplace violence. *IPMA News.* Alexandria, VA: The International Personnel Management Association, pp. 22, 24.

[39]———— (May 2000). Developing an effective plan to prevent violence in the workplace. *IPMA News.* Alexandria, VA: The International Personnel Management Association, p. 23.

[40]Johnson, Pamela, and Julie Indvik (Fall 1999). The organizational benefits of assisting domestically abused employees. *Public Personnel Management, 87*(3): 365–374.

[41]Castelli, *NIOSH condemns workplace-murder epidemic.*

[42]Castelli, Ibid.

[43]Solomon, C.M. (April 1995). Talking frankly about domestic violence. *Personnel Journal*, p. 64.

[44]Ibid.

[45]Pereira, J. (March 2, 1995). Legal beat: Employers confront domestic abuse. *The Wall Street Journal*, p. B–1.

[46]Feliu, A. G. (1994). Workplace violence and the duty of care: The scope of an employer's obligation to protect against the violent employee. *Employee Relations Law Journal, 21*, 381–403.

[47]Martucci, W. C., and D. D. Clemow (1994/5). Workplace violence: Incidents—and liability—on the rise. *Employment Relations Today*, pp. 463–470.

[48]Braverman, Mark (1999). *Preventing Workplace Violence: A Guide for Employers and Practitioners.* Los Angeles: Sage Publications; Labig, Charles E. (1995). *Preventing Violence in the Workplace.* New York: American Management Association; and Denenberg, Richard, and Mark Braverman (1999). *The Violence-Prone Workplace: A New Approach to Dealing with Hostile, Threatening and Uncivil Behavior.* Ithaca: Cornell University Press, pp. 165–169.

[49]DiLorenzo, L.P., and D.J. Carroll (March 1995). Screening applicants for a safer workplace. *HR Magazine*, 55–58.

[50]Feliu, *Workplace violence*, p. 393.

[51]Feisenthal, E. (April 5, 1995). Legal beat: Potentially violent employees present bosses with a Catch-22. *The Wall Street Journal*, B-1, 5.

[52]Nigro, Lloyd G., and William Waugh, Jr. (Fall 1998). Local government responses to workplace violence. *Review of Public Personnel Administration* (): 5–17.

[53]Barrier, M. (1995). The enemy within. *Nation's Business, 83*(2): 18–24.

[54]Trice, Eleanor (October 1997). Can (and should) HR help calm domestic violence? *IPMA News.* Alexandria, VA: The International Personnel Management Association, pp. 15, 17.

[55]Johnson, D.L., J.G. Kurtz, and J.B. Kiehlbauch (1995). Scenario for supervisors. *HR Magazine, 40*(2): 63–68.

[56]Smith, Maureen (October 1998). Violence in the Workplace: are you protected? *IPMA News*. Alexandria, VA: International Personnel Management Association, pp. 12–13.

[57]Ceniceros, R. (January 30, 1995). Preventing workplace violence. *Business Insurance, 3*, 16.

[58]Fox, J. (March 13, 1995). Security: Keeping the homicidal employee at bay. *Forbes, 155*, 24–27.

[59]Rabin, R., and S. D. Sugarman (1993). *Smoking policy: Law, politics and culture*. New York: Oxford University Press.

[60]Teague, S. (January–February 1990). Smoke gets in your eyes: The hazard of second-hand smoke. *Heart Corps*, 60.

[61]Kent, D., and L. Cenci (June 1982). Smoking and the workplace. *Journal of Medicine*, p. 470.

[62]Evans, D. (1994). Employers face difficult questions in initiatives against alcohol abuse. *Occupational Health & Safety, 63*: 58–60.

[63]Nazario, S. (April 18, 1990). Alcohol is linked to a gene. *The Wall Street Journal*, p. B-1.

[64]Newcomb, M. D. (1994). Prevalence of alcohol and other drug use on the job: Cause for concern or irrational hysteria? *The Journal of Drug Issues, 24*: 403–416.

[65]Normand, J., S.D. Salyards, and J.J. Mahoney (1990). An evaluation of preemployment drug testing. *Journal of Applied Psychology, 75*: 629–639.

[66]Greenberg, E. (March 1987). To test or not to test: Drugs and the workplace. *Management Review, 12*: 24.

[67]Donkin, R. (April 1989). New hope for diagnosing alcoholism. *Business & Health*, pp. 20–23.

[68]Klingner, Donald, Gary Roberts, and Valerie Patterson (Summer 1998). The Miami Coalition surveys of employee drug use and attitudes: A five-year retrospective (1989–1993). *Public Personnel Management, 27*(2): 201–222.

[69]Crow, S.M., M.F. Villere, and S.J. Hartman (1994). Planes, trains, and ships: Drug testing is no substitute for drug supervision: Part II. *Supervision, 55*: 14–16.

[70]Kaestner, R., and M. Grossman (1995). Wages, workers' compensation benefits and drug use: Indirect evidence of the effect of drugs on the workplace. *American Economic Review, 85*: 55–60.

[71]Gillian, F. (1995). Recreational drug use may not be the biggest threat. *Personnel Journal, 74*: 21–23.

[72]Pouzar, E. (1994). Drug and alcohol abuse present RM challenge. *National Underwriter, 98*: 13.

[73]_____ (September 2000). Alcohol in the workplace causes headaches. *IPMA News*. Alexandria, VA: International Personnel Management Association, p. 18.

[74]Goldstein, Charles (July 2000). Employee drug-testing in the public sector. *IPMA News*. Alexandria, VA: The International Personnel Management Association, pp. 13–15.

[75]Trenk, B. (April 1989). Clearing the air about smoking policies. *Management Review*, p. 32.

[76]Gilbert, Ron, Edward Hannan, and Kevin Lowe (Fall 1998). Is smoking stigma clouding the objectivity of employee performance appraisal? *Public Personnel Management, 27*(3): 285–300.

[77]Crow, S., and S.J. Hartman (1992). Drugs in the workplace: Overstating the problems and the cures. *Journal of Drug Issues, 22*, 923–937.

[78]Macdonald, S., S. Wells, and R. Fry (1993). The limitations of drug screening in the workplace. *International Labour Review, 132*: 95–113.

[79]Manley, S.A., and G.S. Gibson (1990). Drug-induced impairment: Implications for employers. *Psychology of Addictive Behaviors, 4*, 97–99.

[80]Lavan, H., M. Katz, and J. Suttor (1994). Litigation of employer drug testing. *Labor Law Journal*, pp. 346–351.

[81]Comer, D. R. (1994). A case against workplace drug testing. *Organization Science, 5*, 259–267.

[82]Jacobs, S. (December 11, 1995). New AIDS drugs' aim is "buying time." *The Miami Herald*, pp. C-1, 5.

[83]Stodghill, R., R. Mitchell, K. Thurston, and C. Del Valle. (February 1, 1993). Managing AIDS: How one boss struggled to cope. *Business Week*, pp. 48–54.

[84]Burris, S. (1993). *AIDS law today: A new guide for the public*. Connecticut: Yale University Press.

[85]*School Board of Nassau County Fla v. Arline*, 107 S. Ct. 1123 (1987); and *Shuttleworth v. Broward County*, 639 F. Supp. (S.D. Fla. 1986).

[86]_____ (February 2000). EAPs: An effective response to diversity in the workplace. *IPMA News*. Alexandria, VA: International Personnel Management Association, p. 15.

[87]Carroll, Charles (June 1999). Opening doors to ability: A time of transition: EAP alternatives for the 1990s. *IPMA News.* Alexandria, VA: The International Personnel Management Association, pp. 23, 24.

[88]Wharton, A.S., and R.J. Erickson (1993). Managing emotions on the job and at home: Understanding the consequences of multiple emotional roles. *Academy of Management Review, 18*: 457–486.

[89]———— (December 1999). More workers checked out due to stress, even as work/life programs showed progress. *IPMA News.* Alexandria, VA: International Personnel Management Association, p. 3. Available on-line at: www.cch.com.

[90]Harris, M.M., and L.L. Heft (1992). Alcohol and drug use in the workplace: Issues, controversies and directions for future research. *Journal of Management, 18,* 239–266.

[91]Smith, Maureen (January 1999). Coping with employee stress. *IPMA News.* Alexandria, VA: International Personnel Management Association, p. 17. Also available on-line at: www.ipma-hr.org/cprserie.html.

[92]Perussima, Robert (October 1998). Technology trends: employee self-service. *IIPMA News.* Alexandria, VA: International Personnel Management Association, p. 24; and Platt, James (July 1997). EAP on-line: A new therapeutic intervention for employees. *IPMA News.* Alexandria, VA: The International Personnel Management Association, p. 15.

[93]———— (June 1997). Worksite wellness efforts lower costs and improve productivity. *IPMA News.* Alexandria, VA: The International Personnel Management Association, p. 27.

[94]Holton, R. (September 1988). AIDS in the workplace: Underwriting update. *Best's Review, Property-Casualty Edition,* pp. 96–98; and Solovy, A. (January 20, 1989). Insurers, HMOs and BC-BS plans talk about AIDS. *Hospitals, 63:* 24.

[95]Masi, D. (March 1987). Company response to drug abuse from the AMA's national survey. *Personnel, 63:* 40–46.

[96]Uzych, L. (March 1990). HIV testing: The legal balance between individual and societal rights. *Southern Medical Journal, 83:* 303–307.

13
Organizational Justice

Ronnie Lee McKnight, a prisoner at Tennessee's South Central Correctional Center (SCCC), charged that two prison guards, Darryl Richardson and John Walker, had unlawfully injured him (*Richardson v. The Knight*, 1997). He contended that they had placed him in extremely tight physical constraints, an action that he asserted deprived him of various constitutional rights. The guards defended themselves noting that courts have ruled that prison employees are protected from such charges when they are lawfully carrying out their duties. The challenge in this case is that a private company manages the SCCC and Richardson and Walker are not public employees.[1] Should Richardson and Walker, have the same rights as guards employed by the state of Tennessee? Should McKnight have the same rights as a prisoner in a public correctional facility? Should other citizens (like the media) have the same expectations of SCCC as they would of a state-operated facility?

By the end of this chapter, you will be able to:

1. Define the sanction function.
2. Identify the ways an organization establishes and maintains the terms of the employment relationship between employee and employer.
3. Describe the ways different personnel systems view the sanction function.
4. Discuss the balance the Court examines when deciding whether a public employer has violated an employee's constitutional rights to free speech, freedom of association, or privacy rights.
5. Describe the role of property rights and due process in establishing and maintaining the terms of the employment relationship.
6. Define the concept of organizational citizenship and relate it to employee perceptions of fairness.
7. Discuss how discipline and grievance procedures are connected to the sanction function.

8. Diagram a typical disciplinary procedure and describe various steps in a grievance procedure.
9. Define the terms *reasonable accommodation* and *undue hardship* in the Americans with Disabilities Act, and show the value conflict implied in these terms.
10. Describe how modern technology raises privacy concerns.
11. Describe the rights of employees who have been sexually harassed or who are considered whistle blowers.
12. Discuss the transition from sovereign immunity to qualified immunity for public employees.

THE SANCTION FUNCTION

Every organization, public or private, must establish and maintain *terms of the relationship between employee and employer*. This is the **sanction function**, the last of the four core functions. These terms in an employment relationship are captured in expectations employees have of their employer and contributions employees are willing to make in order to have their expectations fulfilled. Similarly, employers have expectations of employees and make contributions to employees in order to have those expectations fulfilled. The heart of the sanction function involves the interplay of these various expectations and contributions or obligations.

ESTABLISHING AND MAINTAINING EXPECTATIONS

Employee expectations and obligations come from numerous sources, ranging from the law to casual conversations with friends or acquaintances in similar jobs. Employer expectations and obligations are similarly diverse coming from organizational needs, comparisons with other organizations, and the character of the workforce. Regardless of where they originate, there are several formal mechanisms by which these tangible terms, and sometimes the intangible ones as well, are recognized. The first is the personnel manual, which contains the policies, rules, regulations, procedures, and practices that constitute a particular personnel system. For example, there may be a policy giving priority to promoting from within. There may be rules limiting political activity of employees while on the job. There may be a policy about bonuses or pay for performance. These policies and rules constitute some of the terms of the employment relationship.

Second, in some jurisdictions, the **terms of the employment relationship** are established through collective bargaining between employer and union. These terms are contained in working rules mutually agreed upon by employer and union membership. Third, various local, state, and federal laws establish expectations and obligations of employees and employer. For example, local ordinances may authorize merit personnel systems and policies; legislatures establish pay rates for public employees; the Fair Labor Standards Act describes required compensation policies; the Civil Rights Act of 1964 proscribes various forms of discrimination in employment; the Hatch Act and its counterparts in state and local governments proscribe political activity by employees. These and other laws contain provisions that affect the expectations and obligations that employees and employers have of one another.

It may be of interest to see the extent to which the law does play a role in establishing and maintaining the employment relationship. In a 1998 survey of the federal workforce, the Merit Systems Protection Board found that about 14 percent of the respondents believed they had suffered racial discrimination. Some 13 percent said they had been discriminated against because of gender; 11 percent indicated discrimination based on age. About 2 percent reported discrimination based on religion, marital status, political affiliation, or disability.[2] The total number of charges brought in 1999 under federal discrimination statutes was some 77,400.[3] Of those, 37 percent were charges of racial discrimination; 31 percent gender; 9 percent national origin, and 2 percent religion. Twenty-two percent were brought under the ADA; 23 percent were Title VII suits; 18 percent age discrimination; and 1 percent equal pay act claims. The EEOC found "reasonable cause" in only 5.7 percent of the Title VII cases and 4.4 percent of the ADA cases.

Last, the sanction function in public employment differs fundamentally from private employment because public employees have certain rights conferred upon them by the U.S. Constitution. Citizens are protected from government action by the Bill of Rights, including the Fourteenth Amendment. When citizens become employees of the government, they give up some of those rights, but they still have substantially more protection in speech, association, privacy, and equal treatment than do employees of private employers. We will discuss these protections later in the chapter.

Maintaining Expectations

Various processes maintain and enforce the terms established through these four mechanisms. Commonly, we think of employees suing their employer for violating some employee right. But more realistically, an organization's discipline and grievance procedures maintain the terms of the employment relationship or contract. Most disagreements are handled informally between supervisor and employee, but when informal channels are inadequate, formal discipline and grievance procedures involving due process are invoked. Sometimes, if those prove ineffective in resolving differences, the employee complains directly to elected officials or takes judicial action.

An employee is disciplined when the employer believes the employee is not living up to the terms of the employment "contract." Usually, this means that the employee is not contributing to the organization in the way the employer expects. On the other hand, when the employee believes the employer has violated its obligations, the employee "grieves" the employer's action, setting in motion some review. In large measure, the quality of the grievance processes due an employee who is subject to discipline determines whether employees believe they, and their coworkers, have been treated equitably and with dignity. (We will discuss discipline and grievance procedures in more detail later in the chapter.)

The notion that organizational justice is derived from balancing expectations and obligations suggests that the processes which establish and maintain expectations and obligations are as important as what those expectations and obligations actually are—their substance. In the next sections we will discuss the sanction function in alternate personnel systems, then we will review both the substantive and procedural rights of public employees and how those rights are balanced by the values of organizational efficiency and political responsiveness.

THE SANCTION FUNCTION IN ALTERNATE PERSONNEL SYSTEMS

We have talked in general about organizational justice, the mechanisms for establishing the terms of the employment relationship, and various processes for maintaining or enforcing those terms. But there truly are significant differences in the sanction function, depending upon which personnel system the employee is part of. This is because with the sanction function, the rules of the personnel game are established and maintained. This is where the expectations and obligations of employee and employer are determined and enforced. Every so often, one group or another will test its power to influence the rules. This is what inevitably happens with a strike. Regardless of the outcomes on wages, a strike gives the adversaries the opportunity to see where they stand with regard to setting expectations and obligations of employee and employer. Taking a case to court or arbitration can serve the same purpose. Battles between the legislature and executive branches of government are often fought over who has the discretion to set the rules.

The reason why unions were so successful in early years of this century was because they held out the promise of organizational justice for employees. One of the first objectives of a union is to negotiate a grievance procedure that includes a third-party decision-making process—one that takes the employee's grievance *outside* the managerial chain of command.

Civil service systems similarly value individual rights as a way of protecting employees from partisan political pressure. The first objective of civil service reform in the late nineteenth century was to legislate the elimination of politics from administration through the creation of systems in which employees could be dismissed only for *performance* deficiencies, not because they belonged to the wrong party or failed to pay voluntary dues. With regard to the sanction function, however, civil service systems differ from collective bargaining, because civil service systems are founded on dual values—individual rights and efficiency. Thus, even though we often see elaborate due process protections for public employees, we also hear complaints from managers, themselves covered by the same civil service protections, about the red tape and due process that hardly makes it worth the effort, in their eyes, to discipline employees.

Affirmative action personnel systems are driven by the value of social equity and, depending upon the context, individual rights. The expectation in affirmative action systems is that each person will be treated on his or her own merits and performance. But the benign use of racial classifications benefiting minorities at the expense of the individual right of non-minorities are rarely rejected by affirmative action advocates. Affirmative action personnel systems strongly advocate due process as a way of ensuring fair treatment in organizational systems suspected of bias.

When it comes to political personnel systems and also to contracting out, the value of individual rights diminishes in favor of responsiveness and efficiency, respectively. Due process may not be highly valued. Political executives who serve at the pleasure of elected leaders enjoy virtually no employee rights. Their positions do not fall under merit system provisions, and they are hired, moved, and dismissed largely based on a calculation of the political value they bring to an administration. Consequently, they may be less respectful of the rights of others, and see them as impediments to political and administrative action.

Contracting out is often seen as a way of circumventing personnel systems where individual rights have become entrenched at the expense of efficiency and responsiveness. Once a service is contracted out to a private employer, employees will find themselves operating under a new personnel system, usually with fewer employee rights. Depending upon the service, the constitutional protections that employees enjoy under a public personnel system are less likely to apply, and the due process public employees generally enjoy may be sacrificed to the goal of administrative efficiency and profit.

PROTECTING EMPLOYEES' CONSTITUTIONAL SUBSTANTIVE RIGHTS

In much of this chapter we review court cases, and managers may wonder why they should be familiar with these cases when they have attorneys to rely on. In some instances, knowledge of the decisions reached in particular cases is less important than how the court reached a decision. Managerial and judicial reasoning are not necessarily the same because in the balance between individual rights and efficiency, the court places much more value on individual rights than managers do. In a court of law, what may be good for the organization as a whole but bad for some individual employees may not serve as an adequate justification for administrative action. Furthermore, the court has said that failure to know the law may put administrators in legal jeopardy.[4]

Let's look now at some of the legal protections that are incorporated as terms of the employment contract. Once known to employees, these protections affect their expectations and employer obligations. The degree to which the expectations and obligations are mutually accepted will affect the employee's sense of organizational fairness. But, as in so many matters affecting fairness and rights, the formal rules that protect employees may create tension with the flexibility that supervisors need to manage effectively.

Freedom of Speech and Association—The First Amendment

Freedom of Speech.   The First Amendment to the constitution states "Congress shall make no law respecting an establishment of religion, or prohibiting the free exercise thereof; or abridging the freedom of speech, or of the press; or the right of the people peaceably to assemble, and to petition the Government for a redress of grievances." This amendment protects citizens from government's intrusions on the free exercise of religion, speech, political beliefs, and political association. Citing passages from many of the Court's precedents, Justice Brennan in *New York Times v. Sullivan* (1964)[5] indicated the importance of the First Amendment in our form of government. The constitutional safeguard "was fashioned to assure unfettered interchange of ideas for the bringing about of political and social changes desired by the people." The First Amendment "presupposes that right conclusions are more likely to be gathered out of a multitude of tongues, than through any kind of authoritative selection. To many this is, and always will be folly; but we have staked upon it our all." Justice Brennan himself wrote: "We consider this case against the background of a profound national commitment to the principle that debate on public issues should be uninhibited, robust, and wide-open, and that it may well include vehement, caustic, and sometimes unpleasantly sharp attacks on government and public officials" (p. 701).

Commonly, we think that the purpose of the First Amendment is to protect a speaker's right to expression—as an end in itself. Actually, as Cooper observes from his review of judicial opinions, the free flow of information is vital to the *listener's* ability to come to conclusions about government affairs, and this is what justifies the "untrammeled communication of ideas."[6]

While citizens often endorse the First Amendment uncritically, the Court faces a difficult task when applying it to public employment situations. The First Amendment provides the vehicle for classic confrontations between advocates of administrative efficiency and the rights of public employees. On the one hand, government has a duty to conduct its business efficiently, which means requiring respect for hierarchy and organizational loyalty. On the other hand, no one knows better how taxes are being spent than civil servants; and if they feel their jobs will be jeopardized if they speak out, is the public being deprived of information vital to its understanding of government?

In many ways, the balance the Court tries to draw among the values of administrative efficiency and individual rights depends on the extent to which the justices believe that public employees should give up the constitutional rights they have as citizens when they go to work for a public employer; on the extent to which they feel that what goes on *inside* a public agency is a matter of public concern; and on the extent to which they feel the judiciary should be involved in public personnel management at all.

In one of the key free speech cases, *Connick v. Myers* (1983),[7] a 5–4 Court decided that Sheila Myers was appropriately discharged for insubordination when she refused a transfer and then distributed a questionnaire to colleagues regarding the way Harry Connick, the elected district attorney in New Orleans, ran his office. The Court's deference to administrative efficiency is seen in two ways in this case. First, the Court tempered its decision on whether Ms. Myers was speaking out on a matter of public concern by noting that she was a disgruntled employee. In other words, her aims and motives were considered, as well as the content of the information she was providing with the questionnaire results. Further, the majority dismissed the importance of most of the information itself, suggesting that matters of internal agency operations are not a matter of public importance in judging the performance of the district attorney.

Because the Court acknowledged that a few of Myers's questions addressed matters of public concern, they turned to the government's argument on why she should be dismissed. As in all cases, the court always looks for reasons why an action was taken or not taken, and it scrutinizes them. When the court has determined that an employee's constitutional rights are at stake, managerial discretion itself is not a sufficient justification for the disciplinary action.

In this case, the Court concluded: "The limited First Amendment interest involved here does not require that Connick tolerate action which he reasonably believed would disrupt the office, undermine his authority, and destroy close working relationships" (p. 724). Here the Court retreated from previous judgments where *evidence* of disruption would have been required before the employer could have justly considered terminating the employee.

Connick v. Myers points out the difficulty in assessing the whistle-blower's claim. Was Myers a potential whistle-blower who was shut up? Was she simply a disgruntled employee? Does it really matter whether a whistle-blower is a disgruntled employee?

While *Connick v. Myers* involved a public employee's first amendment rights, in 1996 in the case of **Wahaunsee County v. Umbehr**[8] the court held that a private business holding a contract with a public employer has similar rights. Umbehr hauled trash for the county and was a frequent critic of the county commissioners. When the county failed to renew his contract, he successfully alleged that they were retaliating for his criticism and thereby violating his first amendment right to free speech.

Freedom of Association: Patronage versus Civil Service.   Governments have struggled since the early 1800s to draw a balance between a responsive and an efficient government. Advocates of responsiveness have generally favored more political control over public bureaucracies; advocates of administrative efficiency have fought to keep politics out of administration. Political personnel systems fight for the allocation of public jobs on the basis of political loyalty as a reward for service to a political party and as a way of ensuring that newly elected officials can appoint people committed to their goals. For years, limitations on the political activity of employees as well as constraints on political influence over them have been dealt with in legislatures and executive branches of government.

The courts stepped into this battle in the mid-1970s by limiting the patronage practice of discharging public employees on the basis of political affiliation. The Court argued that patronage dismissals violated a public employee's First Amendment right to freedom of belief and association—to belong to a political party of choice and maintain one's own political beliefs. In **Rutan v. Republican Party of Illinois** (1990), a 5–4 Court extended its ruling to hiring, promotion, transfer, and recall decisions.[9,10] The Court said the government must show a vital governmental interest before it could condition personnel actions on political belief and association. The majority claimed that preservation of democratic processes was not advantaged by patronage enough to outweigh a public employee's First Amendment rights.

In an earlier case, ***Branti v. Finkel*** (1980), the Court decided 6–3 that in trying to determine what positions were exempt from restrictions on patronage dismissals, "The ultimate inquiry is not whether the label 'policymaker' or 'confidential' fits a particular position; rather, the question is whether the hiring authority can demonstrate that party affiliation is an appropriate requirement for the effective performance of the public office involved."[11] In light of *Rutan*, this restriction on patronage dismissals would seem to apply to hiring as well.

In a companion case to *Wabaunsee County v. Umbehr* the court reviewed the first amendment rights of contractual and temporary employees in ***O'Hare v. Northlake***.[12] The court ruled that hiring temporary workers based on party affiliation was unconstitutional.

To conclude this discussion of the public employee's rights under the First Amendment, one of the more interesting observations involves the extension of rights to independent contractors and temporary workers. In *Richardson* the court ruled that private prison guards do not have the same rights as public employees. But *Umbehr* and *O'Hare* may be sending a different message. It appears that the practice of contracting out and utilizing non-civil service employees to avoid constitutional obligations afforded public employees may not lead to clear cut conclusions.[13]

Privacy, Drug Testing, and the Fourth Amendment

We have seen that citizens who are public employees often are protected less by the Bill of Rights than are ordinary citizens. The Fourth Amendment to the Constitution protects citizens from unreasonable search and seizure and is a crucial foundation for privacy. It does this in law enforcement cases by requiring the searching authority to obtain a warrant prior to the search. A judge, a neutral party, must be convinced that the searching authority has probable cause to believe that the suspected individual has broken the law, before the warrant is issued.

The Fourth Amendment to the Constitution states: "The right of the people to be secure in their persons, houses, papers, and effects, against unreasonable searches and seizures, shall not be violated, and no Warrants shall issue, but upon probable cause, supported by Oath or affirmation, and particularly describing the place to be searched, and the persons or things to be seized."

But in some non-criminal cases, the government is able to conduct a search without a warrant. These are cases like border searches and searches of employee desks and lockers, and searches of individuals themselves—as in drug testing. In these kinds of situations, no probable cause is required. A balance test is performed weighing the government's interest or special need with the individual's expectation of privacy.

In 1985 the Federal Railroad Administration promulgated rules to curb alcohol and drug abuse by railway employees. Among other provisions, the rules called for drug and alcohol testing for certain railway employees following a major train accident. The Railway Labor Executives' Association, acting on behalf of several unions, charged that the regulations violated the employees' Fourth Amendment rights against unreasonable search and seizure. They claimed a violation because the rules called for the testing of all employees covered by the regulations, regardless of any evidence leading to suspicion that they had broken the law.

In *Skinner v. Railway Labor Executives'Association* (1989),[14] the Supreme Court ruled 7–2 that where "special needs" go beyond normal law enforcement and make impractical the securing of a warrant and establishing probable cause, the Court must balance the government's interest against the privacy interests of the individual in order to determine if the Fourth Amendment has been violated. According to the Court in *Skinner*, regulating the conduct of railroad employees to ensure safe transportation constitutes a compelling government interest, especially because the railroad industry had a history of alcohol and drug abuse by its employees. Further, the Court ruled that the drug testing constituted a minimal intrusion into the privacy of the railroad workers since they knew in advance who would be tested, and when and under what conditions the testing would take place.

The Court's reasoning in its drug testing cases has implications generally for the relationship between the courts and public administrators. In *National Treasury Employees Union v. Von Raab* (1989), the Court said that the intrusion of privacy by United States Customs Service drug testing procedures was minimized by the administrative regulations themselves: "These procedures significantly minimize the program's intrusion on privacy interests."[15] In other words, the Customs Service developed a set of procedures on drug testing that successfully anticipated a constitutional challenge. Those procedures were aimed not only at promoting political responsiveness and administrative efficiency but also at recognizing the individual rights of the employees.[16] In other words, the impact of the Court on public personnel administration is evident in these drug-testing cases, not only in the specific decisions it has rendered, but also in the Court's power to encourage administrative agencies to think like a judge and anticipate judicial challenge as they develop administrative rules and procedures.[17]

PROTECTING EMPLOYEES' CONSTITUTIONAL PROCEDURAL RIGHTS

Property Rights and Due Process

Earlier, we suggested that the sanction function is concerned with both the substance of employee and employer expectations and obligations, and the processes by which these expectations and obligations are established and maintained. Now, we will look at procedural rights and how they are balanced by the value of organizational efficiency.

The process side of this concern is found in two concepts— **property rights** and **due process**. It has become popular to assert that civil service rules "hamstring" management by making it impossible to discipline or discharge employees protected by civil service systems. In one respect, this statement is correct. Public employees have rights to their jobs that exceed those of their private-sector counterparts. Yet this statement is also incorrect, for these rights ultimately are derived from the constitutional requirement of due process, rather than civil service regulations. Constitutional protections accorded *public* employees are an extension of the government's responsibility to guarantee certain freedoms to its citizens. The key here is that the *government* is bound by the Constitution, whether in its dealings with citizens simply as individuals or citizens as employees.

The Fifth and Fourteenth amendments to the Constitution require that a government may deprive an individual of life, liberty, or property only after due process of law. Over the years, the courts have come to conclude that public employees have a property interest in their jobs, if they have been led to expect that they will hold their jobs permanently as long as they perform satisfactorily. Courts have found these expectations implied in civil service system personnel policies and manuals that specify an employee will be discharged for good cause only, or where specific grounds for dismissal are identified, or where progressive discipline is endorsed and steps identified.[18] In other words, a job can be considered a public employee's property, and once that is established, the government—the public employer—can take the property/job only after due process.

One of the efficiency arguments for contracting out for service delivery or hiring temporary workers is that their expectations of due process are less than those of permanent civil service employees. With fewer rights, managerial discretion increases, and flexibility in handling human resources is enhanced. On the one hand, private-sector employees who handle the contract work have no constitutional rights as employees, and in the case of temporary workers, even if a public employer hires them, there are no expectations of job security.

What is due process? Minimal due process requires that an employer notify an employee of the employee's violation and give the employee a chance to state his or her side of the story. Due process comes in degrees, where the amount depends on the scope of the discipline contemplated. The critical step in linking due process with fairness comes when the person or board hearing the employee appeal or grievance is not in the employee's normal chain of command. This conveys the message that the employee will be heard impartially—by an investigator, board, or arbitrator.

A simple written reprimand might appropriately call for minimal due process, but a contemplated firing, which would deprive a public employee of the economic means of supporting him- or herself and possibly create difficulty for the employee when seeking another job (infringe on the employee's liberty to seek employment), would require a pretermination hearing.[19] Once again, we see personnel policies and practices growing out of an attempt to balance an employee's expectations of fair treatment (individual rights) with the employer's necessity to manage the public workforce efficiently.

Organizational Citizenship and Employee Perceptions of Fairness

Due process is not only something that might be required by law. Its presence can lead employees to conclude that their employer is committed in more than words to treating employees fairly.[20] In some ways this is just like the conclusions that citizens would draw about their government knowing that citizenship implies the right to fair treatment protected by due process as well as substantive rights.

Drawing on the concepts of the psychological contract and equity theory, if the employee expects and receives fair treatment, he or she is likely to feel obligated to reciprocate in some way.

Organizational effectiveness hinges on intangible elements of the psychological contract like the willingness to cooperate, courtesy, sportsmanship, loyalty and commitment. These characteristics can be included within the concept of **organizational citizenship**. The importance of procedural justice should not be underestimated in promoting organizational citizenship. According to Neihoff and Moorman, "Procedural justice is instrumental in promoting group concerns because fair procedures communicate the message that the group values each member.[21] More recent research provides some reason to believe that employees perceive procedural justice as an expression of organizational support and in recognition of that support are likely to help others in the organization, exhibit personal initiative, and promote the organization's image.[22]

What exactly is **procedural justice**? It consists of both the policies and methods to make organizational decisions regarding the distribution of rewards and punishments as well as an interpersonal aspect—the way supervisors and managers implement the policies and methods. Moorman's literature review confirms that employee perceptions of substantive justice are influenced by how those decisions are arrived at and carried out.[23] Perhaps most important, his research shows that perceptions of fairness emanating from how supervisors treat employees is a cornerstone of organizational justice and thus, organizational citizenship. While the goal of due process is to treat individual employees fairly, the consequence is the climate that is set and the larger picture that is drawn for all employees regardless of whether they ever utilize grievance or other due process channels or are the recipients of bad organizational news.

Discipline and Counseling of the Unproductive Employee

The employee's sense of fairness is significantly affected by how disciplinary and grievance procedures are carried out, and this puts a premium on the supervisor's role. Disciplinary action is the last step—never the first—in dealing with an employee whose performance is substandard. It assumes that the supervisor of a poorly performing employee has asked a number of questions regarding job design, selection, orientation, performance appraisal, training, and compensation:

Job design	Are the tasks, conditions and performance standards of the position reasonable and equitable?
Selection	Does the employee meet the minimum qualifications established for the position?
Orientation	Were organizational rules and regulations, and position requirements clearly communicated to the new employee?
Performance appraisal	Was the employee's performance adequately documented, and was the employee provided informal and formal feedback on the quality of his or her performance?

Training   Does the employee have adequate skills to perform the required tasks at the expected level of competence?

Compensation   Is good performance rewarded, or are there factors in the work environment that make it impossible or punishing to perform well?

Theoretically, therefore, **discipline** represents the last step in supervising employees because it symbolizes a failure to adjust the expectations/obligations of the employment relationship by less intrusive means. It is primarily a supervisory responsibility, since most performance problems are handled informally within the work unit with minimal involvement by the personnel department.

Figure 13–1 (page 329) shows the sequence of personnel activities that occur prior to disciplinary action. It is the primary responsibility of the employee's immediate supervisor to ensure that each of these steps is followed. Together, they represent the counseling and disciplinary action process.

The personnel manager has three important responsibilities with respect to disciplinary action. Initially, the personnel department is responsible for establishing the process. Once it has been established as part of the agency's personnel rules and regulations, the personnel director is frequently responsible for counseling unproductive employees and for assisting the supervisor in implementing evaluation and training procedures to improve performance or institute disciplinary action. Last, the personnel director is responsible for making sure the system is applied equitably. The following memorandum from the personnel director in Kansas City, Missouri, to department heads, shows that the personnel director has both a facilitating and a policing role in the disciplinary process.

To: All Department Heads
From: Tom F. Lewinsohn, Director of Personnel
Subject: Employee Rights and Obligations

In today's world of work we hear much about employee rights but seldom hear about employee obligations. With our departmental budgets becoming tighter those employee obligations deserve even more critical attention. For their paychecks, which is only one of their rights, employees can be expected to fulfill obligations such as showing up for work regularly and punctually, taking directions from supervisors, doing their jobs correctly, and following rules.

Too often supervisors do not act soon enough in trying to correct employees not living up to their job obligations. Employees failing to show up for work regularly and/or punctually may be accommodated by giving them status as part-time employees which more accurately reflects their availability for work. Some employees not living up to their job obligations are tolerated until their supervisors can no longer bear it. Then, by taking disciplinary action, the supervisors may have overreacted to one offense with no back-up data to support their action. Supervisors must be able to justify their disciplinary actions which may be more often justified and upheld when they acted after having considered the following:

1. Did the employee know that his or her behavior could result in disciplinary action?
2. Was the rule being enforced fairly, and was it applied consistently?
3. Was there an objective investigation of the offense?
4. Does the severity of the discipline reflect the seriousness of the offense and, when possible, take into consideration the employee's service record?

Most of the employees' rights and obligations, listed in the Personnel Rules and Regulations, are sometimes expanded upon by departmental regulations. However, departmental regulations must not conflict with the Personnel Rules and Regulations. Even though departments may become legally bound by their departmental regulations, in cases of appeal of disciplinary action, the departments may lose their enforcement of that disciplinary action if the disciplining supervisor failed to follow departmental regulations.

Employee rights and obligations will become, if they have not already become, a crucial part of managing better with less in the coming austere budget year. It is perhaps the time to rejuvenate the work ethic, "a fair day's pay for a fair day's work," which includes fair and equitable treatment. Also, it may be time for a reminder that no one has a right to a job, only a right to compete for a job and to retain a job with its rights as a result of fulfilling job obligations. TFL:njc

The supervisor and the personnel department play mutually supporting roles for the disciplinary system to work effectively. The personnel manager must help establish a clear and equitable system; the supervisor must provide adequate supervision of employees and enforce work rules fairly. If discipline is required, it is a good idea for it to be handed out by the personnel department on the basis of information provided by the supervisor. This will provide equitable treatment for employees throughout the organization.

Steps In The Grievance Process

Every day, in thousands of instances, employees—public and private—claim they have been treated unjustly. In a very provocative statement, David Ewing, a well-known authority on employee rights, observed: "It appears that very few [nonunion] companies in this country—possibly as few as thirty to fifty—have had effective grievance procedures in place for several years or more.[24] This will come as a surprise to most public employees and their employers, who have had **grievance procedures** for years as an integral part of merit systems.

Figure 13–2 diagrams a typical disciplinary action and grievance procedure. Note that if the employee is a member of a minority group, the affirmative action officer may be involved in the process.

Management should establish with employees grievance procedures that clearly establish the employee's right to file written complaints concerning alleged unfair management practices, and procedures for hearing these complaints in the agency. The specific items that might arise and be subject to a grievance complaint could be defined in personnel rules and regulations. If a collective bargaining agreement exists, the grievance procedure will be defined in the contract. Usually,

FIGURE 13–1 Disciplinary Action and Other Personnel Activities

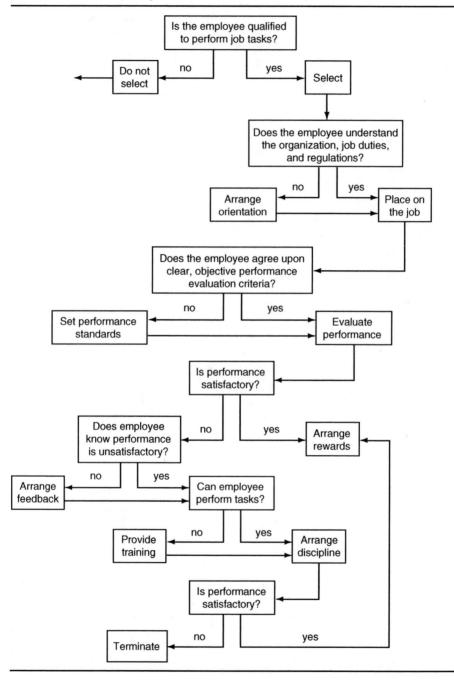

FIGURE 13–2   Disciplinary Action Procedures

Supervisor	Personnel Manager	Affirmative Action Officer
Sets performance criteria	Provides orientation to work rules and regulations	
Monitors employee performance; if performance is unsatisfactory, counsels employee verbally		
If performance remains unsatisfactory, places written notification of performance deficiency in employee's file		Counsels employee as to organizational expectations and sanctions
	Counsels employee as to organizational expectations and sanctions	
Monitors subsequent job performance; if unsatisfactory, recommends disciplinary action	Gets commitment from employee concerning future job performance	Reviews disciplinary or termination action for EEO compliance
	Authorizes disciplinary action or dismissal	

grievances will be limited to topics in the working rules that an employee believes management has violated. Topics such as the following will probably be included as issues contained in a negotiated contract or in personnel rules enforced by a civil service board. Under each possible area of grievance we have given an example drawn from the exit interview files of a state agency in Kansas.

Work assignments	Employees may feel that work assignments are made subjectively.
Promotion	An employee may feel that the promotional criteria established for a position were not valid or not utilized, or that promotional procedures were improper.
Poor supervision	Employees may feel that supervision is inadequate, and that supervisors are biased or incompetent.
Political interference	Conflict arises between elected and appointed officials, or among supervisors.
Sexual discrimination	Gender inequities and sexual harassment often lead to employee perceptions of unfair treatment.

In any of these instances, it is important that the agency have an established informal and formal grievance procedure that would allow employees to bring their charges to the notice of higher ups and get a fair hearing. The following steps might constitute a typical grievance process:

1. *Informal counseling.* The aggrieved employee should meet and discuss the situation with his or her supervisor or the next higher up if the complaint is about the employee's immediate supervisor. The success of this step depends on an organizational environment that encourages employees to speak openly about their concerns.
2. *Formal grievance.* If informal counseling is unsuccessful, the aggrieved employee should have the opportunity to file a formal grievance in writing stating the problem and what the employee thinks ought to be done to correct the situation. If asked by the employee, the personnel department can help the employee prepare the necessary document.
3. *Consultation between supervisor and personnel director.* After the grievance is filed, the personnel department should consult with the employee to verify the situation and then work with the parties to see if an agreement can be reached.
4. *Investigation/adjudication/arbitration.* A number of steps can follow the attempt by the personnel department to work out a solution between the parties. These might include assigning an impartial person—often from the personnel department—to investigate and make a decision; convening a panel to hear the complaint and make a decision; and securing an outside arbitrator to hear the complaint and render a decision.

Employees can seek redress of grievances by following agency procedures. The more due process afforded the employee internally, the less likely it is that an employee will seek an external channel to air a grievance.[25] In fact, some legal proceedings will require that internal grievance procedures be followed before undertaking judicial avenues. In other cases, the external investigating agency or court will incorporate the proceedings of an internal process as part of its own review.

ONGOING ISSUES—SUBSTANTIVE AND PROCEDURAL

As might be expected, several ongoing substantive and procedural issues illustrate how judicial interpretation of the Constitution supports conflicting values (primarily employee rights and organizational efficiency). These include:

- state immunity *from federal statutes*
- employment eligibility under the ADA
- privacy protection of Internet-based communication for public employees
- protection from sexual harassment
- protection for "whistle-blowers"
- employee "comfort" versus workforce diversity programming

State Immunity *from Federal Statutes*

In recent cases, the Supreme Court has demonstrated its conservative philosophy by emphasizing the importance of states' rights as provided in the eleventh amendment. The court held that Congress exceeded its authority when it applied to state employees the Fair Labor Standards Act,[26] the Age Discrimination in Employment

Act,[27] and the Americans with Disabilities Act.[28] The majority ruled that Congress had no evidence that states were discriminating on the basis of age or disability when it passed the law. The rulings do not apply to local governments.

On the one hand, these rulings seem to put other civil rights legislation in jeopardy as applied to state governments. On the other hand, it is not unusual to find that states themselves have statutes that parallel these federal laws. For example, California's statute goes further than the ADA in protecting employees with disabilities.[29]

Employment Eligibility under the Americans With Disabilities Act

The Americans with Disabilities Act of 1990[30] is probably the most significant piece of civil rights legislation since Congress passed the Civil Rights Act of 1964. Its purpose is to eliminate discrimination against individuals with disabilities or against those perceived to have a disability. Individuals recovering from drug or alcohol abuse are considered disabled, and those who are HIV infected are covered as well. The act parallels the Rehabilitation Act of 1973, but the scope is broader, extending coverage to all employers with fifteen or more full-time employees.

The act, which covers both private and public employers, prohibits discrimination in employment against otherwise qualified applicants and employees, and requires that reasonable accommodations in employment conditions and facilities be made for otherwise qualified disabled applicants and employees. Some examples of reasonable accommodation include: (1) making existing facilities used by employees readily accessible to and usable by an individual with a disability; (2) job restructuring; (3) modifying work schedules; (4) reassignment to a vacant position; (5) acquiring or modifying equipment or devices; (6) adjusting or modifying examinations, training materials, or policies; (7) providing qualified readers or interpreters.

The requirement that employers make *reasonable accommodations* for the disabled may be mitigated if the employer can show an *undue hardship*—usually financial—would be incurred. Undue hardship is defined by the ADA as an action that is "excessively costly, extensive, substantial, or disruptive, or that would fundamentally alter the nature or operation of the business." In determining undue hardship, factors to be considered include the nature and cost of the accommodation in relation to the size, the financial resources, the nature and structure of the employer's operation, as well as the impact the accommodation would have on the specific facility itself.

The terms **reasonable accommodation** and **undue hardship** represent Congress's attempt to balance employee and employer expectations and obligations, and the values of individual rights and efficiency. An employee may expect and an employer is obligated to make a reasonable accommodation for an employee who is disabled but otherwise qualified. But efficiency tempers this expectation/obligation; an employer is not obligated to make the accommodation if it forces an undue economic hardship or hardship in service delivery. These terms represent a political compromise over conflicting values and expectations/obligations, and they provide general guidance. The particulars of implementation require administrative interpretation and action, and what is reasonable and undue hardship are being defined administratively and judicially representing a maturation of the law.[31]

Privacy, Technology, and Public Employment

The fourth amendment application to drug testing is just one instance that juxtaposes employer interests in productivity and safety with employee interests in privacy. A 2001 survey of its membership by the American Management Association revealed that 82 percent of the responding organizations used some form of electronic monitoring and/or surveillance.[32] The most prevalent form of monitoring involved Internet connections (63 percent); the least was storage and review of voice mail messages. Forty-six percent of the companies reviewed e-mail. The biggest reasons cited are protection from legal liability (sexual harassment most often) and concerns for the physical security of employees. Ninety-five percent of the companies that monitor employees have a written policy.

Public employees have more privacy rights than their private sector counterparts. The constitution, as well as state statutes and federal law like the Freedom of Information Act[33] and the Electronic Communications Privacy Act,[34] protect these rights. Important here is the rule of thumb that the more compelling the reason an employer has to monitor employee behavior, whether electronically or otherwise, the more likely the court is to defer to the employer. Attempts to prevent behavior like sexual harassment and workplace violence that is injurious to other employees provide a reasonable justification for surveillance.[35] A comprehensive policy that sets out the employer's expectations and is clearly communicated to employees and acknowledged by them provides a crucial base for this aspect of the employer-employee relationship.

Protection against Sexual Harassment

What is **sexual harassment**? The United States Equal Employment Opportunity Commission, responsible for enforcing the Civil Rights Act of 1964, as amended, and various other employment discrimination laws, has issued the following guidelines: Unwelcomed sexual advances, requests for sexual favors, and other verbal or physical conduct of a sexual nature constitute sexual harassment when (1) submission to such conduct is made, either explicitly or implicitly, a term or condition of an individual's employment, (2) submission to or rejection of such conduct by an individual is used as the basis for employment decisions affecting such individual, or (3) such conduct has the purpose or effect of unreasonably interfering with an individual's work performance or creating an intimidating, hostile, or offensive working environment.[36]

In simple terms, sexual harassment is not romance although it certainly can grow out of romantic attachments turned sour. It is the coercive and hostile behavior of one person toward another based on gender. The number of cases of sexual harassment filed with the EEOC has increased from 10,532 in 1992 to 15,836 in 2000.[37] The number of males filing suit has increased from 9.1 percent to 13.6 percent in that same period. But not all cases are pursued beyond a claim and initial inquiry. Of the 15,836, the EEOC found "no reasonable cause" in 44.1 percent of the cases.

It is clear that men and women see sexual behavior differently, sometimes markedly so. Table 13–1 from a U. S. Merit Systems Protection Board report shows some of these differences.[38] Independent analysis of the same survey data led Thacker and Gohmann to conclude that females are more likely than males to

TABLE 13–1   Is it Sexual Harassment

Type of Uninvited Behavior by a Supervisor	Percentage of Women Who Consider it Harassment		
	1980	*1987*	*1994*
Pressure for sexual favors	91	99	99
Deliberate touching, cornering	91	95	98
Suggestive letters, calls, materials	93	90	94
Pressure for dates	77	87	91
Suggestive looks, gestures	72	81	91
Sexual teasing, jokes, remarks	62	72	83
	Percentage of Men Who Consider it Harassment		
	1980	*1987*	*1994*
Pressure for sexual favors	84	95	97
Deliberate touching, cornering	83	89	93
Suggestive letters, calls, materials	87	76	87
Pressure for dates	76	81	86
Suggestive looks, gestures	59	68	76
Sexual teasing, jokes, remarks	53	58	73
Type of Uninvited Behavior by a Co-Worker	Percentage of Women Who Consider it Harassment		
	1980	*1987*	*1994*
Pressure for sexual favors	81	98	98
Deliberate touching, cornering	84	92	96
Suggestive letters, calls, materials	87	84	92
Pressure for dates	65	76	85
Suggestive looks, gestures	64	76	88
Sexual teasing, jokes, remarks	54	64	77
	Percentage of Men Who Consider it Harassment		
	1980	*1987*	*1994*
Pressure for sexual favors	65	90	93
Deliberate touching, cornering	69	82	89
Suggestive letters, calls, materials	76	67	81
Pressure for dates	59	66	76
Suggestive looks, gestures	47	60	70
Sexual teasing, jokes, remarks	42	47	64

*Based on the percentage of respondents who indicated that they "definitely" or "probably" would consider the identified behavior harassment.

define as harassing behaviors that could lead to a hostile work environment, and they are more likely to report the need for emotional or medical counseling as a result of sexual harassment.[39]

While sexual harassment ultimately must be dealt with in the workplace, conflicts involving claims of harassment frequently find their way into the court system as interested parties seek justice through the law.[40] In ***Meritor Savings Bank v. Vinson*** (1986),[41] the Supreme Court established several significant legal guidelines in its interpretation of the Civil Rights Act of 1964, as amended. Mechelle Vinson, who was employed by the bank in 1974, rose through the ranks to assistant branch manager on her merits when in 1978 she was discharged for excessive use of sick leave. Ms. Vinson claimed that during her four years with the bank she had been constantly subjected to sexual harassment. She estimated that over the four-year period she had sexual intercourse with Sidney Taylor, the branch manager, some forty or fifty times. "In addition, [she] testified that Taylor fondled her in front of other employees, followed her into the women's restroom when she went there alone, exposed himself to her, and even forcibly raped her on several occasions" (p. 55). Vinson testified that she was afraid to report the harassment to Taylor's superiors. Taylor denied her charges completely, contending that they resulted from a business dispute.

Even though the conflicting testimony was never resolved, the Supreme Court made several significant legal points in its 9–0 judgment. First, it concluded that an adverse personnel action need not be taken in order to prove that sexual harassment has occurred. It affirmed lower court findings and the EEOC's guidelines that "Title VII affords employees the right to work in an environment free from discriminatory intimidation, ridicule and insult" (p. 59). Further, it affirmed that "a plaintiff may establish a violation of Title VII by proving that discrimination based on sex has created a hostile or abusive work environment" (p. 59). However, it tempered its stance somewhat by saying that in order for a legal violation to occur, the sexual harassment must be "sufficiently severe or pervasive 'to alter the conditions of the [victim's] employment and create an abusive working environment' " (p. 60) [internal cite omitted].

Second, the Court found that when trying to determine the nature of the relationship, "The correct inquiry is whether respondent by her conduct indicated that the alleged sexual advances were *unwelcome*, not whether her actual participation in sexual intercourse was *voluntary*" (p. 60) [emphasis added].

In 1993 the Supreme Court revisited the issue of sexual harassment in ***Harris v. Forklift***.[42] Teresa Harris worked as a manager at Forklift Systems equipment rental company. At issue was whether Harris would have to show that she had suffered psychological injury in order to prevail in her claim that she was working in a sexually abusive and hostile environment. A unanimous Supreme Court found in Harris' favor, indicating that "Title VII comes into play before the harassing conduct leads to a nervous breakdown." A hostile environment exists where a "reasonable person" objectively comes to that conclusion and when a victim subjectively perceives it as such. The Court acknowledged the lack of a cookie-cutter formula for establishing when a hostile environment exists, but it did outline several factors that should be considered: frequency of the conduct, its severity, whether it is physically threatening or humiliating, or a mere offensive utterance, and whether it interferes with an employee's work.

As a footnote, in *Harris* the Court rejected a lower court standard that used the "reasonable woman" to determine whether or not a hostile environment exists. The Court stayed with its frequently relied upon hypothetical "reasonable person." The Merit Systems Protection Board report shows that men and women see these things differently. But the Court is reluctant to acknowledge that justice should be gender specific.

Recent court cases have made clear that employers are always liable for discriminatory acts by supervisors if resulting in a tangible personnel action. If no tangible personnel action is involved, the employer may mount an effective defense if (1) it can show reasonable care in preventing and correcting promptly harassing behavior; and (2) it can show where an employee charging sexual harassment has failed to take advantage of a valid complaint procedure.[43] Finally, in ***Oncale v. Sundowner Offshore Services*** the Supreme Court held that Title VII protects employees from same sex harassment.[44]

Despite *Vinson* and *Harris*, Dresang and Stuiber observe that sexual harassment is not easy to eliminate or even to minimize: "In part, the difficulties of taking corrective action relate to organizational power and societal sex-role stereotypes, forces beyond the easy reach of reformers."[45]

But the problem of sexual harassment involves more than issues of power, stereotypes, and litigation. It would be naive to claim that productivity in organizations is disconnected from personal attraction and cooperation. Productivity is often enhanced by close, affectionate working relationships that develop with an organizational culture that encourages respect, dignity, and tolerance. But the proper relationship between sexuality, productivity, and fair treatment is difficult to realize in any organizational context because of divergent and unspoken expectations and perceptions. The relationship between sexuality, productivity, and equity promises to become more complicated in the 1990s with increasing ethnic diversity and accompanying expectations in the workplace.

Protection for "Whistle-blowers"

The tendency of public organizations and administrators to withhold self-incriminating information from the public is counterbalanced theoretically by **whistle-blowing**. This form of dissent focuses public attention on behavior the whistle-blower considers illegal or unethical. It is this moral imperative, accompanied by the whistle-blower's knowledge that his or her charges will be scrutinized and possibly met with reprisal, that distinguishes the whistle-blower's actions from a simple act of insubordination for private purposes.

Whistle-blowing is a well-publicized phenomenon because it plays upon the public's desire to expose corruption and increase responsiveness or efficiency in government agencies. The Civil Service Reform Act of 1978, which applies to federal employees, includes as a merit principle: "Employees should be protected against reprisal for the lawful disclosure of information which the employees reasonably believe evidences: (a) a violation of any law, rule, or regulation, or (b) mismanagement, a gross waste of funds, an abuse of authority, or a substantial and specific danger to public health or safety." Several additional federal laws passed since 1978 contain protections for whistle-blowers who disclose specific types of information.

Despite these protections and similar ones in several state and local governments, employees usually blow the whistle on their employer only as a last resort, when the conflict between their ethical standards and their perception of their agency's behavior is so great as to leave them no choice. In other terms, whistleblowing results from a perceived gross breach in the employment contract—in this case, the expectations an employee has of his or her employer or co-workers. Often times, this expectation runs counter to the employer's expectation and desire for employee loyalty. Whistle-blowers often exhaust organizational channels for dissent before they "go public" with charges and information.

The U.S. Merit Systems Protection Board surveyed federal personnel specialists in 1980 and again in 1988 regarding the occurrence of prohibited personnel practices. In the 1988 survey, 19 percent of the respondents said they had observed at least one instance of retaliation for whistle-blowing during the previous twelve months. Only half of those surveyed in 1988 believed that protections for persons attempting to expose prohibited personnel practices were adequate—down slightly from 1980.[46]

Comparing the results of a 1992 survey of federal employees with one conducted in 1983, the Merit Systems Protection Board found a similar 20 percent of those surveyed reported having direct knowledge of a wasteful or illegal activity. In 1992, one-third of the employees who reported a wasteful or illegal activity said they had experienced or been threatened with reprisal, up from some 25 percent in 1983.[47] In 1996 that number was 22 percent.[48]

How should whistle-blowing be evaluated?[49] On the one hand, it divides the agency and undercuts its management, and causes serious organizational harm—sometimes for the self-serving purposes of a disgruntled employee. On the other hand, it may prevent managers from hiding information harmful to the agency or its managers, using specious reasons such as security and efficiency. Whistle-blowing represents a classic conflict between individual rights, possibly under the rubric of the First Amendment, and the desire of managers to control the flow of information out of the agency in order to preserve individual careers, administrative efficiency, or political support.

Organizational Justice, Productivity, and Workforce Diversity

It seems clear that over the years the expectations employees have of their employers have risen. Employees expect job security, a decent wage, health benefits, a sound retirement system, safe working conditions, an environment free of unfair discrimination, participation in decisions that affect them, and in some cases, child care and parental leave. At the same time, demands on public employers for productivity have resulted in more work with less staff, declining health benefits, and threats of privatization. These contrasting forces place considerable strain on the sanction function and complicate perceptions of organizational justice and organizational citizenship.

Furthermore, there is substantial sentiment among public managers as well as the public at large that the relationship between the rights of public employees and managerial flexibility has tilted towards the side of employees at the expense of government efficiency and responsiveness.

Recent statements by the U.S. Merit Systems Protection Board, created by the Civil Service Reform Act of 1978 to hear federal employee appeals, are significant in this regard.[50] In 1994, the Merit Systems Protection Board conducted a survey of federal managers asking them about their actions in dealing with poorly performing employees. According to the report, "Our findings demonstrate the need to correct the imbalance between forces discouraging supervisors from firing poor performers and the near total absence of forces encouraging them to act."[51]

The report indicates that the "problems in dealing with poor performers are so pronounced" that several steps should be contemplated including consolidating the paths available to discipline employees; consolidating the opportunities for employees to appeal disciplinary actions; and, finally, permitting poor performance to be considered in reduction-in-force procedures. A similar report published in 1999 reinforces these findings and recommendations and adds: "Agencies need to do a better job of hiring people for supervisory jobs who have an aptitude for the human relations aspects of supervisory work."[52]

But the sanction function is driven by more than demands for individual rights versus productivity or administrative efficiency. Added to this contentious set of factors is the demographic trend toward increasing ethnic diversity in the workforce. Ethnic diversity will complicate employee expectations and what employers can expect from employees. This heterogeneity in expectations and obligations can be expected to place additional strain on the organizational processes aimed at matching them.

It appears that one of the issues that will dominate human resource management is how organizations can effectively manage the relationship between workforce diversity, organizational justice, and productivity. The relationship between any two of these factors might be predictable, but inserting the third adds a dimension of significant uncertainty.

PUBLIC EMPLOYEE LIABILITY

In the 1970s the Court enlarged the scope of its constitutional inquiry, granting more rights to public employees, clients, or beneficiaries of the government, prisoners, and citizens who otherwise might come in contact with government officials. It is one thing for the courts to grant new rights; it is another to enforce recognition of and respect for them. One mechanism to advance these ends is the threat that a public official might be held personally liable for violating a citizen's constitutional rights. Traditionally, administrators came to share the same immunity from civil suits arising out of actions connected with their official functions as had formerly belonged only to legislators and judges and other special classes of public employees. But in order to balance the need to protect the rights of citizens with the need to protect public officials who are required to exercise discretion that affects citizens, the doctrine of **sovereign immunity** gave way to a more limited form of immunity for administrative officials. The revised doctrine, captured clearly now in ***Harlow v. Fitzgerald*** (1982), states that "government officials performing discretionary functions generally are shielded from liability for civil damages insofar as their conduct does not violate clearly established statutory or Constitutional rights of which a reasonable person would have known.[53]

The concept of **qualified immunity** outlined in *Harlow* suggests that in order to perform their job effectively and with only minor fear of being sued, public officials must become aware of the constitutional law that impinges upon their work and the work of their agency. Moreover, the threat of liability for a public official is directly related to the scope of constitutional rights the Court is willing to grant public employees and citizens. The broader the rights, the greater the threat of liability; the narrower the interpretation of rights, the less the threat, because it takes a strong case for a plaintiff to substantiate a claim that a right has been violated.

In the opening to the chapter we saw that the increased use of private contractors to provide public services raises a new set of justice questions. In *Wabaunsee County v. Umbehr* the court ruled that a private contractor does not relinquish free speech rights when it wins a government contract. We have introduced in this section the concept of *qualified immunity* that protects public employees as they carry out their public duties. Does this practice extend to private business holding government contracts?

In 1997 the Supreme Court answered "no" by a 5–4 vote.[54] An inmate claimed that prison guards had used extreme force in violation of his constitutional rights. The guards claimed qualified immunity in a defense that would mimic that of a public prison guard, arguing that without this protection every disciplinary action they took would be subject to a lawsuit and the prison's work would suffer.

The court distinguished between public prison guards and those employed by a private contractor arguing that a competitive market place would encourage appropriate actions with regard to prisoners. Too little discipline, cautioned by the fear of lawsuits, would place the private prison management company in a competitive disadvantage with comparable firms. A vigorous dissent argued that the prison function performed was the same whether public or private, and if prison guards employed by the state enjoyed limited immunity so too should their private management counterparts.

A recent unrelated development is the potential liability that public employers have for criminal acts of their employees. "Typically, these lawsuits claim a failure by the employer to exercise proper care in the hiring, supervision and/or training of an employee" (p. 491).[55] Thus, in contrast to common practice, the public employer may be responsible for the private actions of an employee. For example, a housing authority unwittingly hires as a housing inspector an individual with a history of theft. The inspector is subsequently found guilty of theft and assault of one of the tenants. The tenant sues the housing authority claiming negligence in hiring. The authority put the tenants at risk, and it should have known about the inspector's criminal history. Some state statutes limit the liability of public employers in this regard.[56] But in cases of gross negligence and where constitutional rights have been violated, a victim may sue under Title 42 U.S. Code 1983, which imposes liability on public employees for "deprivation of any rights, privileges, or immunities secured by the Constitution."

The legal issue in these cases relates to the determination of fault and causation and whether a public employer is guilty of "deliberate indifference." Drawing this conclusion from a single bad decision is very difficult to do.[57]

Interestingly, this negligent employee process liability can cause confusion for the human resource manager who also is under notice not to reveal information about discharged employees that might harm their ability to secure another job. Employees have liberty interests guaranteed by the Constitution's Fifth Amendment. The government cannot abridge a person's liberty without due process. The freedom to work is considered a liberty, and if a public employer stigmatizes an employee in the context of discharging or failing to rehire, it may have violated the employee's Fifth Amendment right if due process has not been observed.[58] Sometimes, due process is a simple matter of giving the employee an opportunity to respond in writing to adverse information that may be filed in an employee's personnel records. In other cases, it may require a pre- or post-termination hearing that would allow the employee to respond to any adverse information connected with the discharge.

SUMMARY

In some ways, the sanction function is the most important of the four core functions. Activities designed to fulfill this function aim to establish and maintain the terms of the relationship between employee and employer. These terms consist of expectations and obligations employee and employer have of each other, and they constitute the rules of the game. Expectations and obligations arise from a number of sources. Of these, only public employees enjoy rights stemming from the Constitution. However, practically, these rights are balanced against the duty a public employer has to operate efficiently. In this balance we can see the inevitable conflict between administrative efficiency and individual rights and resultant perceptions about organizational justice.

Recent rulings suggest that the contemporary Supreme Court has tipped the balance in favor of administrative efficiency over individual rights. With the judicial avenue narrowing, the rights of employees are likely to result from new legislation and administrative policy, rules and regulations rather than appeals to constitutional protections.

Internal disciplinary and grievance procedures are mechanisms to enforce the terms of the employment relationship. Increasing diversity of the workforce will bring a broader array of employee expectations and obligations to the workplace. Relatively objective disciplinary guidelines and impartial grievance procedures might be expected to ameliorate the negative impact of these differences and provide a foundation of respect necessary to channel the differences into creativity and productivity. The challenge is to accomplish this in a political environment where public employees are seen as entrenched and as obstacles to government efficiency and responsiveness.

KEY TERMS

discipline
due process
grievance procedure
organizational citizenship
procedural justice
property rights
psychological contract
reasonable accommodation
sanction function
sexual harassment
sovereign versus qualified immunity

terms of the employment relationship
undue hardship
whistle-blowing
Branti v. Finkel (1980)
Connick v. Myers (1983)
Harlow v. Fitzgerald (1982)
Harris v. Forklift (1993)
Meritor Savings Bank v. Vinson (1986)
National Treasury Employees Union v. Von Raab (1989)
New York Times v. Sullivan (1964)

O'Hare v. Northlake (1996)
Oncale v. Sundowner Offshore Services
(1998)
Richardson v. McKnight (1997)

Rutan v. Republican Party of Illinois (1990)
Skinner v. Railway Labor Executives'
Association (1989)
Wabaunsee County v. Umbehr (1996)

DISCUSSION QUESTIONS

1. Define the sanction function, and identify the ways an organization establishes and maintains the terms of the employment relationship between employee and employer.

2. Public employees are granted more rights generally than private-sector employees. Why is this so? Do you think public employees should give up their rights as citizens in their capacity as employees? Do you think public-sector employees should have fewer rights? Do you think that private-sector employees should have more rights?

3. How does the sanction function differ in alternate personnel systems?

4. Discuss the balance the Supreme Court examines when deciding whether a public employer has violated an employee's First Amendment right to free speech.

5. Do you agree with the provisions of the Fourth Amendment? Do you agree that public employers ought to be able to conduct drug screens of their employees? If you answer "yes" to both questions, how do you reconcile the tension between your positions? How does the Court reconcile the tension?

6. Why do you think the Supreme Court considers a person's job as property? Describe the role of property rights and due process in establishing and maintaining the terms of the employment relationship.

7. Is it useful to consider employees as organizational citizens? If so, what expectations might they hold of their employer? And what expectations might the employer have of them in return? Today, it is frequently asserted that in society at large people seem more concerned with their rights than their community or citizenship obligations. Do you think this is true of organizational citizens as well? How do you think the contemporary employment environment affects organizational citizenship?

8. Some have argued that democratic values must be practiced in order to be learned. If democratic values were practiced in organizations, how would the relationship between employee and employer change? What would be the benefits and the costs?

9. Discuss how discipline and grievance procedures are connected to the sanction function.

10. Diagram a typical disciplinary procedure.

11. Are the interests of employee and employer the same in establishing a grievance procedure? Construct a model grievance procedure from the employee's standpoint. Construct it now from the employer's standpoint. Do you have any differences? As an employer, which process would you use to construct a grievance procedure?

12. What rights does the ADA give to employees and how does it balance those rights with the employer's interests?

13. How has modern technology in the workplace raised new privacy concerns? What do you think is a reasonable approach to an employer having access to an employee's e-mail? What do you see as the similarities and difference between an employer having access to employee e-mail and Internet use and the monitoring of phone calls?

14. Describe the rights of employees who have been sexually harassed or who are considered whistle-blowers.

15. What relationship do you see between organizational justice, productivity, and workforce diversity?

16. Use the various court cases described in the chapter to show how the courts reach a balance among the four values.

17. When discussing politics, sometimes we refer to "inalienable rights." What does this mean? Do you think that public employees should have any inalienable rights?

CASE STUDY: JUAN HERNANDEZ VS. THE COUNTY

INTRODUCTION

Metropolitan County is the largest local government in the state. County government is divided into about fifty operating departments and employs about 20,000 people. Among the departments is the Office of Data Processing Center (DPC).

Juan Hernandez, a Hispanic male, was employed by the DPC on July 15, 1982, as a data processing trainee. On May 10, 1983, he was promoted to the position of Computer Operator I and attained permanent status in that position six months later. He remained in that position until his termination on March 9, 1992.

This case study will examine the circumstances leading to his dismissal, his role as a union steward for Local 121 of the American Federation of State, County and Municipal Employees (AFSCME), and the various steps involved in his termination. It will reach conclusions relating to the disciplinary action and grievance process in public agencies in general.

EMPLOYMENT HISTORY

From his initial employment until April 1987, Juan Hernandez's record reflected satisfactory and dependable service. On April 25, 1987, however, he received a written reprimand for failing to satisfactorily back up numerous documents that were lost in a power outage.

Mr. Hernandez reacted to the reprimand by a letter of rebuttal which indicated that he disagreed sharply with management's allegations of his lack of general competence.

In October 1987, he received an evaluation summarizing his performance as "in need of attention." His scheduled merit increase was deferred for three months. Although the overall tone of the evaluation was encouraging, it implied an incompetence in his ability to grasp the concepts of a larger computer system. Mr. Hernandez appealed the evaluation, but withdrew the appeal when he received a satisfactory evaluation along with his merit increase three months later.

In January 1988 the director of operations for the DPC brought about a reorganization that resulted in Mr. Hernandez being switched from the day to night shift. Despite his objections to this change, Mr. Hernandez's employment continued satisfactorily for the next 18 months, until he suffered a severe on-the-job injury on July 26, 1989. A portion of the raised computer floor collapsed while he was on it carrying a box of computer paper. His resultant knee and leg injuries caused Mr. Hernandez to be absent from work for 425 hours.

Upon his return to work on October 27, 1990, he was presented with a formal record of counseling dated July 29, 1989, just three days after his injury had occurred. This record, which was prepared by his supervisor as a summary of the informal counseling that had occurred with him, cited a number of infractions, having to do with failure to make up time for a long lunch; failure to produce a leave slip for his absence; and for improperly printing various forms needed by other departments.

On June 29, 1991, Mr. Hernandez was given a formal record of counseling citing his involvement in a technical failure that occurred in the computer room at the main console. The essence of the incident concerned Mr. Hernandez's evident unfamiliarity with the software that both he and the operators under his supervision were utilizing.

SHOP STEWARD

On July 27, 1991, Mr. Hernandez was elected to the position of shop steward representing the DPC employees with AFSCME Local 121. During his term as shop steward, he aided several employees who were contemplating filing grievances against the DPC on the grounds that the agency was illegally testing computer operators prior to giving them permanent appointments.

TERMINATION

On January 9, 1992, Juan Hernandez was himself given an "unsatisfactory" performance evaluation based on his failure to complete certain training courses, designed to insure his knowledge of the hardware and software both he and his subordinates were utilizing. He refused to sign this evaluation.

On January 23, 1992, he was charged one day without pay for calling in sick the day before the start of his scheduled one-week vacation. Upon returning to work, he submitted a doctor's statement excusing him for the absence. This doctor's statement, coupled with other evidence, would later prove the grounds for his termination.

Mr. Robert Hess, an administrative officer for the DPC, began to compile evidence that Mr. Hernandez had falsified doctors' statements that excused several of his absences. He had observed that the handwriting of doctors' excuses dated June 15, 1991, and January 23, 1992, did not match the handwriting of other excuses obtained from the same doctor for the injuries suffered in his 1989 accident. In addition, the excuses in question were written on Pacific Hospital forms, while the others were not.

Interviews were conducted with the physician, Dr. Herman Wilbanks, and with Mr. Vincent Pico, administrative resident at Pacific Hospital. Dr. Wilbanks denied writing the excuses; and Mr. Pico confirmed that Mr. Hernandez had not been a patient at the hospital on the dates in question.

Mr. Hernandez then altered his story by stating that the excuse that he had submitted for the January 23 absence was a copy of the original. He claimed that his daughter, a pre-med student at Long Beach State University, had copied the original one "as practice for her classes," and he had mistakenly submitted the copy. However, the Los Angeles County Crime Laboratory Bureau confirmed that the handwriting was the same on both forms.

On March 10, 1992, Mr. Hernandez attended a scheduled disciplinary action meeting in the office of the deputy director of the DPC. He was represented by the union. At this meeting, he was given a termination letter and a disciplinary action report effecting his dismissal. He signed the form at the union representative's advice.

APPEAL HEARING

An appeal hearing was held on May 10, 1992. Mr. Hernandez was represented by AFSCME Local 121; the County was represented by the County Attorney's Office.

The impartial hearing examiner concluded that violations 1 through 4 were not substantiated, but that the charge of a false claim of leave was substantiated. Mr. Hernandez's termination was sustained (Exhibit A).

CONCLUSION

Both collective bargaining agreements and disciplinary action procedures provide for progressive discipline of employees for poor performance, and they protect employees against unfair harassment or unsubstantiated allegations.

In the case of Juan Hernandez, the pattern and timing of management's disciplinary action against him are both suspect. A casual review of his record of disciplinary action indicates that it followed on-the-job injuries and his election as shop steward.

On the other hand, it is also clear that Mr. Hernandez's work performance was frequently careless or incompetent. Moreover, his falsification of medical excuses was flagrantly dishonest. Management's efforts to substantiate this required the spending of much time, money, and effort. It was also aided by the fact that the DPC, as a computer-oriented agency, was able to establish objective performance standards (in terms of quantity, quality, and timeliness of production). By monitoring these incidents, it was able to document irregular performance incidents.

Yet despite management's advantages, the only incident of willful misconduct that was upheld was the falsification of medical statements, an infraction relating to personnel rules rather than productivity. The lesson to be learned from this is that management, in the final analysis, when attempting to terminate an employee who is backed by union and legal representation in front of an impartial examiner, must have documentation that unquestionably proves guilt on the part of the employee charged with the violation of a concise, tangible regulation.

Questions

After finishing the case study and studying the exhibit carefully, be prepared to discuss the following questions in a small group and to defend your answers in subsequent class discussion.

1. Did the employer (the Data Processing Center) provide Mr. Hernandez with clear performance standards from the time of his employment to the time of his termination?
2. Did the DPC provide Mr. Hernandez with adequate informal counseling concerning his performance discrepancies prior to initiating formal counseling and disciplinary action?
3. Did the employer adequately document Mr. Hernandez's alleged violation of clear performance standards?
4. Who, if anyone, benefited from the outcome of this case study?
5. What functions and values are present in this case?

6. How important is an impartial hearing examiner in developing a sense of organization justice?

EXHIBIT A: HEARING EXAMINER'S REPORT

MONK, MURPHY, TANNENBAUM AND ENDICOTT
ATTORNEYS AT LAW
HEARING EXAMINER'S REPORT

Date: June 20, 1992

To: The Honorable Samuel Shapiro
County Attorney
County

The Honorable Jeremy Irving
Attorney at Law
AFSCME Local 121

On May 10, 1992, the Hearing Examiner heard testimony and considered evidence relative to the termination of Mr. Juan Hernandez from the County, Data Processing Center.

The following charges were advanced to support termination:

1. Alleged violation of time and leave regulations, as described in the formal record of counseling that Mr. Hernandez received on July 29, 1989.
2. Alleged willful negligence in the performance of Mr. Hernandez's job duties in the improper printing of forms, as described in the formal record of counseling which he received on July 29, 1989.
3. Alleged willful negligence in the performance of Mr. Hernandez's job duties in the failure to properly load programs CICS (S337) so as to prevent damage to the System 3000 Data Base on June 9, 1991, as described in the formal record of counseling which he received on June 29, 1991.
4. Alleged failure to complete required training courses (MVS, Payroll system, OMICROM OMEGAMON, and OPS-JES2) by January 23, 1992, as required by his performance evaluation of January 9, 1992.
5. Alleged falsification of physician's excuses for sick leave for June 15, 1991, and January 23, 1992, as described in the Laboratory Analysis Report dated March 5, 1992, LACPSD Case #101374).

Having evaluated all evidence and testimony presented relative to these charges, the Hearing Examiner finds that insufficient evidence exists to document discharge on grounds 1, 2, 3, or 4. However, under the terms of the collective bargaining agreement between AFSCME Local 121 and the Board of Supervisors of the County, dated October 27, 1991, sufficient evidence has been presented to document discharge on ground 5.

Discharge is hereby affirmed.

NOTES

[1] *Richardson v. McKnight*, 521 U.S. 399 (1997).

[2] U.S. Merit Systems Protection Board (1998). The changing federal workplace: employee perspectives. Washington, DC: U.S. Merit Systems Protection Board.

[3] EEOC charges remain steady (March 2000). *International Personnel Management Association News*, p. 5.

[4] *Harlow v. Fitzgerald*, 73 L Ed 2d 396 (1982) at p. 410.

[5] *New York Times v. Sullivan*, 11 L Ed 2d 686 (1964) at p. 700.

[6] Cooper, Phillip J. (November-December 1986). The Supreme Court, the first amendment, and freedom of information. *Public Administration Review*, 46, 622–628.

[7] *Connick v. Myers*, 75 L Ed 2d 708 (1983).

[8] *Wabaunsee County v. Umbehr*, 116 S.Ct. 2342 (1996).

[9] *Rutan v. Republican Party of Illinois*, 111 L Ed 2d 52 (1990).

[10] Roback, T.H., and J.C. Vinzant (1994). The constitution and the patronage-merit debate: Implications for personnel managers. *Public Personnel Management*, 23, 501–512.

[11] *Branti v. Finkel*, 445 U.S. 507 (1980) at p. 518.

[12] *O'Hare Truck Service v. City of Northlake*, 135 L. Ed. 2d 874 (1996).

[13] Eisenhart, K.E. (1998). The first amendment and the public sector employee: The effect of recent patronage cases on public sector personnel decisions. *Review of Public Personnel Administration*, 18, 58–69.

[14] *Skinner v. Railway Labor Executives' Association*, 103 L Ed 2d 639 (1989).

[15] *National Treasury Employees' Union v. Von Raab*, 103 L Ed 2d 685 (1989) at fn 2.

[16] Golstein, Charles H. (July 2000). Employee drug-testing in the public sector. *International Personnel Management Association News*, pp. 13–16.

[17] Daly, J. (1993). Substance abuse policy adaptation in Florida municipal government. *Public Personnel Management*, 22, 201–214.

[18] Markowitz, D.L. (Spring 1995). The demise of at-will employment and the public employee conundrum. *The Urban Lawyer*, 27, 321.

[19] *Cleveland v. Loudermill*, 470 U.S. 532 (1985).

[20] Moorman, R.H. (1991). Relationship between organizational justice and organizational citizenship behaviors: Do fairness perceptions influence employee citizenship? *Journal of Applied Psychology*, 76, 845–855; Organ, D. W. (1990). The motivational basis of organizational citizenship behavior. *Research in Organizational Behavior*, 12, 43–72.

[21] Niehoff, B.P., and R.H. Moorman (1993). Justice as a mediator of the relationship between methods of monitoring and organizational citizenship behavior. *Academy of Management Journal*, 36, p. 535.

[22] Moorman, R.H., G.L. Blakely and B.P. Niehoff (1998). Does perceived organizational support mediate the relationship between procedural justice and organizational citizenship behavior? *Academy of Management Journal*, 41, pp. 351–358.

[23] Moorman. Relationship between organizational justice and organizational citizenship behaviors.

[24] Ewing, D. E. (1989). *Justice on the job: Resolving grievances in the nonunion workplace*. Boston: Harvard Business School, p. vii.

[25] Ibid.

[26] *Aldine v. Maine*, 527 U.S. 706 (1999).

[27] *Kimmel v. Florida Board of Regents*, 528 U.S. 62 (2000).

[28] *University of Alabama v. Patricia Garrett*, Docket Number 99–1240, Decided February 21, 2001.

[29] Giron, L. (December 31, 2000). State law redefines who has disability. *Los Angeles Times*, p. W1.

[30] Americans with Disabilities Act of 1990, Public Law 101–336, July 26, 1990; Kohl, J.P., and P.S. Greenlaw (1996). Title I of the Americans with Disabilities Act: The anatomy of a law. *Public Personnel Management*, 25, 323–332; Greenlaw, P.S., and J.P. Kohl (1993). AIDS: Administrative decisions and constitutional rights. *Public Personnel Management*, 22, 445–460; http://janweb.icdi.wvu.edu/kinder.

[31] Greenlaw, P.S., and J.P. Kohl (1992). The ADA: public personnel management, reasonable accommodation and undue hardship. *Public Personnel Management*, 21, 411–427; Smith, M. The ADA in the workplace: how has it impacted your organization? *International Personnel Management*

Association News, pp. 6–7; *Sutton v. United Airlines, Inc.* 119 S.Ct. 2139 (1999), and *Murphy v. United Parcel Service, Inc.*, 119 S.Ct. 2133 (1999); see also http://www.eeoc.gov/regs/index.html.

[32]American Management Association (2001). Workplace monitoring and surveillance: policies and practices. New York: American Management Association.

[33]5 U.S.C. 552.

[34]18 U.S.C. 2701.

[35]Cozzetto, D.A., and T.B. Pedeliski (1997). Privacy and the workplace: technology and public employment. *Public Personnel Management, 26*, 515–527.

[36]United States Equal Employment Opportunity Commission. (November 10, 1980). Final amendments to guidelines on discrimination because of sex. *Federal Register, 45*, 219.

[37]Equal Employment Opportunity Commission (2001). www.eeoc.gov/stats/harass.html.

[38]United States Merit Systems Protection Board (1995). *Sexual harassment in the federal workplace: Trends, progress, continuing challenges.* Washington, DC: U.S. Merit Systems Protection Board.

[39]Thacker, Rebecca A., and S.F. Gohmann (Fall 1993). Male/female differences in perceptions and effects of hostile environment sexual harassment: "Reasonable" assumptions? *Public Personnel Management, 22*, 461–472.

[40]Robinson, R.K., B.M. Allen, G.M. Franklin, and D.L. Duhon (1992). Sexual harassment in the workplace: A review of the legal rights and responsibilities of all parties. *Public Personnel Management, 22*, 123–136; Strickland, R. A. (1995). Sexual harassment: A legal perspective for public administrators. *Public Personnel Management, 24*, 493–513.

[41]*Meritor Savings Bank v. Vinson*, 91 L Ed 2d 49 (1986).

[42]*Harris v. Forklift*, 126 L Ed 2d 300 (1993).

[43]*Burlington Industries, Inc. v. Ellerth*, 118 S. Ct. 2257 (1998) and *Faragher v. City of Boca Raton*, 118 S. Ct. 2275 (1998).

[44]*Oncale v. Sundowner Offshore Services, Inc.* 523 U.S. 75 (1998).

[45]Dresang and Stuiber. Sexual harassment, p. 123.

[46]United States Merit Systems Protection Board (1989). *Federal personnel management since civil service reform.* Washington, DC: U.S. Merit Systems Protection Board, pp. 3–8.

[47]United States Merit Systems Protection Board (1993). *Whistle-blowing in the federal government: An update.* Washington, DC: U.S. Merit Systems Protection Board.

[48]U.S. Merit Systems Protection Board (1998). The changing federal workplace: employee perspectives. Washington, DC: U.S. Merit Systems Protection Board.

[49]Brewer, G.A., and S.C. Selden (1998). Whistle blowers in the federal service: new evidence of the public service ethic. *Journal of Public Administration Research and Theory, 8*, 3, 413–439; Near, Janet P., and M.P. Miceli (1995). Effective whistle-blowing. *Academy of Management Review, 20*, 679–708.

[50]United States Merit Systems Protection Board (September 1995). *Removing poor performers in the federal service.* Washington, DC: U.S. Merit Systems Protection Board.

[51]Ibid., p. 10.

[52]United States Merit Systems Protection Board (July 1999). *Federal Supervisors and Poor Performers.* Washington, DC: U.S. Merit Systems Protection Board.

[53]*Harlow v. Fitzgerald*, 73 L Ed 2d 396 (1982) at p. 410.

[54]*Richardson v. McKnight*, 117 S.CT. 2100 (1997).

[55]Walter, R.J. (September-October 1992). Public employers' potential liability from negligence in employment decisions. *Public Administration Review, 52*, 491–496.

[56]Martucci, W.C., and D.B. Boatright (Summer 1995). Immunity for employment references. *Employment Relations Today, 22*, pp. 119–124.

[57]*Board of the County Commissioners of Bryan County, Oklahoma v. Brown*, 520 U.S. 397 (1997).

[58]Shearer, R.A. (Winter 1992). Due process liability in personnel records management: Preserving employee liberty interests. *Public Personnel Management, 21*, 523–532.

14
Collective Bargaining

Collective bargaining is the process by which agency managers negotiate terms and conditions of employment with the recognized representative of public employees. It is a personnel system based on the value of individual employee rights achieved through the collective voice and power of employees. Collective bargaining is primarily focused on the sanction function, in that through collective bargaining the conditions and terms of the employment relationship between employee and employer are determined and maintained. Law and state and federal compliance agencies determine the context for bargaining and resolution of disputes. **Collective bargaining** is a set of techniques under which employees are represented in the negotiation and administration of the terms and conditions of their employment. Because collective bargaining can conflict with other personnel systems, it also focuses conflict over a number of issues: job security with no privatization, employment quotas versus seniority, drug testing versus employee rights, adversarial dispute resolution versus alternative dispute resolution techniques, and win-lose bargaining versus win-win bargaining.

The past fifteen years offer contradictory answers to questions about the future of public-sector bargaining. While the number of public employees covered by collective bargaining agreements has continued to increase, actual union influence over public HRM policy and practice has declined compared to competing values like efficiency, flexibility, and affirmative action. Therefore, it is helpful to examine underlying pressures that shape public collective bargaining today. There are three general groups: *economic* pressure on collective bargaining *outcomes,* *organizational* pressure on collective bargaining *processes,* and *political* pressure on collective bargaining *systems.*

In the final analysis, the strength of collective bargaining will be affected by unions' ability to persuade the public and legislators that strong unions are tied to vital public policy concerns that go beyond the more narrow economic concerns of their current members. Some such concerns that may prove persuasive are: (1) employment access by minorities, women, and persons with disabilities; (2) organizational justice in the allocation of employee benefits, training, and involvement; (3) organizational productivity; and (4) employer-financed retirement and health-care systems. And there are signs of union renaissance in such trends as alternative dispute resolution, gainsharing and labor-management cooperation.

By the end of this chapter, you will be able to:

1. Discuss the history and legal basis of collective bargaining, focusing on differences between the public and private sectors, and between the United States and other countries.
2. Explain the connection between public agencies' legal obligation to protect employees' constitutional rights in the United States, and unions' in their members' individual rights as employees.
3. Describe collective bargaining practices: unit determination, recognition and certification, preparation for negotiation, contract negotiation, contract ratification, contract administration, and unfair labor practices.
4. Discuss the changing context of public-sector collective bargaining in terms of continued economic pressure on collective bargaining outcomes, organizational pressure on collective bargaining processes, and political pressure on collective bargaining systems.
5. Identify some key "crossover issues" that unions might champion to increase their public support: employment access, organizational justice, productivity improvement, and pensions and health insurance.
6. Evaluate specialized collective bargaining issues related to police officers and firefighters.
7. Discuss emergent issues in public-sector bargaining: labor-management cooperation, alternative dispute resolution, and gainsharing.

COLLECTIVE BARGAINING: HISTORY AND LEGAL BASIS

Collective bargaining evolved differently in the United States from Europe, Latin America, and the Caribbean. All private-sector bargaining in the United States is based on a single nationwide body of law and one compliance agency. But in the public sector, bargaining is more complex because there is one law and compliance agency for all national government employees, and separate laws and agencies for state and local government employees in each state—forty-three in all—where collective bargaining is permitted. This section clarifies these complexities.

Private Sector Unions in the United States

In the private sector, collective bargaining began in the late 1800s with the rise of industrial unions (The Industrial Workers of the World and the Congress of Industrial Organization) and craft unions (The American Federation of Labor). In the face of bitter opposition by management, aided in many cases by the federal court system, these unions gained political power and legal protection. The New Deal brought about the passage in 1935 of the **Wagner Act** (or the **National Labor Relations Act**), which recognized the right of all private employees to join unions and required management to recognize and bargain collectively with these unions. It prohibited many previously common practices: blacklisting union members, signing "sweetheart contracts" with company unions, and so on. It established a federal agency—the **National Labor Relations Board (NLRB)**—with the responsibility of certifying unions as appropriate bargaining representatives, supervising negotiations to ensure "good faith" bargaining and adjudicating deadlocks (impasses) that might arise during contract negotiations. This law was counterbalanced (at least from management's point of view), by the **Taft-Hartley Act (1947)**, which prohibited labor unions from engaging in **unfair labor practices** and allowed states to pass **right to work laws** (statutes forbidding unions from requiring applicants to be union members in order to qualify for jobs).

With the change from manufacturing to service that began during the 1960s, the percentage of employees operating under collective bargaining agreements has declined steadily from a high point of about 35 percent in 1957, to a low of about 12 percent today. And with current economic trends (including **outsourcing**, job export, automation, **two-tiered wage and benefit systems**, and continued growth of service jobs in the secondary labor market), it can be expected that labor unions will decline still further.[1]

The Public Sector—Federal

With the exception of a minor provision of the Taft-Hartley Act prohibiting strikes by public employees, and the **Postal Service Reorganization Act (1970)**, which provides for supervision of the U.S. Postal Service collective bargaining by the NLRB, neither the Wagner Act, the Taft-Hartley Act, nor the NLRB is involved at all in public-sector collective bargaining. Rather, a complex of laws that apply differentially to federal, state, and local governments regulate collective bargaining in the public sector.

Collective bargaining developed differently in the public sector for two fundamental philosophical reasons. First, in the private sector, the unitary nature of company management makes it possible for a single union to negotiate bilaterally with a single employer. In the public sector, agency managers are accountable to the chief executive, to the legislature, and ultimately to the taxpayers. Thus, it is impossible to negotiate binding contracts at the negotiating table (especially on economic issues) without their being subject to further negotiation and ultimate ratification elsewhere within the political arena. Second, the strike, as an ultimate weapon for exercising collective employee power by withholding services, is more difficult to justify and apply in the public sector because its direct impact is on the public (possibly involving essential services like police, fire, and sanitation) rather than simply affecting corporate directors or stockholders.

Within the federal government, the development of collective bargaining lagged behind the private sector because the types of jobs were different, treatment of employees by employers was better, and federal agencies were relatively small compared to the large industrial firms organized during the 1930s in the private sector. Civil service employees were largely incorporated into the merit system that arose between 1923 and 1945. At the same time, politicians began to lose interest in protecting civil service employees because their jobs were no longer subject to favoritism. Public employees' unions were recognized as legitimate bargaining agents in 1961. Binding grievance arbitration with management was permitted (though not required) in 1969, and the scope of bargaining was broadened in 1975.

In 1978, Congress passed the **Civil Service Reform Act, (Title VII)**, which created a **labor relations regulatory agency**—the **Federal Labor Relations Authority (FLRA)** formally authorized to mediate disputes between federal unions and agency managers. Though this law clarified such issues as unit determination, scope of bargaining, and impasse resolution procedures, federal agency employees still may not strike or bargain collectively over wages and benefits, both of which Congress sets.

The Public Sector—State and Local

It is more difficult to comprehend and summarize the status of collective bargaining in state and local governments. This is primarily due to federalism, which means that the authorization and regulation of collective bargaining for state and local governments is a state responsibility. Many federal laws (such as affirmative action requirements and the wage-and-hour provisions of the Fair Labor Standards Act) regulate personnel practices in state and local government. But without violating federal law, each state is responsible for developing and administering its own laws to regulate collective bargaining by state agencies, and for local governments within the state.

State governments have often gone beyond the federal government in enacting laws to clarify collective bargaining for their employees and for employees of local governments within their jurisdiction. Forty-three states presently have enacted laws affording at least some public employees the right to "meet and confer" or negotiate on wages and working conditions. Public employees in six states are not covered by any labor relations laws, with the possible exception of no-strike provisions applicable to public employees.

In our federal system of government, both national and state governments have sovereign powers. Local governments are created and regulated by state governments, so they have no sovereignty. With respect to collective bargaining, this has meant that they cannot enter into collective bargaining agreements with employee organizations unless the state has passed legislation authorizing them to do so. Home rule powers make it possible in some cases for a local government to opt out of the state law if state law makes it optional, or to create its own "meet and confer" ordinances. Typically, this has meant that pressure for public-sector bargaining first arose among teachers, police or firefighters in big cities and spread to other areas of a state once the state statutes or constitutional revisions authorized it. In the forty-three states allowing some form of collective bargaining, over 14,000 governments were conferring or negotiating with over 36,000 bargaining units by 1987. In 1985, 62 percent of all federal employees (1,266,000) were **unionized** (covered by a collective bargaining agreement), compared with 40 percent (1,163,000) of state employees and 52 percent (3,868,000) of local government employees.[2] By 1987, the last year for which comparable statistics are available, 37 percent of state and local employees belonged to a union or employee association (5.2 million of 14.1 million).

TABLE 14–1   Public and Private Sector Collective Bargaining in the United States

Sector	Laws	Regulatory Agencies
PRIVATE	National Labor Relations Act Wagner Act (1935) Taft-Hartley Act (1947)	National Labor Relations Board
PUBLIC		
FEDERAL	Title VII of the 1978 Civil Service Reform Act	Federal Labor Relations Authority
STATE AND LOCAL	Each state has its own law	Each state has its own agency

The difference between the number and percentage of employees covered by a collective bargaining agreement and those who belong to the union comprise the group of "free riders." The most heavily unionized groups are mail carriers (90 percent), education (2.7 million of 7.3 million), police (336,000 of 689,000), highway (225,000 of 524,000) and fire fighters (154,000 of 296,000).[3]

The conditions imposed on public-sector collective bargaining make the extent of unionization and the growth of collective bargaining understandable. First, the inability of employees to negotiate bilaterally with management has meant that public-sector unions have developed primarily as interest groups whose objective is to influence the decisions of the legislatures (Congress, state legislatures, city councils, and school boards) that will have the ultimate authority to ratify or reject negotiated agreements, or to set pay and benefits if these are outside the scope of bargaining.[4] Because the Taft-Hartley Act forbids states from enacting **closed shop** provisions applicable to public agencies, public employees are not required to join a union as a condition of employment in a public agency, even though these employees will be covered by the provisions of the collective bargaining agreement negotiated between the union and agency management. These **free riders** benefit from the gains won by the union for its members, but are able to avoid paying dues if they so choose by declining to join the union.

The differences between public- and private-sector collective bargaining laws and regulatory agencies are shown in Table 14–1.

Unions in Europe, Latin America and the Caribbean

Politically, European democracies tend toward a parliamentary rather than Presidential model, with multiple political parties rather than a two-party system as in the United States. At least historically, European political parties tend to represent smaller and more ideologically unified constituencies than in the United States—including organized labor. So European public- and private-sector unions tend to be more ideological and to have a higher political profile than in the United States. They participate in elections, nominate candidates, and sponsor partisan legislation. Frequently, basic employee rights are included in the national constitution (usually as an appended **Labor Code**), including rights to health care, pensions, annual vacations, and severance bonuses based on years of service. Frequently, these basic rights apply to all employees (whether unionized or not). And because the labor code is highly visible and uniform nationally, employees find it easier to approach government in situations where they feel their rights as employees are being violated. These European traditions carried over to Europe's Latin American and Caribbean colonies during the colonial period, and have largely been retained in the English-, French-, and Spanish-speaking countries of the area.

Imagine, then, the plight of an immigrant worker newly arrived in the United States from one of these countries who has trouble with an employer because, for example, he has not been paid in a month even though he's supposed to be paid weekly, is paid at a lower pay rate than other employees doing comparable work, or fired for complaining about unsafe working conditions. Rather than a single labor code and a single agency enforcing employee rights, we offer him a variety of federal, state, and private remedies, depending on the situation:

- If you were discriminated against on the basis of a federal EEO/AA law, contact the local office of the appropriate federal compliance agency (see Chapter 8).
- If you were not paid, or not paid for all the hours you worked, and are not a member of a "protected class" (see Chapter 8), contact the state Department of Labor.
- If you have been discriminated against as a "whistleblower", and your employer is a federal contractor (see Chapter 13), contact the U.S. Department of Labor or the Office of Federal Compliance Programs.
- If none of these remedies apply, you may sue your employer in civil court.

COLLECTIVE BARGAINING, INDIVIDUAL RIGHTS, AND THE CONSTITUTION

Collective bargaining is one method by which terms and conditions of employment are determined. Understanding the unique role of collective bargaining in public agencies means understanding the relationship among union power and individual rights, constitutional protection, and political action.

While collective bargaining contracts demonstrate employee influence on some personnel functions (primarily pay, benefits, promotion and disciplinary action), collective bargaining has no impact on selection (applicants are not eligible for union membership until they are hired and pass their probationary period). Because both managers and unions are required to comply with affirmative action laws, affirmative action has influenced both unions and management much more than collective bargaining has influenced the selection and promotion process.

Public employees' pay and benefits have been particularly affected by collective bargaining. Control over these activities has passed from management to the legislature, which now has three roles in the process: to pass enabling legislation governing contract negotiations, to pass appropriations bills funding negotiated collective bargaining agreements, and to pass substantive legislation incorporating noneconomic issues into the jurisdiction's personnel laws and regulations.

Collective bargaining plays a unique role in the public sector because of its close and interactive relationship with the constitutional rights afforded public employees within civil service systems and because of the union's role in protecting the individual rights of public employees as a dominant value.

In the private sector, only two dominant values are competing in the context of collective bargaining—administrative efficiency and employee rights. And management's only legitimate interest is the "bottom line"—protecting profits by keeping production costs (including wages and benefits) low. In the absence of collective bargaining or employment contracts, most employees are hired and fired "at will" (meaning they may be discharged for any reason or for no reason at all). Similarly, pay and benefits are often negotiated on an individual basis, without general awareness by other employees in the company.

In the public sector, government agencies are required to protect the individual rights of employees. This goal originated with the desire of civil service reformers a century ago to protect public employees from partisan political pressure and to promote efficiency. And in the last few decades, federal courts have recognized that agencies that are constitutionally required to protect the rights of citizens in general cannot violate the constitutional rights of citizens as public employees. But the cumbersome nature of civil service laws regulating disciplinary action, and the need of public managers to maintain efficiency, has meant that elected officials and public managers continue to exert pressures challenging the individual rights of employees. These include contracting, privatization, political appointments and affirmative action (where the rigidities of civil service or collective bargaining systems based on seniority have had an adverse impact on minorities).

In responding to these pressures, public-sector unions have three advantages over their private-sector counterparts. First, public agencies are required to provide services to residents of a particular geographic area. This means that with some exceptions (primarily contracting out or outsourcing), the employer is required to remain in a fixed geographic area. Second, union members are not just employees—they are voters as well. Given the key role of legislative action in ratifying negotiated collective bargaining agreements in the public sector, the strength of union members as political action arms and voting blocks is important in understanding their political strength. Third, unions in the public sector have been able to obtain court opinions enforcing the value of individual rights as it is defined and protected by seniority systems.

COLLECTIVE BARGAINING PRACTICES

Collective bargaining has evolved into a formal and technical process, an administrative ritual that involves a number of prescribed concepts: unit determination, recognition and certification, scope of bargaining, contract negotiation, impasse resolution, ratification, contract administration, and unfair labor practices.

Unit Determination

Before collective bargaining can occur, a primary responsibility of the federal or state collective bargaining agency is to determine appropriate criteria for the formation of unions.[5] The two most commonly used criteria are either to divide employees by agency or by occupation. Agency bargaining establishes each state or local government agency as a separate bargaining unit. While this offers the advantages of working within an existing management structure, it can cause a proliferation of bargaining units and inequities among agency contracts.

An alternative is to group employees into general occupational classes, usually on the basis of the state or local government's job classification system. This will result in the establishment of bargaining units such as health, public safety, teachers, general civil service employees, state university system employees, and so on. This method has the advantage of limiting the number of bargaining units and automatically including employees of new agencies in preestablished units. It also clarifies, on a systemwide basis, which employees are excluded from participation in bargaining units because their jobs are managerial or of a policy-making nature. Its disadvantage is that it lumps workers with different interests and needs into one large bargaining unit, such as all health care workers.

Both agency-based and occupation-based **unit determination** require coordinating mechanisms to ensure that negotiated contracts treat employees equitably. Some public organizations—New York City, for example—have opted to establish a multilevel system of bargaining. Agency-based units bargain over salaries and benefits, while department- and occupation-based units bargain over work rules and grievance procedures.

Recognition and Certification

Once appropriate bargaining units have been established, unions are free to organize employees for the purpose of bargaining collectively. While no uniformity among state laws exists, **recognition** and **certification** procedures are generally similar in all states; New York State's Taylor Law was used as a model by many of them. An employer may voluntarily recognize a union as the exclusive bargaining agent for employees in that bargaining unit without a recognition election *if* the union can demonstrate that a majority of the employees in the bargaining unit want to be represented by that union. If voluntary recognition does not occur, the union can win recognition through a representation election. Here, employees are offered the option of approving any union that has been able to show support (through signed authorization cards) from 10 percent of the eligible employees, or declining union representation. Depending upon state law, winning the representation election requires that the union win a majority of the votes cast or a majority of votes from eligible members of the bargaining unit, regardless of the actual number of votes cast.

Once a union has been voluntarily recognized or has won a representation election, it is formally certified by the labor relations agency as the exclusive agent for that bargaining unit. Certification requires that management recognize this union as the legitimate representative of employees and that it engage in collective bargaining over all items required or permitted by applicable law.

Scope of Bargaining

The **scope of bargaining** is simply the range of issues which applicable law requires or permits to be negotiated during collective bargaining. If the laws specify which issues are included or excluded, the scope of bargaining is considered *closed*. If no restrictions are placed upon bargainable issues, the scope of bargaining is termed *open*. Nonetheless, certain issues like agency structure, agency mission, and work methods or processes are usually excluded from bargaining because they are management prerogatives. The Civil Service Reform Act (Title VII) prohibits covered federal employees from bargaining over wages and other economic issues such as retirement and health benefits, which are established by Congress. Most state collective bargaining laws allow or require bargaining over wages, benefits, and working conditions. Yet the distinction between issues included in bargaining— or excluded from it—is not always clear. Issues that management considers excluded, such as adding drug testing to selection or promotion criteria, are frequently considered bargainable by unions because they affect member rights or important public policy issues. In such cases, their bargainability must be clarified by the state labor relations agency.

Contract Negotiation and Preparations for Negotiation

Contract negotiation usually begins immediately following recognition and certification, or (if the union has previously been certified) in anticipation of the expiration of an existing contract. Local union officials may represent their own membership, or a professional negotiator who has negotiated similar contracts with other state or local governments may be employed. Management is represented by an experienced negotiator supported by a team of experts that will include the personnel manager, the budget officer, a lawyer, and some line managers who understand the impact of contract provisions on agency operations.

In most cases, negotiation occurs "**in the sunshine**." That is, negotiations are conducted in public because states have an open-meetings law that prohibits government officials from determining public policy through back-room deals. Prior to the negotiations, it is important that management's negotiator reach a clear understanding with elected officials concerning their preferred contract provisions and their minimally acceptable contract provisions (particularly with respect to economic issues). And it is important to prepare adequately for negotiations by collecting comparative data on other agencies and contract agreements, preparing spreadsheet analyses of the cost of alternative settlements on economic issues, and estimating projected revenues available to pay the price tag on economic items. Good negotiation is impossible without good research.

Negotiation involves both task- and process-oriented issues. Both sides see it as the opportunity to shape HR policy and practice. As in any strategic contest, each side attempts to discover the other's strengths and priorities, while keeping its own hidden until the opposition appears most willing to concede on an issue. Good negotiations depend on the negotiators' ability to marshal facts, sense the opposition's strengths and weaknesses, and judge the influence of outside events (such as job actions or media coverage) on the negotiations. Good faith bargaining requires negotiators to work for the best deal their side can get, while still remaining receptive to the needs of the other party. Experts agree that interest-based bargaining, also called collaborative or **win-win bargaining** is most satisfactory.[6]

Impasse Resolution during Contract Negotiations

There are two types of collective bargaining impasses: disagreements that occur during the negotiations over the *substance* of negotiations (such factors as pay or benefits), and disagreements over the interpretation of contract provisions that have previously been negotiated and approved. If management and union are unable to resolve differences through two-party contract negotiations, there remain three procedures involving intervention by a third party: mediation, fact-finding, and arbitration. The order in which these are employed, and whether they are used at all, will depend on the provisions of the applicable collective bargaining law.

Mediation is the intervention of a neutral third party in an attempt to persuade the bargaining parties to reach an agreement. This may be an independent individual, or one from a group designated by an agency such as the **American Arbitration Association** or the **Federal Mediation and Conciliation Service (FMCS)**. It is in the interest of both parties to make a good faith effort to reach a voluntary mediated settlement, since this is the last stage at which they will have full control over contract provisions.

If mediation is not successful, negotiations may progress to the second step— **fact-finding**. A fact-finder appointed by the federal or state collective bargaining agency will conduct a hearing at which both sides present data in support of their positions. After these hearings, the fact-finder releases a report to both parties, and to the public, that outlines what he or she considers a reasonable settlement. Although this advisory opinion is not binding, the threat of unfavorable publicity may make either side more willing to reach a negotiated settlement.

If fact-finding is unsuccessful, the final stage may be **arbitration**. Essentially the same procedures are followed as in fact-finding. However, the arbitrator's formal report contains contract provisions that both parties have agreed in advance will be binding. In an effort to avoid having to "split the difference" between extreme positions, the arbitrator may decide in advance to take the "last, best final offer" presented by either side, based on either the entire contract or issue-by-issue. Arbitration of substantive items at impasse during contract negotiation is termed **interest arbitration**, to distinguish it from subsequent arbitration over the meaning of previously ratified contract provisions (**grievance arbitration**) during the contract administration process. The cost of third-party interest dispute resolution during negotiations is usually borne equally by both parties.

Contract Ratification

Once representatives of labor and management have negotiated a contract, both the appropriate legislative body and the union's membership must ratify it before becoming law. For the union, **ratification** requires support of the negotiated contract by a majority of those voting. For management, it requires that the legislature (state, county, school district) appropriate the funds required to finance the economic provisions of the contract. Because all states have laws or constitutional provisions prohibiting deficit financing of operating expenses, revenue estimates impose an absolute ceiling on the pay and benefits that may be negotiated through collective bargaining. Nor is it considered bad faith bargaining for a legislature to refuse to ratify a negotiated contract if projected revenues will not meet projected expenses.

The requirement that a negotiated contract be ratified by the legislature is a sore point for union advocates because it limits the application of binding interest arbitration. Courts have uniformly held that the legislature cannot delegate its responsibility for keeping expenditures within revenues. Although union advocates frequently (and justifiably) protest that the legislature is biased toward management, state laws require that the state or local legislature take all interests into account—including those of the union and its members—in deciding whether to ratify a negotiated contract.

Contract Administration

Once a contract has been negotiated and ratified, both union and management are responsible for administering its provisions. Key actors in implementation include the union steward, a union member who will interpret the contract for the employees and serve as their advocate and representative to management; supervisors, who will be implementing contract provisions relating to everyday employee-employer relations; and the personnel manager, who is management's expert on how the contract affects human resource policy and practice.

Conflicts are bound to arise during **contract administration** because reaching compromises during negotiations often requires agreement on what will later turn out to be ambiguous contract language. For example, labor and management may agree during contract negotiations that the shop steward "may spend a reasonable amount of time not to exceed two hours per week on union activities." Subsequently, differences may arise over such issues as whether the steward is in fact spending a "reasonable" amount of time on union business, or whether management has the right to approve when this time can be taken. Negotiations will then be needed to determine whether the shop steward's or the supervisor's actions constitute a violation of the contract's provisions.

Part of the contract will therefore outline the process for resolving grievances that occur during contract implementation. The process may begin very informally with discussion between union and management representatives. If the issue is not satisfactorily resolved informally, it is written up as a formal grievance and appealed through channels up to a neutral third party outside the agency. Binding grievance arbitration is the norm (in contrast to the lack of binding *interest* arbitration over contract negotiation impasses).

Management should view the **grievance** process as one more potentially beneficial effort by employees to make the organization more effective by calling attention to inefficient or inequitable supervisory practices. It can serve as an internal evaluation device, a means of instituting planned change and a method of redressing inequitable organizational practices. It is recommended that supervisors and public personnel managers know the contract, maintain open lines of communication with employees, meet and deal informally with union representatives over potential grievances, exhibit uniform and adequate documentation for all personnel actions, and keep the record open to unions and employees. One way to keep both parties honest in handling grievances is to require the losing party to pay for the services of a third party arbitrator. This discourages unions from pursuing frivolous grievances just to satisfy a disgruntled member, and it encourages management to handle grievances fairly rather than simply opposing the union on every issue.

UNFAIR LABOR PRACTICES

Federal and state collective bargaining laws all include lists of personnel practices forbidden to labor and management. In this regard, it is most important that management remember that employees have an *absolute* right to organize and bargain collectively in federal agencies, and in those states where enabling collective bargaining legislation exists. Management has no corresponding right to prevent employees from doing so. This means that management cannot seek to influence the outcome of a representation election by coercing, threatening, or intimidating employees. It can present information on the comparative advantages and disadvantages of union membership; also, it can restrict union organizing to public locations (lunchrooms, bulletin boards) that do not interfere with the work of the agency and do not occur on company time.

During negotiations, each party is bound to bargain in good faith. **Good-faith bargaining** means that each party will listen to the other side and will negotiate. A failure to show up for scheduled negotiations, or a "take it or leave it" approach to the negotiations themselves, will likely lead to a formal charge of unfair labor practices being filed with the labor relations regulatory agency. Findings against the agency can result in fines, administrative sanctions, or the invalidation of negotiated settlements or representation elections.

Whether or not public employees should have the right to strike is contested because it pits fundamental rights against each other. On the one hand, public employees are guaranteed constitutional protection of association and expression. In addition, there is strong justification for extending to employees the same right to withhold their services as a bargaining weapon that private employees enjoy. On the other hand, the importance of public services to the public, and the monopolistic nature of most public agencies, strengthens the argument that public-sector strikes are less tolerable or politically acceptable than those in the private sector.

In practice, the outcome of strikes by public employees seems to depend on a variety of fairly predictable factors, among them applicable laws, historical practice, and the relative control of the union over the job market. In the federal government and most states, all strikes by public employees are illegal. In some cases (such as the ill-fated strike of the 10,000 member Professional Air Traffic Controllers Organization (PATCO) in 1981), employees who strike are fired, the union is decertified, and union officers are fined and jailed. Yet in fields where strikes are the norm (such as education), and where there are no available qualified substitutes for union members (such as law enforcement), strikes often occur with impunity. Or they occur under a different guise, such as "sickouts," "job actions," and "blue flu" (where employees are absent or unproductive in concert, without a strike formally being called).

In reality, economic pressures both increase and diminish the likelihood of strikes by public employees. Most employees have lost real purchasing power over the past two decades and see themselves as making sacrifices in order to maintain a high level of public service without tax increases. But management's use of alternatives (such as contracting or privatization) to provide public services frequently reminds public employees (or threatens them, depending on your perspective) that their job security, pay, and benefits within civil service systems and collective bargaining are a better deal than they would ever get if their jobs were contracted or privatized.[7] The threat of privatization or contracting out is also a powerful tool for breaking unions or gaining **givebacks** during contract renegotiation.

PRESSURES ON PUBLIC-SECTOR COLLECTIVE BARGAINING

Three underlying trends help explain why the percentage of employees—public and private—working under collective bargaining agreements has declined from 35 percent in 1957 to 12 percent today:[8] economic pressures on collective bargaining outcomes, organizational pressures on collective bargaining processes, and political pressures on collective bargaining systems.

Economic Pressures on Collective Bargaining Outcomes

The percentage of unionized employees in the United States dropped from one out of three in 1950, to one out of six in 1990[9] due to a number of factors: the erosion of manufacturing in favor of nonunionized service and white-collar employment, the gradual shift of jobs away from the Northeast to the Southeast and Southwest (parts of the country without a strong tradition of industrial unions), and the increased effectiveness of union avoidance strategies developed by employers.

Much current debate about the effectiveness of unions in the new global economy is influenced by beliefs that unions hinder economic competitiveness,[10] employment growth[11] and investment activity by unionized firms.[12] Salaries and benefits are the main reason employees unionize, and there is some evidence that employees who bargain collectively enjoy higher pay and benefits (about 7 percent higher) than their nonunionized counterparts. Yet other factors like urbanization, population, the local economic climate, and the relative demand for employees in the field are more significant determinants of salary. And continued pressure to reduce the cost of government has lessened the impact of collective bargaining on public employee salaries.[13]

But in any event, unions are viewed as a structural constraint that increases employer costs. And collective bargaining outcomes, among other costs, increase competitive pressure on employers. Rising health-care costs (and related workers' compensation, sick leave, and disability retirement expenses) constitute a large share of personnel costs.[14] Total employer liabilities for health-care coverage for current employees are $85 billion for those Americans covered by employer-financed plans.[15] Nationally, medical costs have climbed from $248 million to $600 billion in 1990, growing at twice the rate of inflation even when adjusted for population increases.[16] Like health-care systems, troubled public and private pension systems are rapidly becoming a political issue. The increase in corporate indebtedness and economic restructuring that characterized the 1980s have increased tendencies to borrow against employee pension plans, or to eliminate them altogether. While the Social Security trust fund is currently solvent, demands on the system can be expected to increase as the post-World War II "baby boom" generation enters retirement age.

Organizational Pressures on Collective Bargaining Processes

The focus of union negotiations has generally been on win-lose negotiations over economic issues.[17] The adversarial tactics employed by union negotiators have placed them in a situation where their strategies seem outmoded or even irrelevant to insuring their constituency will receive equitable treatment in an economy where the demand for union jobs has declined significantly. The steady growth of alternative dispute resolution (ADR) techniques in a number of areas (family law, torts, and workplace grievances) is due to realization that adversarial techniques build acrimony, harden bargaining positions, and delay the resolution of the original conflict.

Managers, supervisors, and personnel directors have responded to this realization by creating work systems that enhance involvement and participation. The common thread among these systems is their emphasis on the connection between the quality of the work environment and the quality of individual, team, and organizational performance. Training can also enhance involvement and participation because it includes not only individual job skills but also improvements in employees' work relationships. Examples are team building and organizational development,[18] total quality management (TQM),[19] and training for diversity.[20] In the private sector, employers' team-building and TQM efforts are somewhat hindered by provisions in the Taft-Hartley Act that prohibit employer-sponsored employee associations. This is because, in the "bad old days" of industrial collective bargaining, managers sometimes attempted to subvert collective bargaining by creating a union led by management sympathizers, recognizing it as the official bargaining agent, and signing collective bargaining agreements favorable to management rather than the employees. No such prohibition exists in the public sector (because this Taft-Hartley provision does not apply to public agencies), so competition often exists between employee unions and employer-sponsored quality circles or TQM groups.

Traditional collective bargaining processes also run counter to the current transition from affirmative action compliance to workforce diversity. Workforce diversity has brought about changing definitions of productivity based on the need for variation in managerial styles, and resultant increases in organizational effectiveness.[21] Without an organizational commitment of respect, tolerance and dignity, differences lead only to divisiveness that consumes organizational resources without positive results.[22]

Pressures for public agency accountability and performance have meant increased flexibility in job matching for individual employees (based on competency-based job matching, rank-in-person personnel systems, and individualized development plans); and on competency-based job matching systems (such as results-oriented job descriptions, delegation, and management by objectives). Traditional criteria for determining merit (seniority and "blanket" qualifications standards for a range of positions) are simply not considered valid enough to be used as the sole basis of selection, promotion, layoff decisions, or even work arrangements.

Political Pressures on Collective Bargaining Systems

Economic and organizational pressures, if they are generalized and persistent, soon make themselves visible as political pressures on the validity of collective bargaining as a personnel system. Within the public sector, the perceived anachronism of traditional industries and traditional industrial relations has interacted with demands for "reinventing government." This slogan epitomizes the continued pressure on public agencies to measure outputs, increase efficiency, and enhance political accountability.[23] In public agencies, it has meant the relative ascendancy of political responsiveness and efficiency as values; and the need for personnel administrators to work with other systems (besides traditional civil service and collective bargaining). Critics have argued that the private sector can often provide services more cheaply and efficiently by eliminating "unnecessary" personnel costs and employee protection. And desires for both political payoffs and political accountability make provision of public services through the private sector more attractive. Consequently, much government growth has been through a secondary labor market of part-time, temporary, and seasonal employees, which at least gives the appearance of controlling the size of the public "bureaucracy."[24]

MOVING FROM PRIVATE PRIVILEGE TO PUBLIC INTEREST

The ability of unions to make collective bargaining a continuing alternative public personnel system is at heart a political issue. Advocates of collective bargaining systems must build a constituency that focuses broad public concern on "crossover" issues that political leaders may consider seriously because they invoke genuine public interests, rather than representing merely union efforts to maintain what opponents consider the private privilege of jobs, benefits, and due process protection. Some such concerns are (1) employment access by minorities, women, and persons with disabilities; (2) organizational justice in the allocation of employee benefits, training, and involvement; (3) productivity improvement; and (4) economic necessity for employer-financed retirement and health-care systems.

Employment Access by Minorities, Women and Persons with Disabilities

Traditionally, unions have been perceived as more concerned with the rights of current members than ensuring equality of job opportunity for minorities, women, and persons with disabilities. Indeed, public employee unions have historically opposed promotional opportunities for women and minorities, and have been parties to many lawsuits establishing the relative priority accorded individual rights based on seniority.

This perceived or actual lack of support for social equity may be a function of discrimination within union leadership. A recent study indicates that although women are proportionally represented in leadership positions within Massachusetts AFL-CIO locals, they are overrepresented as secretaries and seriously underrepresented as presidents, or the chairs of key grievance or negotiations committees.[25] This in turn may be due to sex-role stereotypes (for example, the belief that confrontational dispute resolution requires a male personality), which are at variance with the research findings of workforce diversity advocates who have studied the impact of alternative leadership styles on organizational effectiveness.[26]

But whatever the cause, unions can enlarge their base of support by focusing on employment access issues,[27] women,[28] and Americans with disabilities. Unions must sensitize themselves to workforce diversity, to pay equity, and to those employee services that help employees meet family obligations. Because women are the traditional family caregivers, an employer's ability to attract a diverse workforce depends upon the provision of these same services and benefits: flexible benefits,[29] parental leave,[30] child- and elder-care support programs,[31] alternative work locations and schedules, and employee-centered supervision.

However, enhancing the diversity of union membership and leadership will not result in increased political power for public unions unless gains in representation are translated into proportionate gains in dues-paying membership and political clout. This in turn will depend upon two things: the ability of unions to settle the free-rider issue by successful litigation to require free riders to pay their fair share of benefits,[32] and the ability of unions to organize workers around political action as well as internal bargaining issues.[33]

Organizational Justice in Benefits, Training, and Involvement Opportunities

The United States currently is suffering from the absence of concerted public policy that ties together educational development, national human resource development, industrial policy, and economic growth.[34] Public and private employers uniformly express alarm at the ineffectiveness of our educational system in producing the skilled workers needed by high-technology industries. But the organizational implication of economic pressures for increased productivity and lower personnel costs are clearly a "shake-out" between core employees and contingent workers who increasingly work under very different conditions. Though the logic of simultaneously applying different pay, benefit, and retention policies is apparent to personnel administrators and supervisors, it is often hard to explain to contingent workers who find themselves working side-by-side with core employees. **Core employees** are relatively permanent in that they are hired into civil service positions or on long-term performance contracts. These positions usually have pensions, health benefits, vacation and sick leave, and opportunities for training and career development. **Contingent workers** are relatively temporary in that they are hired on a seasonal, part-time or temporary basis. These jobs usually come without benefits or opportunities for career development.

But this threat of being trapped in the contingent workforce is not only an economic condition, but also a psychic tragedy—the loss of dignity, of hope for the future. This is a powerful, explosive issue that political leaders can use to capitalize on racial and ethnic divisiveness, or a national agenda for education, economic reform and job creation. Union members, and adherents of collective bargaining systems, may be able to take advantage of public support for fair and decent wages by supporting pay equity for women, minorities and the disadvantaged—groups that have been traditionally discriminated against in the private sector because market-based pay plans allow employers to pay them less than the wages offered their white male counterparts. Pay equity may be a particularly fruitful issue in state and local government, where employment of women and minorities in service jobs is disproportionately high.[35]

Organizational Productivity

Unions build a broader constituency to the extent that they can demonstrate that union strength is critical to employee involvement,[36] and that employee involvement is critical to enhanced workplace productivity.[37] For example, one recent study investigates the effectiveness of employee participation in achieving product quality improvement in union versus nonunion settings and in programs unilaterally administered by management versus programs with joint union-management administration. Findings suggest that among unionized firms, those with jointly administered programs achieved significantly greater improvements in product quality than did those with more traditional adversarial collective bargaining relationships (that is, with no participation programs), but those with programs administered solely by management fared no better than those with no programs. The gains associated with jointly administered programs in unionized firms were at least equal to the gains associated with participation programs in nonunion firms.[38]

And a related case study indicates that enhanced industrial productivity may be possible by combining the advantages of company-based employee involvement programs with those of independent local unions, especially in a high-tech industry that has moved away from adversarial management employee relations.[39] But obviously, more research and experimentation are needed into the impact of workers councils, quality management teams, and independent local unions (ILUs) on organizational productivity in the United States.[40]

EMPLOYER-FINANCED EMPLOYEE RETIREMENT AND HEALTH-CARE SYSTEMS

Thus far, the development of a contingent workforce with few (if any) traditional benefits like holidays, vacations, sick leave, health insurance or retirement has focused on either the business justification for this change (minimized costs and increased flexibility) or the consequences for individual employees. Yet this trend has serious related public policy issues, including the solvency of Social Security and public health systems. Union strength will increase to the extent that voters view dismantling of private pension and health benefit systems as major public issues.[41]

CONTRACT ADMINISTRATION ISSUES FOR POLICE AND FIREFIGHTERS

Somehow, collective bargaining for police officers and firefighters is more contentious and detail-oriented than most HR directors or managers expect. This is due to the environmental context—these are high-profile public services with diverse expectations of accountability for public service. And it's due to the organizational context. Police and fire departments are hierarchical organizations, yet actual firefighter and police work requires highly skilled individuals accustomed to making decisions on their own. Generational change and the availability of advanced technical and professional education has created an upcoming cadre of firefighters and police officers who are more qualified—at least in terms of formal education—than many of their supervisors. And many of these supervisors feel that subordinates often give insufficient deference to organizational hierarchy or its collective wisdom. The nature of work assignments is also an issue. These are not 9-to-5 jobs. Police officers may work a rotating schedule requiring constant changes between day, afternoon, and night shifts. On-call and overtime status are frequent issues because of emergencies or court appearances. Firefighters normally work a 24-hour shift while living at the station house, with several days off from one work day to the next. Finally, this is a male-dominated, testosterone-rich environment, where aggression and confrontation are often considered normal ways of resolving workplace issues. And issues do arise that can be categorized along common themes:

- ADA: what constitutes a serious disability; light duty assignments; fitness for work.[42]
- FLSA: covered or exempt; implications for comp time, holiday pay, on-call status,[43] and overtime.[44]
- Drug testing, particularly related to accidents, disabilities and job retention.[45]
- FMLA: implications for sick leave and job retention.[46]
- Seniority: conflict with AA over eligibility for promotion or reassignment.[47]

While management deals with these issues as best it can on a daily basis, the same conflicts among personnel systems and values that characterize the rest of public sector HRM also affect police and firefighters. That is, "civilian" employees—usually hired as temporary or part-time employees—are replacing sworn police officers or firefighters/EMTs/paramedics in office positions.

EMERGENT ISSUES

Despite its uncertain future, public sector collective bargaining shows significant changes. These include increased labor management cooperation for productivity improvement, alternative dispute resolution, and gainsharing.

Labor-Management Cooperation

Public sector labor and management teams from 27 cities, counties and states attended a program on labor-management cooperation at Harvard University. Teams, made up of unions, city managers, department heads, and other administrators learned how to create and sustain labor-management initiatives that improved services and morale through labor-management cooperation.[48] And Detroit Mayor Dennis Archer noted recently, "Seven billion dollars in new development commitments, apprenticeship programs for workers, renovated recreation centers, increased support for neighborhood institutions—all this is evidence of the power of partnership."[49] A recent Department of Labor report indicated that ". . . labor-management cooperation that engaged employees in decisions around service planning and implementation typically resulted in:

- *Better Service:* services frequently became faster; often new or expanded services were offered, and all were responsive to citizens.
- *More Cost-Effectiveness:* Money was saved and money better spent.
- *Better Quality of Work Life:* Employees gained more involvement and greater opportunities to contribute and learn skills. They gained greater job security and found greater respect.
- *Improved Labor Management Relations.* Less conflict, faster conflict resolution, more flexible contracts, and emphasis on mutual responsibility for service improvement.[50]

Alternative Dispute Resolution

Diverse organizations oriented toward team-based productivity improvement require methods of resolving disputes that are more appropriate to their culture and structure than traditional grievance resolution. Fortunately, contemporary organizations have been successfully experimenting with **alternative dispute resolution (ADR)** techniques that meet these criteria. Generally, these include any procedure, agreed to by the parties to a dispute, in which they call upon the services of a neutral party to assist them in reaching agreements and thus avoid litigation. The most popular variants are mediation and arbitration, but they include a range of procedures:

- *Open door policy:* Encourages employees to bring grievances of any kind to their managers with the assurance that no retaliation will result.[51]
- *Negotiation:* A process of explicit bargaining between parties to a dispute in an effort to reach a settlement without outside intervention.
- *Ombudsman:* Use of a manager with strong communication skills, respected by labor and management, with broad authority to hear disputes and facilitate resolution.[52]
- *Peer review panel:* Use of an informal panel representing labor and management, to determine if existing policy was accurately and equitably applied.[53]
- *Mediation:* Active assistance by a neutral third party in reaching a settlement. Emphasizes informality, confidentiality, and flexibility to resolve a particular dispute, or to preserve and improve long-term relationships.[54]
- *Arbitration:* A process by which both sides usually commit themselves in advance to the binding decision of a neutral arbitrator, referee, or private judge, typically through procedures specified by the American Arbitration Association.[55]

This development was spurred by the **Alternative Dispute Resolution Act of 1998**, which encouraged use of alternative methods of workplace dispute resolution throughout the Executive Branch.[56] Today the American Arbitration Association estimates that more than 400 employers—with workforces ranging from 800 to 300,000 workers—use some form of ADR to resolve many of their employment disputes. They report significant savings in legal fees, quicker dispute resolution, and a decrease in litigation since beginning ADR programs.[57] Public sector applications include the State of South Carolina[58] and the U.S. Postal Service.[59]

Gainsharing

Gainsharing is a group bonus plan in which monetary savings from improved performance are shared between the organization and employees of the better performing unit. Under gainsharing, standard hours of direct labor in each unit of output are measured and compared with historically based long-term standard performance levels. Payouts are based on the value of productivity improvement.

Gainsharing differs from motivational programs like TQM, quality circles, or self-directed work teams in that there is a direct link between financial rewards and productivity. There are three commonly followed gainsharing variations:

- *Simple financial measure gainsharing (Scanlon Plans):* pay bonuses are based directly on productivity increases without allowance for factors beyond employees' control.
- *Productivity-measure gainsharing (Improshare and similar systems):* pay bonuses are calculated based on a formula for productivity improvement.
- *Multiple factor gainsharing:* pay bonuses are based on a mixture of short- and long-term indicators. They can also be financial (e.g., "cost reduction") or nonfinancial (e.g., "client loyalty").

Gainsharing, properly designed and implemented, focuses on three general principles: employee involvement, bonus payments, and worker identification with the employer. And a considerable body of research indicates that it increases productivity and profits. Kaufman's study of 104 U.S. organizations that had introduced Improshare plans showed a median productivity growth of 4.17 percent in the first 3 months, 4.9 percent in the first 6 months, and 8.31 percent in the first year. Median increases over the first three years ranged from 5 to 15 percent during a period when there was an average annual growth rate of 2 percent for all manufacturing industries.[60] A 1992 American Compensation Association study of variable pay plans, including 348 variants of gainsharing, reported an average 129 percent return on investment in gainsharing, and average gains to employees in the United States of over $2,200 per year.[61] There have also been significant public sector applications, including city services in Charlotte, Phoenix, Baltimore and Coral Springs (Florida).[62]

While it may be conceptually simple and intuitively attractive, adoption of gainsharing by an employee does require top-level support for key policy decisions like the organization's objective, composition of the gainsharing team, frequency of payments, whether to include gainsharing as part of formal collective bargaining agreements or as separate contracts, whether all members of the team should be paid the same sum or a percentage of salary, and what relative percentage of gains should be paid to employees, the organization—or rebated to taxpayers in the form of tax cuts.

Once these policy issues have been considered, the next stage is consultation with representatives from unions, supervisors, personnel and budget staff, and citizens. The purpose of this consultation is to explain gainsharing, to adapt the proposal to suit the organization, and to gain commitment from various "stakeholders". Once buy-in has occurred, labor and management need to work together to design performance measures that are realistic, measurable, and participative. They need to train those involved. And finally, the system needs to be implemented by establishing baseline productivity measures, collecting information on performance improvements, displaying the results, checking assumptions for validity, making payments, and monitoring to see when changes are needed in the performance indicators.

SUMMARY

Collective bargaining is law, process, and ritual. As law, it provides the constitutional and statutory foundation that enables employees collectively to negotiate the terms and conditions of employment with managers (and indirectly, with legislators and the public). Second, it is the standardized procedures by which this collective negotiation takes place. And third, it is a ritual through which employees demonstrate their relative power (through the sanctions process) over employment policy and practice.

In the final analysis, the strength of collective bargaining as a public personnel system will be affected by unions' ability to persuade the public, and its leaders, that strong unions are tied to vital public policy concerns that go beyond the more narrow economic concerns of their current members. Some concerns that may prove persuasive are (1) employment access by minorities, women, and persons with disabilities; (2) organizational justice in the allocation of employee benefits, training, and involvement; (3) organizational productivity; and (4) economic necessity for employer-financed retirement and health-care systems. Signs of union rebirth are evident in emergent trends within the public and private sector toward alternative dispute resolution, labor-management cooperation, and gainsharing.

KEY TERMS

alternative dispute resolution (ADR)
Alternative Dispute Resolution Act of 1998
American Arbitration Association
arbitration
certification
Civil Service Reform Act of 1978 (Title VII)
closed shop

collective bargaining
contingent worker
contract administration
contract negotiation
core employee
fact-finding
Federal Labor Relations Authority (FLRA)
Federal Mediation and Conciliation Service (FMCS)

free riders
gainsharing
givebacks
good-faith bargaining
grievance
grievance arbitration
"in the sunshine" (negotiations)
interest arbitration
labor code
labor relations regulatory agency
mediation
National Labor Relations Act (Wagner Act)
National Labor Relations Board (NLRB)

outsourcing
Postal Service Reorganization Act (1970)
ratification
recognition
right to work laws
scope of bargaining
Taft-Hartley Act (1947)
two-tiered wage and benefit systems
unfair labor practices
unionized
unit determination
win-win bargaining

DISCUSSION QUESTIONS

1. Why is the history of collective bargaining in the public sector different from that in the private sector?
2. Why is the legal structure of collective bargaining more complex and confusing in the public sector than in the private sector?
3. What are the reasons for the current crisis among public-sector unions?
4. What are some crossover issues that unions might focus on to change the public perception that their primary objective is economic benefits for their members, rather than public policy issues affecting a broader segment of society?
5. Should management's strategy toward collective bargaining be (a) opposition to unions and avoidance of collective bargaining, or (b) acceptance of unions' legitimacy and participation in collective bargaining? What factors will influence which option management chooses to pursue?

CASE STUDY: GOOD MANAGEMENT OR BARGAINING IN BAD FAITH?

BACKGROUND INFORMATION

You are the new city manager for Sunbelt City. It is small (50,000 population), but growing at about 10 percent annually, as retirees and business owners move south seeking warmer winters and lower taxes. The city currently employs about 100 sworn police officers. The city charter classifies police officers as within the civil service system. Because public-sector collective bargaining is authorized for local governments in this state, those officers in nonsupervisory positions are also represented by the PBA (Police Benevolent Association).

Sunbelt is governed by a five-member elected city council. Last November, three incumbent council members were defeated by newcomers who ran on a platform of keeping taxes down by making government more effective and efficient. The two remaining council members also favor this objective.

The council has enthusiastically supported your strategy of reducing the city budget by bargaining hard with unions over salary and fringe benefits. By using the veiled threat of privatization or outsourcing as a "hammer," you have successfully renegotiated contracts for the city's solid waste and public works employees. Under the new contracts, trash collectors now work a full eight-hour day instead of being allowed to go home when their routes are finished. And the public works department is now operating under a two-tiered contract that protects salaries and benefits for current employees, but requires new employees to enter at lower salaries and to pay a higher proportion of their health benefit costs.

Now you face a challenge. A new council member suggests that you use the same strategy in renegotiating the contract with the PBA, up for renewal this year. You immediately sense trouble ahead as other council members have indicated a similar interest. Threatening solid waste and public works employees with privatization is one thing—it's been done all over the country, and many private trash haulers and maintenance companies do a thriving business. But what are the alternatives to police officers hired through a civil service system? And will any alternative satisfy voters and the rest of the council, given that Sunbelt residents want both lower taxes and high-quality police protection? You hire a collective bargaining consultant and labor negotiator to provide you with expert advice in the matter. The consultant recommends that you consider three options: (1) hard bargaining with the PBA, (2) contracting for police services with the county sheriff's office, or (3) contracting with a private security firm.

THE CHOICES

Hard bargaining means taking bargaining positions that reduce pay and benefit costs, such as: (a) proposing a tiered contract offering lower pay and benefits to new officers than current ones; (b) routinely challenging police officer requests for disability retirement and workers' compensation for injuries suspected of being caused by outside employment; (c) hiring civilian employees to do office work and putting all sworn police officers on the street; and (d) proposing early retirement provisions to reduce lower personnel costs by reducing the number of senior officers. This is politically the least risky option, but it will work well only if citizens are convinced the quality of law enforcement will not suffer, and if PBA negotiators fear that one of the other two options will be imposed if they do not agree to "giveback" contract provisions that reduce pay and benefit costs.

Contracting with the county sheriff's office means changing the city charter by abolishing the police department and contracting with the county sheriff's office for police services. The contract would need to be carefully negotiated to include (a) reimbursement to Sunbelt for any capital equipment (such as police buildings or vehicles) sold to the county; (b) qualitative and quantitative measures of service (such as number of officers, response time, and responsiveness to the council); and (c) provisions for city police officers to join the county sheriff's department (this would involve complex negotiations over seniority, pay, and benefit packages for both organizations). This option offers probable dramatic short-term cost savings. But the down side is less control over quality of service, no assurance that costs for contracting will remain lower than the cost of the Sunbelt police department, and a large one-time lump-sum payment of accrued annual leave to those Sunbelt police officers who elect to retire rather than join the county sheriff's department.

Contracting with a private security firm offers the greatest potential benefits and risks. Private security corporations already provide security at many condominiums and public facilities, operate county and state correctional facilities, and are starting to move into municipal law enforcement. Informal negotiations with officials in private security firms lead you to believe that they will offer to provide sworn law enforcement officers at less than half the cost of the current police department's budget, largely because of lower pay and benefit costs. Not only will payroll costs be lower, but also administrative expenses are capped by the contract, and legal liability risks are covered by the contractor's bond. The risks are also great. Public opinion will probably be against hiring "rent-a-cops" to replace sworn police officers, and the PBA will use this opposition to build a firestorm of political opposition to the proposal. Certainly the quality of service will be in doubt, and the training and fitness for duty of sworn officers may be questionable if, as rumored, the security company hires retired police or corrections officers because they are already certified.

THE OUTCOME

You decide on the first option (hard bargaining), backed by credible statements that if hard bargaining is unsuccessful you intend to pursue council approval for either of the other two options. The PBA fights back hard, stirring up public opinion against you, directly lobbying the council against your proposal, and filing an unfair labor practice charge with the state collective bargaining regulatory agency, alleging that your purported threat to contract out for law enforcement services is in fact a refusal to bargain in good faith. Several weeks later, the hearing officer decides that you have not violated the requirement for good faith bargaining. But in the meantime, PBA and public pressure have forced two council members to publicly come out against the contracting option. And the county sheriff's department becomes the subject of investigation by the State Attorney General's office and the State Department of Law Enforcement, when it is alleged that sheriff's deputies are guilty of widespread bribery and extortion efforts to protect drug dealers and gambling interests in the county. The PBA agrees to a contract that is essentially the same as the previous one, with a cost-of-living increase in pay and no changes in benefits. As a condition of ratification, the PBA insists privately to council members that you be fired. The council fires you at the same time it approves the collective bargaining agreement with the PBA.

Questions

1. What does this case study show about the current strengths and weaknesses of public-sector collective bargaining as a public personnel system?
2. Looking back at the situation, are there any options that would have been better for you to select than the three you were offered by the consultant?
3. What arguments could you have presented to make a stronger case for hard bargaining or contracting out?
4. Is there anything else you could have done to handle this situation better, or were you simply a victim of bad timing and corruption in the county sheriff's department?

NOTES

[1]Kochan, T., and H. Katz (1988). *Collective bargaining and industrial relations.* Homewood, IL: Business One Irwin.

[2]Union Recognition in Government. (January 18, 1988). *Government Employee Relations Report, 71,* 208.

[3]U.S. Department of Commerce, Bureau of the Census (1991). *Labor-Management Relations in State and Local Government, GC87(3)*–3. Note: the Bureau of the Census discontinued publication of this volume of the *Census of Governments* report, effective 1991.

[4]Chandler, Timothy, and Rafael Gely (December 1996). Toward identifying the determinants of public-employee unions' involvement in political activities. *American Review of Public Administration, 26* (4): 417–438.

[5]A good general reference for public-sector unit determination is: Gershenfeld, W. (1985). Public employee unionization: An overview. In Association of Labor Relations Agencies (1985). *The evolving process: Collective negotiations in public employment.* Ft. Washington, PA: Labor Relations Press.

[6]Fisher, Roger, and William Ury (1991). *Getting to Yes.* New York: Penguin Books.

[7]Naff, K. (January-February 1991). Labor-management relations and privatization: A federal perspective. *Public Administration Review, 51,* 23–30.

[8]Berman, Evan, James Bowman, Jonathan West, and Martin Van Wart (2001). *Human Resources Management in Public Service: Paradoxes, Processes and Problems.* Thousand Oaks: Sage Publications.

[9]Coleman, C. (1990). *Managing employee relations in the public sector.* San Francisco: Jossey-Bass.

[10]Mishel, L., and P. Voos (1992). *Unions and economic competitiveness.* Armonk, NY: M. E. Sharpe.

[11]Leonard, J. (Winter 1992). Unions and employment growth. *Industrial Relations, 31,* 80–94.

[12]Hirsch, B. (Winter 1992). Firm investment behavior and collective bargaining strategy. *Industrial Relations, 31,* 95–121.

[13]Derber, M. (1987). Management organization for collective bargaining in the public sector. In B. Aaron, J. Najita, and J. Stern (Eds.). *Public sector bargaining* (2nd ed.). Washington, DC: BNA.

[14]Blostin, A., T. Burke, and L. Lovejoy (December 1988). Disability and insurance plans in the public and private sector. *Monthly Labor Review,* pp. 9–17.

[15]Allan, I. (1988). Financing and managing public employee benefit plans in the 1990s. *Government Finance Review, 4,* 32.

[16]Luthans, F., and E. David (1990). The health-care cost crisis: Causes and containment. *Personnel, 67,* 24.

[17]Nigro, Felix, and Lloyd Nigro (2000). *Public Personnel Management.* Itasca, IL: Peacock Publishers.

[18]French, W., and C. Bell (1990). *Organizational development* (4th ed.). Upper Saddle River, NJ: Prentice Hall.

[19]Deming, W. (1988). *Out of the crisis.* Cambridge, MA: MIT Center for Advanced Engineering Study.

[20]Solomon, J. (February 10, 1989). Firms address workers' cultural variety: The differences are celebrated, not suppressed. *The Wall Street Journal,* p. B-1.

[21]Loden, M., and J. Rosener (1991). *Workforce America! Managing employee diversity as a vital resource.* Homewood, IL: Business One Irwin.

[22]Thomas, R. (1990). From affirmative action to affirming diversity. *Harvard Business Review, 68,* 107–117.

[23]Osborne, D., and T. Gaebler (1992). *Reinventing Government.* Reading, MA: Addison-Wesley.

[24]Chandler, T., and P. Feuille (June 1991). Municipal unions and privatization. *Public Administration Review, 51,* 15–22.

[25]Melcher, D., J. Eichstedt, S. Eriksen, and D. Clawson (1992). Women's participation in local union leadership: The Massachusetts experience. *Industrial and Labor Relations Review, 45,* 267–273.

[26]Rosener, J. (November-December 1990). Ways women lead. *Harvard Business Review, 68,* 119–126.

[27]Mladenka, K. (June 1991). Public employee unions, reformism, and black employment in 1,200 cities. *Urban Affairs Quarterly, 26,* 532–548.

[28]Riccucci, N. (1990). *Women, minorities and unions in the public sector.* Westport, CT: Greenwood.

[29]———. (July 1990). Cafeteria plans, wellness programs gaining in popularity. *Employee Benefit Plan Review,* pp. 90–92.

[30]Taylor, P. (May 23, 1991). Study of firms finds parental leave impact light. *The Washington Post,* p. A9.

[31]———. (March 1987). Child care and recruitment boost flexible plans. *Employee Benefit Plan Review,* pp. 32–33.

³²Voltz, W., and D. Costa (March 1989). A public employee's "fair share" of union dues. *Labor Law Journal, 40*, 131–137.

³³Masters, M., and R. Atkin (1990). Public policy, bargaining structure, and free-riding in the federal sector. *Journal of Collective Negotiations in the Public Sector, 19*, 97–112.

³⁴Dunlop, J. (Winter 1992). The challenge of human resources development. *Industrial Relations, 31*, 1, 50–79.

³⁵Orazem, P., P. Mattila, and S. Weikum (Winter 1992). Comparable worth and factor point pay analysis in state government. *Industrial Relations, 31*, 1, 195–215.

³⁶Herrick, N. (1990). *Joint management and employee participation: Labor and management at the crossroads.* San Francisco: Jossey-Bass.

³⁷American Productivity Center (1987). *Participative approaches to white-collar productivity.* Washington, DC: U.S. Department of Labor, Bureau of Labor-Management Relations and Cooperative Progress.

³⁸Cooke, W. (1992). Product quality improvement through employee participation: The effects of unionization and joint union-management administration. *Industrial and Labor Relations Review, 46*, 1: 119–127.

³⁹Jacoby, S., and A. Verma (Winter 1992). Enterprise unions in the United States. *Industrial Relations, 31*, 1: 137–158.

⁴⁰U.S. Department of Labor (1989). *An Orientation to Joint Labor-Management Initiatives.* Washington, DC: U.S. Department of Labor, Bureau of Labor-Management Relations and Cooperative Programs.

⁴¹U.S. Congress, House, Select Committee on Aging, Subcommittee on Human Services (March 9, 1992). *Left at the gate: The impact of bankruptcy on employee and retiree benefits.*

⁴²IPMA (September 1999). ADA does not trump CBA. *IPMA News.* Alexandria, VA: International Personnel Management Association, p. 9; Smith, Maureen (November 1999). Impact of the ADA in the workplace: how has it impacted your organization. *IPMA News.* Alexandria, VA: International Personnel Management Association, pp. 6–7; Ott, Tina (December 1999). Under ADA officer has no right to moonlight. *IPMA News.* Alexandria, VA: International Personnel Management Association, pp. 9–10; IPMA (December 1999). Denver police department required to consider reassignment as reasonable accommodation. *IPMA News.* Alexandria, VA: International Personnel Management Association, p. 10; Ott, Tina (July 1998). Attendance required under ADA. *IPMA News.* Alexandria, VA: International Personnel Management Association, p. 10; Chiapetta, Tina Ott (April 2000). Severe depression not a disability. *IPMA News.* Alexandria, VA: International Personnel Management Association, p. 7; Chiapetta, Tina Ott (April 2000). ADA protects officer with HIV. *IPMA News.* Alexandria, VA: International Personnel Management Association, p. 7; Ott, Tina (March 1999). Firefighting not essential function of assistant fire chief. *IPMA News.* Alexandria, VA: International Personnel Management Association, p. 6.

⁴³IPMA (October 1999). Pagers, beepers & on-call pay. *IPMA News.* Alexandria, VA: International Personnel Management Association, p. 7; Ott, Tina (July 1998). On-call time not compensable. *IPMA News.* Alexandria, VA: International Personnel Management Association, p. 10; Ott, Tina (March 1999). Short response time does not make on-call time compensable. *IPMA News.* Alexandria, VA: International Personnel Management Association, p. 6.

⁴⁴Chiapetta, Tina (September 1999). FLSA requires weekly overtime. *IPMA News.* Alexandria, VA: International Personnel Management Association, p. 9; Chiapetta, Tina Ott (October 1999). Who is exempt? *IPMA News.* Alexandria, VA: International Personnel Management Association, pp. 8–9. *IPMA* (November, 1999). Solutions to FLSA problem needed! *IPMA News.* Alexandria, VA: International Personnel Management Association, p. 10; Ott, Tina (July 1998). EMS employees entitled to overtime. *IPMA News.* Alexandria, VA: International Personnel Management Association, p. 11; Ott, Tina (October 1998). Employers can force employees to take comp time before vacation. *IPMA News.* Alexandria, VA: International Personnel Management Association, pp. 9–10; Chiapetta, Tina Ott (August 2000). Forced compensatory time. *IPMA News.* Alexandria, VA: International Personnel Management Association, p. 9; Ott, Tina (March 1999). Second circuit rules on salary basis test. *IPMA News.* Alexandria, VA: International Personnel Management Association, p. 6; Ott, Tina (January 1999). Ninth circuit interprets salary basis test after Auer decision. *IPMA News.* Alexandria, VA: International Personnel Management Association, p. 13.

⁴⁵Chiapetta, Tina Ott (July 1999). Recent drug use negates ADA protection. *IPMA News.* Alexandria, VA: International Personnel Management Association, pp. 11, 13.

[46]IPMA (December 1999). States immune from employee suits under FMLA. *IPMA News*. Alexandria, VA: International Personnel Management Association, p. 10; Chiapetta, Tina Ott (January 2000). No FMLA claim when employee unable to perform essential functions. *IPMA News*. Alexandria, VA: International Personnel Management Association, p. 10; Ott, Tina (June 1998). Employer can rely on employee's doctor for FMLA opinion. *IPMA News*. Alexandria, VA: International Personnel Management Association, p. 6.

[47]Ott, Tina (November 1998). Court says no to race/gender conscious promotions. *IPMA News*. Alexandria, VA: International Personnel Management Association, p. 8.

[48]IPMA (July 1999). State and local government labor-management teams attend first joint SLG-LMC/Harvard executive program. *IPMA News*. Alexandria, VA: International Personnel Management Association, pp. 7–8.

[49]IPMA (June 1999). "The power of partnership:" A success story from Detroit, Michigan. *IPMA News*. Alexandria, VA: International Personnel Management Association, p. 6.

[50]U.S. Department of Labor (May 1996). *Working together for Public Service: Report of the U.S. Secretary of Labor's Task Force on Excellence in State and Local Government through Labor-Management Cooperation.* Washington, DC: U.S. Department of Labor.

[51]Barrier, M. (July 1998). A working alternative for settling disputes. *Nation's Business, 86(7):* 43–46.

[52]Hayford, S.L. (January 2000). Alternative dispute resolution. *Business Horizons, 4:* 111–118.

[53]Verespej, M.A. (February 2, 1998). Sidestepping court costs. *Industry Week*, pp. 68–72.

[54]CPR Institute (1998). *Introduction.* Available online at: www.cpradr.org/cprintro.htm; Mareschal, Patrice (Fall 1998). Providing high quality mediation: Insights from the Federal Mediation and Conciliation Service. *Review of Public Personnel Administration*, 55–67.

[55]Carver, Todd, and Albert Vondra (May–June 1994). Alternative dispute resolution: Why it doesn't work and why it does. *Harvard Business Review, 70*, pp. 120–130.

[56]United States Congress (1998). Alternative Dispute Resolution Act of 1998. Available online at: www.cobar.org/focomms/adr/adract1998.htm; and Ford, J. (July 31, 2000). Workplace ADR: Facts and figures from the federal sector. Available online at: www.conflict-resolution.net/articles/Ford3.cfm?plain+t.

[57]American Arbitration Association (2000). Resolving employment disputes. Available online at: www.adr.org/rules/guides/resolving_employment-disputes.html.

[58]Loftis, Deme, and Deborah Drucker (April 1997). Increasing the use of alternative dispute resolution in the South Carolina state employee grievance process. *IPMA News*. Alexandria, VA: International Personnel Management Association.

[59]Carnevale, David (1993). Root dynamics of alternative dispute resolution: An illustrative case in the U.S. Postal Service. *Public Administration Review, 53:* 455–461.

[60]Kaufman, Roger (January 1992). The effects of IMPROSHARE on productivity. *Industrial and Labor Relations Review, 45(2):* 311–322.

[61]Hattiangadi, Anita (1998). *Raising productivity and real wages through gainsharing.* Washington, DC: Employment Policy Institute.

[62]Charlotte (NC) (n.d.). *A guide to setting business unit targets.* Human Resources Department, Employee Incentive Program; Fox, James and Bruce Lawson (August 1997). Gainsharing program inspires pride, creativity and productivity among Baltimore county employees. *IPMA News*. Alexandria, VA: International Personnel Management Association, pp. 25–27; Coral Springs (FL) (1995). *Employee gainsharing program, Policy #06.11.08, Administrative Policy Manual.* Information is also available online for agency members through IPMA's Center for Personnel Research: www.ipma-hr.org/research/personnel.html.

Index